LOT SMITH

G 6-2019

LOT SMITH

MORMON PIONEER and AMERICAN FRONTIERSMAN

CARMEN R. SMITH and TALANA S. HOOPER

GREG KOFFORD BOOKS
SALT LAKE CITY, 2018

ISBN 978-1-58958-692-5 (paperback)
Also available in ebook.

Greg Kofford Books
P. O. Box 1362
Draper, UT 84020
www.gregkofford.com
facebook.com/gkbooks
twitter.com/gkbooks

Library of Congress Cataloging-in-Publication Data

Names: Smith, Carmen, 1916-2018, author. | Hooper, Talana S. (Talana Smith), 1953- author.
Title: Lot Smith : Mormon pioneer and American frontiersman / Carmen Smith and Talana Hooper.
Description: Salt Lake City : Greg Kofford Books, 2018. | Includes bibliographical references and index.
Identifiers: LCCN 2018033371 | ISBN 9781589586925 (pbk.)
Subjects: LCSH: Smith, Lot. | Mormon pioneers--Biography. | Frontier and pioneer life--Utah. | Frontier and pioneer life--Arizona.
Classification: LCC BX8695.S7525 S65 2018 | DDC 289.3092 [B] --dc23
LC record available at https://lccn.loc.gov/2018033371

To my husband, Omer J. Smith
—Carmen R. Smith

To my husband, Steve,
and my children, Melynde, Ryan, James,
Lorianne, Julee, and Morgan
—Talana S. Hooper

Contents

Introduction,   ix

1. Mormon Battalion,   1
2. Minute Men,   19
3. Utah War,   37
4. Escape Capture,   49
5. Peace,   61
6. Civil War Captain,   73
7. British Mission,   91
8. Last Utah Years,   109
9. Journey to Arizona,   117
10. Arizona Stake President,   131
11. Sunset's Succor,   147
12. Circle S Ranch,   161
13. A Wanted Man,   173
14. Resettlement of United Order,   187
15. To Yavapai County,   205
16. Under Arrest,   215
17. Marked Man,   227

Epilogue: Reinterment,   239

Appendix A: Utah War Participants with Lot Smith,   243
Appendix B: Members of Lot Smith's 1862 Civil War Company,   245
Appendix C: Wives and Children of Lot Smith,   247
Appendix D: Lot Smith Timeline,   249

Bibliography,   257
Index,   277

Major Lot Smith, in charge of a Command of Utah troops in the Echo Canyon War. Steel engraving by Chas. B. Hall, NY, reprinted by permission of the Utah State Historical Society, Salt Lake City.

Signature of Lot Smith, Letter to John Taylor, July 12, 1879, John Taylor 1808-1887. LDS Church History Library, Salt Lake City.

Introduction

I live for those who love me, for those who know me true,
For the heavens that shine above me and await my coming, too,
For the cause that needs assistance,
For the wrongs that lack resistance,
For the future in the distance,
For the good that I can do.[1]

Lot Smith's last and fifty-second child was born six months after his father was killed by a renegade Navajo in Arizona. This son, James "Jim" Martin Smith—my grandfather—longed throughout his life to learn anything and everything about the father he never had the privilege to know. He sought and acquired stories of his father for years and learned that his father's life had generated many myths and legends. Lot Smith was a daring man of strong passions and character who had a temper to match his fiery red beard. Ten years after his death, the *Deseret News* published: "Like all brave and martial men, [Lot Smith] could not tolerate a coward. He had no patience with them, and of course, they thought him to be the most tyrannical of men. But with those who possessed bravery and honesty he was true as steel."[2]

Smith was born in New York in 1830, not far from where the Mormon church had been organized only one month before. At the age of sixteen, Smith volunteered to serve in the Mormon Battalion—an experience that significantly shaped his life. He developed endurance and an ability to survive on shortages of food, water, and clothing. In the Territory of Utah, Smith joined the cavalry corps known as Minute Men, or Life Guards, of the Nauvoo Legion. This group defended the Mormon pioneers in the Rocky Mountain region. Smith fought in several skirmishes that arose between the settlers and the Indian tribes of the area. Smith was appointed Color Bearer General of the Nauvoo Legion with the rank of captain when he had barely reached manhood. Three years later, he was elected as Davis County's first sheriff, a position he served in for roughly ten years. As a captain of the Life Guards in the

---

1. George Linnaeus Banks, "What I live For."
2. *Deseret News*, April 5, 1902.

fall of 1856, Smith was among the leaders who helped rescue the Willie and Martin Handcart Companies in the blizzards of Wyoming.

Smith is best remembered for his role in the Utah War of 1857 when the US Army was sent to invade Utah Territory. His reputation of fearlessness was reinforced by the daring acts of burning the supply wagons of the US Army and working alongside legendary Mormon gunfighter Porter Rockwell to stampede the US Army's cattle. Smith's next military campaign in 1862 was not against the US Army but was a part of the Union Army during the American Civil War. Communication across the country was vital to the preservation of the Union. Commissioned by President Lincoln, Smith led the Utah Volunteers in protecting, repairing, and rebuilding the transcontinental telegraph lines and mail lines from Fort Bridger to Independence Rock.

Brigham Young had long sought to colonize in the Arizona Territory. After several years of failed efforts, he appointed Smith to the task. Leading the missionary colonists on the seven-week journey to the site designated by Young at Sunset Crossing on the Little Colorado River, Smith instituted the United Order, the Mormon communitarian system, within a stable society. He established a dairy in Pleasant Valley at Mormon Lake, initiated the Circle S Ranch, was called as the first Latter-day Saint stake president in the Arizona Territory, and developed goodwill with the Hopis and Navajos. When Apostle Wilford Woodruff fled to Arizona, Smith and the settlers helped Woodruff elude capture by federal authorities several times.

Polygamous men in Arizona and Utah became targets for arrest, including Smith, who had eight wives. Smith, along with apostle Moses Thatcher and the three other Arizona stake presidents, was commissioned by President John Taylor to purchase land in Mexico as a refuge for polygamous families. When he eventually returned to Arizona, he still faced arrest and further dangers as a stockman. As he defended his ranch interests against those who would rustle his stock or steal his range rights, he acquired the reputation as the most feared gunman in Arizona with several notorious acts wrongly credited to him, including participation in the Mountain Meadows Massacre, acting as one of Brigham Young's destroying angels, and the branding of his wives. Near his home in a remote four-mile box canyon, Smith suffered the bullet which took his life. Ten years after his death, his body was exhumed from Arizona and reinterred in his old hometown of Farmington, Utah.

*****

My grandfather passed his passion to know his father onto his posterity and extended family. Jim Smith's oldest son, my father Omer, recorded the stories and enlisted the help of my mother Carmen to research Lot Smith's history in libraries around the country. When Omer unexpectedly passed away, Carmen continued to research, interview, and compile for another thirty years. Many anxiously awaited this biography. When my mother's eyesight, and therefore her ability to use the computer, began to fail, I resolved to not allow all the love, sacrifice, and labor of my mother, father, and grandfather to collect and preserve Lot Smith's story to be wasted. As a legendary, Old West figure entwined in the early events of Mormon history, I felt that his incredible story was worth every effort to preserve. As I became more familiar with Lot Smith's narrative style—so compelling and touched with humor—I wished he had taken the time to write more of his life and keep a journal. However, he was much too active *living* to write about life. I feel deep gratitude for his contemporaries who wrote of him and for those who preserved his letters.

My mother and I gratefully acknowledge those who have graciously assisted over the years in acquiring the substance for this biography and—in her words—"who made research so exhilarating": archivists Ron Esplin, Irving Golding, Randy Dixon, Ron Barney, and Gladys Noyce at the LDS Church History Library; the late A. J. "Jeff" Simmonds at the Merrill-Cazier Library at Utah State University; Chad Flake at Brigham Young University Library; and John Irwin and Bonnie Greer at Northern Arizona University Special Collections. We feel indebted to many members of the Lot Smith family, especially Alden B. Smith II, Alvin V. "Mike" and Fern Steed, Karl Smith, Willard Smith Jr., Kenneth B. Smith, Jessie Smith, Arza Lavell Smith, Georgia Smith Buss, Nona Smith Rhead, Dan DeWitt, Alene Sessions, Rock M. Smith, Ralph Smith Burton, Grant Gill Smith, Ellis Craig, and Bert Smith. We also deeply appreciate others who have supported the research and project, including Maury Jones (Snake River Expedition), Glen Leonard (Farmington), Ken Evans of Homolovi Ruins State Park (northern Arizona and Sunset), Southwest Indian mission president Ralph Evans, Southwest Indian mission president S. Eugene Flake, the late Charles S. Peterson for enthusiastic support, Ruth Dorsett for housing in Salt Lake City, and the expertise of JoJean Loflin and Brian Whitney.

Talana S. Hooper
Gila Valley, 2015

CHAPTER 1

Mormon Battalion

Lot Smith, the fifth of seven children born to William Orville Smith and Rhoda Hough Smith, was born May 15, 1830, in a log cabin in the tiny wooded village of Williamstown, Oswego County, New York. According to his descendants, when Lot Smith was asked of his early childhood, he replied that he was just a blue-bellied Yankee. The term *blue-bellied* referred to the New Haven Colony in Connecticut, home for generations of Smith's mother's people, the Houghs.[1] These early people had Puritan roots and chose to be governed by strict "blue" laws based on the admonitions in Holy Writ.[2] As with most Yankees, Smith's father taught his sons the rudiments of making a living from the land. Before Lot was ten, William O. allocated a few acres to him to be planted in corn.[3]

Their life changed when they embraced a new religion in 1839.[4] In April 1830, the month before Lot Smith was born, the Church of Christ (now known as The Church of Jesus Christ of Latter-day Saints) had been organized in Fayette, Seneca County, New York, sixty-five miles southwest of the Smith's homestead. Followers became commonly known as Mormons, named as such for Joseph Smith's "gold bible"—The Book of Mormon. Roughly thirty-five people joined the Mormon Church in the area of the William O. Smith family.[5] The Smiths and Houghs attended the small Richland Township branch.[6] In this branch, the Smiths became

---

1. Donald Lines Jacobus, *Families of Ancient New Haven,* 4.

2. Whitney R. Cross, *The Burned-Over District,* 6.

3. Alice Ann Richards Smith, letter to Lula Greene Richards, July 21, 1921.

4. Records of the 56th Quorum of the Seventy of the LDS Church list the baptism of Jesse Wells Smith, Lot's brother, on November 18, 1837, by James Blakeslee. If Blakeslee baptized him, the year is almost surely 1839, for Blakeslee spent the entire year of 1837 in Upper Canada and did not return to Oswego County until the fall of 1839. Ambrosia Branch Records lists baptisms: Emily Jane, April 17, 1839; Joel Hough, April 18, 1843; Jesse Wells Smith, November 18, 1837; Abiah Ann Smith April 17, 1841.

5. Minutes of the Ward Teachers Meetings of the Farmington Ward 2 (1868–73), February 4, 1872.

6. James Blakeslee, letter to Parley P. Pratt, Journal History of the Church (hereafter cited as Journal History), October 12, 1839, 2.

acquainted with the Woodruff family, where Wilford Woodruff served as a teacher.

In June 1841, the Smith family left New York to gather to Nauvoo, Illinois, with other faithful Saints. Members of the family included father William (41), mother Rhoda (39), Emily Jane (19), Joel (17), Jesse Wells "Nick" (15), Abiah Ann (13), Lot (11), William "Bill" James (8), and Hyrum (6). They drove their wagon approximately thirty miles toward Rome, then westward on the old Iroquois Trail to Buffalo, traveling for seven weeks along the shore of Lake Erie to Kirtland, Ohio. While there, they met in the Kirtland temple for a Sunday meeting. The wagons continued through Ohio, onto the National Road through Indiana, and into Illinois. After a journey of nine hundred miles, the Smith family reached Nauvoo in early August.[7]

Most of the incoming Latter-day Saints flocked to the Illinois side of the Mississippi River where the prophet Joseph Smith (no relation) resided. However, the William O. Smiths chose the west side of the Mississippi in Iowa for their home. Three miles west of Montrose was a cluster of Latter-day Saints known as Hawley Settlement. William O. built his family a log cabin one mile west of Hawley Settlement (renamed Ambrosia) from the timber on Sugar Creek. On the morning of September 24, Lot's Hough grandparents arrived from New York in the village. The first winter (1841-1842) that the Smiths were in Iowa was comparatively mild, but the following season was less hospitable. Ice on windows was half an inch thick by November and did not melt until April.[8]

Persecution and distrust of the Mormons followed the Saints as they continued to gather in Illinois and across the river in Iowa. After the prophet Joseph and his brother Hyrum were both murdered on June 27, 1844, the William O. Smith family mourned with their fellow Saints. Hostilities worsened between the Mormon and non-Mormon residents. Consequently, the Latter-day Saints began preparations to leave and travel west across Iowa. The exodus began in February 1846. As each group of Saints crossed the Mississippi River, they camped temporarily just north of the Smith home in the Sugar Creek Camp.[9]

The Smith family did not join the exodus west until after the dedication of the Nauvoo Temple. They gathered with the Ambrosia Latter-day

---

7. Joseph Lee Robinson, *History of Joseph Lee Robinson (February 18, 1811– January 1, 1893)*, 10.

8. Belle Bailey, "Severe Winters," 1.

9. Stanley B. Kimball, "Nauvoo West: The Mormons of the Iowa Shore," 140.

Saints on May 6 at Montrose, Iowa, in a wagon company led by Captain Daniel C. Davis. During the northward journey, Lot's uncle Riley Hough's first bugle call of the day roused the camp at six o'clock. Subsequent bugle calls announced morning prayer, cooking breakfast and milking, hitching up the teams, starting the day's journey, and halting. The Davis Camp wagons first passed through Charleston over a roadbed of logs withed together with willows and then moved on toward Farmington on planks laid for some miles. The company endured fierce storms of lightning, thunder, wind, and hail that scattered their stock and blew down their tents, but they persisted. The wagons on the prairie—saturated with spring rains—sank hub-deep in the sod-covered quagmire and required double teams at nearly every ravine. On May 16, the Ambrosia Saints arrived at Garden Grove on Grand River where they held Sunday services the next day. Among the speakers were Lot's father and Captain Davis. The following day, the Davis Camp planted their temporary settlement in a spot named Hickory Grove about twenty miles away from Garden Grove.

Two months later, in July 1846, Brigham Young dispatched Samuel L. Gully as a special messenger to the Hickory Grove Camp. Gully arrived late in the evening, after the camp had retired to bed, but they all were nonetheless called to assemble by Hough's bugle. Gully informed the group that Captain James Allen of the United States Army had advised Young that the president of the United States had authorized the muster of five hundred Mormon volunteers into the war between Mexico and the United States. Young had vigorously sought recruits for two weeks; yet more were needed. Five hundred men were to be provisioned and paid to march westward. Their wages, Gully explained, could aid the fifteen thousand destitute Latter-day Saints who were stranded beside the Missouri River, assisting them in moving westward in the spring. Pay was seven dollars per month with rations furnished, including a clothing allowance and the promise of their guns and equipment at discharge. The term of service was twelve months. Furthermore, Young had information from a reliable source that Senator Thomas H. Benton of Missouri intended to charge the Mormons with treason if they refused to volunteer, granting him authority to organize a militia to exterminate them. Gully closed his speech with Young's earnest appeal that the Mormon men volunteer to prevent the spilling of blood. Young said that the Church's opportunity to serve in the US Army "was like a ram caught in a thicket and it would be better to sacrifice the ram than to have Isaac die."[10]

When Gully finished, the camp exploded into indignation. They had just been driven from their homes. Why should the Saints volunteer for a government whose president had refused Joseph Smith's pleas for justice? Yet how could they ignore the counsel of their current leader? After Captain Davis reemphasized the urgency of Gully's message, a dozen or so men volunteered. Gully urged the volunteers to hurry westward to the Missouri River to join the battalion before their departure. The entire Hickory Grove group broke camp and accompanied the volunteers to the river. The day before they arrived at the Bluffs, another call came for more volunteers. Lot's father stated that others might do as they pleased, but as for him, he would not volunteer—neither would he encourage any of his sons to enlist.[11] However, sixteen-year-old Lot did volunteer to join the group of seventeen men and boys.[12]

About noon on Sunday, July 19, the Davis Camp wagons pulled up at Miller's Hollow—later known as Council Bluffs and Kanesville.[13] Captain Davis told the Hickory Camp volunteers to hustle to the rendezvous on the Missouri River near Trader's Point. Smith and the others hiked eleven miles down the Missouri River for muster the next day. As some of the last to arrive, the Hickory Grove volunteers completed the ranks of Company E under the leadership of Captain Davis.[14] Lot's name was recorded as Luther Smith. Whether Luther was a nickname, or if he used the name to not displease his father, Smith was now one of the youngest privates in the Mormon Battalion.

The Hickory Grove Camp volunteers hiked downriver through rain to the whitewashed log trading post at Sarpee's Point to receive their personal supplies. Trader Peter Sarpee supplied the Mormon Battalion enlist-

10. Samuel Hollister Roger, *Journal of Samuel Hollister Rogers*, July 5, 1846.

11. James Van Nostrand Williams, "Life Sketch of James Van Nostrand Williams," 24.

12. Williams, 25. Along with Captain Davis (42), other recruits were Edward Bunker (23), Edwin Calkins (26), Newman Bulkley (28), Abraham Day (28), Daniel Q. Dennett (37), Isaac Harrison (30), Charles Hopkins (36), Hiram Judd (24), Zodak K. Judd (18), William Lance (Lancehall) (17), Harlum McBride (21), David Pettigrew (54), Alva Phelps (31), Thomas Richardson (42), and James V. Williams (15).

13. Williams, "Life Sketch of James Van Nostrand Williams," 25.

14. Zodak Knapp Judd, "Reminiscences of Zadock Knapp Judd," 17.

ees with one blanket each, as well as coffee, sugar, flour, and bacon drawn in bulk for each six-man mess. Sarpee also provided utensils for each mess of one tin pan, one frying pan, one spoon, and one butcher knife. Each man received a tin cup.[15] Rain continued the next morning. In sodden clothing, Smith's Company E formed a column and marched five miles to join the other four Mormon companies who were camped at Mosquito Creek. From there, the battalion began their southward march along the Missouri River's east bank toward Fort Leavenworth—headquarters of Stephen W. Kearny's Army of the West.

Eight days later the battalion marched double file onto the main street of St. Joseph, Missouri, where many of the residents were astonished that the Mormons had responded to the government's offer to accept volunteers.[16] They taunted the Mormon soldiers with phrases like, "You'll never see California," and "The government intends to send you to Old Mexico, and you never need expect to see home again."[17] On the evening of July 30, a wild windstorm tore through the encampment. Lightning struck and trees crashed to the ground in every direction around the camp, but not one tree fell within the camp—only the tents were blown down.[18] Early the next morning, the battalion marched through the riverside town of Weston, Missouri, in a double column with three fifers and two drummers at the head.[19] The next afternoon, the battalion crossed over the Missouri to Fort Leavenworth.

On August 4, Smith with the boys of Companies C, D, and E crowded around the quartermaster's storehouse for issuance of arms. Smith was issued a musket. Additional equipment included a large cartridge box with a heavy two-and-a-half-inch-wide leather belt to carry over the left shoulder, a similar belt with bayonet and scabbard attached to carry over the right shoulder, and a wide waist belt. Each soldier was also issued a knapsack for clothing with straps over the shoulders and under the arms with a long strap to hold the soldier's bedding. Also to be swung over the shoulder: a powder flask, a round three-inch canteen which held three

15. Henry Bigler, "Extracts From the Journal of Henry W. Bigler," 36.

16. Elijah Allen, "Elijah Allen Autobiographical Sketch, circa 1848"; William Hyde, *The Private Journal of William Hyde*, 19–20; Henry Standage, diary, July 30, 1846.

17. Allen, "Autobiographical Sketch."

18. Henry Standage, diary, July 30, 1946; Azariah Smith, journals, July 30, 1846.

19. William Bryam Pace, journal. 10–11.

pints of water, and a haversack to carry rations.[20] Altogether, the soldier was nearly covered from shoulder to waist, "harnessed like a mule" and "burdened too much to either fight or run."[21]

After almost two weeks at the fort, the Mormon Battalion marched out of Leavenworth down the dusty Santa Fe Trail to join General Kearny in the conquest of California in the Mexican-American War. The battalion companies wound over the prairie in alphabetical order to the Kansas River. "The road was a foot deep with sand and dust," Henry W. Bigler later wrote.[22] The soldiers learned what it meant to carry a heavy musket and all the encumbrances of a foot soldier on a hot, dusty day.[23] At the Council Grove camp, Lieutenant Andrew J. Smith brought orders that he was to lead the battalion to Santa Fe. With him was surgeon George B. Sanderson of Missouri. A letter also arrived from Young that cautioned the soldiers about remedies for illness. He said to "let calomel alone, and to use faith, that there was no promise of life if we did use it."[24] The column of infantry had hardly left Council Grove before Doctor Sanderson prescribed his cure-all drug: calomel. The soldiers followed Young's counsel and threw away the paper cachets that contained the powders.[25] When the doctor discovered their actions, he swore he would cut the throat of anyone who refused his calomel and arsenic.[26]

The daily marches were extended from twelve to fifteen miles, and then to twenty to twenty-five miles. On September 8, the battalion began a more than one-hundred-mile march up the Arkansas River. At this point, Lieutenant Smith reduced the food rations to two-thirds.[27] To shorten the distance to Santa Fe by a hundred miles, Lieutenant Smith led the battalion on a waterless fifty-mile march across the Cimarron Desert, a dangerous section of the trail inhabited by marauding Comanche.[28]

---

20. Judd, "Reminiscences," 24.

21. Azariah Smith, journals; James S. Brown, *Giant of the Lord*, 40.

22. Henry William Bigler, *Diary of a Mormon in California*, August 13, 1846.

23. Robert W. Whitworth, "From the Mississippi to the Pacific, An Englishman in the Mormon Battalion, the Journal of Robert Whitworth," August 15, 1846.

24. Henry Standage, diary, August 29, 1846.

25. Henry Standage, diary, September 12, 1846.

26. Hyde, *Private Journal*, September 3, 1846.

27. Daniel Tyler, *A Concise History of Mormon Battalion in the Mexican War 1846–1847*, 161.

28. Rogers, *Journal*, September 16, 1846.

Early in the morning of September 17, Howard Egan and John D. Lee drove a mule-drawn trap into camp. Lee and Egan had been sent as agents to receive the pay due the battalion. Since the paymaster had no cash to disburse, Lee and Egan accompanied the battalion to Santa Fe.[29] After they crossed the Arkansas River, the thirsty soldiers gratefully found rainwater still standing in several buffalo wallows mixed with buffalo urine and dung. Only a few sickened.[30] For the next five days, the Mormon foot soldiers slogged up the Cimarron River bottom, pulling their weakening mule teams through the heavy sand.[31] As they continued across the desert, only the wide path of wagon ruts marked the trail. Two tiny elevations known as Rabbit Ears peeped over the horizon to guide the travelers.[32] About ten days out of Santa Fe, the soldiers' march increased to an average of twenty-seven miles a day. The soldiers were sore-footed and gaunt, their coats were worn through, and their shoulders galled from carrying muskets and cartridge boxes.[33]

The battalion camped near Wagon Mound, a landmark that resembled the silhouette of a covered wagon and team. Lieutenant Smith proposed that the fifty ablest men from each company take the best teams and proceed by forced march the last hundred and forty miles to Santa Fe. All sick, disabled men and weakened teams were to be left behind.[34] The soldiers grieved at the separation and named the place the Vale of Tears. The column of the forward division wound up the valley of the Pecos River past an adobe and stone ruin of many compartments now known as Pecos National Historical Park. The tall doorways in the sometimes thirty-foot-high walls were topped with lintels carved with strange writing. Some of the battalion members attributed the building to the Nephite civilization referred to in The Book of Mormon.[35]

The battalion arrived in Santa Fe on October 9. Three days later, a new commander for the Mormon Battalion was announced. Captain

---

29. Henry Standage, diary, September 17, 1846.

30. Rogers, *Journal*, September 18, 1846; Henry Standage, diary, September 18, 1846.

31. Alexander Majors, *Seventy Years on the Frontier, Alexander Major's Memoirs of Lifetime on the Border*, 75.

32. Tyler, *History of Mormon Battalion*, 161.

33. Hyde, *Private Journal*, September 30, l846.

34. Hyde, October 3, 1846.

35. Robert S. Bliss, "Journal of Robert S. Bliss with the Mormon Battalion," October 11, 1846.

Philip St. George Cooke, now Lieutenant Colonel appointed by Kearny, replaced Lieutenant Smith. While in Santa Fe, Colonel Cooke suspected that a company of U. S. cavalry might steal some corral fence poles to use for firewood, and ordered Lot Smith to bayonet any thieves. The task proved impossible. While Smith guarded one side, the cavalry hitched poles on the other side and rode off. When Cooke saw the poles gone, he asked Smith why he had disobeyed orders. Smith replied, "If you expect me to bayonet United States troops for taking a pole on the enemy's ground to make a fire of, you mistake your man."[36] Smith expected punishment but was only placed under guard.[37] The battalion remained in Santa Fe about ten days while Cooke tried to assemble adequate supplies for the march westward; however, he was only able to gather a sixty-day ration of flour, sugar, coffee, and salt; a thirty-day ration of salt pork; and a twenty-day ration of soap.[38] As the battalion prepared to leave Santa Fe, Doctor Sanderson determined the fitness of the men for further service. The eighty-six disqualified men, along with most of the women and children, were ordered to Bent's Fort [Pueblo, Colorado] to winter on the Arkansas.[39] On the same day, the enlisted men each drew two dollars and sixty cents in cash and the balance of two-and-a-half-months' pay in checks.[40] Lee and Egan left to carry the payroll to Council Bluffs.[41]

The battalion soldiers marched out of Santa Fe to begin their trek down the Rio Grande and on across the continent to the Pacific Coast. In addition to the assignment to bring a fighting force to California, Cooke received orders from General Kearny to lay out a wagon route across the continent.[42] The general sent to Cooke three experienced guides to assist: Pauline or Paulino Weaver, Antoine Leroux, and Jean Baptiste Charbonneau. Since Colonel Cooke had been unable to obtain sufficient provisions in Santa Fe, two days after departure he cut the rations from two pounds of beef per day to a pound and a half and reduced flour from a pound to three quarters.[43] Before the battalion turned from the

---

36. B. H. Roberts, *The Mormon Battalion: Its History and Achievements*, 85.

37. Roberts, 85.

38. Tyler, *History of Mormon Battalion*, 174.

39. Andrew Jensen, *Documentary History of the Church*, October 15, 1846. .

40. Elijah Elmer, journal, October 16, 1846.

41. Tyler, *History of Mormon Battalion*, 174.

42. Philip St. George Cooke, *The Conquest of New Mexico and California: An Historical and Personal Narrative (1878)*, 86.

43. Guy M. Keysor, journal, November 7, 1846.

Rio Grande, the commander twice more cut the rations. Consequently, as they marched through the towns along the Rio Grande riverside, the hungry soldiers traded clothing, combs, pocket mirrors, brass buttons, and the like for peaches, grapes, apples, melons, and onions.[44] The heavy-laden wagons sank a foot deep in the soft sand in the march along the Rio Grande. With long ropes attached to the wagons, as many as thirty men heaved and hauled with the mules. Near the current town of Derry, New Mexico, the colonel further lightened the baggage wagons by discarding one-third of the tents, one-third of the mess pans and heavy camp kettles, and all the tent poles. The soldiers cooked nine to a mess, slept nine to a tent, and muskets were used for tent poles.[45]

The battalion made the arduous fifteen-mile climb out of the valley of the Rio Grande up to the semi-arid high plateaus of what is now western New Mexico to a waterhole hidden under the north rim of a steep-walled canyon. Members of the battalion named it the Lost Well. At the base of the north wall, a nine-foot wide round hole provided a seemingly inexhaustible supply of water. Huge masses of volcanic rock blocked the passage of men and animals through the short canyon to the waterhole.[46] Cooke sat for two hours on an overhang above the well, directed the watering, and cursed its slowness.[47]

Water determined the battalion's route. The command camped at Ojo de Vaca (Cow Spring) beside the Copper Mine Road that led south to Janos in Sonora and north to the Santa Rita copper mines. With no known water on the proposed route, Cooke and his council decided to turn south to Janos in the morning.[48] David Pettigrew and Levi W. Hancock, both older men of Company E, could not support the decision. They believed Doctor Sanderson and some of the officers wanted to go deeper into Mexico for tobacco, wine, whiskey, and other amenities of civilization. That night the two visited each tent in the encampment and asked each mess to pray that the battalion might not go farther into Mexico but on to California.[49] The next morning, the battalion had hardly marched two miles before the road veered slightly to the southeast. Cooke

44. Bigler, *Diary,* October 29, 1846.

45. Tyler, *History of Mormon Battalion*, 202.

46. For expanded details, see Carmen Smith, "The Lost Well of the Mormon Battalion Rediscovered," *Utah Historical Quarterly* 57(3): 277–86.

47. David Pettigrew, journal, November 13, 1846.

48. Philip St. George Cooke, "Cooke's Journal," November 19, 1846.

49. David Pettigrew, journal, November 20, 1846.

called a halt. He looked down the road to the southeast and then to his intended direction to the west. He then rose in his stirrups, and ordered his bugler to blow the right, saying that he was not going all around the world to get to California. He was ordered to go to California, and would go there or die in the attempt.[50] Pettigrew heard the end of the pronouncement and exclaimed, "God bless the Colonel!" The colonel's pleased look at Pettigrew's remark is one of the few instances when his face betrayed anything but sternness in the battalion's presence.[51]

The battalion experienced extreme temperatures as they crossed the desert. The sun blistered the soldiers' faces in the day and, at night, water froze an inch thick.[52] After two full days of marching without water, Charbonneau promised the battalion they would find water in six miles.[53] They marched twelve miles before suffering a painful disappointment.[54] There was water—or rather, there *had* been about a barrelful of water in a hole in some rocks at the foot of a mountain (probably Black Mountain). But the rocks contained no water when the infantrymen arrived. The colonel and his staff had reached the water first and served themselves. Then they had allowed their mounts to finish it off. The foot soldiers crowded around the hollow and dipped with spoons and sucked through quills for a mouthful of water.[55] The lack of water began to be critical to survival.

The soldiers arrived at a mile-wide and thirty-mile long smooth bed of white sand called Las Playas (Sand Beaches). Smith recalled:

> One day when we had marched a long distance without water, and nearly famished, we beheld a dry lake at a distance, sometimes called a mirage. It looked so much like a lake of water to those who never saw one that we had full assurance of speedy relief. . . . It stimulated us to press on, but to our horror it was only dry land, and we traveled fully six miles across this delusion and still found no water, and night had fully come.[56]

---

50. Bigler, *Diary*, November 20, 1846.

51. Tyler, *History of Mormon Battalion*, 207.

52. Cooke, "Cooke's Journal," November 19, 1846.

53. Cooke, November 22, 1846.

54. Henry Standage, diary, November 23, 1846.

55. Tyler, *History of Mormon Battalion*, 208; Frank Alfred Golder, Thomas A. Bailey and J. Lyman Smith, *The March of the Mormon Battalion From Council Bluffs to California, Taken from the Journal of Henry Standage*, November 23, 1846.

56. Andrew Jenson, *Latter-day Saint Biographical Encyclopedia*, 1:803. See also Henry Standage, diary, November 23, 1846.

When the men found willow or wire grass, they began to dig. Private Smith helped dig with energy. A ragged shirt hung from his shoulders, an Indian blanket wrapped around his lower torso substituted for pantaloons, and rawhide cut from the hocks of an ox encased his feet.[57] Smith recalled: "[D]igging down about eight feet . . . we found abundance [of water] to supply all our wants."[58]

Smith was sent with a keg of water on a mule to the many soldiers who lay back on the trail. He was ordered to give the first drink of water to the last man and then to continue back to the company. He passed the first few soldiers but soon relented to the pleading men.[59] Four battalion men—William J. Johnston, Azariah Smith, Henry Bigler, and a battalion member identified only as Brown—related their experience with Smith and the keg of water. They told that one of the men played dead until Lot poured a little water on his mouth. Suddenly revived, the man grabbed the canteen and began to gulp. He held on so forcefully that Lot dragged the man along the ground and finally put his foot on his chest to pull the canteen away.[60] Lot Smith later related:

> I watered them all and had some left, so I had a drink when I got through a distance of twelve or fourteen miles. I was careful in giving them water, though many drank quite heartily. The Lord surely blessed my little keg of water in a marvelous manner. For my disobedience to orders, I was tied behind a wagon and made to walk in trying circumstances which rather humiliated me, but I felt that I could not have done less.[61]

Henry W. Jackson of Company D said that Smith was tied to the wagon "until the forenoon march was ended. Colonel Cooke, informed of the situation, countermanded the order of Lieutenant George P. Dykes, sparing Smith the [afternoon's] unjust punishment."[62]

The men were not fully recovered from the ravages of thirst as they left Las Playas. After they passed through Animas Valley and on to the current

57. Journal History, April 9, 1902; *Deseret News*, April 16, 1902. This footwear had been made by skinning a section of hide from above and below the gambrel joint of an ox leg so that it retained the shape of a tube. The lower end was sewed shut with sinews. The natural crook in the hide partially fit the heel. See Tyler, *History of Mormon Battalion*, 245.

58. Jenson, "Lot Smith," *Biographical Encyclopedia*, 1:803.

59. Jenson, 1:804.

60. Samuel Claridge Young, "Treasures of Samuel Claridge Young," 36.

61. Jenson, "Lot Smith," *Biographical Encyclopedia*, 1:804.

62. Celia Smith, *The Story of Eliza Ann Dibble and Her Three Husbands*.

southwest corner of New Mexico's border with Arizona, they ascended the rugged Guadalupe Mountain Range. On November 28, they camped on the continental divide: the "American Back Bone."[63] The steep descent from the Backbone was pronounced impossible by the guides. Yet, for a half-mile, the soldiers let down all the wagons with ropes. Only one wagon slipped into the ravine and was demolished into kindling wood and scrap metal.[64]

The Mormon Battalion's only battle was fought in the San Pedro Valley. Before the battalion left the Missouri River, Brigham Young had promised that "not one of those who might enlist would fall by the hands of the nation's foe, that their only fighting would be with wild beasts."[65] Though Smith's role in this battle is not recorded, no one escaped the excitement. The battalion marched in loose order alongside the San Pedro River where some abandoned ranch cattle remained—mostly bulls. Cooke permitted those in the front guard who carried Yeagers to lay in a supply of beef.[66] The ruckus caused other bulls to rush out of the river bottom. One bull caught Amos Cox and ripped a four-inch gash under his thigh with its horn as he was tossed ten feet in the air over the beast's back.[67] Although the bull was shot twice, he dashed through the column and escaped. Another bull attacked the rear wheels of a loaded wagon so forcefully that it lifted the wagon and pushed it off the road. The same bull then plunged into a six-mule team, disemboweled a mule, and ran off. After the dust and smoke of the chaos cleared, someone showed Cooke the heart of one of the bulls that was shot through with two balls. Another had been shot six times.[68]

As the battalion marched closer to the Mexican fort at Tucson, Cooke learned that Commandant Comaduran would not allow the American battalion to pass through the town. Since any other route would cause in-

---

63. Henry Standage, diary, November 28, 1846; Journal of Robert S. Bliss, November 29 and December 1, 1846.

64. Brown, *Giant of the Lord*, 65–66.

65. Tyler, *History of Mormon Battalion*, 118.

66. Guy Messiah Keysor, "Battalion Journal"; Elijah Elmer, journal, December 11, 1846. A Yauger/Yeager/Yager (from the German Jaeger) is a .54 caliber US Rifle, the first general issue percussion rifle manufactured by a government arsenal. William Dresser, letter to Carmen Smith, National Rifle Association of America, July 9, 1974.

67. Cooke, *Conquest*, 219.

68. Tyler, *History of Mormon Battalion*, 219–20.

convenience and delay, Cooke decided to proceed through Tucson despite the threat. [69] Colonel Cooke held a parley with Mexican soldiers sent from the presidio of Tucson on December 15. The Mexican sergeant and soldiers again informed the colonel that his battalion was not to pass through Tucson. [70] When a treaty of the surrender of Tucson was finally negotiated, the Mormon Battalion marched eighteen miles to Tucson the next day without food or water. [71] No surrender took place. The commandant, his troops, and most of the inhabitants had fled. [72]

The Mormon soldiers established camp a half-mile beyond the town near a canal of water. [73] Cooke and some of the soldiers returned to the presidio where a small ceremony completed the formal possession of Tucson. Christopher Layton and Samuel Lewis of Company C stuck a fifteen to twenty-foot maguey stalk that bore the American flag into an old cannon barrel and, according to his descendants, raised the first flag of the United States in Tucson, Sonora, Mexico. [74]

The battalion left the Tucson campsite on December 18 to begin a march northwest across the desert to the Gila River. Water for both men and mules was almost nonexistent. The battalion abandoned all semblance of military order; each man traveled when he could and rested when he had no strength. [75] At the end of the second day, Sergeant Elijah Elmer pronounced the previous forty-eight hours as "the hardest pull we have had yet for man and beast." [76] Cooke described his soldiers: "They are almost barefooted, carry their muskets, knapsacks, etc., and do not grumble." [77] The more than hundred-mile journey toward the Gila River so exhausted the men that Cooke remarked that "any other company under like circumstances would have mutinized." [78]

---

69. Cooke, "Cooke's Journal," December 9, 12, 13, 1846; Bigler, *Diary*, December 12, 1846; Hyde, *Private Journal*, December 13, 1846.

70. Cooke, *Conquest*, 148; Henry Standage, diary, December 15, 1846.

71. Cooke, *Conquest*, 151; Henry Standage, diary, December 16, 1846.

72. David Pettigrew, Journal, December 16, 1846.

73. Cooke, "Cooke's Journal," December 16, 1846.

74. Max T. Layton and Ed Moody, interview by Carmen R. Smith, February 18, 1974. In author's possession.

75. David Pettigrew, journal, December 17 and 18, 1846.

76. Elijah Elmer, journal, December 19, 1846.

77. Cooke, "Cooke's Journal," December 20, 1846.

78. Hyde, *Private Journal*, December 20, 1846.

The battalion reached and trailed down the Gila River. On December 28, the colonel sent five guides to travel three hundred miles down the Gila and over the desert to the ranch of Juan Jose (John Trumbull) Warner in California to bring back fresh mules and eight to ten beeves.[79] After they crossed the Colorado River, the troops traveled over the hundred-mile Colorado Desert where they endured more hot days, cold nights, hunger, and thirst. At some point along the march, Smith and others were so hungry that when they found a pepper tree, they peeled the bark off and ate it. It did not agree with Smith and he never wanted pepper again. Legend holds that throughout the rest of his life, Lot did not allow pepper at his table.[80] The soldiers anxiously awaited the beef from Warner's Ranch. At each day's campsite, Smith climbed the nearest eminence to look westward for any rising dust of the coming beef.[81] Finally, on the evening of January 15, a train of ten beeves and forty-two mules arrived.[82] A butchered beef fed the men.

The battalion arrived at Warner's outpost ranch and, after a week, ascended a bluff and viewed the Pacific Ocean for the first time. Like Smith, many of the soldiers had never seen an ocean. The marching halted for twenty minutes and hardly a diary failed to express joy and wonder at the ocean view.[83] Several more miles brought them to the Mission of San Diego de Alcala (San Diego). The battalion encamped on a flat a mile below the mission—a collection of whitewashed adobe buildings with disintegrating walls and neglected gardens.[84] The date was January 29, 1847. Colonel Cooke's Orders No. 1 dated the following day gave an apt description of their march:

> The lieutenant-colonel commanding congratulates the battalion on their safe arrival on the shore of the Pacific ocean, and the conclusion of the march of over two thousand miles. History may be searched in vain for an equal

---

79. Cooke, "Cooke's Journal," December 28, 1846. The word "beeves" is the plural of "beef."

80. Maude S. Burton, as told by Melissa Packer Smith, September 24, 1980.

81. Alden B. Smith II, interview by Carmen R. Smith, audio recording, January 9, 1984. In author's possession.

82. Henry Standage, diary, January 15, 1847.

83. Henry G. Boyle, reminiscences, January 27, 1847.

84. Cooke, "Cooke's Journal," January 29, 1847; Journal of Robert S. Bliss, January 29, 1847; Nathaniel V. Jones, diary, February 1, 1847.

march of infantry. [85] Nine-tenths of it has been through a wilderness where nothing but savages and wild beasts are found, or deserts where, for want of water, there is no living creature. There, with almost hopeless labor, we have dug deep wells which the future traveler will enjoy. Without a guide who had traversed them, we have ventured into trackless prairies where water was not found for several marches. With crowbar and pick and ax in hand we have worked our way over mountains which seemed to defy aught save the wild goat, and hewed a passage through a chasm of living rock more narrow than our wagons. To bring these first wagons to the Pacific, we have preserved the strength of our mules by herding them ever over large tracts, which you have laboriously guarded without loss. The garrisons of four *presidios* of Sonora, concentrated within the walls of Tucson, gave us no pause. We drove them out with their artillery, but our intercourse with the citizens was unmarked by a single act of injustice. Thus, marching half naked and half fed, and living upon wild animals, we have discovered and made a road of great value to our country. Arrived at the first settlement of California after a single day's rest, you cheerfully turned off from the route to this point of promised repose to enter upon a campaign, and meet, as we believed, the approach of the enemy; and this, too, without even salt to season your sole subsistence of fresh meat.[86]

General Kearny ordered Cooke and his battalion northward to garrison the San Luis Rey Mission strategically located between San Diego and Los Angeles. The battalion cleaned out the mission's filthy, flea-ridden rooms and, for some time, forty-five men of Smith's Company E crowded into one windowless 18 x 20 ft. room with no fireplace, where they cooked, ate, and slept until Cooke gave them permission to use some of the other empty rooms.[87] The battalion had been six weeks at San Luis Rey (February 3 to March 19) when the closing acts in the conquest of California began to be played out. The Mormon Battalion marched to Los Angeles and was crucial in foiling John C. Fremont's unauthorized grasp for power in the emerging government of California when their presence forced Fremont to surrender in early April.

Lot Smith attended at least one bullfight in Los Angeles. A contemporary, Elizabeth Kane, wrote that Smith "put down a bullfight."[88] Smith

---

85. The Mormon Battalion's infantry march was not exceeded until 1934–35 when Mao Zedong led a one-year, six-thousand-mile march from southern to northwestern China.

86. Cooke, "Cooke's Journal," January 29, 1847.

87. Bigler, *Diary*, February 3, 1847; Henry Standage, diary, February 14, 1847.

88. Elizabeth Wood Kane, *Twelve Mormon Homes Visited in Succession on a Journey Through Utah to Arizona*, 23–24.

told the Spaniards that their bullfights were cruel and cowardly. To show true bravery, he said, they should ride the bull instead of killing it. The men answered that no one could ride a maddened bull. According to Kane, Smith then leaped upon the bull and, by holding onto its horns, rode it around the ring until the bull tossed him into the canopied box of the town's leading family.

The wagon road route established by Cooke and the Mormon Battalion along the thirty-second parallel profoundly affected the history of the Far Southwest. Thousands of gold seekers traveled the route to reach the California gold fields in 1849 and 1850. Political leaders promoted the building of a southern transcontinental rail line on the route, thus necessitating the Gadsden Purchase in 1853. The Mormon Battalion's year of service ended and they were discharged on July 16, 1847. Four days after the discharge in Los Angeles, Smith was one of eighty-one battalion soldiers who enlisted for six months' more service to be known as the Mormon Volunteers who were ordered to San Diego where they spent time furbishing the town. [89] Henry G. Boyle wrote: "We did their blacksmithing, put up a bakery, made and repaired carts, and, in fine, did all we could to benefit ourselves as well as the citizens. . . . The citizens became so attached to us that before our term of service expired, they got up a petition to the governor of California to use his influence to keep us in the service."[90]

The Mormon Volunteers were relieved of duty on March 14, 1848. Smith and his friends Harlum McBride, Edwin Calkins, and Edwin Walker sought work. The group of young men took a job building four miles of adobe wall fence at Williams's Ranch located some eighty or ninety miles northwest of San Diego.[91] Meanwhile, gold had been discovered in northern California by fellow members of the battalion. When some of their former comrades brought the news to the ranch, Smith and his companions headed to the goldfields.[92] They passed Sutter's Fort and headed twenty-five miles up the American River to Mormon Island located ten or fifteen miles below Coloma.[93] Profitable placers had already been claimed, so Smith and his companions continued northward and eventually settled on Feather River. The boys found merchandise, food,

89. Tyler, *History of Mormon Battalion*, 298; Military Service during the Mexican War, 1846–1848, Davis Company A, Mormon Volunteers.

90. Henry G. Boyle, quoted in Tyler, *History of Mormon Battalion*, 330–31.

91. Andrew Jackson Workman History, 168.

92. Workman, 168.

93. Workman, 169.

lodging, and services exorbitantly priced. Flour was a dollar a pound.[94] According to Smith's son Alden, his father did not dig or pan gold; he instead raised vegetables in the Feather River Valley where no irrigation was necessary, freighted garden produce and supplies to the isolated miners, and took gold in pay.[95]

By the end of the season, they had made their pile and planned to reunite with their families in the Great Salt Lake Valley. The group included Lot Smith (18), Harlum McBride (25), Edwin Calkins (28), Jerome Zabriskie (20), Andrew J. Workman (24) and his brother Cornelius Workman, Philo Carter (20), Philander Fletcher (25), Edwin Walker (20), and Hyrum Fellows (18).[96] They started out in November 1848. Fifty miles into the journey along the new wagon road through the Sierra Nevadas, Calkins tried a short cut on an Indian trail. He did not return. After they hunted for Calkins for two or three days, his companions came across a "Digger Indian" riding Calkins's horse.[97] They shot him and took the horse. After this incident, the young men returned down the mountain to Mormon Island to buy more arms and ammunition and return to their course. However, they learned that they had started too late in the season to cross the snowy Sierras.[98] Still determined to go, they decided to take the southern route that was open all year. They retraced their route to the Williams Ranch near San Bernardino and, after a few weeks there, met with Ebenezer Hanks, a former sergeant in the Mormon Battalion, who had arrived from Great Salt Lake City. He informed the boys that their party was too small to defend themselves against Indians on the southern route. While they worked and waited to join a larger company, five thousand dollars in gold dust was stolen from the Workman brothers.

---

94. Workman, 168.

95. Alden B. Smith II, interview by Carmen R. Smith, audio recording, January 9, 1984. It is likely that Smith provided produce to Mary Ann Blanks Smithson Harmon, who operated the first hotel in Auburn—a gathering place for Latter-day Saint missionaries. One of her daughters, Paralee America, would become the mother of Mary Merinda Garn who later married Smith.

96. Andrew Jackson Workman History, 168. All had reenlisted under Captain Daniel C. Davis as California Volunteers except Cornelius Workman.

97. "Digger Indian" was a pejorative used to refer to any number of American Indian peoples, especially of the Great Basin, California, and the Southwest, who dug roots for food.

98. Andrew Jackson Workman History, 169.

They did not want to return to Great Salt Lake City empty-handed, so the group returned to the mines for more gold.[99]

At the end of the summer in 1849, the group again headed for Utah over the Sierra Nevadas. Smith added several California horses to his string and for several weeks on the trail, the young men evaded robbers and Indians. As Smith's two pack mules heavily laden with gold crossed a river, one of the mules lost its footing. Too loaded to rise, it drowned. In only a moment of misfortune, Smith lost thousands of dollars and one good mule.[100] The small company rode their horses over the route that offered grass and water with only two small tracts of desert to cross until they reached the settlements of the Saints.[101] Smith and his group likely arrived in November 1849.[102] More than three years had passed since adventure and duty had called Smith from Hickory Grove to join the Mormon Battalion. His experiences would impact the rest of his life with his fellow Saints.

99. Workman, 170.

100. Kate B. Carter, *The Mormon Battalion*, 139. Though circumstances point to the Feather River, some versions mention the Malad River, which at that time was a large river capable of floating away a wagon.

101. Hubert Howe Bancroft, *Reproduction of Hubert Howe Bancroft's History of Utah 1540-1886*, 751.

102. William Holmes Walker, *The Life Incidents and Travels of Elder William Holmes Walker*, 16. Through research in DUP publications, a fall 1849 arrival date of Mormon Volunteers who served with Smith was found for Jerome Zabriskie, Philo Carter, and Harlum McBride. These men may have been in the same group.

CHAPTER 2

Minute Men

Smith's family lived in North Cottonwood (renamed Farmington) located sixteen miles north of Great Salt Lake City.[1] Smith's father had built two cabins on North Cottonwood Creek (later named Big Creek). The double (two-log-length) cabin of Lot's older brother, Joel, stood vacant awaiting Joel's return from the gold mines.[2] To the south, in a two-room log cabin by a large spring, lived Lot's oldest sister Emily Jane and her husband Allen Burk.[3] Lot would live with his sister and her husband, along with his younger brother Hyrum.[4] His father had died the previous midsummer and had bequeathed a yoke of steers to Lot upon his return from California.[5] Smith's mother had already passed away in January 1845 back in Iowa.[6]

Soon after his arrival, Smith continued south toward Great Salt Lake City to seek the office of President Brigham Young. Upon finding the Church office, a one-story, twelve-by-eighteen-foot adobe building with a slanting board roof covered with dirt and brush, nineteen-year-old Smith brought in his California earnings and offered his entire six or seven thousand dollars' worth of gold to the Church.[7] Though funds were critical to the new settlement, Young accepted only one-third of the gold and advised Smith to give one-third to his family and keep one-third to further his own interests.[8] Smith purchased a sixty-acre farm in the northern part of North Cottonwood which he soon traded in partial payment for Thomas Grover's farm on Cherry Creek (later Steed Creek) in the south-

---

1. Glen M. Leonard, *A History of Farmington, Utah, to 1890*, 24.

2. Joseph Lee Robinson, *History of Joseph Lee Robinson*, July 1, 1849.

3. Leonard, *History of Farmington*, 23.

4. 1850 Utah Census.

5. Robinson, *History of Joseph Lee Robinson*, July 1, 1849.

6. George Alma Smith, records, LDS Family History Library.

7. Daniel H. Wells, "Narrative," 124; Andrew Jenson, *Biographical Encyclopedia*, 1:629.

8. Nannie Smith Ashcroft [Lot's daughter], "Lot Smith," 1, and Miss Nona Smith [Lot's granddaughter] as quoted in Philip Smith, "Lot Smith," 3; Zelda E. Tidwell, "William Orville Smith 1800-1849," 1.

Lot Smith's two-story stone home in Farmington, Utah. Left to right: Jane Walker Smith in buggy, Jane Hess (granddaughter of Lot and Jane), Lucy Effie Smith Palmer (youngest daughter of Lot and Jane), Nephi Palmer (husband of Effie), Alta and Andrea Palmer (daughters of Jane's daughter, Margaret). Courtesy Zelda E. Tidwell.

ern part of town.[9] There he built an impressive two-story stone house that overlooked his pasture and the creek.

On February 2, 1850, Governor Young called for volunteers to rescue the colonists in Fort Utah in what would be known as the Provo War.[10] Mormons had accidentally killed the Ute called "Old Bishop," an incident later credited with inciting warfare.[11] When the Utes demanded the mur-

---

9. Production of Agriculture in the County of Davis, State of Deseret, during the year ending June lst, 1850, Schedule; Stephen E. Grover and Dean R. Grover, *Thomas Grover, His Ancestors and Descendants*; Margaret Steed Hess, *My Farmington, A History of Farmington, Utah, 1847–1976*, 62.

10. Writer's Program (US) Works Progress Administration (WPA), Utah, "Provo: Pioneer Mormon City," 55.

11. Marilyn McMeen Miller and John Cafton Moffitt, *Provo, A Story of People In Motion*, 8; George Washington Bean, *Autobiography of George W. Bean, a Utah Pioneer of 1847 and His Family Records*, 56. The Ute "Old Bishop" acquired his title because of his resemblance, both in looks and in gestures, to Bishop Newell K. Whitney, the second presiding bishop of the Church.

derer, and no reparation was offered by the Whites, Big Elk's Timpanogos Utes camped about a mile upriver from Fort Utah and attacked almost daily. The seventy Ute warriors also held James Bean's double log cabin located on a low hill. From the cabin, the Utes could fire on any advance to their river bottom position.[12] The settlers in the fort looked for assistance from the Nauvoo Legion of Utah Territory.[13] Smith was among the volunteers who enlisted to help in the conflict under Captain George D. Grant.[14] About one hundred men of Captain Grant's Minute Men—both infantry and cavalry—began a thirty-mile forced march southward on February 7, arriving after midnight.[15]

Throughout the day of February 15, Nauvoo Legion forces on both sides of the river tried to dislodge the Utes, but the Utes resisted every attack. The next morning, the Utes shot and killed Joseph Higbee, and several others were wounded.[16] In midafternoon, Captain Grant asked for volunteers to attack Bean's cabin in a swift charge. To approach the rear of the cabin, the men would be exposed to the Ute gunfire. Fifteen men were chosen with Lieutenant William H. Kimball in command. Among them were Lot Smith, Robert T. Burton, James Ferguson, John R. Murdock, Ephraim K. Hanks, A. J. Pendleton, Orson K. Whitney, Elijah "Barney" Ward, Henry M. Johnson, and Isham Flynn.[17] The volunteers followed the course of the river under cover for a short distance, and then followed a short ravine that partially concealed them. When they reached more level ground, they spurred their horses and dashed for the rear of the cabin.[18] The Utes sent a barrage of gunfire from inside the cabin through chinks between the boards. Several horses were shot, and the charge was briefly curbed. Smith and Burton raced toward the cabin on unharmed mounts. Through a burst of bullets from the Utes' river bottom camp, they charged around the corner into the passageway between the sections of the cabin amid bullets splintering the wood. Inside the cabin on their horses, both Smith and Burton expected hand-to-hand fighting, but the

---

12. Peter Gottfredson, *History of Indian Depredations in Utah*, 29; J. Marinus Jensen, *History of Provo, Utah*, 49; Bean, *Autobiography*; Orson F. Whitney, *History of Utah*, 426.

13. Whitney, *History of Utah*, 424–25.

14. Gottfredson, *Indian Depredations*, 29.

15. Jensen, *History of Provo, Utah*, 48.

16. Whitney, *History of Utah*, 427; Bean, *Autobiography of George W. Bean*, 62.

17. Whitney, *History of Utah*, 427–28.

18. Whitney, 428.

Utes had fled. Miraculously, not one man had been killed in the charge.[19] In a second charge of Captain Conover's men, Jabez Nowlin was wounded just as he entered the passageway to join Smith and Burton. The rest of the detail was held down by gunfire from the river bottom and gathered at the rear of the log house. Some of the men sawed a hole in the back wall to enter.[20] When it was ascertained that assault was unfeasible, the militia left the hard-won cabin.[21]

General Daniel H. Wells arrived at three o'clock Sunday morning and ordered a force to garrison the fort stockade. At daylight, a few defected Utes at the fort discovered that Big Elk's Utes had stolen away in the night, leaving behind their dead and dying. With the rest of the militia and Grant's larger force of mounted Minute Men, Wells followed the fleeing Utes southward. The Utes were cornered at dusk on the promontory that ran out from the southern end of Utah Lake near Peeteetneet (Payson). The warriors were killed, leaving the women and children to be taken prisoner by the general. The securing of Bean's cabin by Smith and Burton became the defining event of the Provo War. Their swift charge established the two as heroes and began a lifelong friendship between Smith and Burton.[22]

After the Provo War, Smith joined the Life Guards of the Nauvoo Legion, also known as Minute Men. The Minute Men were a cavalry corps used from 1847 to 1869 throughout the Rocky Mountain region. Handpicked and organized into companies of sixty, the expert horsemen were first-class marksmen schooled to the hazards and hardships of the frontier. They kept their powder dry, their firearms in good condition, and their horses ready to saddle and ride at a minute's notice.[23] Smith's first call to military action came on September 17 through October 5, 1850.[24] A band of Shoshones to the north threatened a massacre following the accidental killing of their chief, Terakee (White Cloud). Only two hours after receiving notice, three companies of mounted Minute Men, one of infantry, left Great Salt Lake City and North Cottonwood; among them were Smith and Harlum McBride.[25] They arrived in Ogden the next morning just before sunrise—but not before the enraged Shoshones had burned

19. WPA, "Provo, Pioneer Mormon City," 57.

20. Whitney, *History of Utah*, 428.

21. Whitney, 429.

22. Journal History, February 9, 1850, 3.

23. Solomon F. Kimball, "Our Pioneer Boys," 671.

24. Utah State Archives & Records, Service No. 3424B: September 17, 1850.

25. Willard Richards, letter to Lorin Farr, September 17, 1850, Journal History.

Urban Van Stewart's house and grain, killed the millwright, and pillaged the town.[26] A vigorous pursuit forced the Shoshones to abandon much of their stolen property but not the horses. The chase ended at the ford of Bear River.[27] After a six-day standoff, the troops returned to their homes without recovery of the horses.[28]

The day after their return, Smith and McBride, with twenty-five Minute Men under lst Lieutenant William H. Kimball, were ordered to Ogden to further deal with the Shoshones.[29] The guards headed north for a double mission. First, they were to warn the passing immigrants on the California route that both Bannocks and Shoshones had attacked wagon trains and stolen stock; second, they were to seek peace with both tribes.[30] Since both bands of Indians had departed, no parley could be arranged.[31] After ten days, Smith returned to North Cottonwood.

Private Smith's next opportunity for military service came in February of the next winter.[32] A band of Gosiutes from Skull Valley had raided the Mormon settlements in Tooele Valley. After the Gosiutes stole a large number of cattle, twenty-five men of Captain James Ferguson's Company B of the Battalion of Life Guards left for Skull Valley.[33] After a weeklong search, they found no trace of the stolen cattle, so the men returned home. Porter Rockwell was sent as a follow-up in April. He captured and held some thirty Gosiutes for information and as hostages. However, he failed to disarm his prisoners. The hostages shot their guard, and most of them escaped. Rockwell called for reinforcements.[34] Smith was one of twenty-five men under Captain Ferguson sent to assist Rockwell's command.[35]

26. Heber C. Kimball and Willard Richards, letter to Brigham Young, September 17, 1850, Journal History; *Deseret News*, September 21, 1850, in Journal History.

27. James Henry Martineau, autobiography, 8.

28. September 17–September 22, 1850 Pay Roll of Capt. George D. Grant's Company (A) Life Guards, Nauvoo Legion employed in the Expedition against the Shoshone Indians during the Month of September 1850.

29. Utah State Archives & Records, Service No. No. 3424B: 1850 September 25.

30. Special Orders No. 12, Nauvoo Legion Orders Spl & general, September 23, 1850.

31. James Ferguson, letter to Jefferson Davis, Secretary of War, March 2, 1850, Nauvoo Legion Letterbook, 46. In Nauvoo Legion (Utah) records.

32. Utah State Archives & Records, Service No. 3432: 1851, February 19–27.

33. Utah State Archives & Records, Service No. 3432: 1851, February 19–27.

34. Harold Schindler, *Orrin Porter Rockwell, Man of God, Son of Thunder*, 200–201.

35. Utah State Archives & Records, Service No. 3430: 1851, April 23–May 1.

On May 31, 1851, Smith and Ephraim Hanks were appointed Color Bearers General of the Nauvoo Legion with the rank of captain.[36] Smith enjoyed the distinction for fifteen years. They carried the flags at the head of military parades in Great Salt Lake City on majestic horses. Smith's most-remembered color-bearer horse was his steel-gray Arabian named Stonewall that he had acquired from Brigham Young. At first, the stallion could not be controlled. Since Smith possessed an unusual ability to calm and train horses, he asked Young if he could break it. Young said he didn't want Smith to risk his life, but finally relented. Not long after, Smith returned with Stonewall and astonished Young with an impressive show. The horse seemed to trust Smith implicitly as he "seized the horse by the hind legs [and] raised him up and down in wheelbarrow fashion, crawled between his legs, walked under him, made [the horse] lie down, sat upon him, and then walked across him."[37] When Smith bade Young farewell and started to leave, the horse followed him and could not be brought back until Smith returned. Young said, "Lot, because you broke that horse in such a wonderful manner, I will make you a present of him."[38]

In September 1851, Smith was appointed sergeant in Company B of the Battalion of Life Guards. The following summer, Smith joined twenty men on an expedition to explore the vicinity of Lake Sevier for lead that was much needed for ammunition, and also to quietly search for silver.[39] Smith and Burton left Great Salt Lake City in Albert Carrington's company and were joined by Miles Weaver and Barney Ward. The expedition thoroughly explored the mountain ranges from Salt Creek (Nephi) to Chicken Creek, the Sevier, Fillmore, and on to Beaver Creek. The trio of Smith, Burton, and Ward were sent on several exploratory tours by themselves, but no lead or silver was found.[40]

War brewed with Ute chief Wakara (Anglicized to Walker) in 1853. Smith joined an expedition under Major James Ferguson in April to strengthen Utah Territory's southeastern settlements.[41] Chief Wakara and his warriors began attacking the Mormon settlements in quick succession in July and into October—burning mills, stealing stock, and wounding

36. Executive Record Book A 1850–1854, 310; Nauvoo Legion Muster Rolls 1851–1853.

37. William S. Burton, quoted in Margaret M. Fisher, *Utah and the Civil War*, 101–2.

38. Fisher, 101–2.

39. Journal History, June 2, 1852; Utah State Archives & Records, Service No. 187.

40. Albert Carrington, *Diary of Albert Carrington*, 126–31.

41. Carrington, 126–31.

and killing settlers.[42] Despite hostilities, Young sought peace and sent Wakara a gift of tobacco and offered beef cattle and flour.[43] During the war, Governor Young also attempted to gain control of the two gentile outposts in Utah Territory: Fort Bridger and Green River. After Young unsuccessfully attempted to establish a trading post on Green River, he revoked all territorial licenses to trade with the Indians.[44] He then sent a forty-man expedition to enforce the embargo. Second Lieutenant Smith accompanied Major Ferguson on the twenty-day expedition.[45] Before Smith's battalion arrived at the fort, Jim Bridger had fled and left his partner Luis Vasquez and his Mormon clerks in charge.[46] Major Ferguson promoted Smith to First Lieutenant during or after the three-week tour to Fort Bridger.[47]

In the spring of 1854, Smith was elected as Captain of Company B of the Life Guard Calvary.[48] He was then asked to serve his first tour in the corps of guards that accompanied President Young on his travels. The guards repaired wagons, ferried rivers, warded off hostile Indians, and generally contributed to the welfare and comfort of Young and his company. Although peace had already been made with Wakara, Young planned a trip south to ceremonially negotiate peace and to visit the settlements.[49] To help prevent future problems with the Utes, Young promoted defense during the tour. He exhorted the settlements to fort up and to build strong walls around the cities as he traveled south.[50]

At Meadow Creek, Young's caravan arrived at the wickiup of Wakara. With ceremony beloved of the Utes, a deputation of mounted chiefs from Wakara's camp rode forward and saluted the caravan with singing and gunfire, but Young's party did not go out to meet them.[51] Instead, Young directed his guards to form a corral of the wagons and carriages forty

---

42. Richard W. Young, "The Nauvoo Legion," *Contributor* 9(4): 163–66.

43. Young, 163. For a comprehensive look at the Walker War, see Morris A. Shirts and Kathryn H. Shirts, *A Trial Furnace, Southern Utah's Iron Mission*, 317–36.

44. Kate Carter, *Heart Throbs of the West*, 3:321.

45. *Report of a Detachment of Cavalry sent on an expedition to Fort Bridger and Green River August 21st, 1853* [to September 10, 1853], #3505B, Military Records Section Archives, Utah State Historical Society.

46. Hope A. Hilton, *"Wild Bill" Hickman and the Mormon Frontier*, 40.

47. *Expedition to Fort Bridger and Green River August 21st, 1853*, #3505B, listed Smith as First Lieutenant. The payroll listed Smith as Second Lieutenant.

48. Certificate of election, Special Collection, University of Arizona.

49. Bean, *Autobiography*, 93–94.

50. Wilford Woodruff, *Wilford Woodruff's Journal*, May 3, 5, 6, 1854.

51. Woodruff, May 11, 1854.

rods from the Utes' camp.[52] Young then sent a message to Wakara that he had arrived and would be ready to receive him at a stated time. Wakara, who felt rebuffed at Young's lack of acknowledgement of his ceremonial welcome, sent back word that if Governor Young wanted to meet that he must come to Wakara's camp. Young quipped, "If the mountain will not come to Mahomet, Mahomet must go to the mountain."[53]

Young presented himself at Wakara's wickiup with a large escort of his council and his well-mounted guard including Lot Smith. Wakara sat inside his wickiup "like a prince" in the center of a buffalo robe.[54] The Ute chief received the company with great ceremony. Through the interpreter, Wakara said that Brigham was a big chief and that Wakara was a big chief; Wakara put up his two thumbs to illustrate that the two men were equal.[55] Despite all the talk, official peace was not proclaimed that day. In meeting the next morning, Wakara said, "Wakara talk with Great Spirit; Great Spirit say—'Make peace.'"[56] Each took a puff as the calumet passed, peace was proclaimed, and the fighting ended officially. Wakara with his wife and about thirty splendidly mounted Utes accompanied Young's caravan for much of the remainder of the journey.[57]

During the next few days, the company traveled through the southern settlements and arrived on May 19 at Harmony on Ash Creek, the southernmost settlement of Young's colonies.[58] There the company fed and lodged with John D. Lee.[59] From there, the caravan continued north. When they reached the Sevier River, it was flooding. The guards made quick work of rafting over the river before breakfast. They arrived May 30 in Great Salt Lake City, where Young called for a celebration.[60] "A very interesting party [was] got up by the president at the Social Hall for his Company that went south with him. It continued till midnight when we all returned to our homes."[61]

52. Journal History, May 11, 1854.

53. Solomon Nunes Carvalho, *Incidents of Travel and Adventure in the Far West,* 189.

54. Wells, "Narrative," 125–32.

55. Wells, 125–32.

56. Carvalho, *Travel and Adventure,* 193.

57. Carvalho, 193.

58. Journal History, May 19, 1854; "Return of Brigham Young," *Deseret News,* June 8, 1854, in Journal History.

59. Juanita Brooks, *John Doyle Lee,* 178.

60. Journal History, May 26, 27, 30, 1854.

61. *Wilford Woodruff's Journal,* June 12, 1854.

Smith had been keeping company with nineteen-year-old Lydia McBride and romance blossomed.[62] The week following his appointment as Color Bearer, Smith and Lydia rode from North Cottonwood into Great Salt Lake City to be married. In Young's Log Row home built along the street south of the temple block, Smith and Lydia stood together with her Uncle Reuben McBride and some of Young's wives as witnesses.[63] President Young pronounced Lot Smith and Lydia Minerva McBride husband and wife for time and all eternity on June 3, 1851.[64] Smith also began to keep company with Jane Walker. In Lydia's words, although she "did all [she] could to keep him from having her as his wife, it was no use."[65] Eight months later, Smith and Jane were married on February 14 in the endowment rooms of the two-story red sandstone Council House. Jane's brother-in-law Heber C. Kimball performed the ceremony. Witnesses were Willard Richards and Thomas Bullock.[66]

Lydia accompanied Smith to the Council House, where they were both endowed on August 9, 1852.[67] However, Lydia could not tolerate a second wife and soon left with their firstborn son. She later described her feelings:

> We lived together, my husband and myself, until a woman by the name of Jane Walker came into my life, when I stood it as long as I could and then quit, going to my father's home in Fillmore, Utah. [Lot] married this Walker woman . . . and all three of us lived together in Farmington until the next Fall when I quit, as I wouldn't live in the same house with her. If [Lot] had got another house for her, then things would have been different. I shouldn't have come away.[68]

Even long after his death, it was rumored that Smith branded his wives. According to a second-hand account, Amasa L. Clark of Farmington re-

62. Deposition, Case of Lydia M. Smith #15411, September 17, 1900, Military Records, National Archives, Washington, DC.

63. Deposition, Case of Lydia M. Smith, September 17, 1900.

64. Church of Jesus Christ of Latter-day Saints, *Endowment House Sealing Book A, A1, 1851-1854*, film 64, 301. The next recorded marriage was solemnized an hour later at 3:25 p.m. in Brigham Young's office, the usual site of marriages at that time.

65. Deposition, Case of Lydia M. Smith, September 17, 1900.

66. Jane Walker Smith, Mexican War, Claim of Widow for Service Pension, Affidavit, November 11, 1899.

67. Utah and Nauvoo Temple Records #1286A, 48. Jane had already been endowed before her marriage (February 2, 1852), Church of Jesus Christ of Latter-day Saints, *Endowments of the Living, 1851-1884*.

68. Deposition, Case of Lydia M. Smith, September 17, 1900.

called Smith "standing at the pulpit. He always took his coat off and laid it on the chair as he walked to the pulpit. He said anything he owned or possessed, he always branded, including his wife."[69] His sense of humor entertained his friends, but his less intimate acquaintances were aghast, and horrified women decried him a wife beater—their worst condemnation.[70]

Jane told how she was "branded." The incident happened after Lydia left in the fall of 1852 and before Smith married his third wife. Jane was gathering fresh eggs for a dinner she was preparing for Smith and two friends when they came in from branding. She saw several eggs in the manger that she could not reach from the outside of the corral. Smith had cautioned her about the temperament of his stallion, but the horse, who dozed in the far corner of the corral, looked peaceful enough. Jane attempted to pass quietly and collect the eggs. The horse, not as drowsy as he appeared, suddenly shrieked and charged Jane. Lot, without dropping his branding iron, jumped and ran between his wife and the stallion. When she ducked under the fence, he pushed her through with the branding iron. The men at the branding fire watched as Jane twisted to check her nice skirt that she wore for company. The branding iron had cooled enough that it didn't even scorch it. One of the men laughed and said, "That's one that won't get away from you; she's branded!"[71]

By the mid-1850s, Farmington had grown into an attractive, productive community. The settlers built a wall for protection. Every able-bodied man, including Smith, worked on it in proportion to their land holdings. George Quincy Knowlton wrote: "This wall was made of mud shoveled into forms and trampled solid by the bare feet of people."[72] After a year's work, the wall was over two and a half miles long and ten to twelve feet high.[73] Before a civil government could be organized in Farmington, the bishop and the ward teachers divided the town into districts, hired water masters, and settled differences. In February 1855, the 40th Quorum of the Seventy was organized in Farmington with Ezra T. Clark as Senior

---

69. Davis County Sheriff Kenneth Hammon, interview with Carmen R. Smith, July 18, 1974. Clark was a youngster when Smith first came to Farmington.

70. Frederick S. Buchanan, ed., *A Good Time Coming: Mormon Letters to Scotland*, 104.

71. Charlie Ashurst to Nephi Lot Smith, interview by Omer J. and Carmen R. Smith, audio recording, June 1, 1972.

72. George Quincy Knowlton, *History of Farmington, Utah*, 56.

73. Leonard, "History of Farmington," 87.

President.[74] As one of the seven presidents of the Seventy, Lot Smith regularly attended the quorum meetings from 1855 to 1867.

By 1854, Pennsylvania Dutch and Scandinavians had begun settling in Farmington.[75] Most of the small group of primarily Danish Scandinavians hardly understood or spoke English. Smith suggested that if the visits of the ward teachers were to be effective, the Scandinavians should be visited by someone who could speak or understand their native language. Smith then began visiting the Scandinavians with Madse Christensen, a Danish immigrant, as his partner.[76] His reputation for ethnic tolerance became widely known. In an 1857 speech in the Tabernacle, Heber C. Kimball decried intolerance among the settlements and cited Lot Smith as an example of acceptance.[77]

In Utah's first general election in August 1854, Smith was elected as Davis County's first sheriff. Smith's service as sheriff constituted his major contribution to Farmington and Davis County and was fraught with challenges and risks typical of the Western frontier, but few incidents were chronicled. Except for a short interim in 1859 and calls to military service in 1857–58 and 1862, Smith served as sheriff for approximately ten years.[78] In addition to the challenges Smith faced as sheriff, he dealt with personal distresses in his family. The same day he became sheriff, his older sister Abiah Ann Smith McBride died and left three small children.[79]

---

74. Andrew Jenson, *History of Seventy Quorums*, 241.

75. Leonard, "History of Farmington," 32–35.

76. Minutes of the Ward Teachers Meeting of the Farmington Ward 1 (1862–68), December 7, 1862.

77. Brigham Young, *Journal of Discourses*, 4:223.

78. Civil records are scant and do not report that Smith was elected as sheriff in August 1856 to the next two-year term. Yet, he served during 1856 and was absent from September 27 to December 5, 1857 in the Utah War (Davis County Court Records, #0484.601, Family History Library, 51). Philemon C. Merrill may have been appointed during Smith's absence. Possibly elected in the 1858 election, Merrill was serving as sheriff on February 19, 1859, until his resignation when he moved to Weber County. Smith was appointed by Judge Stoddard the following month on March 7 (Davis County Court Records, #0484.601, Family History Library, 51). Two years later, on March 11, 1861, Smith was sheriff under Judge Samuel Richards (Minutes of Probate Court 1854–1869, Farmington, 35).

Court minutes show that Smith served as sheriff after his service in the Civil War on October 13, 1862, November 1, 1862, and March 26, 1863, under Judge Thomas Grover (Minutes of Probate Court 1854–1869, Farmington, 47).

79. Personal Family Records of Emily Jane Smith Burke.

About two months later, a wagonload of hay tipped over on October 27 and killed Smith's brother Hyrum who was only nineteen years old and engaged to be married.[80] Perhaps it was because of the Biblical injunction to raise up seed to a deceased brother that Lot soon began to court Hyrum's fiancée, Julia Ann Smith.[81] Lot and Hyrum had first become acquainted with the vivacious eighteen-year-old Julia at the home of Lot's friend Robert T. Burton.[82] After his brother's tragic death, Lot proposed, but Julia was loyal to the memory of Hyrum. According to a descendant of Julia's, it took more than a year for her to accept Lot as her husband. Lot sought help from both President Young and his wife Jane.[83] Both obliged. Jane said to Julia, "Oh come on, Julia; marry Lot and we'll all have fun."[84] Young married Smith and Julia Ann in his office on the main floor of his newly built Beehive House. Young expressly stipulated that the children would belong to Lot's brother Hyrum.[85] Julia then moved into the big stone house with Jane.

An extravagant social festivity was held February 6 and 7, 1855, to celebrate the service of the Mormon Battalion. Almost ten years had passed since nearly five hundred men had responded to Young's call to serve in the Mormon Battalion. Lot Smith and Henry S. Dalton made certain that all widows and wives of the battalion members in Davis County were invited to the celebration.[86] The attendees crowded Brigham Young's Social Hall for the festival. Elaborate decorations by David Candland, Great Salt Lake City's official party host, adorned the walls of both the lower and upper floors. The programs for both days began at 2:00 p.m. and ended between 2:00 a.m. and 5:00 a.m. Nearly one thousand people attended

---

80. Personal Family Records of Emily Jane Smith Burke.

81. For more about the Levirate Law and Hebrew marriage practices in Mormon theology, see Brian C. Hales, *Joseph Smith's Polygamy, Vol. 3: Theology*, 34–36.

82. Julia lived in Great Salt Lake City with her mother and stepfather Samuel Burton Jr., who was Robert T. Burton's father.

83. Frank Sharar, oral interview notes by Carmen R. Smith. In author's possession.

84. Vera Beamish, interview by Kenneth Smith, audio recording. In author's possession.

85. The record is scanty and inaccurate. Index said Book 1, p 25. Record found Book A 32 and S 25, "Record of Sealings by Proxy 1854 to 1857": Lot Smith b. April 15, 1830, Julia Ann Smith b. March 6, 1837, solemnized by Brigham Young in President's office, November 4, 1855. Jessie Smith gives the date of November 25, 1855. The later date is probably a second sealing that fulfilled the requirement that earlier wives be present and give consent.

86. *Deseret News* 4, no. 46. January 18, 1855, January 26, 1855.

the two-day festivity. Bands played and the people danced.[87] Before dinner the first night, the counselors in the First Presidency—Jedediah M. Grant and Heber C. Kimball—spoke. After dinner, President Young commented that the celebration was the best party he had ever seen in his social hall.[88] He further remarked: "The Mormon Battalion will be held in honorable remembrance to the latest generation; and I will prophesy that the children of those who have been in the army, in defense of their country, will grow up and bless their fathers for what they did at that time. And men and nations will rise up and bless the men who went in that Battalion."[89] The battalion veterans recounted their shared hardships and many anecdotes of assistance, fellowship, and sympathy.[90] The battalion commemoration was cherished by the participants as one of the most memorable events in the early history of Utah Territory.

The mid-1850s presented challenges to Utah. Smith's neighbor Thomas Steed described the situation in Farmington. Grasshoppers devastated the crops in both 1854 and 1855.[91] Farmington's "winter of 1854–55 piled snow three and four feet high and stock died by the hundreds."[92] The following winter of 1855–56 was worse. Snow fell as much as ten feet in Farmington. That winter nearly all the cattle left to range outside Farmington died. Steed found his cattle together in a place sheltered by bushes where they had gathered in a close circle and lain to die.[93] The few remaining animals could hardly work, weakened by lack of forage. To attend the Church's General Conference in April, most of the Saints walked.[94] The residents shared their food with those who had none, and no one died from lack of provisions.[95]

A general reformation took place throughout the church in the beginning of 1856.[96] President Young declared, "I shall take my knapsack

---

87. Item 976 in Peter Crawley, *A Descriptive Bibliography of the Mormon Church*, 3.

88. Daniel Tyler, *A Concise History of Mormon Battalion in the Mexican War 1846–1847*, 351.

89. Tyler, 354.

90. Tyler, 355–63.

91. Thomas Steed, *The Life of Thomas Steed*, 18.

92. Hess, *My Farmington*, 46.

93. Steed, *Life of Thomas Steed*, 20.

94. Steed, 20.

95. Jesse W. Crosby, in *Annals of Wyoming* 10, 11 (1938–39): 210.

96. For a history of the religious reformation in Utah, see Gustive O. Larson, "The Mormon Reformation," 45–63.

under my arm and I will travel through this territory and preach reformation unto this people until they do repent."[97] Young's forty-year-old
counselor Jedediah Grant took up the crusade. He first visited the Saints
in Davis County. On September 17 and 18, he preached in Farmington's
courthouse. On September 19, Thomas Steed said: "[A]s a Ward, [Grant]
weighed us in the balance and found us wanting in great many things. He
then called upon us to know if we were willing to repent and renew our
Covenant again before God; and we arose en mass to show our willingness to be obedient to the call of the man of God who had come to us
armed with the Spirit and power of the Lord Almighty."[98] The next day,
Smith was among the 406 Farmington residents gathered at the millpond
to be rebaptized.[99]

During the fall of 1856, President Young recalled the Territory's
highest-ranking field grade officers from missions in England. Those who
returned in early October included Brigadier General George D. Grant, his
adjutant James Ferguson, William H. Kimball, Cyrus Wheelock, Joseph
A. Young, and Chauncey Webb—all led by apostle Franklin D. Richards,
newly released European Mission President. To greet and honor Brigadier
General Grant with a 113-mile escort to the City, Major Burton and a
small party of the mountain boys gathered at Fort Bridger on October
1. Though the records do not name the party members, the group would
have likely included Burton's close associate in the military, Lot Smith.
The returning missionaries brought disturbing news. The James G. Willie
and Edward L. Martin handcart companies, who had started late in the
season from Iowa with short supplies, were now out on the Wyoming
plains headed west to the Great Salt Lake Valley. Disaster was imminent
due to the lateness in the season. The escorts and missionaries left Fort
Bridger on October 4 for the City.

The next morning President Young addressed the circumstances of
the handcart companies during General Conference. Young called for
men to volunteer to help bring in the Saints. Stressing urgency, Young
called for the volunteers to leave quickly despite the temperate weather.[100] On Monday evening, October 6, the Minute Men known as "the
boys" and their leaders met in Young's office to receive instructions and

---

97. Robinson, *History*, 69.

98. Steed, *Life of Thomas Steed*, 20.

99. Farmington Ward Membership Records; *Deseret News*, October 1, 1856,
reported that 445 were re-baptized.

100. Leroy R. Hafen and Ann W. Hafen, *Handcarts to Zion*, 122.

blessings.[101] As captain of Company B of the Life Guards Cavalry, Lot Smith would have been in this group. Early in the morning of October 8, the rescue group left the City. They camped that night at the foot of Big Mountain and elected George D. Grant as captain with assistants William H. Kimball and Robert T. Burton.[102] The trip to Fort Bridger from Big Mountain was slowed by a drop in the temperature followed by heavy snowfall. It required four days of travel before the rescue party reached Fort Bridger. Three days later they reached the vicinity of Green River, with no sign of the emigrants. At this point, an anxious Grant sent scouts to go as far as Devil's Gate in search of the oncoming companies.[103]

After another heavy snowfall at South Pass on October 17, the weather on the east side of the mountain turned even colder, the nights more bitter, the snow deeper. On October 19, when the rescue party was about fourteen miles farther east below the mouth of Willow Creek on the upper reaches of the Sweetwater, the scraping wagon axles pushed snow in front of the wagons which forced a stop. The rescuers were unaware that they were hardly a day's journey from Willie's handcart company.[104] When the express team found Willie's company, the rescue party broke camp—snowbound or not—and pushed on. The evening of the next day, October 21, they reached the Willie camp—its people huddled in willows near the fifth crossing of the Sweetwater. Bonfires soon blazed for the freezing Saints. The several wagons loaded with food and provisions brought for the two handcart companies could not fill the needs of the approximately 340 members of the Willie Company. The rescuers could only dole out inadequate but deeply appreciated flour and warm clothing with a promise of more to come.[105]

Captain Grant and his party—including Burton and Smith—left William Kimball with Willie's Company and pushed eastward five more days through more storms and deepening snow to search for Martin's company. They passed the place now known as Three Crossings on the Sweetwater, Split Rock, and reached Devil's Gate on October 27 to find

---

101. Rebecca Bartholomew and Leonard J. Arrington, *Rescue of the 1856 Handcart Companies*, 8.

102. Bartholomew and Arringron, 9-10; Hafen and Hafen, *Handcarts to Zion*, 125.

103. Hafen and Hafen, 125.

104. Janet Burton Seegmiller, *"Be Kind to the Poor": The Life Story of Robert Taylor Burton*, 151.

105. Scegmillcr, 14.

the first express men who awaited further orders.[106] Alarmed, Captain Grant sent a second express to ride eastward to search for the Martin handcarts and "not to return until [the emigrants] were found."[107] The express traveled as quickly as their mounts permitted to find the Martin handcarts strung out along the trail and stalled near the last crossing of the North Platte River at Red Buttes/Bluffs Camp now known as Bessemer Bend. Pinned down by a blizzard, they had not moved for nine days.[108] Paul Gourley and his daughter Nichalous of the Martin Handcart Company tell that Lot Smith was one of their first rescuers.[109] Nichalous wrote, "When they arrived at Green river, Joseph A Young, Lot Smith and Angus Wheelock were sent ahead to meet the companies and let them know that relief was coming." She continued, "The three men who came ahead brought a few crackers in their pockets. The children [including Nichalous] were in a wash eating bark off the willows. When they saw the men on horses appear over a hill. The children became very frightened and ran for camp thinking the men were Indians."[110]

Aghast at the shattered spirit of some of the Saints, the rescuers encouraged the company to start traveling again toward the supply wagons. Daniel Jones, Joseph A. Young, and Abel Garr continued eastward to the two stranded wagon companies of Captains William Benjamin Hodgett and John A. Hunt that were trailing the handcarts with orders for them also to start westward. Smith helped bring the Martin Company forward. For two days the Martin handcarts traveled westward. On one of those days, Jones, who was leading Captain Hunt's wagons forward, caught up with the Martin handcarts as they labored up a long muddy hill. Jones left the wagons and went to assist. He recalled,

---

106. Seegmiller, 17

107. Seegmiller, 17–18.

108. George D. Grant, as quoted in Riverton Wyoming Stake, *Remember: The Willie and Martin Handcart Companies and Their Rescuers—Past and Present*, 25.

109. Paul Gourley and his eleven-year-old daughter Nichalous Gourley (Teeples) remembered Joseph A. Young, Lot Smith, and Angus Wheelock. In Raymond W. Madsen, "Scottish Convert Made Long Ocean Journey to Join Ill-Fated Handcart Group," 6; Nichalous Gourley Teeples, "Experience of the Paul Gourley Family 1856 with the Martin Hand-cart Company." Since Paul Gourley served under Smith the following year in the 1857 Utah War, the identification of Smith is positive.

110. Nichalous Gourley Teeples, "Experience of the Paul Gourley Family 1856 with the Martin Hand-cart Company."

A condition of distress here met my eyes that I never saw before or since. The train was strung out for three or four miles. There were old men pulling and tugging their carts, sometimes loaded with a sick wife or children—women pulling along sick husbands—little children six to eight years old struggling through the mud and snow. As night came on the mud would freeze on their clothes and feet. There were two of us and hundreds needing help. What could we do? We gathered on to some of the most helpless with our riatas [lariats] tied to the carts, and helped as many as we could into camp on Avenue hill.[111]

Wagons were sent from Devil's Gate with provisions and met Martin's handcarts at Greasewood Creek. When the group arrived at Devil's Gate, there was room for only a third to shelter in the stockade. Many of the others were so weak they could barely scrape away the snow to set up tents. The Minute Men drove the stakes into frozen ground.[112] The Saints moved to a cove, thereafter known as Martin's Cove, to shelter from the wind strong enough to blow off a wagon cover. There they could await wagons and provisions from their fellow Saints, then ride to Great Salt Lake City.[113] The struggle to convey the handcart companies to the valley was filled with heartbreak as death took more. Of the more than one thousand persons who launched out with the Willie and Martin handcart companies, about 190 died.[114]

As Smith became established in the Rocky Mountains, he continued to advance his military career in the Provo War and as a member of the Nauvoo Legion cavalry in disputes with the Utes, Shoshones, and Gosiutes. These experiences, combined with his service as Davis County sheriff and as a rescuer of the handcart companies, prepared him for the demanding role he would take the following year in the Utah War.

---

111. Daniel W. Jones, *Forty Years Among the Indians*, 66.
112. Bartholomew and Arrington, *Rescue of the 1856 Handcart Companies*, 22.
113. Bartholomew and Arrington, 23.
114. Riverton Wyoming Stake, *Remember,* cover flap.

CHAPTER 3

Utah War

A succession of government-appointed territorial officials sent to Utah led to many conflicts with the Mormons. Some appointees were upright and honest; others were openly dishonorable. Any disagreements between the appointees and the Saints were featured prominently—but not neutrally—in the nation's newspapers. The situation in Utah became increasingly tense. Young had chosen a military man, Daniel H. Wells, as his second counselor in the First Presidency of the Church on January 4, 1857, to replace Jedediah Grant, who had passed away in December. Wells was designated Lieutenant General of the Utah Militia. He resumed his military duties, reactivated the Nauvoo Legion throughout the territory, and installed new local officers.[1] Lot Smith was elected on June 27, 1857, as a major of the First Battalion of Life Guards.[2]

Young planned his annual 24th of July picnic and extended invitations to the Saints to celebrate with him at Silver Lake up Big Cottonwood Canyon; over 2,500 people responded.[3] Major Lot Smith, who commanded five platoons, was stationed at the gate at the mouth of Big Cottonwood Canyon with orders to guard access and make certain that no one preceded the carriages of the First Presidency on the route. Hundreds of waiting wagons crowded the slopes around the entrance to the canyon. Smith also posted sentinels on the way up the mountain to preserve order and to assist in case of mishaps.[4] While the crowd awaited the coming of Young, several bands played.[5] When Young arrived, Major Smith, on horseback with his guards, led the procession up the dugway.[6]

At Silver Lake throughout the next day, the celebrants raised the stars and stripes, listened to speeches and prayers of thanksgiving by their leaders, socialized, and danced to the music of six bands in three separate

---

1. Nauvoo Legion General Orders No. 1, April 11, 1857.

2. Muster Roll, Field and Staff of the 1st Regiment, 1st Brigade, 1st Division, Nauvoo Legion, August 27, 1857.

3. Wilford Woodruff, journal, July 23, 1857.

4. Special Orders No. 5, July 15, 1857, Nauvoo Legion Orders.

5. Journal History of the Church, July 22, 1857 (hereafter cited as Journal History).

6. Woodruff, journal, July 23, 1857.

plank-floor boweries.[7] At about noon, four horsemen arrived posthaste at the campsite. Two were mail carriers—Bishop Abraham O. Smoot and Judson Stoddard. They were accompanied by Porter Rockwell and Judge Elias Smith. In only twenty days the mail carriers had rushed across the continent from Fort Leavenworth, Kansas, to bring Young alarming news.[8] The US government had refused to give Utah's mail carriers the mails from the East in order to keep the Territory uninformed that an army of 2,500 soldiers was being assembled to subdue the Utah Territory and supplant Young as governor by Alfred Cumming of Saint Louis. The advance guard was already en route. President Young did not immediately inform the celebrants about the report.[9] He retired to his tent to allow the Twelve Apostles to ask questions as to what he intended to do. In the meantime, the dancing continued. At the eight o'clock prayer break, Wells broke the news to the attendees.[10] Despite the news, the dancing continued until a late hour.[11] Early on the morning of July 25, Major Smith's cavalrymen again took stations along the return route and the descent began. Young was the last to leave, escorted again by Lot Smith and members of his guard.

As the US Army advanced across the plains toward Utah, Young gathered the outlying settlements to the Great Basin. On September 8, the US Army Assistant Quartermaster, Captain Stewart Van Vliet, arrived in Salt Lake City to a cordial welcome.[12] The captain had intermingled with the Mormons at Winter Quarters and relations were friendly. In honor of Van Vliet, master chef David Candland invited the Minute Men, including Lot Smith, to dine at the Globe Bakery, a popular eating place next to the Council House.[13] Van Vliet felt the united fervor of the Mormons and heard the impassioned accusations of injustice. The Latter-day Saints did not intend to be routed again from their homes. The expulsions from Missouri and Illinois still blazed in the Mormon minds. Young proclaimed to Captain Van Vliet: "[W]hen those troops arrive, they will find Utah a desert. Every house will be burned to the ground, every tree cut down and every field left waste. We have three years' provisions on hand, which

---

7. *Deseret News*, 7:165.

8. Woodruff, journal, July 24, 1857.

9. Bryant S. Hinckley, *Daniel Hanmer Wells*, 94.

10. Kate B. Carter, *Heart Throbs of the West*, 7:95.

11. Andrew Jackson Allen, "Diary," 16.

12. Journal History, September 8, 1857.

13. John D. T. McAllister, *Autobiography and Diary*, September 11, 1857.

we will 'cache,' and then take to the mountains and bid defiance to all of the powers of the government."[14] Van Vliet was persuaded that President Buchanan had misjudged the situation. As Van Vliet left Great Salt Lake City on September 14 and traveled eastward, he met each segment of the army and tried to persuade them that to invade Utah Territory was folly.[15]

The afternoon of Van Vliet's departure, Young proclaimed martial law.[16] Nauvoo Legion Commander, Lieutenant General Wells, departed September 27 for Fort Bridger with important papers that Young desired to be delivered to the advancing army.[17] Major Lot Smith accompanied the commander and a large contingent of men.[18] Companies of fifty to a hundred men hastened up Echo Canyon behind the staff of the general. Their urgency was fueled by rumors that the army was advancing by rapid forced marches.[19] Wells ordered troops to build rock parapets atop the high cliffs of Echo Canyon, to position huge boulders to be cast down at will on the army, and to construct levees to flood the route and push the army against the boulder-topped bluffs.[20] Hosea Stout wrote: "[B]efore we return it will be determined whether a legalized government mob can force themselves on us against our will and contrary to all law or not. We go in the name and Strength of Israels God."[21]

Commander Wells and two apostles, George A. Smith and John Taylor, along with troops arrived September 30 at Mormon-held Fort Bridger. Wells entrusted General Lewis Robison, who had authority at Fort Bridger, to deliver Young's important letter packet to the enemy's camp.[22] Wells

---

14. Edward Tullidge, *History of Salt Lake City*, 174–175.

15. Journal History, September 25 and 28, 1857.

16. Tullidge, *History of Salt Lake City*, 166.

17. Tullidge, 169.

18. *Contributor*, 3:270.

19. George A. Smith, journal, September 27, 1857.

20. Tullidge, *History of Salt Lake City*, 169. The breastworks and dam in the bottom of the canyon are located about 1.25 miles east of the Echo exit on old Highway 30. The fortifications begin about three-quarters of a mile up the canyon from the current rest area and continue for about one and a half miles. There were supposedly sixteen fortifications; thirteen are currently pictured in the information center at the rest area.

21. Juanita Brooks, *On the Mormon Frontier, the Diary of Hosea Stout*, 638.

22. The packet of letters included five things. First, it included a letter of Young dated September 29, 1857, citing the section of the Territorial Laws that referred to the manner in which the governor might be succeeded. On that authority, Young stated that he was still the Governor of Utah, not having been removed by

then chose the two majors of the 1st and 2nd Battalions of Cavalry—Lot Smith and J. D. T. McAllister—to accompany Robison. Robison was also assigned to travel fifteen miles up Ham's Fork, survey the position of the army's encampment, travel back across country toward Bridger, and report the route.[23] Robison, McAllister, and Smith were joined by Porter Rockwell and left Bridger the morning of October 1.[24] Apparently, the group split. Robison and Rockwell made the survey while Smith and McAllister headed for the army's camp at Ham's Fork to deliver the papers.[25] Henry S. Hamilton, one of the bandsmen of Colonel E. P. Alexander's camp, reported the delivery of the letter packet to Colonel Alexander:

> A delegation of Mormons came to our camp, bearing with them the following order from Brigham Young. . . . We were somewhat surprised that our colonel tolerated such impudence, and did not take them prisoners; but he treated them courteously, even ordering out the band to entertain them. On their departure he instructed them to inform Mr. Brigham Young that [the Colonel's] orders to proceed to Salt Lake City came from an authority much higher than [Young's]–from the President of the United States; that [the army] were there as escort to Governor Cumming, who was to supersede him, and they would better not come with any more such orders.[26]

Upon his return to camp, Smith was invited to dinner with the commanding general and his aides.[27] Recalling the conversation, Smith wrote:

> During the meal General Wells, looking at me as straight as possible, asked if I could take a few men and turn back the trains that were on the road or burn them. I replied that I thought I could do just what he told me to do.

---

the President of the United States. Young further demanded immediate retreat or delivery of arms and ammunition to Quartermaster General Robison at Fort Bridger and a retreat the following spring. Second, it included the Proclamation of September 15, 1857, that forbade US troops to enter Utah Territory and ordered Mormon troops to be ready to repel the US troops. Third, the packet included a proclamation of martial law throughout the territory. Fourth, there was a letter to Mr. James Rupe, wagonmaster traveling with the army, that warned him to "take care of his men." Rupe had been appointed general agent for Majors & Russell to accompany the trains. See Raymond W. Settle and Mary Lund Settle, *War Drums and Wagon Wheels,* 56. Fifth, the packet included Wells's letter of transmittal.

23. George A. Smith, Journal History, October 25, 1857.

24. McAllister, *Autobiography and Diary,* October 1, 1857.

25. Hubert Howe Bancroft, *History of Utah 1540-1886,* 515; Journal History, October 1, 1857.

26. Henry S. Hamilton, *Reminiscences of a Veteran,* 81–82.

27. *Contributor,* 3:271–72.

The answer seemed to please him, and he accepted it, telling me that he could furnish only a few men, but that they would be sufficient, for they would appear many more to our enemies. As for provisions, none would be supplied, as we were expected to board at the expense of Uncle Sam. As this seemed to be an open order, I did not complain.[28]

The request made by General Wells sent Smith into a leading role in the most dramatic acts of the Echo Canyon War.

Majors Smith and McAllister formed the vanguard of patrols from the Latter-day Saint men who had arrived at Fort Bridger. Smith selected forty-three men for the mission.[29] (See Appendix A.) He chose as his officers Captain Horton D. Haight and Lieutenants Thomas Abbott and John Vance, and he requisitioned the best available horses.[30] With the company ready to leave Fort Bridger for the field, General Wells's farewell to Smith's men was a wise forewarning: "Boys, don't let them pen you! don't let them pen you!! boys don't let them pen you!!!"[31] In the late afternoon of Friday, October 2, Smith rode eastward at the head of his company toward the approaching army.[32] Historian Edward Tullidge described Smith's entry into the Utah War:

> Among all the warriors of the Mormon Israel, there was, perhaps not one so fitted to open this very peculiar campaign as Lot Smith. His lion-like courage and absolute fearlessness of personal danger when most in its presence, marked him out as the man of men to execute an exploit of such daring as that designed to astonish the American nation into a realization of the Mormon earnestness, yet at the same time to do it without the shedding of a drop of 'the enemy's' blood.[33]

Smith's company traveled most of the night and crossed Ham's Fork where they stopped on the south side near Black's Fork to camp in the hills below the soldiers' rendezvous camp located about four miles upriver.[34] Very early the next morning, Smith and his company rode to the army's camp where he and his forty-three Mormons looked at the

---

28. *Contributor*, 3:272.

29. Thurzal Q. Terry, *Great Utah War*, 8.

30. Carter, *Heart Throbs of the West*, 3:19.

31. Terry, *Great Utah War*, 8.

32. Smith's *Contributor* story dated his departure from Fort Bridger as Saturday, October 3. Diaries of his company specified Friday, October 2.

33. Tullidge, *History of Salt Lake City*, 173.

34. Henry Ballard, Private Journal, 5; Terry, *Great Utah War*, 9; Philo Dibble, journal.

182 wagons loaded with supplies, well-guarded by many soldiers. Smith saw no opportunity to burn any wagons. One of the army waggoneers, William Clark, reported that "Lot Smith, a Mormon captain with two hundred mounted men came riding into camp, stopped awhile, then rode off toward Green River."[35]

Smith met a small train of six corn wagons under the leadership of Rankin. Smith told Rankin to head back east, but as soon as Smith was out of sight, the train went west again. US troops met Rankin's train, took out the lading, and left the wagons standing.[36] Smith's company camped that night on Green River not far from the troops that had taken the lading.[37] The following day the company continued eastward and met Benjamin F. Ficklin, who was unknowingly allied with the US army.[38] Smith inquired of him where Majors and Russell's supply trains were. Knowing Smith's intent to burn the supply wagons, Ficklin declined to betray their location.[39] Later in the day at Green River, Smith found the Tenth Infantry of the army, or part of it, with a light battery camped near the road. Smith recalled:

> On the road, seeing a large cloud of dust at a distance up the [Green] river on the old Mormon road, I sent scouts to see what caused it. They returned, overtaking me at Sandy [Fork], and reported a train of twenty-six large freight wagons. We took supper and started at dark. After traveling fourteen miles, we came up to the train, but discovered the teamsters were drunk, and knowing that drunken men were easily excited and always ready to fight, and remembering my positive orders not to hurt anyone except in self-defence, we remained in ambush until after midnight.[40] I then sent scouts [Henry Day and Henry Jackson] to thoroughly examine the appearance of their camp, to note the number of wagons and men and to report all they discovered. When they returned and reported twenty-six wagons in two lines a short distance apart [about 150 yards apart], I concluded that counting one teamster to each wagon and throwing in eight or ten extra men would make their force about forty. I thought we would be a match for them, and so ordered an advance to their camp.[41]

---

35. William Clark, "A Trip Across the Plains in 1857," 192.

36. Philo Dibble, journal, 9; Hamilton Gardner, ed., "A Territorial Militiaman in the Utah War, Journal of Newton Tuttle," 306.

37. *Contributor*, 3:272

38. Tracy Albert, "Journal of Captain Tracy Albert," 5n14.

39. Captain Jesse A. Gove, *Utah Expedition, 1857–1858,* 73.

40. *Contributor*, 3:272.

41. Kate B. Carter, *Heart Throbs of the West*, 10:235–36.

As Smith and his troops neared the train, they discovered there were twice as many wagons and double the men. Smith's men thought he would make casual inquiries and pass their advance upon the train as a joke, but Smith felt it was not a time for joking. Smith led his company forward until their horses' heads were lit by firelight. When he looked back at his twenty men, he realized that the end of his troops could not be seen in the darkness; it looked as though there could be a hundred or more. Smith asked for the captain and John Dawson stepped forward. Smith told Dawson to quickly get all his men and their personal property out of the wagons for he "meant to put a little fire into them." Dawson exclaimed, "For God's sake, don't burn the trains," to which Smith replied that it was for His sake that he was going to burn them. [42] Dawson stated that he didn't think Smith had enough men to burn the wagons. Smith bluffed that if he didn't have enough, all he had to do was whistle.[43] The teamsters were very frightened as they came forward to stack their guns and huddle under guard until they realized they would not be harmed. Then they laughed and said they were happy for the wagons to burn so they wouldn't have to drive them anymore. A tar rope in one wagon was to be used, as it was said, to hang Brigham Young; it made a great bonfire instead. [44]

When an army messenger came into camp, Smith demanded his dispatches, and the man replied that they were only verbal. Smith said: "I told him if he lied to me his life was not worth a straw. He became terrified, in fact I never saw a man more frightened. The weather was a little cool but his jaws fairly clattered." The verbal orders were that they were not to sleep and were to keep a night guard because there were Mormons in the field; they would be escorted in the morning. While Smith and his company were involved with the first train, a guard came from the second train. Smith told the guard to go back and not to move until he came to take care of the second train. The guard returned to his train, squatted by a wagon wheel, and never moved until Smith arrived.

Smith and Dawson went to the second train where Dawson shook the wagon master's wagon and yelled for Bill (R. W. Barret). Groggy with sleep, Bill grumbled until Dawson exclaimed, "Damn it man, get up, or you'll be burned to a cinder in five minutes!"[45] Smith's men carried out the same itinerary with the second train and were spread thin guarding, but

42. *Contributor*, 3:272–74.
43. Carter, *Heart Throbs of the West*, 10:236.
44. Terry, *Great Utah War*, 10.
45. *Contributor*, 3:272–74.

the teamsters never figured it out. Smith asked Dawson about his freight since he needed overcoats for his men. Smith also asked if there was any powder in the wagons. If so, Smith would take Dawson with him to fire the wagons. Dawson was terrified at that dangerous proposition and searched diligently for overcoats and powder. He found a lot of saltpeter and sulphur that were almost as hazardous as powder. Smith said they would have to take the risk of injury anyway. Dawson begged Smith, "For the good Lord's sake don't take me, I've been sick and am not well yet, and don't want to be hurt."[46] Smith said, "There were many such laughable incidents connected with the adventures of the night, if we had dared to laugh."[47]

Smith respected Dawson's frank desire to not torch the wagons and instead took his Irish follower, Big James, who was not afraid. They both made torches and when the train was ready to fire, a Ute came asking for two wagon covers, some flour, and soap. When Smith filled his order, the Ute was elated. Smith and Big James then rode with their torches from wagon to wagon and set the wagon covers on fire in the blowing wind. To Smith, the covers seemed to catch fire very slowly. When he said so to his companion, Big James swung his long torch overhead and said, "By St. Patrick, aint it beautiful! I never saw anything go better in all my life."[48]

Smith's account continued: "On completing this task, I told [Dawson] that we were going just a little way off and that if he or his men molested the trains or undertook to put the fire out, they would be instantly killed. We rode away, leaving the wagons ablaze."[49] The wagon masters abandoned their teams and cattle and walked the twenty miles to Camp Winfield. The bright red tongues of flame from Dawson's and Barrett's fifty-one wagons could be seen from a distance of twenty-one miles.[50] With the burning wagons at their backs, Smith and his men proceeded in the pre-dawn darkness to the bluffs of Green River. Smith sent Edwin Booth alone with a message to General Wells detailing their activities to that point.[51] When the troops rode on to Sandy, they stopped only long enough to get breakfast. Without further rest after their all-night rigors,

---

46. *Contributor*, 3:272–74.

47. *Contributor*, 3:272–74.

48. *Contributor*, 3:272–74.

49. *Contributor*, 3:274.

50. James A. Oliver, *Biography of Samuel Bateman, 1832–1881*, 40.

51. *Contributor*, 4:27.

they went up to the road to encounter another wagon train at a place now known as Simpson's Hollow. [52]

The train captain, Lew Simpson, was out watering the cattle at a creek a mile and a half from camp. Smith's troops disarmed the teamsters and Smith rode out to meet Simpson. Smith demanded Simpson's pistols. Simpson replied:

> "By God, sir, no man ever took them yet, and if you think you can, without killing me, try it." We were all the time riding towards the train, with our noses about as close together as two Scotch terriers would have held theirs— his eyes flashing fire; I couldn't see mine—I told him that I admired a brave man, but that I did'nt like blood—you insist on my killing you, which will only take a minute, but I don't want to do it. We had by this time reached the train. He, seeing that his men were under guard, surrendered, saying: "I see you have me at a disadvantage my men being disarmed." I replied that I did'nt need the advantage, and asked him what he would do if we should give them their arms. "I'll fight you!" "Then," says I, "we know something about that too—take up your arms!" His men exclaimed, "Not by a damn sight! We came out here to whack bulls, not to fight." "What do you say to that, Simpson?" I asked.
>
> "Damnation," he replied, grinding his teeth in the most violent manner, "if I had been here before and they had refused to fight, I would have killed every man of them."[53]

Simpson was terribly distressed over the capture of his train. He was the son-in-law of Mr. Majors, who owned the wagons about to be burned. Smith offered to leave Simpson a wagonload of provisions for his teamsters. At that offer, Simpson said, "You will give me two, I know it by your looks!"[54] Smith told them to hurry to remove their personal belongings and leave with their two wagons. Smith told, "Simpson begged me not to burn the train while he was in sight, and said that it would ruin his reputation as a wagon master. I told him not to be squeamish, that the trains burned very nicely, I had seen them before, and that we had'nt time to be ceremonious."[55] Smith considered Simpson the bravest man he faced during the war. Smith then told his men to get to work. After getting pro-

---

52. Among the personnel of the twenty-four wagon train were a couple of young men—twelve-year-old William F. "Buffalo Bill" Cody and James Butler "Wild Bill" Hickok. William F. Cody [Buffalo Bill], *Story of the Wild West and Campfire Chats by Buffalo Bill*, 436.

53. *Contributor*, 4:27–29.

54. *Contributor*, 4:27–29.

55. *Contributor*, 4:27–29.

visions, they broke up the ox yokes and bows, piled them on the wagons, and set them afire. [56]

The Mormon troops rode south about two miles to rest when a most distressing event occurred. Most of the men were standing in a group dividing out some gun caps. [57] While Smith was reloading his pistol, one of the company's Yeager rifles discharged and the heavy ball passed through Orson P. Arnold's thigh, which broke the bone in a dreadful manner, and then hit Philo Dibble on the side of the head and passed through Samuel Bateman's hat. As Arnold fell with his leg under him, Smith caught him and straightened his leg. The jagged bone pierced the skin and blood gushed out. Smith, with others, laid their hands upon Arnold and invoked a blessing from heaven to save his life, for they knew they could not. Expecting troops from the camp to overtake them at any moment, Smith immediately sent two men to the river for poles to make a litter to carry Arnold to safety. As Smith and a doctor's son set the bone and bandaged the wound with shirts of the men, a picket guard ran into camp blurting that two hundred cavalries were almost upon them. [58] Smith said:

> Under the circumstances nothing could have produced greater consternation. One of the men moved that we surrender. I told them that I would say when to do that. He then proposed that we *run*. I replied that I would kill the man that made that motion, myself, if he dared to try it. Then I made my first war speech. I told the men that we were not out here of our own choice, on our own business. Our people and their rights were being assailed. It was the Lord's work that they were engaged in, and we were called by Him to protect our homes and our religion. If He suffered those troops to come near us, we would trust in Him and whip them, no matter about their numbers. The boys gathered around me and said that I had spoken right, that they would stand by me if I would stand. I was well repaid for stiffening my knees, for poor Orson looked up and said he knew I would'nt run away and leave him to die. [59]

The group began their thirty-mile journey over a trackless desert, carrying on their shoulders the wounded Arnold on poles toward a safe place on Green River. Since their only water was that which was carried in their canteens, they ran out of water by nightfall. The men had been without sleep for more than forty hours, and Smith suggested the group stop to lie

---

56. "Interesting From Utah," *The New York Times*, July 8, 1858.
57. Terry, *Great Utah War*, 11.
58. Fred Abbott, audio recording, June 25, 1960; Terry, *Great Utah War*, 12.
59. *Contributor*, 4:27–29, 48.

down and rest until morning. However, some suggested that part of the group could go ahead for water and return to meet the group carrying the litter. All agreed. After only a mile, however, one of the litter poles broke and the other almost fell to the ground. Arnold, who had been sleeping, was jarred awake and began to suffer painfully. Smith sent the rest of the men on to get water, which was at least an eight miles distant. They journeyed back and met the group on the plain in darkness with no direction of fire, road, or landmarks. Smith said, "I only know of one way to account for the incident. We had to have the water or the boy would die, and a Power greater than we *knew* it."[60]

The men were totally exhausted and fell asleep as soon as they dismounted their horses. Smith took off the saddles and guns and looked after the horses. With sleep overwhelming him, he thought of a fellow too short to help carry the stretcher who would be fresher compared to anyone else. He awoke him and asked him to watch the horses, and promptly fell asleep. Although he was aware the man just turned over, he could not arouse himself. Before daylight Smith's company headed out toward Green River. Their picket guard advised to make a five-mile circuit around the river to avoid enemy soldiers he had seen on the banks. Smith gave the choice to his men, but said that he himself was not going to lengthen the journey, and he headed for a small grove of cottonwoods on the river bottom. He said that "it would take a right smart lot of soldiers" to get him out of that grove. The group left the wounded Arnold in the care of two men on the bluffs and followed Smith to the river. While Smith was in a tree surveying the situation, a picket guard dashed into the grove to say that two soldiers were chasing two of our men toward the group. Smith said, "Without thought I sprang down, caught up my gun and ran; my men following me. In a minute or two I stopped short, and asked him if he said that two of our men were being chased by *two* soldiers. He said, 'yes.' 'Then I hope they will catch them, I don't want any two men that any other two can chase.' They all laughed."[61] The truth of the matter was that two Mormon men were chasing two mountaineers. The mountaineers agreed to take care of Arnold, and did so for ten days until General Wells sent a wagon to convey him home. Smith's men were glad to find that the "enemy" soldiers seen on the riverbank were fellow soldiers under the leadership of Captain Haight. William A. Hickman came to tell Smith that there was a large herd of cattle located where they had burned the first

60. *Contributor*, 4:27–29, 48.
61. *Contributor*, 4:27–29, 48.

wagon trains. Accordingly, Smith's troops gathered the hundred and fifty head and turned them over to Hickman, who took them to the Salt Lake Valley. Several of the teamsters accompanied Hickman, saying that they had had enough of government bull whacking to last a lifetime. [62]

On Wednesday, October 7, Smith and company moved upriver about eight miles from the trading post of Baptiste "LeChat" and camped for the day.[63] When they ran short of provisions, Smith was glad to meet Simpson, who shared supplies from those Smith had given them. Smith met a man who had been a prisoner at Fort Bridger when Smith left there. The man commented that he thought Smith and his command of five hundred were a fine group of men. Smith wrote: "General Wells had told us that our numbers would be magnified in the eyes of the enemy, and it proved to be so. We passed during all the fall for from five hundred to a thousand men, while in fact the whole number never exceeded at any time one hundred, and generally was not half that many."[64]

Smith and his cavalry had been successful in their exploits to hinder the progress of the US Army toward the Territory and were eager for another encounter. Fortunately for both the army and the Mormons, no more supply trains were burned. They next turned their attention to the army's stock and would barely escape capture.

---

62. *Contributor*, 4:27–29, 48.

63. Gardner, "A Territorial Militiaman," 305.

64. *Harper's New Monthly Magazine* reported that Smith's company, which burned the three wagon trains, numbered five hundred. *Harper's New Monthly Magazine* 16 (December 1857–May 1858): 258.

CHAPTER 4

Escape Capture

The war continued. General Wells wrote Smith of his pleasure in Smith's successes and continued with instructions: keep a good lookout both in the rear of his company as well as ahead, obtain food and clothing from any trains if possible, remain in the rear of the enemy's camp, burn wagons, stampede stock, and keep the foe weary with night surprises.[1] Resolved to follow orders, Smith decided that taking the army's cattle could hamper their progress as effectively as anything else. He sent twelve men from the camp on the Sandy River to get the rest of Simpson's cattle. The twelve men hurried back toward the Sandy River when they found two hundred soldiers following them.[2] Smith was undaunted. When he learned from scouts that all the soldiers had left Green River to head west, he and his company started after dark for Green River. There, three of his men learned from Baptiste "LeChat" that the army teamsters had taken a hundred head of cattle and started for Ham's Fork. Smith and company rode all night in an unsuccessful attempt to overtake them. They camped that night on Black's Fork.[3]

Early the next morning in fog, Smith and Mark Bigler were climbing a nearby lookout peak to survey the situation when they discovered a group of men on the summit only three hundred yards above them. They assumed they were enemy troops by their actions. Since it was three miles back to camp, they knew they could not escape by running. They were soon overtaken by thirty men who were under the leadership of Orrin Porter Rockwell and Thomas Rich.[4] Had the men on the summit been US soldiers instead of fellow Saints, Smith would have been captured. With the seventy-four men under Rockwell and Smith combined, the Mormon troops proceeded up the river to ascertain the army's situation on Ham's Fork. On a bluff, they sighted a herd of 1,400 cattle below on the bottom lands within sight of the army's camp. Smith prefaced the following incident with: "Rockwell and I were good friends, on the following basis: I did

---

1. *Contributor*, 4:47–48.

2. James A. Oliver, *Biography of Samuel Bateman*, 43.

3. Oliver, 43.

4. *Contributor*, 4:48.

as I pleased, and he, regularly, damned me for it."[5] As they looked over the herd, Smith declared that they would take the cattle. Rockwell felt that the cattle were left there as a trap to catch Smith; the willows were sure to be full of artillery, and all would be killed. Smith told Rockwell to go ahead and sit by—he would take the cattle on his own. Rockwell roughly replied that he would see Smith in limbo first. While Rockwell stopped to glass the location, Smith started rushing down the steep bluff with only a third of the men able to keep up. Porter joined in a terrible rage, swearing—at Smith for going so fast and at the men for not going fast enough. They ran their horses for two miles to reach the herd. The army guards saw them coming and quickly started the herd toward their camp but they were intercepted, and the Mormons turned the cattle back. Then Smith's men gave such a shout that the cattle stampeded and trod over many, killing half a dozen of the slower animals. The guards, as well as Captain James Rupe, were as frightened as the cattle. When Rupe recovered a little, he asked Smith to leave him enough cattle to take his wagons to camp. Smith gave him twenty head.

Then Rupe's men made an astonishing request. They asked Smith if they could have their guns back. This request led to the discovery that the men had thrown away their guns when they saw the Mormon troops coming down the bluff like wild men. Someone had said their lives would be spared if they were unarmed. Smith told them to get their guns; he and his troops had all they wanted. Rockwell told Rupe to tell the Colonel that the Mormons were going to kill every one of them if they did not release their three prisoners. The frightened guards then ran their teams towards camp. Some of the cattle dropped dead, but they continued their dash until they were within their lines. Smith and Rockwell joined their men with the stock and divided the cattle into manageable herds. With only the stars to guide them through the night, Smith and Rockwell piloted the cattle westward.[6] At ten o'clock they stopped, tied their horses to sagebrush, and camped without feed or water. At daylight, the men lost no time in moving to the river, killing a cow, and appeasing their hunger. Smith returned to his men on Ham's Fork, and after resting the herd, the guards pushed the cattle on toward Fort Bridger accompanied by Rockwell.[7] The company divided the day after Smith's return. Rich's company returned to the Muddy, and Smith's men, who included those

---

5. *Contributor*, 4:48–50.
6. *Contributor*, 4:48–50.
7. Andrew Jackson Allen, "Diary," 23.

left by Rockwell, returned to Ham's Fork to eat supper and hide in the hills for the night.[8]

Back in Great Salt Lake City, Young strategized. He had a few ideas to expedite desertion of the US troops. For example, if a thousand men, mostly soldiers, could be persuaded to desert "with all the ammunition they can carry," it would greatly benefit the Mormons.[9] He suggested that Lewis Robison inform soldiers and bullwhackers that they could have protection and gainful employment in Salt Lake City—a good incentive since some of the bullwhackers had been forced by circumstances to volunteer into the army. To further encourage desertion, Young gave Wells these precise and detailed—if somewhat unrealistic—instructions:

> [H]ave bro. Lot Smith, or some other clear spoken and loud voiced person who is also a good rider, be furnished with a good horse and instructed at once to proceed to the enemy's camp and upon the first opportunity, at about dusk on a still evening, approach within hailing distance on the windward side, and on a point or rise of ground, if any, and shout something as follows: "Attention the camp" (to be repeated perhaps, once or twice, till attention is attracted) "all who wish to fight the Mormons had better stay where they are, and all who do not wish to fight are advised to make for Salt Lake City at every opportunity, where they will be well treated, furnished with employment and permitted to proceed to California when they please."[10]

US Captain Jesse Gove wrote: "My company and Capt. [Franklin] Gardner's were ordered out to go down the creek to have a brush with Lot Smith and some 60 Mormons who were approaching our trains."[11] On October 15, Smith and four men started up Ham's Fork to reconnoiter the enemy at their camp. After he had gone ten miles and had not discovered the army's camp, Smith sent a man back to tell the others to follow.[12] He felt that his command was quite strong with Rockwell's reinforcements, so they started

---

8. Hamilton Gardner, ed., "A Territorial Militiaman," 309.

9. Nauvoo Legion Letter Book, Nauvoo Legion (Utah) records, 1851–1870.

10. Nauvoo Legion Letter Book.

11. Jesse A. Gove, *Utah Expedition*, 78. This incident would have to have been on October 15, though Gove reported it under an October 16 journal entry and reaffirmed it in his sentence previous, noting that Captain Marcy's command returned. Since Smith and company departed immediately for Bridger on the 16th without waiting for nightfall, the confrontation with Gove and Gardner would have been October 15. The date is confirmed by Sam Bateman's October 15 entry: "We traveled up Ham's Fork and suddenly came upon the soldiers about 8 or 9 o'clock at night." Samuel Bateman, *Diary*, 44.

12. Hamilton Gardner, ed., "A Territorial Militiaman," 309.

trailing a detachment of troops after dark and unexpectedly came upon a large force—too close for comfort. [13] Smith, mounted on a government mule, quickly led his men out of sight over rough ground so the enemy could not discern how many men were in his group. [14]

After the capture of the army beef two days before, the army thirsted for vengeance against the Mormon raider Lot Smith and "the rascals that come out on the hills boldly, knowing that we have no mounted troops."[15] The army's leaders planned to search for Lot Smith but did not tell their troops for fear of spies in their camp. Instead, they suggested that they were seeking a road to Henry's Fork for winter quarters. Captain Randolph B. Marcy formed a makeshift cavalry of mules with harness bridles and a few saddles. Bugle calls that night assembled volunteers for a mounted expedition to head out at four o'clock in the morning.[16] In the predawn darkness, Captain Marcy led more than sixty of his men a few miles up Ham's Fork hoping to surprise and capture Smith. When he didn't discover his quarry upriver, Marcy headed downriver to look for Smith's early morning campfires.

Smith recalled: "[S]uddenly we heard the tramping of animals, and the picket guard reported a hundred or more horsemen on the march."[17] Unaware of the cavalry, he assumed that the dust and noise was the mules being taken to grass downriver. In the early light, Smith's men followed the noise of the tramping mules down the narrow valley between the steep hills and banks of Ham's Fork. If possible, Smith intended to take the mules in the same manner he had taken the cattle. Within a few miles, Smith's men drew close before being discovered. When Captain Marcy and his men unexpectedly realized their closeness, they scrambled into line.[18] Marcy demanded that Smith and his troops surrender.[19] Smith called back that he never surrendered.[20] While the soldiers slipped off their mules and dropped onto one knee with their guns in position to fire, Smith's men

---

13. Bateman, *Diary*, 44.

14. *Contributor*, 4:167–68.

15. Gove, *Utah Expedition*, 71.

16. Joseph Parry, journal, 20–21.

17. *Contributor*, 4:168.

18. *Contributor*, 4:168.

19. Parry, journal, 20–21.

20. Parry, 20–21.

remained on horseback—in edgy attention.[21] George A. Smith reported their conversation:

> The Captain said, "I suppose you are Capt. Lot Smith."
> "Major," [Smith] replied. "Yes. What is your name?"
> "Captain Marcy. I saw[,] Capt. Smith[,] that you could not see very well this morning."
> Lot replied, "I think I could see as well as you with your blind bridles."[22]

Smith wrote:

> He [Marcy] then said that the soldiers he commanded were United States troops, and asked me what armed force it was I had. I told him they were from Utah. "What is your business here?" he inquired. "Watching you. What is your business?" I asked. He said they were looking out a way into Utah. "Nonsense," said I, "you have left the main road to the valley long ago. It passes through Echo Canyon. I have been that way myself many a time."

Smith knew that Marcy was out hunting him. Marcy's troops knocked powder down into their guns, ready for a fight while the two leaders continued in mundane conversation.[23] He was following the orders he had received from Alexander as he left camp. The orders were to not fire unless the Mormons fired. With every stratagem he could command, Marcy prolonged the conversation for forty-five minutes. He knew—and Smith did not—that two companies of infantry were advancing at double quick time down the valley to entrap Smith.[24]

One of Smith's men, James P. Terry, added another bit of the conversation during the delay:

> [Marcy] invited Lot to go and visit Colonel Alexander and see the Hickman boys, as the [army] had them prisoners.[25] He said the Colonel would be pleased to see us but Captain Smith declined the invitation as he was not

---

21. Thurzal Q. Terry, *Great Utah War*, 15.

22. George A. Smith, Journal History of the Church, October 25, 1857 (cited hereafter as Journal History).

23. *Contributor*, 4:168.

24. George A. Smith, Journal History, October 25, 1857.

25. Unknown to Smith, Alexander released Thomas J. Hickman—a nonmilitary man—to carry his protest of burning the wagons and grass and stampeding the cattle. See George A. Smith, Journal History, October 25, 1857. On that day (October 16) Bill Hickman was on his way with Lewis Robison and Joshua Terry to treat with Washakie the Shoshoni Chief.

anxious for an introduction to Colonel Alexander. He thought he might see the Hickman boys at some other time.[26]

The conversation continued with the minds of both men busy with matters other than talk. While Marcy calculated the time required for the infantry to come down from the camp to seal off any escape to the north, Smith considered how he could remove his men from Marcy's control. At one point, Smith casually half dismounted, leaving one foot in the stirrup as he tightened his saddle's cinch.[27] Near the end of the conversation, Marcy said that the officers did not want to battle the Mormons. Smith replied that "the Administration seemed to want them to, and that their coming here, put us in the position of a man holding off the hand that clutched a knife with which to cut his throat. We had a good hold of that arm raised against us, and would keep it."[28]

The pleasantries ended, and Smith unexpectedly rode forward directly through the ranks of Marcy's stunned men while Smith's troops skirted to the right. Caught off guard, Marcy trailed some distance behind and ordered Smith's troops to stop.[29] Smith ignored the command. As they hurried away, he told his men that although they had come to catch mules, they had no time to stop for mules or anything else; it was all they could do to keep from being caught themselves. Within three minutes the whole force of the army's infantry arrived with drums, fifes, bugle calls, and shouts. By the time Smith's men met up with the rest of their command, their only route of escape was either up a steep mountain or through the infantry's line.[30] Terry said, "[H]ad we been five minutes later or they [the infantry] that much sooner we would have been completely penned in at this time as the footmen were coming down on our left and Marcy and his 'jack-ass cavalry' were coming up on our right."[31]

At that point Smith called, "[F]ollow me, boys, and I will take you out of this."[32] Smith crossed the river, but his horse struggled to climb the steep bank on the other side. He knew the rest could not do it. As the infantry almost encircled the Mormons, Smith raced upriver to find where the bank was cut by a ravine. Smith said, "Just as we all got across

---

26. Terry, *Great Utah War*, 16.
27. Terry, 16.
28. *Contributor*, 4:168.
29. Oliver, *Biography*, 44.
30. *Contributor*, 4:168–69.
31. Terry, *Great Utah War*, 16.
32. Parry, journal, 20–21.

and had safely clambered up the bank, the cavalry came upon us and commanded us to halt. The boys sent back their compliments, more expressive than elegant, and the main body gave up the chase, as we leisurely rode up the hill."[33] Smith's men dismounted in the protection of the rocks to let their winded horses blow and looked across at the troops who minutes before had them entrapped. Smith imagined how chagrined they must have felt that his troops had slipped through their fingers.[34] Feeling safe, some of the men gathered around a small spring to relax after the narrow escape.[35] Suddenly, Lieutenant Thomas Abbot galloped in wildly and shouted the unbelievable fact that the troops were upon them! The enemy troops jumped off their horses and commenced firing. Smith said, "If ever I was mad, that was the time. Luckily for us they were in short range and over shot the mark—except Mark Hall of Ogden, who got a bullet through his hat. Two horses were shot; a gray one falling near me. The troops thought I had fallen and shouted exultantly. I felt happy to know that they were mistaken." [36] Instead of capturing mules, Smith and his men barely escaped capture by seven hundred soldiers of the US Army in Camp No. 67 on Ham's Fork.[37] Smith then tried to lure the enemy troops out of the rocks where he declared he could whip them, but they refused to take the challenge.[38]

Both hunger and lack of provisions compelled the Mormon troops toward Bridger. After sundown, they reached their camping place where some of their fellow brethren were preparing some beef. Newton Tuttle wrote, "We had eaten nothing since the day before about three P.M., and then not more than half a meal."[39] When Smith saw that the meat was going to be rationed, he put a stop to it and said, "Boys here's meat, help yourselves," which they did with vigor.[40]

Smith promptly dispatched information to Wells of his encounter with Marcy and then continued toward Fort Bridger. An October 17 letter from Wells to Major Smith approved Smith's retreat, promised flour, ordered him to burn no more trains, and commanded him to join his

---

33. *Contributor*, 4:169.
34. *Contributor*, 4:169.
35. Parry, journal, 20–21.
36. *Contributor*, 4:169, 224.
37. Oliver, *Biography*, 45.
38. Oliver, 45.
39. Gardner, "A Territorial Militiaman," 310.
40. Terry, *Great Utah War*, 18.

fellow commander McAllister; however, an ugly storm prevented the delivery of both the letter and the flour.[41]

During winter maneuvers, the Latter-day Saint troops had been instructed to never camp twice in the same spot. They carried only bedrolls tied behind saddles, scanty provisions, minimum cooking utensils, and no tents. Smith and his men cooked, ate, and slept unprotected in the open. As Smith's men arrived on the Muddy on their way to Bridger, the temperature plummeted and the wind hurled snow. As the blizzard raged around them, Smith and his men, without food, shared bedrolls and sleeplessly cowered through the night. The storm worsened all the next day. Driven by hunger on October 18, Smith's men pushed on through the storm toward Fort Bridger. Despite the danger, Smith and his men survived the storm. At Fort Bridger, they discovered that their fellow Saints had burned everything (after the supplies of grain and vegetables had been cached) except a blacksmith shop. Food for Smith's men had not yet arrived. Blacksmith James Turner could not restrain his tears as he watched Smith's men scrounge in a barrel at the side of the forge for scraps of discarded food.[42] In the afternoon, Smith's company traveled to Island Field (located between Willow Creek and Black's Fork) three miles downstream from Fort Supply and dug for leftover potatoes and turnips to appease their hunger.[43] Ten inches of snow lay on the ground the next morning.

The next day, Samuel Bateman and Henry Cahoon took a wagon and four-mule team, pushed through the snow to Fort Bridger, and returned about ten or eleven o'clock at night with a light load of provisions. Evidently, supplies had arrived after the departure of Smith and his men. The camp devoured all the supplies before morning.[44] Smith reported: "We fell back on Fort Supply, eating the beef we had borrowed and sampling some half-cooked government beans," which just about busted Smith's stomach.[45]

Wells's letter to Smith that ordered him to follow the army northward caught up with him at Island Field.[46] Smith prepared to take the fifty best horses and men and go up to Bear River to join McAllister and "head

---

41. Daniel H. Wells, letter to Lot Smith, October 17, 1857.
42. Oliver, *Biography*, 45–46.
43. Henry Ballard, Private Journal, 6.
44. Oliver, *Biography*, 46.
45. *Contributor*, 4:224.
46. Gardner, "A Territorial Militiaman," 310.

off the soldiers that were still going up Ham's Fork."[47] Only thirty men were to remain at Fort Supply and Bridger. The weakest animals and most worn men were to be sent to the camp of General Wells at the head of Echo Canyon. Bateman, in a borrowed overcoat with the toes of his shoes exposing his bare feet to the snow, left reluctantly with tears in his eyes.[48] All the horses had been put out to pasture on the hills where the wind had swept off the snow. When a small company of men came into camp, one man with a fine, fat horse wanted to pasture his horse with the rest. Since Smith wanted to bring his own horse back from the band, he offered to ride the man's horse out and return with his own. The man told Smith that anyone who attempted to ride his horse without a saddle would likely get his neck broken. Smith took the risk. He mounted the horse and rode quietly away—much to the disappointment of some who wanted a bit of entertainment. The man did not know that Smith was generally known as the best horseman in the country.[49]

On October 20, Smith, ready with his fifty, received a letter from Wells. It countermanded his earlier orders to go northward and advised Smith that the army was retracing down Ham's Fork.[50] While at Bridger, Smith became ill with a violent cold, so he sent Lieutenant Abbot with a platoon to check on the army's movements. The platoon escaped an ambush of forty men by rolling off on the sides of their horses with bullets cracking over their heads.[51] The army's march on Ham's Fork allowed the militia to recuperate. Young ordered those with the longest terms of service to come to the City for refitting.[52] Then, Young wrote Wells and his counselors, John Taylor and George A. Smith, to come in for rest and leave the command temporarily to Grant and Burton. Smith wrote: "I made a trip to General Wells' camp on Black's Fork, being at the time suffering from severe cold and sickness." He continued, "[I]nstructions were issued to let the [US] troops winter in the ruins [of Fort Bridger] if they wished to." After nursing his illness a few days at Bridger, Smith was again called to the front.[53]

---

47. Ballard, Private Journal, 6.
48. Oliver, *Biography*, 50.
49. Henry Standage, diary, 114-15.
50. Gardner, "A Territorial Militiaman," 311.
51. *Contributor*, 4:224.
52. Daniel H. Wells, letter to Robert T. Burton, October 18, 1857.
53. *Contributor*, 4:225.

Governor Young was determined that the army would not advance past Fort Bridger. All the supplementary Mormon troops in Echo Canyon were advised. Lorenzo Brown recorded: "All our horsemen are sent out with orders to throw lead as soon as the troops pass Bridger."[54] Orders of November 6 sent Smith's company of twenty men out on Bear River to see that none of the army passed.[55] The company had just left camp when an express recalled them. It was rumored that Marcy had gone over onto Yellow Creek to explore another route to enter the valley, so Smith and a number of the boys were ordered instead to intercept his progress.[56] While Smith and his men ate before moving out, Major Joseph Taylor arrived in camp, having just escaped from army captivity. Among other items of intelligence, Taylor pronounced the rumor of an alternate route false.[57]

On November 9, Smith and company stopped at Cache Cave. During the next day's snowstorm, they caught up with Wells's staff at Brown's station.[58] Wells ordered Smith to Bridger Butte located four or five miles southwest of the fort to relieve Ephraim Hanks's men who had been sent to watch and report on the army as it neared Bridger. Smith's company of twenty-six left for Bear River with a baggage wagon loaded with provisions and destined for Colonel Thomas Callister's camp.[59] Snow impeded Smith and his men on the way to Callister's camp and Bridger Butte. The chill and fierce winds froze several men's faces, ears, and feet. Smith ordered Captain Thomas Rich to follow the rear and allow no one to stop for any reason.[60] Smith and his company arrived at Burton's camp to find Bear River so frozen that they rode their horses over.[61] Smith wrote: "When we arrived, John Woolley said my nose was frozen. I told him I didn't think it possible, for it was so short. He was not satisfied until he pinched it. But some of the boys had to be careful how they handled their ears, as they were stiff as sticks and discolored to blackness."[62]

The next day, Robison and Burton assisted Smith in moving the wagonload of supplies through the snow to Callister's camp at Pioneer

---

54. Lorenzo Brown, Journal, Vol. 1, 297.
55. Henry Ballard, Private Journal, November 6, 1857.
56. Oliver, *Biography*, 47.
57. Oliver, 48.
58. Oliver, 48.
59. Henry Ballard, Private Journal, 9.
60. *Contributor*, 4:225.
61. Oliver, *Biography*, 48.
62. *Contributor*, 4:225.

Hollow.[63] The group arrived exhausted in the evening to find Callister's provisions nearly depleted.[64] Smith and his twenty-odd men left Pioneer Hollow carrying little or no food supply, as none of the wagon's provisions were allocated to his company. They moved Friday through the cold and snow to the Muddy. There some of the boys found and broke open some bones lying on the ground and ate the marrow. Brigham Young Jr. and Stephen Taylor proposed that the two of them return to Echo Canyon to send out provisions.[65]

On November 14, Smith and his men arrived at Bridger Butte to re-place Hanks's men.[66] From the vantage of the Butte, they watched the US Army as it moved slowly through the deep snow toward Bridger. During the week or ten days that Smith and his boys kept watch at the Butte, Bateman wrote: "[T]he only thing we had to subsist upon was raw wheat like we fed our horses. Occasionally we killed a rabbit, but we got so hungry that some of the boys made an attack upon the enemy's cattle to get some beef but only obtained an old mule."[67] In the three-day struggle to advance the last seven miles to Fort Bridger, the army endured a wild snowstorm and their teams froze dead in their tracks.[68] Yet the US soldiers had coats and boots. They had bedding and tents (some with stoves) in which they sheltered at night and built fires to warm themselves.[69] In con-trast, Smith and his men endured the same vicious weather unprotected on windswept Bridger Butte. The chaplain of the group prayed for twenty feet of snow to stop the army. It snowed, and although the snow was not quite that deep, it was soon evident that the army was stopped for the winter.[70] With the US troops settled at Fort Bridger, Smith moved to a stationary camp back between the Muddys and sent men every day to the Butte. John Vance, Thomas Abbott, and Sam Bateman took turns with three other boys as scouts to keep watch on any movement of the enemy.[71]

---

63. Burton said General Robison accompanied Major Smith. A. P. Rockwood said Robison *and* Burton accompanied Smith. Albert P. Rockwood, diary, 1847–1853.

64. Samuel Bateman, *Diary*, 48–49.

65. Bateman, *Diary*, 49.

66. Bateman, *Diary*, 49.

67. Bateman, *Diary*, 49.

68. William Wallace Hammond, Biography, Works Progress Administration, 2:157.

69. Henry S. Hamilton, *Reminiscences of a Veteran*, 86–88.

70. *Contributor*, 4:225.

71. *Contributor*, 4:225.

They ran out of provisions again and finally obtained part of a nearly dead steer. They ate some of it boiled, but it made the men sick. When they hung the remains in a cedar tree, even the crows wouldn't eat it.[72] Guard duty for Smith's company lasted a few days less than three weeks. Smith recorded: "The word came to us to leave ten men on the Yellow Creek Mountains to guard the army. The detail of this illustrious little band was made, and the rest of us turned toward home."[73]

Smith and his command had successfully stampeded the army's cattle and had barely escaped capture. They had endured several harsh Wyoming winter storms with scant provisions and kept guard on Bridger Butte. Now they looked forward to more peaceful pursuits when the war ended the next spring.

72. Bateman, *Diary*, 50.
73. *Contributor*, 4:225–26.

CHAPTER 5

Peace

Smith and his men became part of the last troops to come into the City and arrived December 5. Smith had been under extreme tension for the past ten weeks and as he traveled home, fatigue overwhelmed him. When they reached President Young's office, Young stepped out to say about ten words. Smith wrote: "[Young's words] had the effect to dispel every sense of weakness or weariness. I was ready that moment to return to the mountains. . . . [I]t was not the words but the spirit which dictated them that touched the key note of my heart." [1]

The Latter-day Saints felt a great sense of victory in the burning of the wagons and supplies of Johnston's army by Smith and a mere handful of their own men. Militia men expressed the triumph as they composed ten verses of "The Song of 1857" to the tune of "Yankee Doodle." [2] Three verses pertained directly to Smith:

"And when within two hundred miles,"
    the officers were saying,
"It won't be but a little while
    'til Mormons we'll be slaying,
We'll hang each man that has two wives;
    we've got the rope quite handy."
That is, I mean they would have done,
    but Smith burned it on the Sandy.

Chorus (after each verse):

There's a great commotion in the East
    about the Mormon question.
The problem is, to say the least,
    too much for their digestion.
When Alexander heard of this,
    it really made him wrathy.

---

1. *Contributor*, 4:226.

2. A combination of versions can be found in the notebook of William Luck (LDS Church History Library); Rolla Virgil Johnson, *Life Review of a Mormon*, 19–21; and Fred Carroll who learned it in the Mexican Mormon Colonies. See also Lester A. Hubbard, *Ballads and Songs From Utah*, 436-39; Thomas E. Cheney, *Mormon Songs From The Rocky Mountains*, 88–89.

"Who'll bring these burners in?" he said.
    "I will," said Captain Marcy.
"I'll bring those burners in," he said,
    "and by the necks we'll stretch them."
That is, I mean he might have done,
    but my, he couldn't catch them.

Chorus

Soon after this Lot and his boys
    rode out for fun and revelry;
To their surprise they happened on
    a lot of jackass cavalry.
"Will you fight?" says Smith. "Oh no,
    but set a trap to catch us."
Our backs were turned, they popped away
    but oh, they didn't hit us.

Chorus

James P. Terry in closing his 1857 diary wrote: "I never traveled with or would wish to travel with a better officer than [Lot Smith]. He was a boy with the boys, divided what he had to the last with his men and fared just as they did. He was always on hand to do more than his part of standing guard or anything else that needed to be done."[3] George Frederick Hamson was one of Smith's ten men that remained on Yellow Creek Mountains. His two wives had both given birth in Hamson's absence. According to Hamson's descendants, while he was still out on military service, Lot Smith rode up to Box Elder (present-day Brigham City) thirty-five miles distant from Farmington to visit the Hamson wives. They invited him to dinner and told him that one of the babies had died. Smith returned to Farmington and took a fresh milk cow, probably a two-day trip, back to Box Elder. He put the cow in the corral and left without telling the wives or waiting for thanks.[4]

After Indians attacked the Salmon River mission on February 25, drove off oxen, cows, and horses, and killed two men in the process, Major Smith received orders written March 9 from Lieutenant General Commander Wells to raise fifty men and to join the Salmon River Expedition to bring the Saints from Fort Limhi.[5] Smith's next assignment with Major Howard

---

3. Thurzal Q. Terry, *Great Utah War*, 18–19.
4. Leonard Valgene Hamson, interview by Carmen R. Smith.
5. Salmon River Mission Journal; Deposition of Thomas S. Smith in Fort Limhi Massacre, April 15, 1858, Brigham Young Letterpress; Nauvoo Legion

Egan was outlined in a March 30, 1858, letter from Wells to Colonel Callister. Among the six battalions organized, both Smith's and Egan's cavalry battalions were to scout, guard their horses, watch the US Army's movements day and night, and never open fire except in self-defense. [6] Smith and Daniel D. McArthur left the city with their battalions on April 3 with faces to a cold, raw wind.[7] The deep snow in Echo Canyon was impassable for wagons, but did not prevent the mounted men of McArthur and Smith from making their way the next day. Smith camped in Echo Canyon above Weber Station. While military units waited along the length of Echo Canyon, Colonel Thomas L. Kane persuaded the new governor Alfred Cumming to come into the City without the army. Cumming left Camp Scott with Kane on April 5 in a closed carriage with views only through the front.[8] At Yellow Creek, Cumming was welcomed heartily by William H. Kimball's official escort.[9]

On April 5, Wells instructed Callister, commander of forces in Echo Canyon, to impress the unfriendly merchant Abel Gilbert of Gilbert and Gerrish (on his way east with a pass to the army at Bridger ruins) with the "largeness of our forces," but not to betray fortifications.[10] After putting on a show for Gilbert, the troops provided a similar spectacle for the new governor as he passed along the same route later in the evening in the opposite direction. As Cumming came along the canyon and saw the whole snowy canyon hillside lit up in a blaze of glory with every hut apparently occupied, he appeared to be nothing short of amazed. He was apparently even more astonished with frequent encounters with groups of armed soldiers.[11] Unknown to him, they were all the same group who scurried

---

Letterbook, 253. In Nauvoo Legion General Orders No. 1 of March 6, 1858, Smith was assigned as one of ten majors. Record of Orders & Returns, Courts Martial, &c. of 2nd Brigade, 1st Division, Nauvoo Legion. Head Quarters, 14th Ward G.S.L. City, July 1857, 28.

6. Nauvoo Legion Letterbook, "ORDERS.58," 265–66.

7. Journal of Lorenzo Brown, 1:308.

8. Clarence Merrill Autobiography, *Our Pioneer Heritage* 9 (1966): 312–29.

9. Governor Cumming, journal, quoted in Elizabeth Cumming, *The Genteel Gentile, Letters of Elizabeth Cumming, 1857-1858*, 47–49; Journal History of the Church of Jesus Christ of Latter-day Saints, April 3, 1858 (hereafter cited as Journal History).

10. Daniel H. Wells, letter to Thomas Callister, April 5, 1858.

11. Alfred Cumming, letter to A. S. Johnston, April 15, 1858, quoted in J. Cecil Alter, *Utah, The Storied Domain*, 43.

ahead in the dark to repeatedly meet and salute his carriage.[12] Smith and his fifteen to twenty men did their part to impress Cumming with their numbers. They built a large bonfire in front of a hill in Echo Canyon.[13] The men marched and rode horses past the bonfire in view of Governor Cumming. Once out of the firelight, they hurried around the hill in the dark to make another appearance in the firelight.[14] The men shouted orders back and forth, whooped and hollered, shot their guns into the air, and dodged out of sight only to reappear.[15]

Governor Cumming arrived in Great Salt Lake City on April 13, made his inspections, and found the law books and records safe and in order—not burned as had been reported.[16] The Echo Canyon War could have been considered ended. Albert Sidney Johnston, however, had not yet been defused. Young was not to be taken by surprise. On April 10, Wells's adjutant James Ferguson, sent Callister orders that he and Smith were to continue on duty "till properly relieved," that they were never to camp twice in the same place, and that no cavalry was to be stationed east of the Weber.[17] Not until April 20 did Smith come into Great Salt Lake City with part of his cavalry from the Weber.[18] Judge Delana R. Eckles had indicted Smith and other prominent Mormons for treason in March—Smith for burning the wagon trains—and also a $1,000 reward was offered for Smith's capture.[19] The offer of the reward had been confirmed the week before Smith came into the valley when Ben Simon reported to Young that a white man from Johnston's camp was offering $150 to the Indians for any Mormon and $1,000 for Smith.[20]

Also, the week after his return to Great Salt Lake City, Smith heard that he had reportedly chased the new gentile marshal Peter K. Dotson

---

12. "Clarence Merrill," in *Our Pioneer Heritage* 9 (1966): 312–329.

13. Chloe Knowlton Hess of Farmington, Utah, reported that as a child her father, Benjamin F. Knowlton, showed her the big rocks collected on the west side of the canyon readied to roll down on the army and the spot in the canyon where he marched around the hill with Smith. Interview by Omer J. and Carmen R. Smith, May 1979. In author's possession.

14. Austin and Alta Fife, *Saints of Sage & Saddle*, 86.

15. "A Menacing Bunch," *Deseret News*, July 18, 1977; Louis Evans, interview by Omer J. and Carmen R. Smith, October 6, 1980.

16. Journal History, April 13 and 19, 1858.

17. Nauvoo Legion, Letter Book, 273.

18. Lewis Robison, journal, April 20, 1858.

19. J. Cecil Alter, *Utah, The Storied Domain*, 260.

20. Journal History, April 9, 13, 1858.

into the army's camp. Marshal Dotson and about a dozen others, including US officials, had visited the camp of Ute Chief Little Soldier on April 26 to persuade the Utes to steal horses from the Mormons and trade them to the army.[21] In addition, Dotson and the officials carried writs for the arrest of Young and sixty-six other men.[22] Simon had told Dotson that Ephraim Hanks was out to catch him and the other US officials.[23] The army's reaction is captured in Captain Gove's protest that "three or four hundred Mormons under the command of the rebel Lott Smith were within a few hours' ride of them with the intention of capturing his whole party."[24] US Army Captain Albert Tracy reported that Dotson related that he and his party "had ridden all night to escape a body of some 500 Mormons who had resolved on his capture."[25] The number of Mormon pursuers increased with each retelling of the story.

Rather than submit to armed subjugation, President Young directed the Saints in Great Salt Lake City and northern settlements to abandon their homes and move south. A few men were to be left behind prepared to set the buildings afire and leave a bare and burned land to the invading army.[26] Smith's families were among the Farmington Saints that moved to Clover Creek located south of Utah Valley between Mona and Nephi.[27] When Governor Cumming returned in May from Camp Scott where he had gone to fetch his wife, he found the muddy roads clogged with bedraggled Saints and their children streaming southward. Johnston's army did eventually march into Great Salt Lake City—but peacefully. On June 26, 1858, the twenty-five-hundred-man army marched through the silent and deserted streets of Great Salt Lake City.[28] Smith's station that day is not known. In Farmington as the army marched through the deserted village, the homes were banked with straw to be set afire by men including Smith's brother-in-law, Allen Burk.[29] A few men were left to guard the streets of Great Salt Lake City. The army settled forty miles distant in

21. Journal History, May 4, 1858.
22. Cumming, *Genteel Gentile*, 60.
23. Journal History, May 4, 1858.
24. Journal History, May 4, 1858.
25. Albert Tracy, "The Utah War, Journal of Albert Tracy, 1858–1860," 9.
26. Journal History, April 30, 1858.
27. Margaret Steed Hess, *My Farmington*, 412.
28. Robert T. Burton, *Autobiography*, June 26, 1858.
29. Ada Arvilla Burk Earl, *Autobiography*.

Cedar Valley, where they established Camp Floyd, and the Saints returned to their homes.

Edward Tullidge stated that Young's "proclamation [that they would leave the land burned and wasted] and the order of Lieutenant General Wells, followed so quickly by the burning of the supply trains, ultimately brought the Peace Commission, and the Proclamation of pardon to the entire Mormon people."[30] Woodruff reported that the wagon master of the train that Smith burned stated, "[I]t was well for the mormons for if this train had not been burned the Armey would probably have pushed on[,] had a fight & blood been spil[l]ed."[31] Seymour B. Young wrote: "Captain Lot Smith will ever stand out prominent as the one man who did more to check the army and prevent its advance into Salt Lake valley during the winter of 1857 than any other man, save it be Brigham Young, under whose orders he was acting."[32]

When the Utah War officially ended, Lot Smith returned to peaceful pursuits in Farmington—his family, horses, and farm—and as Davis County Sheriff. Twenty-seven-year-old Smith had courted Laura Burdick, a nineteen-year-old brunette with dark eyes, olive skin, cheeks that never needed coloring, and a queenly posture.[33] Little is known of their courtship except that some years previously, Laura and her friend had watched a military drill in Farmington. Laura remarked that she "admired the man with a red beard [who] rode a fine horse. Someday, she prophesied, she'd marry him. The two girls gleefully laughed at such a prediction."[34] During the winter break in the war, Smith had called on the widow Jerusha Burdick in Farmington and asked for Laura's hand.[35] Smith escorted his bride-to-be to Young's office on the main floor of his residence. Smith and Laura watched as the bookcase in the back of the room moved to reveal a narrow stairway between the walls. The couple climbed to an upper, all white room where sat most of the Apostles. There, Lot Smith and Laura Louisa Burdick were married January 3, 1858, by Brigham Young with Daniel Wells and Wilford Woodruff as witnesses.[36] Smith stayed with his friend Burton for

---

30. Edward W. Tullidge, *History of Salt Lake City*, 175.

31. Wilford Woodruff, journal, November 12, 1858.

32. Seymour B. Young, "Lest We Forget," 29.

33. Eva Augusta Rice, "Sketch of the Life of Laura Louisa Burdick Smith."

34. Eva Rice Howell, letter to Carmen R. Smith, October 29, 1970.

35. Howell, October 29, 1970.

36. Christian L. Christensen, "Sealings of couples, living and by proxy 1851–1889," C:262.

several days both before and after his wedding. During this time, he and Laura attended a military ball on Christmas Eve at the Social Hall, where dancing continued until 4:00 a.m. Christmas Day. They also attended another ball at Ballo's Hall on January 5.[37] Three months after his marriage to Laura, Young sealed all three wives—Laura, Jane, and Julia—to Smith, in the Endowment House witnessed by W. W. Phelps and S. L. Sprague.[38]

Smith became a member of a prayer circle—a distinct honor.[39] By 1858 each member of the Quorum of the Twelve was counseled by the First Presidency to gather members to form a prayer circle. The purpose of a prayer circle was "to produce greater union among the Saints, and the spirit of forgiveness and mutual reciprocity of feeling and a more complete reliance upon the Lord."[40] Smith also joined many of his Farmington neighbors as they expanded eastward into Morgan County and the higher Weber River Valley. He bought one of the best water rights in the narrow valley from his Farmington neighbor, Judson Stoddard. A log cabin sat on a side hill and overlooked the valley with springs below.[41] Julia was the wife chosen to live at his newly purchased property in the area later known as Stoddard. It was more than an adventure when Smith transported Julia and her belongings to Weber Valley. As they wound up the narrow gorge of Weber Canyon, they had to cross the river several times. Julia was terrorized. With each plunge of the team into the river, she screamed in hysteria. Her descendants said that Smith finally tied her into the wagon.[42]

After the departure of General Johnston, President Young scheduled a picnic on October 19, 1859, for his clerks on Antelope Island—the largest of Great Salt Lake's islands.[43] Antelope grazed the island's slopes, as did intelligent, sure-footed horses—foaled and adapted to the rocky west side cliffs and rough hills. Young's invitation included Sheriff Lot Smith and

37. John Daniel Thompson McAllister, diary, December 24, 1857; Robert T. Burton, diaries, January 5, 1858.

38. Burton, diaries.

39. Nannie Smith Ashcroft, "Lot Smith," 1.

40. Brigham Young, letter to George Q. Cannon, Washington, DC, First Presidency Letterbook #18, 4:884.

41. Andrew Jenson, *Encyclopedic History of the Church of Jesus Christ of Latter-day Saints*, 589.

42. Grace Smith [wife of Lot's grandson], interview by Carmen R. Smith. In author's possession.

43. Journal History, October 19, 1859.

other noted horsemen.[44] Smith intimately knew the five-by-fifteen-mile island with springs and unexcelled pasture. He and his brother Jesse "Nick" Wells had caught and tamed some of the island's finest wild horses.[45]

On the appointed day of the picnic, the clerks and their families in carriages and wagons crossed the lakebed to the island. For the major entertainment of the outing, Young scheduled a morning roundup and branding of some of the island's nearly one thousand horses. The horses had not felt a rope on their necks for more than four years and were wild as deer. Sons of the First Presidency—Heber P. Kimball and Brigham Young Jr. with Stephen Taylor—joined the roundup crew.[46] The horses ridden by the roundup men "were island-raised, long-winded, swift-footed, and their speed on a long run was something wonderful."[47]

Early in the morning, the horsemen in groups of three scattered over the island. The city folk watched as they rode out and kept watch for their return. Before long, about seventy-five of the fastest horses, coats white with foamy sweat, thundered into the corral. The city-folk had never seen such a wondrous sight.[48] Led by Smith and Stoddard, four of the mounted men entered the corral where the wild horses milled in confusion—wild-eyed and snorting. The animals started on the run around the corral. Smith picked a horse and roped its front foot. Before the horse could fall, his partner dropped a loop onto the same animal's neck. The downed horse was quickly branded and turned loose. The horse was hardly on his feet before Stoddard and his partner had another horse ready for the branding iron. And so it continued until all the band had been branded and turned out of the corral to make room for the next group of horses.[49] The long runs of fifteen to twenty miles enabled the horsemen to select the best horses. Those in the lead made invaluable saddle mounts.[50]

Ten days after the roundup on Antelope Island, Utah held its first hanging. The man sentenced to be hanged was a twenty-seven-year-old New Yorker, Thomas H. Ferguson, who had left home for the West at age twenty-one and met with misfortune. He ended up in Great Salt

---

44. Annie Call Carr, *East of Antelope Island*, 30.

45. Zelda E. Tidwell, "Jesse Wells Smith 1826–1896," 2.

46. Benjamin Brown, *Antelope Island Mountain*, quoted in Carr, *East of Antelope Island*, 25–40.

47. Carr, 31; John R. Young, *Memoirs of John R. Young*, 121.

48. Benjamin Brown, "Antelope Island Mountain," 31.

49. Brown, 31–32; Kate Carter, *Heart Throbs of the West*, 233.

50. Brown, 32; Young, *Memoirs*, 121.

Lake City, where he began a bout of heavy drinking.[51] On the night of September 16, 1859, a little shop on Main Street (East Temple) was robbed of five-or-six-hundred dollars' worth of goods that included a quantity of champagne. The following day when Ferguson entered the saloon next door looking like he had imbibed the entire previous night, saloonkeeper Alexander Carpenter accused him of being one of the robbers. The angry Ferguson shot Carpenter fatally in the chest.[52] A jury found Ferguson guilty of murder, and he was sentenced to be hanged. Territorial Marshal Dotson requested twenty armed men of the militia to keep peace during the execution. Instead of twenty, General Wells's adjutant, James Ferguson, ordered a much larger force of fifty mounted men and fifty footmen under Major Lot Smith.[53]

On the day of execution, the somber cavalcade started at 11 o'clock a.m. from the basement jail in the county courthouse. Dotson (who had earlier fled from Smith) may have felt a bit unsettled as he rode in the procession; he was preceded and flanked right and left by Smith's escort of one hundred men in ranks.[54] Behind them rolled a wagon carrying the convicted Ferguson, who sat alone in front of his coffin. At the place of execution, the condemned man mounted the steps of the scaffold and addressed the assemblage in a forty-five minute speech. After H. Jacobs prayed with him at his request, he said, "Gentlemen, I bid you farewell." The white cap was drawn over his face and, according to a *Deseret News* report, "the rope which held the fatal drop, was cut and Ferguson was launched into eternity."[55]

In addition to his duties as sheriff, Smith had other civil appointments in the town and county including maintenance of fences and county roads, and was appointed Davis County Commissioner.[56] He was also elected as a representative to the Territorial Legislature in 1860. Smith was appointed by Judge Richards as Assessor and Collector of Taxes in Davis County for 1861.[57] Smith, however, asked his Deputy Sheriff William Budge to assess and collect. He was more suited to stock work than with tax collection. To

51. *Deseret News*, 9:280, in Journal History, October 28, 1859.
52. Journal History, September 17, 1859.
53. Journal History, October 19, 1859.
54. *Deseret News*, 9:280, in Journal History, October 28, 1859.
55. *Deseret News*, 9:280, in Journal History, October 28, 1859.
56. Davis County Court Records, Film #0484.601, 41; Nona Smith Rhead, *Lot Smith*, 3.
57. Davis County Court Records, Film #0484.601, 85.

save stock feed for winter, the court appointed Smith and Rosel Hyde to see that no surplus cattle were turned in to Farmington's Big Range during the summer months.[58]

In May 1861, Smith was invited to accompany Young again on a tour to the southern Utah settlements—his third trip as an escort for Young. When the cavalcade reached Fillmore, Smith visited his wife Lydia and his nine-year-old son Lot Samuel, who were living with her father. Lydia agreed to return to Farmington with Smith on one condition: she would have her own separate residence. Smith was pleased to comply, and the couple made plans for her to join him on his return trip. The caravan moved southward and stopped along the way to meet with the Saints at Cove Creek, Pine Creek, Beaver, Parowan, Cedar City, Santa Clara, and the most southern settlement of the territory, Tonaquint.[59] Then they proceeded to Washington, Toquerville, Virgin City, and Grafton.[60] Homeward bound, the wagon train arrived back at Fillmore on June 6, where Lydia and her son joined Smith to return home to Farmington.[61]

Hardly a month after his return with Lydia, Smith learned that his wife Julia was being escorted to the East by the US Army. The army had orders to transport at government expense anyone who wished to escape to the States. The company included Smith's wife Julia, their daughter Phoebe, Julia's mother Louisa Mercy/Maria Chapin, and Louisa's husband. Smith quickly obtained the help of Porter Rockwell and Bill Hickman and rode in pursuit. At about noon on July 26, the three horsemen caught up to the army's contingent on its way to Fort Bridger. They kept a discreet distance and traveled alongside the army escort all the way to Green River.[62] Along the way, the three men met George Goodhart of Soda Springs, Idaho, a young employee of the American Fur Company who was on his way to deliver a message to some trappers. Goodhart came upon the gentle horses of Smith, Rockwell, and Hickman. After he examined their hobbles to ascertain that the horses belonged to White men, he rode on toward the campfire and called to the three men. They invited him to camp with them and shared their supper of venison. Goodhart told:

---

58. *Minutes of the Davis County Court* 1 (1852–1869): 101, March 10, 1862.

59. Journal History, May 20 to May 27, 1861.

60. Journal History, May 29, 1861.

61. Journal History, June 6 to June 8, 1861.

62. Patience Loader Rozsa Archer, *Recollections of Past Days: The Autobiography of Patience Loader Rozsa Archer.*

After supper I told them how glad I was not to have come across any of them damn Mormons. They asked me why. I told them that the Mormons killed people on sight, murdered the emigrants and that I was more afraid of them than of the savage Indians. . . . Next morning . . . at breakfast I told them everything bad I had ever heard about the Mormons and how I hoped I would not come across any of them. . . . After breakfast I saddled my horse. One of the men tied a good lunch on my saddle. After I was on my horse, Hickman said to me, "How have we treated you?" I told him, "Fine." I could not be treated better, and I also told him how pleased I was to have found them. Then he said, "Tell your company we treated you to the best we had and we are Mormons . . . Port Rockwell, Lot Smith and Bill Hickman." My heart seemed to jump to my mouth. I leaned over and ran my horse as fast as he could go. I expected to be shot every minute, but no shot came.[63]

After the three horsemen trailed the army escort to some point beyond Green River, they successfully secured Julia, who returned with Smith to Utah. He immediately built Julia a new house at Stoddard. Bargain prices from the army's abandonment of Fort Crittendon allowed him to build an impressive two-story house which featured a veranda below and a balcony above, both enclosed with an ornamental balustrade.

When Smith had returned from the war, he was hailed as a hero, indicted for treason, and had a $1,000 reward on him. He expanded his land holdings, married another wife, escorted Brigham Young, brought two wives back home, and continued his duties as sheriff. He next would fulfil an important assignment from President Abraham Lincoln in the Civil War. During this service, he would be subjected to many life-threatening experiences.

---

63. Carter, *Heart Throbs of the West*, 428, 429.

CHAPTER 6

Civil War Captain

The overland telegraph line was completed to Great Salt Lake City on October 18, 1861.[1] Six days later, the line was completed across the entire continent. The American Civil War was raging; protection and maintenance of the transcontinental mail and telegraph service was vital to the preservation of the Union. Vandalism had paralyzed the lines. Brigham Young, who worried that US troops would be headquartered in Salt Lake City to guard the lines, telegraphed Utah's congressional delegate in Washington, DC that the militia of Utah was ready to protect the mail if called upon.[2] Thirty-two-year-old Major Lot Smith was out on Little Mountain east of Great Salt Lake City the morning of April 26, 1862, with Colonel Burton and his company, who were escorting officials William H. Hooper and Chauncey W. West eastward.[3] The travel was not easy. The massive snowfall of the winter was thawing under spring rains and had turned the mountain into a mushy mound of melting snowdrifts and soft mud. In the evening, while the company camped near the telegraph station a half-mile up Echo Canyon, Burton telegraphed Young.[4] Unknown to Smith, Young had been trying to contact him. The day before, General Wells had written an order to Major Smith to gather about twenty men as quickly as possible with such short notice and report to Great Salt Lake City.[5] Before Wells could dispatch his letter to Farmington, a telegram addressed to the president of The Church of Jesus Christ of Latter-day Saints arrived at 8:25 p.m.:

> By express direction of the President of the U.S. [Abraham Lincoln] you are hereby authorized to raise, arm & Equip one Company of Cavalry for ninety 90 Days Service. . . . The company will be Employed to protect the property of the Telegraph & Overland Mail. Companies in or about Independence

---

1. Andrew Jenson, *Chronology of the Church of Jesus Christ of Latter-day Saints, 1805–1884.*

2. Brigham Young, letter to John M. Bernhisel, April 14, 1862; *Utah Historical Quarterly*, 33:59.

3. Pencil notation in one of two copies of Burton's small Civil War diary: "Lot Smith with me." Robert T. Burton, *Autobiography*, 15–16.

4. Robert T. Burton, diaries, April 29, 1862.

5. Daniel H. Wells, letter to Lot Smith, April 28, 1862.

Rock where depredations have been committed & will be continued in Service only, until the U.S. troops can reach the point where they are so much needed. It may therefore be disbanded previous to the Expiration date of ninety 90 days. . . . [U]ntil the proper Staff officers for subsisting these men arrive you will please furnish subsistence for them yourself. —By order of the Sec'r of War.[6]

General Wells quickly penned a postscript to the order he had just dictated to Smith stating that President Young had just received a telegram with authorization to raise a hundred-man company to protect the US mail service. He asked Smith to report for duty the following evening or sooner if possible.[7] However, not until Burton had telegraphed the next evening from Echo Canyon could Young notify Smith of his assignment. Smith left immediately to ride forty miles through the night—back through melting snow, mud, and wild water. By forenoon the next day, Smith was mustering approximately one hundred officers and men, mostly drawn from his Life Guards, at the Council House in the City.[8] (See Appendix B for a list of men in Smith's command.)

With the oath administered to the officers, Major Smith in command of the 1st Battalion, 1st Regiment of Cavalry, 1st Brigade of the Great Salt Lake City Military District became Captain Lot Smith of the United States Army commissioned by President Abraham Lincoln.[9] This military service under Smith's leadership constituted Utah's formal contribution to the nation's Civil War effort. Captain Smith mustered seventy-two privates into the service of the United States and administered their oath to support the Constitution.[10] The company was organized into two platoons led by Lieutenants Joseph S. Rawlins and J. Quincy Knowlton.[11]

---

6. Telegram from President Abraham Lincoln to President of The Church of Jesus Christ of Latter-day Saints, April 26, 1862. Brigham Young Collection, Box 16, F 219.

7. Daniel H. Wells, letter to Lot Smith, April 28, 1862.

8. The government prescribed $146 per month to each soldier, 25¢ per day for clothing and bedding, and 40¢ per day for use of horses and equipment. James C. McFarland, *A Warrior for his People*, 3.

9. Utah State Archives & Records, Service No. 1506; Margaret M. Fisher, *Utah and the Civil War*, 24.

10. Summary Report 1862, Utah State Archives and Records, Service No. 716. J. H. Standifird said Daniel H. Wells mustered the men; Smith administered oath to support the Constitution. John Henry Standifird, diary, 3.

11. Utah State Archives & Records, Service No. 1506.

The next day at one o'clock, the cavalry lined up in the street in front of the Lion House for review by Young.[12] Now under orders to protect government property instead of destroying it as required in the Utah War, Smith complied with the government's request. On May 1, Captain Smith and 105 men rode out of the city to begin their assignment. The cavalry rode to the mouth of Parley's Canyon only to find the canyon road too damaged by flooding to be passable.[13] The next morning, they moved northward to try the route through Emigration Canyon. There the soldiers met President Young, Wells, and members of the Quorum of Twelve Apostles who had come to give a farewell blessing. Young read the telegram from the War Department to the assembled troops. He stressed that loyalty to the union of the country was the first requirement of the men, "and that they must defend the union at all hazards, even to the sacrificing of their lives."[14] Then he began to counsel them, cautioning them to abstain from the use of liquor and profanity. He added: "When you are offered the United States uniform, do not wear it."[15] After the Civil War service, some of Washakie's Shoshones related that they had surrounded Smith's men in ambush. Had they been in US soldier uniforms, the Shoshones likely would have killed them.[16]

The men worked their way over Little Mountain and Big Mountain. They rebuilt washed-out dugways and bridges over swollen streams. All too often, the men pulled out wagons mired to their axles in mud and the bogged mules hitched to them. The baggage wagons had to be unloaded and the baggage repacked, not once but many times.[17] Captain Smith refused to see the cold mud, icy water, and snow as hardship. His constant good humor and positive attitude elevated his men. As they dried out around the campfire, the camaraderie of the group created an *esprit de corps* and made the trying circumstances more tolerable.[18] Captain Smith opened and read the sealed orders from the First Presidency. The troops were given detailed instructions first to "recognize the hand of Providence" in their behalf and to be righteous, kind, and longsuffering in word and

---

12. Fisher, *Utah and the Civil War*, 24.

13. *Deseret News*, May 7, 1862; Journals of US Volunteers, Service No. 1507.

14. Fisher, *Utah and the Civil War*, 25.

15. Fisher, 99.

16. Fisher, 99.

17. Journals of US Volunteers, John H. Standifird, Harvey C. Hullinger, May 3, 4, and 5, 1862.

18. Standifird, diary, May 5, 1862.

deed both in private and public. The orders continued with a list of unacceptable items such as card playing, liquor, swearing, and gambling. They were told to improve the roads they traveled and to build corrals and storehouses when possible. The last instruction included, "Morning and evening of each day let prayer be publicly offered in the command and in all detachments thereof, that you may constantly enjoy the guidance and protecting care of Israel's God and be blest in the performance of every duty devolved upon you."[19]

On their way, the men traveled through Silver Creek Canyon, walled on both sides by high mountains covered with dense brush and a washed-out road.[20] At the mouth of Echo Canyon, the men crossed the creek three times, built two bridges, swam the mules over, packed the baggage on their backs, and drew the wagons over by hand. A valuable horse drowned, but they finally made camp a little above Cache Cave that night. It had taken ten days to conquer the hundred miles that could be covered in good weather by an express rider in one day. In accordance with Young's counsel, Captain Smith designated a camp one mile outside Fort Bridger.

The mail and telegraph route to be protected by Captain Smith's troops included mail stations strung one about every ten miles along the route from Fort Bridger to Independence Rock.[21] At Fort Bridger, Smith's men were called to their first encounter with a local tribe of Indians. The hysterical mail carrier wrote that the troops had arrived just in time to save the fort. He told how the previous day the departing mail stage had been attacked about four miles eastward. Smith detailed Lieutenant Rawlins and sixteen men to proceed with all possible speed to the scene of the attack. Apparently, there had been no ambush; the mail stage had seen an Indian woman, fired on her, and fled back to the fort.[22]

Smith set out to survey the route and conditions of the stations. He left ten men at Fort Bridger to receive and guard the oncoming supply wagons.[23] They found that "the citizens . . . [were] considerably alarmed for fear of the Indians."[24] Smith's cavalry crossed over Ham's Fork and moved toward Green River. At Lewis Robinson's ferry, the troops' wagons were swamped and most of their hardtack ruined. They laid over on Little

19. Brigham Young, letter to Captain Lot Smith and company, April 30, 1862.
20. Standifird, diary, 3, 4.
21. Joseph A. Fisher in Fisher, *Utah and the Civil War*, 37.
22. Journals of US Volunteers, May 11, 1862.
23. Harvey Coe Hullinger, diary, May 12, 1862.
24. John H. Standifird, diary, May 12, 1862.

Sandy while wagons returned to Ham's Fork for more supplies.[25] The men then rode onward to the deserted Pacific Springs Station. Against gale force winds, the cavalry pushed their horses over South Pass.[26]

At the Seminole cutoff on May 19, they met their first westward-bound wagon train. The train's report was chilling. Not a man could be found at any of the stations from the Sweetwater eastward to the Platte.[27] Smith and his US soldiers faced more wind and blowing snow as they traveled past Warm Springs and Ice Springs. At the mail station at Three Crossings of the Sweetwater, they found the paper mail "shamefully used, every sack emptied and contents scattered about the premises and emigrants helping themselves to whatever they wish[ed]."[28] The crude log structure and pole fence at the Split Rock Station had not been burned, only deserted. The mail sacks were burst open and the mail strewed about.[29]

In the morning of May 21, Captain Smith encountered homeward-bound Colonel Burton and his command at Plaunt's Station located at the parting of the Mormon and Oregon Trails. Plaunt's Station had been burned when about twenty-five of a native tribe had surrounded the four-teen men in the station for a night and then drove off the stock in the morning.[30] Burton reported that on his first pass of Plaunt's station, he had found only part of the horse stables still standing. On a lone post, "[a] notice was found . . . saying that depredations had been committed on the mail route by Indians or Mormons or both, warning emigrants not to travel in small parties &c., with four names to it, Tim Goodale [a mountaineer] among them."[31]

Three men—Stephen Taylor, Heber P. Kimball of Burton's command, and Seymour B. Young of Smith's command—were sent to Goodale's camp. They carried a warrant for Goodale's arrest and orders to bring him in for a court martial. Goodale arrived the next day. Thoroughly fright-ened, he disavowed any knowledge of the notice and denied any part in

25. Journals of US Volunteers, May 15, 1862.

26. Robert G. Cleland, *This Reckless Breed of Men*, 60.

27. Cleland, 60.

28. Robert T. Burton, diaries, May 22, 1862.

29. Harvey Coe Hullinger, diary, May 20, 1862.

30. John H. Standifird, diary, May 21, 1862.

31. Robert T. Burton, diaries, May 21, 1862. Goodale was related to Young's family: "At Fort Bridge and at other times I met and briefly knew . . . Tim Goodell (my mother's cousin)." Scrapbook of John R. Young.

it since he could neither read nor write. Goodale was pressured until he feared for his life. He finally convinced the court of his innocence.[32]

After Goodale's court martial, Captain Smith left some of his men at Devil's Gate twenty miles farther eastward and continued on to Independence Rock. He left a small detachment to guard the telegraph office near Sweetwater Bridge where mail was found scattered, and then he established command headquarters at Devil's Gate.[33] The mail stations were not yet wholly reestablished and sufficiently guarded. While Smith's command guarded one station, the Indians stole mail livestock from another.[34] Smith's company began to rebuild the former Wheeler and Merchant Station and construct corrals. They put together a large raft to ferry emigrating Mormon wagons.[35] At Devil's Gate on May 29, Captain Smith received orders from newly arrived US Brigadier General James Craig from the East to proceed westward with fifty men to guard the Ham's Fork Station where sixty horses of mail stock had been stolen. Smith departed the next day and left Lieutenant Rawlins and twenty-nine men at Devil's Gate.[36] Smith pushed westward with half his men and repaired broken telegraph lines. At Ice Springs they again found scattered mail.[37] He left 1st Sergeant Riter and ten men at Green River and rode onward to Ham's Fork.[38] With a squad stationed at Ham's Fork, the protection of the overland mail and telegraph route became more secure, and the personnel of the mail stations began to return.[39] The mail carrier's agent arranged to bring horses to restock the corrals of the mail stations.

On June 7, Smith and part of his company arrived at Pacific Springs where they met General Craig and the Ohio Volunteers the following day.[40] The general assigned the Utah Volunteers to guard the mail route between the first crossing of the Sweetwater and Green River. Several days later, General Craig sent orders for Captain Smith's entire company

---

32. Fisher, *Utah and the Civil War*, 45–47.

33. R. H. Attwood, *Journal of the Utah Volunteers*, May 26, 1862.

34. Robert T. Burton, diaries, May 27, 1862.

35. Harvey Coe Hullinger, diary, May 27, 1862; W. C. Coleman, journal, April 30, 1862.

36. Attwood, *Journal of the Utah Volunteers*, May 29, 1862; Harvey Coe Hullinger, diary, May 29, 1862.

37. Attwood, *Journal of the Utah Volunteers*, May 31, 1862.

38. Atwood, June 4, 1862.

39. Harvey Coe Hullinger, diary, June 8, 1862.

40. Attwood, *Journal of the Utah Volunteers*, June 7, 1862.

to ride to Fort Bridger, establish headquarters there, and guard the line from Green River to Great Salt Lake City.[41] The next day, however, after a morning interview with the general, Smith returned to his camp to find a letter from Ben Halliday that reported the loss of four mules from the Big Sandy Station. Somehow the message had been delayed three days, which made recovery of the stock next to impossible. Nevertheless, as ordered, Smith with Lieutenant Knowlton and twenty men left Pacific Springs immediately for Big Sandy.[42] This pursuit was Smith's ninth expedition against American Indians—his first as captain of the US Volunteers.

At Big Sandy, Smith and his men found that the trail of the thieves led northward. They rode hard on the route toward the Wind River Mountains in the forenoon of the second day, June 11, and reached the North Bend of Green River (Three Forks of Green River) where the rustlers had crossed. They had traveled 150 miles in two days, to no avail.[43]

They turned back and had not proceeded far before they sighted a half-grown grizzly cub on the opposite side of the river. Captain Smith, Lieutenant Knowlton, and Sergeant Howard Spencer started in pursuit. They swam their horses over the river to the opposite shore and discovered the cub was not alone—its mother was there. The captain and his comrades gave chase as the bears scrambled up the bluff. The horses gained on the bears until they were within shooting range. Then the bears raced downhill toward the river. Overtaken, the big bear turned on Smith, caught his horse by the tail with her forepaws, and held on. Smith turned in his saddle and used the butt of his gun to beat her off. She let go and made for the willows. Overtaken a second time, the bear whirled and caught Smith's stirrup. While their comrades across the river watched, the contest continued back to the river. The bears received an occasional shot, which only made them fiercer. They whirled to charge the horsemen. At the river, the men killed the smaller bear. The jerked meat would make good eating. To secure the cub, a man from the company swam across the river with a rope tied to his body trailing a series of ropes tied together. Captain Smith attached one end of a rope to the bear and the other end around the neck of his horse. He mounted and plunged into the river. The heavy pulling through the swift current rolled Smith's horse over, feet upward. Smith disengaged himself from the horse and managed to swim

---

41. Attwood, June 9, 1862.
42. Attwood, June 10, 1862.
43. Lot Smith, letter to Brigham Young, June 16, 1862.

ashore. The boys hauled the horse out onto land, but not before the animal nearly drowned.[44]

Their arrival back at Pacific Springs on June 14 coincided with the onset of a violent two-day blizzard. During the second night in sleet and rain, high wind tore down all the tents but one. The gale was so fierce they could not set up the tents again. The next morning, a bright sun arose on an amiable landscape—calm and serene. Yet, the storm left grim reminders. Not one hair remained on either mane or tail of Peter Cornia's horse, and Knowlton's horse had chilled to death.[45] Captain Smith immediately sat with a scribe to report to Young:

> On Monday 8th Inst. I had an interview with Br. General Craig who arrived by Stage at the Pacific Springs Station. He expressed himself much pleased with the promptness of our people in attending to the call of the General Government[,] also the exertions we had made to overcome the obstacles on the Road, spoke in high terms of our people generally, informed me that he had telegraphed President Lincoln to that effect and intended writing to him more fully by Mail, was much pleased with the Corral and Houses we were building at Devils Gate, wished us to leave a Guard there, and desired us to contribute as much as possible to our own comfort and render all the assistance possible to the Mormon Emigration.[46]

Smith continued in his report that the general had given him authority to act according to his discretion for the public good and that Craig thought the Mormons were his most efficient troops at the time.

The few days that Lieutenant Colonel William Oliver Collins's Ohio Volunteers and Smith's Utah Volunteers shared camps at Pacific Springs and South Pass generated several stories. One of Smith's men Lewis Huffaker told of a competition between legendary frontiersman Buffalo Bill and Lot Smith:

> Buffalo Bill first tested [exhibited] his deftness. He sat on his horse mounted in the saddle. The horse he was to lasso was put to a run. Bill threw the rope and caught the running horse around the neck and held him with the assistance of [a dally around] the horn of his saddle.
>
> Lot Smith cried, "I can do better than that." He stood on the ground, sent out the rope [Smith was left-handed] and caught the running horse with

---

44. Fisher, *Utah and the Civil War*, 100; Journal History of the Church of Jesus Christ of Latter-day Saints, July 9, 1862 (hereafter cited as Journal History).

45. Fisher, *Utah and the Civil War*, 100; Attwood, *Journal of the Utah Volunteers*, June 15, 1862.

46. Smith, letter to Brigham Young, June 16, 1862.

the loop in the rope by one of the [front] feet. There was a knot at the end of the rope that Lot Smith held; dropping the rope to the ground, he placed his foot on the knot and held the horse secure.

Buffalo Bill said that was the best he had ever seen.[47]

Captain Smith again reported to Young from Pacific Springs some ten days later on June 27 that his command had been attached to Colonel Collins' regiment in General Craig's division. He also reported that his men had built a log house with bake houses, a large corral at Devil's Gate, and a bridge on the Sweetwater. He had received orders to march to Fort Bridger and guard the line from Green River to Salt Lake City.[48] Smith's company arrived at Fort Bridger and established camp on the creek above it. While there, his command celebrated the Fourth of July. Early in the morning, muskets were fired continuously for half an hour. The buglers played "The Star-Spangled Banner," "Hail Columbia," and "Yankee Doodle," and, at eight, the command marched with flying flags into Fort Bridger. They marched through the fort and encamped about a half mile east. In midafternoon Smith's troops feasted on a dinner of bread, fresh beef, and coffee.[49]

That same day Smith received a request from the US Army sergeant in charge of Fort Bridger. Five mounted US soldiers had deserted at the North Platte Bridge and were headed westward. Colonel Collins wanted them captured. Captain Smith detached Lieutenant Knowlton with ten men to accompany the sergeant on what was to become known as the Bear Lake Expedition.[50] The expedition left with five days' provisions. When those five days passed without their return, Smith was concerned and said to those in camp "that surely some one or two of the party would get out alive and soon make a report of the results of the expedition."[51] To the relief of all, nine days later all arrived safely back at Fort Bridger.[52]

As the term of enlistment of the Utah Volunteers neared its end, Smith was still on duty at Fort Bridger. Then, on July 19, an unknown tribe raided the camp of mountaineer Jack Robinson only six miles above

47. Smith, letter to Brigham Young, June 16, 1862.

48. Smith, letter to Brigham Young, June 27, 1862.

49. *Deseret News*, 12:32, in Journal History, July 4, 1862.

50. Attwood, *Journal of the Utah Volunteers*, July 4, 1862; Seymour B. Young in Fisher, *Utah and the Civil War*, 60.

51. Fisher, 68.

52. Fisher, 60–68. The personnel are listed in Kate B. Carter, *Treasures of Pioneer History*, 5:395.

Fort Bridger. They stole more than two hundred horses along with mules and cattle.[53] Smith's US Volunteers received notice the next day and responded. Only an hour and a half after Sunday afternoon's bugle call to assemble, sixty-two mounted volunteers were ready to depart Fort Bridger.[54]

Accompanied by Robinson's son-in-law, Mr. Robert Hereford, the expedition left Fort Bridger to follow the tracks of the stolen horses. On the afternoon of their first day, Smith and the Volunteers rode northward thirty-five miles. At the Muddy River they found two abandoned ponies and three of the stolen colts. Apparently the raiders were pushing the stolen animals to their limit and abandoned any animal that could not keep up.[55] On day two, the volunteers swam their horses across Ham's Fork and continued northward along the west side of Green Valley and rode to a spot near present-day Fontenelle on the Green River. On day three, they came upon the raiders' first camp and were astonished at how quickly they had moved with so large a band. They realized the chase would be longer than anticipated and would require more provisions. Captain Smith and Lieutenant Knowlton rode ahead to Lander Road but were unsuccessful

----

53. Fisher, *Utah and the Civil War*, 71. Young's account is also recorded in "Lest We Forget." The number of stolen horses, usually reckoned at two hundred, is approximate. Seymour B. Young guessed the number of horses at three hundred.

54. The roll included: Lieutenants J. Quincy Knowlton and Joseph Rawlins; Sergeants S. H. W. Riter and Howard O. Spencer; Corporals Andrew Bigler, William A. Bringhurst, Hiram B. Clawson, Newton Myrick, and Seymour B. Young; Privates "Wood" Alexander, William C. Allen, John Arrowsmith, Isaac Atkinson, Lachoneus Barnard, John R. Bennion, Samuel Bennion, Edwin Brown, Charles Burnham, John Cahoon, Thomas S. Caldwell, Theodore Calkins, Francis R. Cantwell, Jesse J. Cherry, H. B. Clemens, Peter Cornia, George Cotterell, James H. Cragun, Charles Crismon, Joseph Fisher, Moses W. Gibson, Joseph Goddard, William Grant, James Green, Thomas H. Harris, James Hixon/Hickson, Lewis A. Huffaker, James Imlay, Lars Jensen, Hiram Kimball Jr., James Larkins, William Longstroth, Thomas Lutz, Donald McNichol, Edward A. Noble, Lewis Osborn, Hugh D. Park, Francis Prince, William H. Rhodes, Landon Rich, Alley S. Rose, Emerson D. Shurtliff, James "Jimmie" Sharp, Harlow E. Simmons, Joseph Taylor, Joseph Terry, Mahlon Weiler, and James H. Wells; Wagoners Henry Bird, Solomon Hale, Mark Murphy, and Alfred Randall; Others Joseph H. Felt, Samuel H. Hill, and Ira N. Hinckley. Fisher, *Utah and the Civil War*, 71, 72.

55. Elias Smith, ed., "The Expedition After Indians," 52. Seymour B. Young's account in Fisher, *Utah and the Civil War*, is very similar.

in obtaining provisions. The expedition camped for the night on the Big Island in Green River.[56]

The command rested their horses all morning on day four while three men—Knowlton, Seymour Young, and Sol Hale—rode back upriver to Lander Road in another attempt to purchase supplies but their efforts were fruitless. The command rode to a small stream near the base of the Green River Mountains and discovered the raiders' hastily-abandoned second campground. Evidence indicated that a fight had occurred at the camp. An emigrant's cap lay on the ground, pierced by a bullet. Beef of five oxen lay strewn on the ground, unfit to eat after two days' exposure in the hot sun.[57] Advantage fell to the thieves, who could travel more quickly because their meat was on the hoof, while the troops had to haul their provision on packhorses.

On day five, and on half rations, Smith's company started at daylight and traveled to the north fork of Green River, crossed, and rested their horses. Five miles farther they found where the thieves struck and crossed the south fork of Lewis Fork (Snake River). They tracked the thieves twenty-one miles onward to a rim (elevation 7,921 ft.), the beginning of the narrow trail to and along the Hoback River. Captain Smith, Mr. Hereford, and the sixty-two men continued along the treacherous trail of Hoback Canyon, which stretched thirty miles and appeared in some places to be a thousand feet above the swift torrent below. At the middle fork of the Hoback River, the men swam their horses over the river and camped just north of present-day Bondurant. That day they found tracks and the remnants of a sage hen—both so fresh that the thieves' party appeared to be no more than six hours ahead.

That evening, Smith and his men camped at the junction of the Snake and Hoback Rivers.[58] A council was held and all agreed that the men must ride more swiftly if they were to overtake the thieves. Many of the horses had not been shod before leaving Fort Bridger and had very tender feet.[59] Consequently, on day six, twenty of the most sore-footed horses and riders turned back toward Fort Bridger.[60] The forty-three remaining men continued up the Snake River through a dense forest and into a large,

---

56. Elias Smith, "The Expedition After Indians," 52.

57. Smith, 52.

58. Smith, 52.

59. Fisher, *Utah and the Civil War*, 75.

60. Those who left under Lieutenant Rawlins included Corporal Myrick and privates Allen, Arrowsmith, Bess, Brown, Burnham, Cantwell, Cottrell, Cragun,

grass-covered valley called Strawberry Flat immediately south of what is now the town of Jackson, Wyoming. While the horses nipped the grass, the men ate strawberries.[61] The band of stolen horses had scattered in the clearing and confused the trail, which delayed the pursuers. When the trail was found again, it continued northward to the main fork of the Snake River where it divided into three channels about ten miles below the Three Tetons. The depth of the first stream (about one hundred feet wide) was not difficult to cross; the second, deeper with a swifter current, caused Smith to pause.[62] He ordered his comrades to remove their clothing, bind it to their saddles with their belts, and swim their horses over. When the men were stripped and ready to jump their horses into the stream, Smith stopped them. Smith's legendary comments may have historical validity: "Wait," he commanded. "Let me try it first." He plunged his horse over the small bluff and into the stream. Both horse and rider disappeared in the deep water. According to legend, when Captain Smith surfaced, he said, "We won't cross here. It's a sunnuvabich."[63]

Smith searched and found a better crossing at a gravelly sand bar about three hundred yards upstream. Again, he led the way; the men followed in single file. With difficulty, several members of the command successfully reached the west bank of the river. Unfortunately, Donald McNichol's horse panicked. The horse was swept downstream into a deep underflow and disappeared. McNichol—the best swimmer in the group—had not followed orders to strip. Encumbered with his clothing, boots, and six-shooter, he rose with difficulty to the surface of the turbulent river. He made no call for assistance. Although Smith and Howard Spencer ran down the bank of the stream, they could only watch the swift current carry him away to sink beneath its surface. Sobered by the loss of their comrade, the rest of the men sloshed up the bank of the river and dressed.[64]

When the adjutant called roll after the crossing, there were two men besides McNichol who did not answer. No one had seen Seymour Young and Sol Hale since the force had scattered in search of the trail in Strawberry Flat. Smith called for volunteers to go back on the trail. Sergeant Spencer

---

Eardley, Green, Hickson, Huffaker, Imlay, Jensen, Park, Prince, Rhodes, Rose, and Terry. Fisher, 75.

61. Dr. Seymour B. Young, "Lest We Forget," 612.

62. Elias Smith, ed., "The Expedition After Indians."

63. Arthur Dwight Smith, interview by Omer J. and Carmen R. Smith, February 27, 1980.

64. Smith, "The Expedition After Indians."

said he would go alone if he could borrow Sergeant Riter's mount. The big sorrel mare had demonstrated her strength and ability in crossing the swollen stream with ease. Spencer rode back about four miles and met the two coming on. Near Strawberry Flat, Young had collapsed and lain beside his horse near a stream. Hale had stayed with Young and shot and roasted a ground squirrel for him.[65] Somewhat revived, Young accompanied Hale onward to catch up with the command. After the happenings of the day, to make an evening meal for forty-three men from a scant eight pounds of flour seemed only a small inconvenience.[66] The loss of a comrade distressed Smith, and Hale reported that Captain Smith walked the camp all night, brokenhearted.[67]

On day seven, the men again started tracking northward up the densely-wooded valley of the Snake River (current Jackson Hole). They found more stolen mares—all pitifully jaded from overheating. The hungry men were also lucky enough to find and dispatch a skinny cinnamon bear.[68] By eating every scrap, they made it serve for two skimpy meals—their first food since the eight pounds of flour the day before.[69] The saddle horses also suffered from the extended chase. Not six horses were fit to travel another day at the same speed. Captain Smith asked his command whether they still wanted to pursue the thieves or withdraw from the chase and hunt game for food. Hereford, the one most concerned with the recovery of the horses, expressed complete satisfaction that everything possible had already been done. The men traveled eight miles farther, hoping to sight game before they abandoned pursuit entirely.[70]

Homeward bound on Saturday July 27, their eighth day, Captain Smith's comrades traveled to the south fork of the Snake River. Here, the men of the captain's mess put together a large raft of quaking aspen logs to ferry the entire company. After McNichol was drowned, Smith made sure that everyone undressed. Smith's messmates (Sergeant Spencer, Corporals Andrew Bigler and Young, Privates Peter Cornia, Jimmie Sharp, and Thomas Caldwell) placed their baggage on the raft and climbed aboard to cross. When the raft pulled up to the south shore, one of the men aboard

---

65. Heber Q. Hale, *Biography of J. H. Hale*, section on Solomon H. Hale, 182.

66. Seymour B. Young remembered years afterward that it was Lieutenant Quince Knowlton who rescued him.

67. Seymour B. Young, "Captain Lot Smith (Concluded)."

68. A cinnamon bear is a North American black bear with reddish-brown hair.

69. Smith, "The Expedition After Indians."

70. Smith, "The Expedition After Indians."

caught the limb of a cottonwood tree which had fallen on the edge of the stream. As he held on, the raft tilted and tipped the men's clothing, two saddles, and cooking utensils into the water. Before the men could secure the raft to tie up, the force of the current swept it away downstream, but not before non-swimmer Caldwell managed to scramble aboard. Smith plunged in, swam to the raft, and climbed aboard. Smith and Caldwell floated until the raft lodged on an island midstream about a mile down-river. The large raft was abandoned, and Smith and Caldwell put together a smaller raft. William Longstroth swam to the island with a rope over his arm. Pulled across by their comrades, the three landed safely at their north-side camp.[71]

Of Smith's seven-man mess that had crossed to the south shore and lost their clothing, only the captain and Caldwell had safely returned to the north shore. This left five men on the south shore with no equipment. Two of the men, Bigler and Cornia, one entirely nude and the other with scant underclothing, attempted to avoid an all-night onslaught of mosquitoes by hurrying upstream in the half dusk, loosening a log, jumping astride it, and pushing it with poles across the river to the north-side camp. The other three—Spencer, Young, and Sharp—faced the night with no food, no bedding, no means to make a fire, and nothing more than underclothing to protect them from the hordes of mosquitoes. At daylight, the trio found a log upstream. They straddled the log and poled across. As the log touched the north bank, Spencer and Young both jumped off, but the swift current quickly swept the log downriver with non-swimmer Sharp still astride. Luckily, the log struck a sandbar.[72] The command was grateful to be safely in camp again without further loss of life. In the afternoon, they traveled twelve miles northwest through a violent hailstorm to the north fork of the Snake River. A swan, a badger, and a porcupine killed during the day eked out three scanty repasts. Very little was discarded. Smith's seven-man mess shared the hide of the badger with the hair singed off and broiled it over coals until it thickened.[73]

On July 29, the group traveled a few miles and again crossed two branches of the river.[74] After another harrowing crossing, the men desperately needed food. They turned to Hale to petition Captain Smith for per-

---

71. Smith, "The Expedition After Indians."

72. Young, "Lest We Forget."

73. Young, "Lest We Forget." Young reported that Captain Smith went without food when it was limited.

74. Young, "Lest We Forget."

mission to kill one of the horses. Smith consented and requested Hale to select the animal, shoot it, and see it properly apportioned to the messes. Hale selected H. B. Clemons's horse because it was the plumpest. With the horse tethered to a sage brush, Hale leveled his six-shooter and took aim. But Hale did not fire. Instead, he dropped his arm and said, "Darned if I can shoot the poor old horse." Another hungry trooper James Larkins did not hesitate. The horse was soon carved up and each man roasted a portion to eat.[75]

While the others rested after the meal, Captain Smith, Lieutenant Knowlton, and Hereford began to explore. They discovered they had landed on an island. They also found the Big Snake on the other side of the island far too large and its current too strong to be fordable. This meant they had no choice but to re-cross. Experience, though, had taught its lessons. This time, a rope attached to a heavier raft with the non-swimmers aboard was pulled by men on shore. The men moved onward and next confronted a very deep watercourse. A substantial raft was needed to carry both baggage and non-swimmers. Smith's men, strengthened with more horse meat, worked all day hauling logs with their saddle horses from a little clump of trees several miles away.[76]

The next morning, day twelve, Hereford began to superintend the construction of the raft—binding the timbers firmly together with thongs cut from the hide of the butchered horse. His instructions, however, were laced with his habitual profanity—profanity that Smith would not tolerate. Hereford had already been reproved for his language on several occasions. That morning, Smith emphasized to Hereford that unless he ceased his blasphemy, no one would be crossing the river.[77] Ultimately, the raft was built and the crossing accomplished. The company came upon one of the swamps common along the river course in the Teton Basin. The slough was so extensive that the men had to lay down willows for nearly a mile to be able to walk and carry their saddles and baggage. The horses struggled through the quagmire as best they could. The company then rode west through Teton Pass to the outlet of Market Lake, near present-day Victor, Idaho. Here the men ate the last of the horsemeat.[78]

On day thirteen, the company swam the outlet and traveled southwest twelve more miles over the Big Hole Mountains. The men again

75. Young, "Lest We Forget."
76. Smith, "The Expedition After Indians."
77. William A. Bringhurst, letter to *Deseret News*, April 1902.
78. Smith, "The Expedition After Indians."

rested with no food. Smith and Young rode forward fifteen miles in search of provisions and came upon eight wagons camped for their midday meal. The miners were suspicious since they had recently had a horse and five cattle stolen and one man killed. They threatened to hang Smith and Young from a wagon tongue. Captain Smith cautioned the prospectors that the best thing for them to do would be to furnish some flour and bacon because he and Young were only two of a band of forty Utah Volunteers of the US Army coming their way. He stated they were very much in need of food and, if harm came to himself and his comrade, vengeance might be taken upon those who did them injury. The miners furnished a hundred pounds of flour and a side of bacon, although at a high price. Smith stayed with the emigrants while Corporal Young packed the flour and bacon on his horse and rode the captain's horse back to the camp of his comrades. When Smith, under guard and afoot, and the emigrants reached his camp to find the men busily frying bread and bacon, the emigrants turned generous and furnished two large camp kettles, soup bones, and plenty of beef with salt and pepper. The famished men feasted until midnight on brimming kettles of soup rich with meat and dumplings.[79]

The following day, the fourteenth day of the expedition, the men crossed the Snake River at Jacob Meeks's ferry immediately north of present-day Blackfoot, Idaho.[80] Captain Smith bought from the ferrymen several sacks of flour, a dressed beef, and two wagons with harnesses for the pack animals to pull. Smith paid for the supplies with an order on the US government. The ferryman asked what to do if the government didn't honor the order. Smith replied, "You can hang me to the nearest tree if the United States government does not honor that order!"[81] The requisition was honored.

Even though the mountain boys no longer faced hunger or life-threatening rivers, Captain Smith continued to preserve their strength. In easy stages, the company traveled southward by way of Fort Hall, past the trapper's lodge at present-day Pocatello, Soda Springs, and on down through the Malad Valley. They crossed Bear River and continued on toward Great Salt Lake City.[82] From the Weber River where they camped on

---

79. Young, "Lest We Forget."

80. Hale, *Biography of J. H. Hale*, section on Solomon H. Hale. Seymour B. Young stated that the supplies were purchased at the Snake River ferry called Eagle Rock (present-day Idaho Falls). Seymour B. Young, "Lest We Forget."

81. Fisher, *Utah and the Civil War*, 92.

82. Young, "Lest We Forget."

Friday, August 8 (day twenty), Captain Smith sent a messenger to inform Brigham Young of their approach. There had been concern for Smith's company, which was long overdue. The *Deseret News* had published daily reports, and a worried President Young had sent some of the earlier returned Volunteers in search of the missing men.[83] About four o'clock on Saturday afternoon, August 9 (day twenty-one), Captain Smith led his US Volunteers into Great Salt Lake City. The emaciated, ragged, half-clad band had shared their few clothes with each other. Only Crismon was fully clad—courtesy of an emigrant at the solicitation of Hale.[84] The three-week Snake River Expedition was judged "the most hazardous ever performed in the West by United States troops in defense of their country."[85]

Smith had given valuable service in the cause of the Union Army during the Civil War and would soon be elected as a Brigadier General and serve a two-year mission for the Church in the British Isles.

83. Journal History, August 13, 1862.
84. Fisher, *Utah and the Civil War*, 93; *Deseret News*, August 13, 1862.
85. Fisher, *Utah and the Civil War*, 10.

CHAPTER 7

British Mission

Captain Smith returned home to rest, food, and the comforts of civilization. He received a warm welcome from Jane, Laura, and Julia, but immediately missed Lydia. Only a few days before his return, Lydia had left again to join her father and brother in Fillmore. With her went their oldest son, Lot Samuel, and their newborn babe who he had not seen but named for his friend Robert Taylor Burton. After Smith had brought Lydia back to Farmington in 1861, she had lived contentedly by herself for nine months. Yet Smith desired his wives and children to live together amicably in the same house. He had asked Lydia to move into the big house to live with Jane and Laura. Though, just as before, Lydia could not cope and left.[1]

In 1863, Smith helped haul rock to build the new Farmington chapel.[2] On January 9 and 10, 1864, the Farmington rock chapel was dedicated with Brigham Young and several apostles in attendance. Between the Sunday morning and afternoon meetings, a council meeting was held "relating to difficulties between Lot Smith and his wives which was amicably settled."[3] Wilford Woodruff reported Young's speech of the afternoon: "We should never let our families see us mad. We should always be kind and mild with them and do what was right and not neglect our prayers or to ask a blessing at the table, but set a good example before our families. He said the sins of omission would lead to the sin of commission."[4]

Young planned an outing to the newest colony, which had been established the previous year at Bear Lake more than two hundred miles north.[5] The 1864 trip was Smith's fourth and last opportunity to serve as a guard for President Young. He received a note from John R. Winder that requested his companionship on the trip to Bear Lake if it was convenient—and to keep it "mum."[6] The company left Great Salt Lake City on May 16,

---

1. Lydia M. Smith, Pension Records, September 17, 1900.
2. Thomas S. Smith, Diaries (1855–64), journal 2.
3. Journal History of the Church of Jesus Christ of Latter-day Saints, January 10, 1864 (hereafter cited as Journal History).
4. Journal History, January 10, 1864.
5. Andrew Jenson, *Encyclopedic History of the Church*, 46.
6. John R. Winder, letter to Major Lot Smith, May 11, 1864.

1864. The personnel included Brigham Young, Heber C. Kimball, John Taylor, George A. Smith, Wilford Woodruff, Joseph Young, and others. The mounted guard, which included Smith, followed. The trip turned out to be quite memorable. Apostle Charles C. Rich's son Joseph had reported sightings of a serpent-headed, long-necked monster in the depths of Bear Lake.[7] A *Deseret News* article later told that a long, heavy rope was taken on this expedition to "catch the Bear Lake monster."[8]

The caravan traveled northward and held meetings in the settlements along the route. It increased in numbers to 153 men as it proceeded through Cache Valley to Franklin. At Franklin, it was planned to drive through the uninhabited country to Paris on the shores of Bear Lake in one day. The plans, however, were thwarted. First, the carriage of George A. Smith, who weighed in excess of three hundred pounds, broke down.[9] Then, up the mountain between Cache Valley and Bear Lake Valley, George A.'s second conveyance collapsed, and everyone indulged in a good laugh. George A.'s only alternative was to ride a horse. Members of the Twelve Apostles gathered round as Young supervised Apostle Smith's mounting on the largest saddle horse in the entourage to the amusement of all.

After pushing over the summit, the cavalcade struck deep mud.[10] Horses, wagons, and carriages sank into the depths. The mounted guards came to the rescue. With brute force, thirty men dragged the horses several rods before they regained their feet. The sight of the dignified leadership spattered with mire and stumbling through mud engendered more laughter. Then word came that George A.'s horse was totally spent. To transfer him to another animal, the guards built a scaffold. By this time, circumstances had become so preposterous that the laughter was unrestrained.[11] Finally, at 3:00 a.m., the caravan pulled into Paris.

After resting a day, the company drove to the point on the lake (near present-day Fish Haven) where sightings of the monster had been reported. No monster appeared.[12] After the Sunday meeting, the presidential party departed the Bear Lake colony. Charles C. Rich furnished ox teams to haul

---

7. *Deseret News*, November 25, 1868; May 26, 1869; October 28, 1869.

8. Brigham Young, letter to President David P. Kimball, February 23, 1871.

9. Solomon F. Kimball, "Thrilling Experiences," 241.

10. Kimball, "Thrilling Experiences," 241–42.

11. Kimball, 242–43.

12. The large rope brought for the capture of the monster was left behind. Brigham Young, letter to David P. Kimball, February 23, 1871. See also Kate B. Carter, "The Bear Lake Monster," *Our Pioneer Heritage*, 8:593.

George A. through the mud to the summit of the mountain. The mountain again caused many problems, but not for George A. He rode with "a smile on his countenance that made all who beheld it feel good through and through."[13] Only the ox teams followed the muddy canyon floor. The lighter horse-drawn vehicles hugged side hills so steep that the guards lashed poles to the carriage beds and bore down on the upper end of the poles to prevent the carriages from tipping over. The company continued through the rain. At last, on May 26, they arrived back in Great Salt Lake City.[14]

In the spring of 1865, the Southern Ute families were hungry and discontent. When a young Ute of Black Hawk's band was whipped by a Mormon man in Manti, the Ute Chief Black Hawk attacked the next day and continued a quick succession of raids. The Black Hawk War began. Daniel H. Wells reorganized the Nauvoo Legion to assist in the conflict. On May 19, 1866, Lot Smith's troops elected him to the rank of Brigadier General.[15] That summer, Smith assisted in further organization of the Nauvoo Legion. He and other officers toured county militias for muster, inspection, and drill.[16] The entire territory joined in defense against Black Hawk's guerilla warfare. During the summer of 1866, as many as twenty-five hundred men of the militia were under arms.[17] In July, Smith mustered a sixty-man cavalry company from Davis County under Captain Andrew Bigler for ninety days of service.[18] After Smith recruited, armed, and supplied the troops, he accompanied the cavalry for two days as they traveled alongside the bays and inlets on the west side of Utah Lake. By 1868, every able-bodied man in the Sanpete Valley had been ordered to military service. The settlers abandoned their small settlements and moved into well-guarded forts with posted pickets. Their cattle were carefully guarded in these forts, and Black Hawk's raids began to be less successful. The Black Hawk War officially ended on August 9, 1868, with a peace treaty in Strawberry Valley. Chief Black Hawk, accompanied by seven or eight warriors and escorts of two to six settlers, visited every town and village from Cedar City in the south to Payson in the north. He told the

---

13. Kimball, "Thrilling Experiences," 244.

14. Andrew Jenson, *Documentary History*, 392.

15. Journal History, May 19, 1866. After election as Brigadier General, Smith no longer served as Color Bearer.

16. Journal History, November 4, 1867.

17. Hamilton Gardner, *Pioneer Military Leaders of Utah*, 71.

18. Peter Gottfredson, *Indian Depredations*, 199–200.

residents that before he went home to die, he desired to be at peace with the palefaces.

Also during the war, the School of the Prophets in Utah met for the first time in Great Salt Lake City in the ornate rooms of City Hall.[19] Among others, Lot Smith, Bishop John W. Hess, and Arthur Stayner were the three chartered members from Farmington. During this period, the purpose of the school was to combat the power and influence of the increasing "gentile" (non-Mormon) population.[20]

Ten years had passed since Smith had married Laura Burdick when he began to court nineteen-year-old Alice Ann Richards. She was the daughter of deceased Willard Richards, former counselor and first cousin to Brigham Young. When Alice Ann's father had died in 1854, her mother had married Willard's nephew, Franklin D. Richards. In 1860, Franklin had moved the family to Farmington.[21] Smith first met Alice Ann around 1858 as he rode his horse in Great Salt Lake City and saw her carefully carrying home a cup of yeast from her grandmother's house. Alice Ann immediately recognized the "church hero" and was intimidated. She commented that he was riding a good horse. Smith admitted that it was a fine horse, but that it had only one fault—it didn't seem to appreciate a pretty little girl like he did.[22] Years later, Smith took Alice Ann to a military ball.[23] While courting Alice Ann, Farmington's second Quorum of the Seventy, the 74th, was organized with Lot Smith serving as president of the quorum.[24]

By May, romance had blossomed into marriage plans for Smith and Alice Ann. The wedding party traveled the sixteen miles to Great Salt Lake City early Saturday morning, May 30, 1868. In the back seat of a two-seated carriage drawn by Smith's two matched gray stallions sat Alice Ann and her sister Mary. In the front seat sat the two grooms-to-be—twenty-nine-year-old Elias Van Fleet and thirty-eight-year-old Lot Smith. Smith had made arrangements for the early morning ceremonies with Daniel Wells, who met them as they drew up to the Endowment House. Before

19. For more information about the School of the Prophets, see John R. Patrick, "The School of the Prophets"; and Devery S. Anderson, *Salt Lake School of the Prophets*.

20. Klaus J. Hansen, *Quest for Empire*, 143.

21. Minerva Richards Knowlton, "History of Nanny Longstroth Richards."

22. Knowlton, "History of Nanny Longstroth Richards."

23. Alice Ann Richards Smith, journal extracts, December 26, 1867.

24. 74th Quorum of the Seventy Meeting Minutes, March 29, 1868 and March 31, 1868.

they could alight, Heber C. Kimball arrived and, in Alice Ann's words, "seemed quite shocked."[25] She continued: "In a humorous way but rather serious too, he [Kimball] said, 'It is my privilege to marry Dr. Richards' daughter.' . . . [B]efore anything further happened, President Brigham Young arrived, and he decided it was his right to marry his niece. He said to Lot, 'Why didn't you get my consent to marry my niece?'"[26] Evidently, Smith had secured permission to take another wife without naming her. Alice Ann continued: "And he [Young] said much more, and he was surely stern to the men and lovely to we sisters."[27] The parties entered the Endowment House to be married and sealed by Brigham Young with witnesses Daniel H. Wells and Wilford Woodruff.[28] Alice Ann moved into the large two-story stone house in Farmington as the fifth wife of Smith and lived with Jane, Laura, and their nine children. Julia resided at Stoddard in Morgan County; Lydia was in Fillmore.[29]

A year later, on May 10, 1869, history was made as the golden railroad spike was driven to complete the transcontinental railway on Promontory Hill northwest of Ogden. Celebrations were held simultaneously in Salt Lake City and most of the communities in the Territory.[30] After the arrival of the first company of emigrant Saints on the rails from Great Britain in a journey of only about twenty-three days, the *Deseret News* printed: "By its aid our missionary operations at home and abroad will be greatly promoted. Our Elders can travel with expedition and ease to the most distant parts, perform their missions, return with equal facility, bringing with them fruits of their labors."[31] Fifteen days after the railway was connected, Smith received a mission call by formal letter from Brigham Young. [32] The *Deseret News* announced on the same day: "At a council of the First Presidency and Twelve Apostles the Elders whose names are herewith given were called to go on missions."[33] Smith's name was among the eight listed. Four days later, Smith rode to the Historian's Office to be

25. Alice Ann Richards Smith, *Living Words of Alice Ann Richards Smith*, 38.

26. Smith, 38.

27. Smith, 38.

28. Church of Jesus Christ of Latter-day Saints, *Sealings of Couples,* film, E:139.

29. *Sealings of Couples,* film, E:139.

30. Kate B. Carter, *Our Pioneer Heritage*, 12:336.

31. Quoted in *Church News*, May 12, 1979, 10.

32. Brigham Young, letter to Lot Smith, May 25, 1869.

33. *Deseret News*, May 25, 1869.

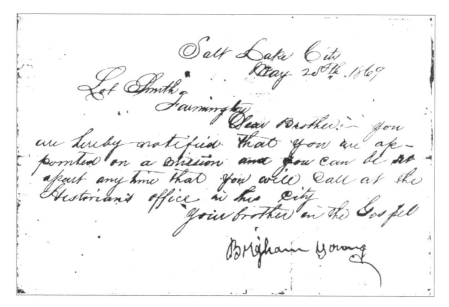

Smith's "Appointment to go upon mission." Special Collections, University of Arizona.

set apart for the British Mission and receive a blessing from his long-time friend and mentor, apostle Wilford Woodruff.[34]

Smith hastened to prepare for a two-year absence from his family, which now consisted of four wives and fourteen young children—not including Lydia. Smith first procured enough flour to supply his families for a year. He then asked his brother William "Bill" James (who was pioneering the new settlement of Bloomington on Bear Lake) to manage his farmlands in his absence. "Bill consented and [his] family moved to Lot's farm for a part of their keep as fee for the family service. The . . . fee amounted to sufficient wheat for their flour. The only other income came from the butter and milk they sold from the cows."[35] Bill was assisted by their half-brother, twenty-one-year-old red-bearded Nathaniel, who lived in Stoddard on property Lot had shared with him.[36] Smith finished arrangements for his family in less than a month after receiving the appointment to fill a mission.

---

34. Christian L. Christensen, Missionary Register 1860–1959, vol. 2, Book B, 13, line 490.

35. William James Smith, Biography.

36. Nathaniel worked for Lot until Lot went to Arizona. Nathaniel moved to Preston, Idaho in 1918.

On June 21, Smith boarded the Union Pacific Railroad in Ogden. In seven days, Smith traveled across almost the entire continent, in contrast to his six-month march with the Mormon Battalion that crossed only half that distance. Smith arrived in New York City early in the morning of June 28. He went to Stevens House on Broadway, where he awakened the elders who were boarding at the hotel.[37] The next day, Elders Lot Smith, Albert P. Dewey, George H. Barton, George H. Peterson, and John Quincy "Quince" Knowlton each paid fifty dollars for cabin passage and embarked on the Inman line's SS *City of Washington*, a British-flagged combination steam and sailing ship.[38] The ship steamed up the coast toward Nova Scotia where the Gulf Stream would take them eastward to the British Isles.[39]

The first few days on the Atlantic Ocean were mild. Then the sea roughened. Winds increased to a gale, and the seas began to roll in huge waves under a hard, driving rain. That night, Smith joined the other sea-sick passengers.[40] Two days later, the wind and the rain began to subside. Although the sea was still rough, Elders Smith and Barton recovered. As the ship neared the Irish Coast on the morning of July 9, the sea became peaceful. The next morning in clear weather, the *City of Washington* steamed up Saint George's Channel along the Welsh coast and around Holyhead's point and lighthouse. Around midnight the ship steamed up the River Mersey to Liverpool, the second largest seaport of the British Empire, where the voyage ended.

A steam tug took the elders ashore. The five Elders walked through the crowded streets of Liverpool and hired a horse-drawn cab to take them to the mission headquarters. There the new elders met Albert Carrington, President of the British and European Missions. The president told them to buy new clothes and advised them of lodging.[41] The next morning, the elders went to the tailor's shop to be measured for English trotter suits. The suits cost £4–18 each or about $25.[42] The quintet explored the city during the remainder of the day. The next day, the missionaries donned their new tight-legged trousers, frock coats, narrow-toed shoes, and beaver hats.[43]

---

37. Albert P. Dewey, British Mission Journal, June 28, 1869.

38. George Barton, diary, June 29, 1869; Alma Eldredge, diary, July 1, 1869, 36.

39. Dewey, journal, July 1–2, 1869.

40. Dewey, journal; and George Barton, diary, July 5–8, 1869.

41. Dewey, journal, July 11, 1869.

42. Barton, diary, July 12, 1869; Alma Eldredge, diary, June 6, 1870; Dewey, journal, July 12, 1896

43. Jacobs, diary, July 21, 1867.

President Carrington assigned Smith to be a traveling elder to the Glasgow Conference in Scotland, the northernmost field in the British Isles.[44] In 1869, the Glasgow Conference consisted of nineteen branches with a fluctuating membership of 978.[45] Smith boarded the train on July 23 and rode eight hours for 225 miles.[46] He stepped from the train at Glasgow's Caledonia Railway Central Station and walked to Glasgow's Latter-day Saint headquarters located in Kingston.[47] At the conference house, Smith met two Scotsmen from Utah: forty-three-year-old Hamilton G. Park and James Sharp, who had been Smith's messmate during the 1862 Snake River Expedition. Sharp directed the Glasgow Conference as he awaited the arrival of Henry C. Jacobs, who had been appointed as the new president of the conference.

When President Jacobs arrived, he began a tour to the east coast with President Sharp and Elder Smith on August 7. The threesome left Glasgow and rode the train through Stirling, Perth, Forth Valley, and arrived in Dundee on the eastern coast—the third most populous city in Scotland— where they visited the Saints in and around Dundee. On the fourth night, they slept with Mr. Adamson at Mill O'Machie. On Saturday, August 14, they walked twenty-five to thirty miles to the coal mining district of Cowdenbeath for Sunday's meetings, then walked six miles to Burntisland and on to the small branch at Musselburgh. [48] Later that week President Sharp, his mission fulfilled, bid goodbye to his native Scotland.[49]

Lot Smith began proselyting with Hamilton Park among the miners and ironworkers of Motherwell, located twelve miles up the River Clyde. Smith and Park encouraged the members to observe the Word of Wisdom. They strove to convince the Scottish Saints that they should abandon "the prevailing evil"—whiskey and tobacco—for financial, intellectual, and spiritual reasons.[50] On his return, Smith received a five-month assignment as a traveling elder to Edinburgh in a region steeped in history. Smith arrived on September 2 at Edinburgh with tall buildings and ancient cobbled streets. He inquired about and visited every known Saint in the district and held meetings when possible. Back in Glasgow at his

---

44. *Latter-day Saints' Millennial Star*, 31:484.
45. British Mission Statistics Record, 114.
46. Dewey, journal, July 31, 1869.
47. Henry Chariton Jacobs, diary, July 31, 1869.
48. Jacobs, diary, August 14, 1869.
49. Jacobs, diary, August 14–20, 1869.
50. Hamilton G. Park, letter to Brigham Young, October 15, 1869.

first district meeting on October 10, Smith, among others, reported the Church activity in the north.[51]

Smith was next accompanied by President Jacobs to the east coast for two weeks. Smith introduced Jacobs to the Saints in Edinburgh, Musselburgh, Tranent, and the ancient seaport town of Dysart. Though pressed by stringent economy, Dysart and its vicinity held some of Scotland's most faithful Saints. From Dysart the pair visited Cowdenbeath and Dunfermline. The Church's struggling branch at Dunfermline had been undermined with jealousy and backbiting. The two missionaries managed to restore a semblance of unity and left the branch somewhat repaired. At Dundee on October 24, Smith spoke to the Saints and "talked freely upon the first principles [of the gospel]," and President Jacobs gave his customary Word of Wisdom speech.[52] The president and Smith continued up the northern seacoast to visit Arbroath and Mill O'Machie before the two returned to Glasgow. Of this tour President Jacobs reported to the *Latter-day Saints' Millennial Star* on November 8:

> I have just returned from a very successful tour through the north, where we had a splendid time in visiting the Saints and putting things in order. I felt that the Lord was with us (Brother L[ot] Smith and myself) all the time, for our tongues were loosened on all occasions, and the Saints seemed to enjoy our visit exceedingly.[53]

Elder William Douglas was sent to meet Elder Smith a few miles eastward of Cowdenbeath in the small colliery district of Boreland near Dysart. They met at the home of the poor but hospitable coal mining family of Charles Wright Spence and his wife Elizabeth.[54] Their eleven children ranged in age from twenty-one-year-old Jane to baby Margaret.[55] Elder Smith blessed nine-month-old Margaret Morrison Spence on that day, November 1, 1869.[56] All the Spence sons were coal miners, and the long hours of labor provided only a scanty living. Emigration to Utah was impossible for the impoverished family.[57]

---

51. William M. Douglas, diary, October 10, 1869.

52. Jacobs, diary, October 24, 1869.

53. *Latter-day Saints' Millennial Star*, 31:759.

54. William M. Douglas, diary, November 1, 1869.

55. Charles Wright Spence family group sheet, courtesy Lucille Satterfield Beem.

56. Record of members collection 1836–1970, CR 375 8, Reel 6328, Dysart Branch.

57. Lucille Satterfield Beem, "My Grandfather—Alexander Morrison Spence," 1–2.

Elders Smith and Douglas visited members in the area who had not been contacted by the Church for as many as two years. They visited members in Clackmannan, Kelty, and Kirkaldy. None of the impoverished Saints in Kirkaldy were able to furnish a bed, so the two elders lodged at the local hotel.[58] After visiting the Saints in Armadale, the two elders arrived back in Glasgow on November 15. During the rest of the week, Smith and Douglas visited local members, attended the weekly singing held at Brother Crawford's, and assisted in sending out the *Millennial Star*. Saturday evening, November 20, the three missionaries—Smith, Douglas, and Jacobs—attended Hengler's circus at West Nile Street.[59] Jacobs wrote on December 2 that Elders Park, Smith, Douglas, and himself "were enjoying excellent health and were actively engaged in spreading the principles of the gospel."[60]

In early December, Smith took the train with Elder Douglas for his third tour of the north, which lasted a month. Elders Smith and Douglas continued to visit the branches, search for members, and hold meetings. At a meeting on December 12 in Arbroath, numerous interested strangers joined the members. "The little room was filled, it being the largest meeting held there for some time among the Saints."[61] After a week in Dundee, the companions made a two-day visit to Dunfermline where the members still harbored ill feelings toward one another. Douglas wrote: "This little branch being in rather peculiar feeling one toward another, we advised them to live their religion."[62] The next three days were spent in Cowdenbeath and they revisited the families at Kelty, "the brethren again being anxious to see us."[63] On Christmas Day, Smith and Douglas traveled to Dysart and again visited the Spence family.[64] Despite a sudden storm, about a dozen Saints came to a meeting in Brother Spence's house.[65] Three men were advanced in the priesthood and both elders

58. William M. Douglas, diary, November 12, 1869.

59. William M. Douglas, diary, November 15–20, 1869.

60. *Deseret News*, December 23, 1869, in Journal History, December 2, 1869.

61. Douglas, diary, December 4–12, 1869.

62. Douglas, diary, December 21, 1869.

63. Douglas, diary, December 23, 1869.

64. Douglas, diary, December 25, 1869. Jacobs wrote that the Scots never paid any attention to Christmas.

65. Douglas, diary, December 26, 1869.

spoke.[66] Elders Smith and Douglas returned to Glasgow via visiting in Bathgate, Blackbrau, and Armadale.

On Sunday, January 2, 1870, the Scotland Mission Conference commenced in one of Glasgow's most distinguished buildings, the Victoria Hotel.[67] Elder Smith reported that during the last six months in the north around Edinburgh, he "had found many good, faithful Saints, who were willing to do what they could for the advancement of the Kingdom of God but a few were lukewarm and indifferent."[68] On January 3, all twelve elders escorted President Carrington to the railway station to entrain for Liverpool. They then began a four-day tour of the Scottish mission. After the first day of sightseeing, the elders scattered to eat with the members. The following day, Smith accompanied the group on a one-day tour of Edinburgh. The elders returned at 8:00 p.m. to Glasgow, where they were welcomed by a roomful of members hosting a soiree which included refreshments, singing, and recitations until two o'clock in the morning. To conclude their tour, the missionary group visited Argyle Arcade, Buchanan Street, and the bazaar at St. George's Square.[69]

In Glasgow, Smith learned he would begin the new year of 1870 with an assignment to the south on the west coast of Scotland in and around Glasgow. Smith requested a list of members from the mission president, and he and the other elders began to search for lapsed or lost members. At this point, the missionaries visited the poor and administered to the sick. On Saturday, January 8, Elders Smith, Douglas, Park, and Jacobs went to visit a Sister Hoggan and found her and several of her children very low with fever.[70] All of them were crowded into a little one-room back place called a den to give her a blessing. President Jacobs had never encountered such wretched destitution; he suddenly became ill. While Douglas and Park went on a short tour north, Smith remained in Glasgow and preached the entire Sunday evening meeting, to the ailing president's relief.[71]

---

66. Record of members collection 1836–1970, CR 375 8, Reel 6327.

67. Scotland Mission Conference statistics show an income of £277.5.80 and a total membership of 807 in twenty-one branches.

68. *Latter-day Saints' Millennial Star*, 32:38.

69. Douglas, diary, January 4–6, 1870.

70. Membership records of Dunfermline recorded that Lot Smith blessed the baby girl of a tailor James Hoggan and his wife, Janet Brown, on June 30, 1869, a likely incorrect date as Smith did not arrive in Scotland until July 23, 1869.

71. Jacobs, diary, January 8–9, 1870.

On Friday, January 28, Smith and President Jacobs went to see Brother Herwood, who was bedfast. They administered to him, and he was almost instantly relieved. Visits to the sick, infirm, and troubled continued to increase. The following week on February 3, the two "visited several very poor old Saints to comfort them and do them good."[72] The next day, they visited a Sister Hyslop, who had finally heard from her husband Lester who was at sea. He was alive but ill. That same day they continued to a little place called New Farm Rutherglen where Smith and Jacobs administered to a poor old sister who had been afflicted with palsy for six years. She was now almost speechless and as helpless as a child.[73] After the district meeting on February 7, the two again were "out among the sick where we done our best for their welfare."[74] During that week, Smith became ill. On the following Monday, however, President Jacobs noted "Bro. Smith is better this morning."[75] That afternoon, the two went to see Sister Hyslop and called on others.

In late February, heavy snowfall left the elders housebound. One of elders suggested that they write the meeting address on some tracts, "The Only Way to be Saved" by Lorenzo Snow, and distribute them. The four Elders sat up until midnight writing on the pamphlets. The next morning, all four braved the snowy streets to offer the tracts to homes in Glasgow. Douglas reported that of the sixty tracts delivered by himself and Smith, "only a few doors shut in our faces. Some of the people would not read them after they saw the name Latter-day Saints on them."[76] On March 8 and 9, the president and Elder Smith began calling to collect the tracts which had been distributed. "When we collect [the tracts] we have many good chances of bearing our simple testimony and explaining our principles to them, which is a great comfort to us. Many say they have read and are well pleased, 'but they have a church of their own.'"[77]

Later in March, Smith and Jacobs went to Rutherglen where they discovered that the Moyes family's baby who had been ill had died. They attended the baby's funeral the next day. In those days among the poor

---

72. Jacobs, diary, February 3, 1870.

73. Jacobs, diary, February 4, 1870.

74. Jacobs, diary, February 7, 1870.

75. Jacobs, diary, February 14, 1870.

76. Conflicts exist between the diaries of Jacobs and Douglas here and for the next week or more.

77. H. C. Jacobs, letter to President A. Carrington, March 11, 1870, *Latter-Day Saint's Millennial Star*, 32:188.

in Scotland, sometimes only the missionaries and the immediate family attended the funerals at the cemetery. For those who could afford no better, the body was placed in a casket with a hinged bottom that dropped the corpse into the earth after the funeral. During the rest of March and into April, Smith and the president continued to hold meetings, visit the members, administer to the sick, and distribute and collect tracts.[78]

When George Romney, President of the Liverpool Conference, arrived on April 14 in Glasgow, the Scotland elders chose to celebrate by visiting Loch Lomond and climbing adjacent Ben Lomond. From Loch Lomond, they boarded a steamer and enjoyed a close-up view of the lake's islands and shoreline of mountains and inlets. The five missionaries hiked five miles to the summit of Ben Lomond (3,192 feet), where Elder Park offered a prayer from the cold, windswept summit.[79]

Elder Smith continued his missionary activities in Motherwell, Lanark, and the Whifflet—a small ironstone mining village. In the Whifflet they arrived at David McNeil's cottage and had quite a long talk with him before going to bed.[80] One of the McNeil sons, John, soon immigrated to Utah to earn money for the rest of the family to immigrate and later had dealings in Utah with all three elders—Smith, Douglas, and Park.[81] On May 31, Smith learned that he was to be transferred to Birmingham as Conference President.[82]

During the last year of his mission, Smith served as president of the Birmingham Conference—described by Andrew Jenson as "one of the best and largest conferences, or districts, in the British Mission" and by Orson F. Whitney as "a Mormon stronghold second only to London in importance."[83] Smith arrived at the Birmingham Conference headquarters on June 8, 1870. He sat up late that night to visit his good friend Albert P. Shumway (the outgoing conference president), Elder Alma Eldredge, and Bishop W. W. Cluff.[84] President Smith would be assisted in his new responsibilities by two traveling elders—fifty-two-year-old Birmingham native Joseph Argyle from Bountiful, Utah, and twenty-six-year-old Elijah

78. Jacobs, diary, March 12–April 13, 1870.

79. Douglas, diary, April 16, 1870.

80. Douglas, diary, May 2–3, 1870.

81. See Frederick S. Buchanan, *A Good Time Coming*, 136–38.

82. Jacobs, diary, June 3, 1870.

83. Andrew Jenson, *Encyclopedic History*, 67; Orson F. Whitney, *Life of Heber C. Kimball*, 277.

84. Alma Eldredge, diary, June 8, 1870.

Box, who was the son of Birmingham converts.[85] Five days after Smith's arrival, five branches from the Leicester Conference were added to the Birmingham Conference.[86]

The first Birmingham Conference under his administration convened Saturday afternoon, July 16, in Temperance Hall on Temple Street. On the stand sat the new British mission president, Horace S. Eldredge, with the presidents of eight conferences in Britain. President Smith read the financial and statistical report of the conference and presented the Church authorities of both Utah and Europe for the sustaining vote of the membership.[87] The visiting elders offered spiritual messages in three sessions, and the following Monday evening the Birmingham Saints presented a concert in the Hockley Chapel on Farm Street.[88] Six months later, at Smith's second conference, a greatly increased attendance of five hundred met again at Temperance Hall. President Eldredge, plagued by a lung complaint from the cool, damp climate, spoke only a short time.[89] The nine presidents of the conferences offered inspiring messages in the evening session. The following evening, a concert and recitations entertained a large attendance of about four hundred.[90]

In October, Smith attended his first mission-wide conference in the great city of London. The Saturday before the conference, President Smith and five other conference presidents accompanied President Eldredge on a visit to Westminster Abbey.[91] Conference convened on October 9 in the rented McDonald Music Hall—a large hall with two galleries that surrounded three sides. Eldredge again was so hoarse and coughed so much that he could speak but little. Smith was one of the six conference presidents

---

85. Joseph Argyle, Manuscript, June 21, 1870. In May 1871 Caleb Parry replaced Joseph Argyle.

86. The branches of Coventry, Leamington, Rugby, Loxley, and Welford were added to the Birmingham Conference. Herefordshire Conference was attached shortly before President Shumway left.

87. *Latter-Day Saints' Millennial Star*, 32:476. Birmingham Statistical Report June 30, 1871: membership 845, thirty-two persons baptized during past six months. Statistical Report for December 1871: membership 941, twenty persons baptized during the past six months.

88. *Latter-Day Saints' Millennial Star*, 32:476.

89. Horace Sunderlin Eldredge, diary, September 25, 1870; Andrew Jenson, "Horace S. Eldredge," *Latter-day Saint Biographical Encyclopedia*, 1:197.

90. *Latter-Day Saints' Millennial Star*, 32: 634, 635.

91. Horace S. Eldredge, diary, George Barton, diary, and Albert P. Dewey, Mission Journal, October 8, 1870.

who spoke in his stead in the evening meeting. In his speech, he pointed out that the Saints had been commanded to seek knowledge out of all good books. He expressed his pleasure that some of the "public journals" had spoken out against the poor treatment of the Saints in the United States.[92]

After the conference, President Eldredge and the six conference presidents, including Smith, began a tour that lasted several days. The first day they visited the Zoological Gardens, and then they returned to Albion Hall, London Wall for an evening concert given by the Church members. They next visited the London Tower and the Crystal Palace, spent an evening at the Alhambra Theatre, and ended their sightseeing at St. James where they listened to Christy's Minstrels, an American troupe of unusual musical ability.[93]

Birmingham had a reputation for rioting and disturbance. Unrest caused by racial, economic, and religious tensions spawned torchlight parades of protest, demonstrations, strikes, and riots. The crowded living conditions with shared ash pits, privies, and washhouses fostered a desperate lifestyle of drunkenness, abuse, violence, and thievery.[94] One incident reported by a Smith descendant illustrates Smith's resolve in dealing with Birmingham's more uncouth characters. As Smith spoke one evening at a public meeting, a burly heckler in the congregation repeatedly called out, "Give us a sign! Give us a sign! Wait a minute. Can you raise the dead?" and similar taunts. Smith ignored him until he called out, "Can you cast out devils?" With that remark, President Smith strode down the aisle and replied, "No, I can't cast out devils, but I can cast out the imps." And he threw the man out.[95]

The Church members of Birmingham, although not affluent, constituted an entirely different element. The faithful Thomas Ash family portrayed the plight of many of the Latter-day Saint families of Birmingham. The Ash family cherished the visits of the missionaries including Smith, Charles Shumway, and Abraham Halliday. Extreme poverty forced frequent trips of the Ash family to pawnshops with some of their scanty clothing for means to subsist until they earned more money. When the missionaries visited the family, Thomas—as usual—serviced the elders'

---

92. *Latter-Day Saints' Millennial Star*, 32:687.

93. Horace S. Eldredge, diary, Albert P Dewey, Mission Journal, and Barton, diary, October 10–15, 1870.

94. Steven R. Sorensen, "Alma Ash."

95. Louise Marie "Tude" Smith Stoddard Krumperman, Lot Smith Family Reunion, 1929.

shoes. The three-generation Latter-day Saint family listened to tales of life in Utah, and the younger family members often lined up the chairs and played the favorite game of the children of English converts—"Going to Zion." The Ash family, like many of the Latter-day Saint converts, looked to emigrate to Utah—a dream of a promised land and a better life outside of the severe destitution that they experienced. The Ash family's desires were fulfilled about fifteen years later.[96]

President Smith visited the conferences in the nearby districts. At the Manchester Conference held January 1, 1871, Smith "bore powerful testimony to the divine authenticity of the latter-day work."[97] At the Sheffield Conference in February, Smith "delivered a very interesting and instructive discourse, bearing a faithful testimony to the truths of the Gospel."[98] At the Bradford Conference in May, Elder Milton B. Shipp and President Smith did most of the speaking at Sunday's three meetings.[99] Smith attended the Leicester Conference held in Red Cross Street Chapel in June, where he spoke on "the establishment of the Church in these days, the early revelations to the Prophet Joseph Smith, and of the first principles of the Gospel."[100] Smith's counselor Joseph Argyle described the Birmingham Conference: "Many of the Saints are very poor and have had to suffer for lack of the necessaries of life this winter through the severe frosts." He continued to say that in earlier days, thousands were baptized. However, since that time, the Saints have suffered persecution, mainly from Christian ministers and reverends. Despite the circumstances, "[t]he Elders declare their willingness to go with brother Smith and myself, as soon as the weather will permit, and warn the people." [101]

During his year as conference president in Birmingham, President Smith became acquainted with George Thomas Baugh, his wife Elizabeth Ann Fereyhough Baugh, and their eighteen-year-old daughter Alice Mary while they served as resident caretakers at the Conference House. The Baugh family sailed on June 21 to America where they settled in Logan, Utah.[102] During Smith's final days in England, he held his final

---

96. Alma Ash immigrated around 1885 and sent for his father's family. See Sorensen, "Alma Ash."

97. *Latter-Day Saints' Millennial Star*, 33:29.

98. *Latter-Day Saints' Millennial Star*, 33:108.

99. Horace S. Eldredge, diary, May 27, 1871.

100. *Latter-Day Saints' Millennial Star*, 33:444.

101. *Latter-Day Saints' Millennial Star*, 33:187.

102. Alice Baugh Smith, "Pioneer Personal History."

Birmingham Conference on Sunday, July 16, again in Temperance Hall. The following evening in the Hockley chapel, the Birmingham Saints bid farewell to their departing conference president with songs, glees, duets, and recitations until a late hour.[103]

On the afternoon of Wednesday, July 26, Smith began his return trip to America. He had stewardship of ninety-three immigrating Saints—all in good health and fine spirits—and was assisted by returning missionaries John Jaques, Albert P. Dewey, Albert P. Shumway, George W. Groo, and Joseph Argyle.[104] Henry Jacob Faust of Utah and his wife were also aboard.[105] Smith and the Saints sailed from Liverpool on the combination sail and steamship SS *Nevada* of the Guion line.[106] On the first night, Smith and others addressed the Saints and gave "some excellent instructions . . . upon matters pertaining to the welfare of the company upon the journey."[107] For the first few days, cold weather chilled the Saints. Then headwinds caused the ship to roll, pitch, and heave. Only six of the passengers attended evening prayers—the rest were seasick.[108] The breeze slackened for two days and allowed the Saints to hold meetings in the steerage before violent rolling and pitching cancelled the respite. Brother Faust and Elder Groo were the sickest, and Smith did not boast of the soundness of his stomach.[109] Beautiful weather returned. During the remainder of the twelve-day voyage, the elders held meetings in the cabin and supervised meetings in the steerage on Sunday afternoons and testimony meetings on weekdays. As was the custom with Utah-bound Latter-day Saints, careful organization promoted orderly activities, much to the admiration and gratitude of the ship's captains.[110]

The ship arrived at New York City the morning of August 5. During the inspection of the Saints by the doctor and examination of the luggage by the customs officers, Captain William Forsyth entertained the elders at dinner in his quarters.[111] Afterward, both the elders and their charges disembarked and went to Castle Gardens for the night. On August 8,

103. *Latter-Day Saints' Millennial Star*, 33:476–77.

104. *Latter-Day Saints' Millennial Star*, 33:425, 440.

105. *Deseret News*, 20:329, in Journal History, August 16, 1871.

106. *Latter-Day Saints' Millennial Star*, 33:456,

107. J. Jaques, letter, July 27, 1871, *Latter-Day Saints' Millennial Star*, 33:491.

108. Joseph Argyle, Manuscript, July 27, 1871.

109. J. Jaques, letter, August 8, 1871, *Latter-Day Saints' Millennial Star*, 33:554.

110. Philip A. M. Taylor, "Mormons and Gentiles on the Atlantic," 209–10.

111. Argyle, diary, August 7, 1871.

Smith and the emigrant Saints boarded the train for the west. Except for one night spent in a large station room in Pittsburgh, the British Saints slept in the railcars until they reached Utah. At Omaha, Nebraska, on August 12, they boarded two Utah Southern cars sent from Utah. The two cars were attached to a slow-moving freight train that frequently slowed to four miles an hour and sometimes even less on difficult grades.[112] During the four-day journey from Omaha to Ogden, the company entertained themselves with singing and enjoyed the scenery.[113]

In the late afternoon of August 16, 1871, Smith and the other missionaries met a warm welcome in Ogden. A special car attached to the Utah Central Railroad brought Brigham Young, George A. Smith, George Q. Cannon, Horace S. Eldredge, Robert T. Burton, and others to meet and welcome the elders and the immigrating company.[114] According to the *Deseret News*, Elders Smith, Jacques, Dewey, Shumway, and Argyle "looked excellently, all being much heavier than when they left, except Lot Smith." [115] Elder Smith's company of ninety-three Saints arrived "in excellent health, having had a prosperous voyage across the ocean and a pleasant journey from New York to this point. Not a death occurred during the entire journey."[116] Though the other elders boarded the Utah Central to ride on to Salt Lake City, Smith and Burton stopped off in Farmington where Smith "received a warm reception, the leading citizens and people generally having turned out to meet him."[117] Smith's feelings about his mission were recorded the following year in a meeting of the 74th Quorum of the Seventy in Farmington: "Some thought it would be trying to be absent from home so much on missions, but it was the pleasantest time of his life when on his Mission, and he thought it was the case with every Elder who had done his duty."[118] Smith would spend only five more years in Utah.

---

112. J. Jaques August 18, 1871 letter, *Latter-Day Saints' Millennial Star*, 33:586.

113. J. Jaques August 18, 1871 letter, *Latter-Day Saints' Millennial Star*, 33:586; Joseph Argyle, diary, August 13, 1871.

114. Robert T. Burton, Diaries, August 16, 1871.

115. *Deseret News*, 20:329, in Journal History, August 16, 1871.

116. *Deseret News*, 20:329, in Journal History, August 16, 1871.

117. *Deseret News*, 20:329, in Journal History, August 16, 1871.

118. 74th Quorum of the Seventy Meeting Minutes, December 14, 1872.

CHAPTER 8

Last Utah Years

Upon his return from England, Smith learned that he had been selected ten days earlier to serve as councilor in the Utah Territorial Legislature scheduled to convene the following January. Circumstances in the Territory had changed significantly during Smith's two-year absence. Governor J. W. Shaffer—openly hostile to the Mormons—had abolished the Nauvoo Legion.[1] Efforts to annihilate the Mormon system of plural marriage had escalated. Federal Judge James B. McKean, who had arrived in Salt Lake City in August of the previous year, had proceeded to reopen charges and indict every possible Mormon on any charge whatsoever, including polygamy. Those indicted included Smith's friends, Robert T. Burton, J. D. T. McAllister, and Alexander F. Macdonald.[2] The Latter-day Saints knew that trial before Judge McKean and his packed non-Mormon juries meant conviction and harsh sentence. Therefore, the indicted Latter-day Saint men limited their public activities to avoid arrest.

Smith returned to attend Farmington's priesthood meetings and took his former place among the ward teachers.[3] He also resumed his attendance at the School of the Prophets until its closure in August 1872.[4] The Farmington ward teachers minutes of September 24 reflected the alarm of Smith and his friend Arthur Stayner, noting, "Br. Lot Smith said now is the time to prepair for war," and adding that "the powers of the devel was never more stronger than at the present."[5]

The *Deseret News* editorials of September 28 were ominously foreboding. Commentaries catalogued the "Doings of the Ring" led by Judge McKean, his Prosecuting Attorney R. N. Baskin, and US Marshal M. T. Patrick. Baskin and McKean attempted to put a stranglehold on the Mormons by focusing on Brigham Young. If they could arrest Young,

---

1. Kate B. Carter, "The Year of 1870," *Our Pioneer Heritage*, 14:8.

2. Robert T. Burton, diaries, October 21, 1871.

3. Minutes of Ward Teachers, September 10, 1871.

4. *Historical Department Journal*; Francis W. Kirkham and Harold Lundstrom, *Tales of a Triumphant People*, 48–49; Andrew Jackson Allen, diary, August 3, 1872.

5. Christian L. Christensen, Minutes of the Ward Teachers 2, September 24, 1871.

Lot Smith (ca. 1870). LDS Church History Library.

turmoil would follow.[6] That same day, Smith, along with Bishop Hess, Stayner, and twenty other Farmington men "visited the City to see Pres. Young and render him any assistance that might be needed."[7] The Federal Justice Department met in an unfinished hayloft courtroom in the upper story of the former Faust and Houtz stables. The meeting attracted an armed and angry throng of Mormons who were concerned with the threat to President Young. They milled around in the muddy street below the hayloft. Amidst the uproar, Smith was highly visible. Attorney Baskin

6. *Deseret News*, in Journal History of the Church, September 28, 1871 (hereafter cited as Journal History).

7. Journal History, September 28, 1871.

attributed the daily crowd of "hundreds of men, many of whom were armed and whose demeanor was most threatening towards the court," to Lot Smith.[8] After the excitement abated and the angry throng dispersed, Patrick quietly arrested Young on a charge of lascivious cohabitation with his wives. A few days later, Attorney Baskin issued a second warrant for Young's arrest on charges of the 1857 murder of Green River trader Richard Yates.[9] The US Marshal knew that the arrest of Young would cause great excitement and a possible confrontation, so he appointed nearly one hundred deputies.[10] When Burton learned of the hundred Deputy US Marshals ordered to arrest Young and possibly himself, he fled north to Smith's home in Farmington.[11] Thereafter, Burton began to be guarded constantly for a year and a half by various friends—Smith among them. On January 2, 1872, Young was arrested for the murder of Yates. Judge McKean refused a $500,000 bail, and the US Deputy Marshal guarded the president in his own house.[12]

During this tense time, the Twentieth Session of the Territorial Legislature convened on January 8, 1872. Forty-two-year-old Smith represented Davis and Morgan counties as councilor in the Utah Territorial Legislature.[13] Smith arrived at the red sandstone City Hall on the southeast corner of State Street and First South. He climbed the stairs to the upper story councilor room, ornate with wide, elegant moldings and luxurious furnishings. The assemblage was called to order. The Council elected officers pro tem, checked credentials, took the oath prescribed by law from Territorial Secretary George A. Black, and proceeded to organize. The Journal of the Legislative Assembly recorded: "On motion of councilor Lot Smith, J. D. T. McAllister was elected Sergeant-at-Arms."[14] Smith was named to six of the twenty-four committees and was later added to two more. The first committees on which Smith served included Petitions and Memorials, Elections, Library, Penitentiary, Unfinished Business, and Counties.[15]

When both branches of the Legislature were organized, Governor George L. Woods read his prepared message to a joint session. After he

---

8. R. N. Baskin, *Reminiscences of Early Utah*, 55.

9. Preston Nibley, *Brigham Young the Man and His Work*, 479.

10. Baskin, *Reminiscences of Early Utah*, 55.

11. Robert T. Burton, diaries, October 21, 1871.

12. Andrew Jenson, *Chronology of the Church*, January 2, 1872, 84.

13. *Journals of the Legislative Assembly*, 1.

14. *Journals of Legislative Assembly*, 6

15. *Journals of Legislative Assembly*, 14.

proposed several items, the governor read in a clear, forcible manner his condemnation of Utah's marriage customs and the lack of a civil statute defining marriage rights.[16] Though angry, the legislators referred the governor's proposals to committees for consideration—according to protocol. They realized that the greater autonomy of statehood appeared to be the only option to escape the interference of federal appointees. Utah Territory had already applied for statehood in March 1856 and again in January 1862. In January 1857, Smith had been one of the Davis County delegates who met with others to draft resolutions to establish a state government.[17] They had applied for admission into the Union by taking a census of the territory, adopting a State Constitution, and petitioning Congress. It had all been in vain. The US Government had responded to these efforts by placing the proposed State of Deseret/Territory of Utah under direct control of federal appointees. The discussion at the School of the Prophets that night had lasted until a late hour. The next morning in priesthood meeting in Farmington, as president of the 74th Quorum of the Seventy, Smith had said:

> What have we to fear if we are living just as God wishes us to? he will not turn away from us. he placed us here that we might choose the good from the eavil, he has said that he will have a tryed people, it is our slackness and carelessness which has brought about so much of this trouble. we should have kept the enemy out. let us wake up and stand like men of God. I thank God that I have the spirit yet to say that I am for the Kingdom of God.[18]

The Legislature began another attempt to gain statehood. The following Monday, January 15, 1872, the House sent to the Council an act already passed that provided for the election of delegates to a convention to prepare a constitution for the admission of Utah into the Union as a state.[19] It was promptly vetoed by the governor. Amended to read "An Act for Holding a Convention to prepare a Constitution for Admission of Utah as a State," Governor Woods again blocked the Legislature.[20] An act empowering a two-thirds majority to overrule the governor's veto was quickly vetoed. Governor Woods's authority to block any legislation left the Legislature powerless. To circumvent the standoff created by the governor's vetoes, Joseph W. Young proposed a resolution to be submitted

---

16. *Journals of Legislative Assembly*, 18–21.
17. *Latter-Day Saints' Millennial Star*, January 20, 1857.
18. Christian L. Christensen, Record of members, January 14, 1872.
19. *Journals of Legislative Assembly*, 35.
20. *Journals of Legislative Assembly*, 49, 66.

to the people so they could decide whether they would vote for holding a convention to draft a constitution and elect delegates.[21] The resolution passed, and a Constitutional Convention was scheduled to be held shortly after the adjournment of the Legislature.

In other business on Monday January 15, Smith suggested amendments to the "Act relating to damage done by animals." The proposals were sent to the Committee on Agriculture, Trade, and Manufacture, and Smith was added to the committee. [22] Smith's bill, renamed "An Act establishing estray pounds, and prescribing regulations for conducting the same," eventually passed.[23] He presented his second bill (C. F. No. 14) on January 30—"a bill for 'an Act in relation to Obnoxious Weeds,' was read, and, on motion of Councilor [Jacob G] Bigler, was referred to the Committee on Agriculture, Trade and Manufactures."[24] On February 16, 1872, Councilors Moses Thatcher and Lot Smith were added to the Committee on Education for the consideration of a bill relating to an appropriation for the Deseret University.[25]

During the time he served at the Legislature, Smith often guarded Robert Burton. Many times Smith spent the night at Burton's as a guest-guard.[26] On February 14, 1872, despite the US Marshal's use of Fort Douglas troops to help make arrests, Burton was honored by members of the LDS Fifteenth Ward with a benefit party at the courthouse. Among many notables—George A. Smith, John Taylor, Daniel H. Wells, Wilford Woodruff, Orson Pratt, and A. Cannon—Lot Smith was one of the speakers, and there was singing until 1:00 a.m.[27]

The Twentieth Session of the Territorial Legislature adjourned on February 16. Three days later, Smith was one of seven delegates from Davis County who attended the Constitutional Convention in the Representatives Room of the city hall to draft a state constitution to present to the US Congress for admission as a state.[28] Smith was one of nine men on the

---

21. *Journals of Legislative Assembly*, 67.

22. *Journals of Legislative Assembly*, 36.

23. *Journals of Legislative Assembly*, 100, 132, 133.

24. *Journals of Legislative Assembly*, 72.

25. *Journals of Legislative Assembly*, 157.

26. Robert T. Burton, diaries, 1872.

27. Robert T. Burton, diaries, February 14, 1872.

28. Andrew Jenson, *Chronology of the Church*; Christensen, Minutes 2, February 25, 1872.

Committee for Public Institutions.[29] After they labored over statutes for almost two weeks, the delegates adopted a constitution and a memorial to Congress asking for the admission of Utah into the Union as a state. The congressional special committee once again denied Utah's admission.

Judge McKean's crusade against the Mormons collapsed on April 15, 1872, when the US Supreme Court overturned McKean's judicial proceedings in Utah for the previous eighteen months.[30] The US Supreme Court's condemnation of trial by packed juries of non-Mormons made polygamy no longer vulnerable to the law.[31] Sometime later, the US Attorney dismissed the cases against some sixty Mormon men. Mormon tempers cooled, and their fears subsided. Opposition to Mormon polygamy, however, did not abate.

Smith returned to the quieter life of Farmington. During this time, Smith built a three-story barn in Farmington.[32] On June 16 Brigham Young sent a telegram to all the bishops urging liberal donations to the immigration for the poor from the Old Country.[33] That same day in Farmington's Sacrament Meeting, Smith showed support for Young's request when he spoke of how the Saints in the European countries were unable to emigrate—despite their faithfulness—because of poverty, and how they were surrounded with "the wickedness & corruption of the world."[34]

Smith renewed his acquaintance with Alice Mary Baugh and arranged for their marriage. On April 29, 1872, Alice Mary was married to Smith in the Endowment House by President Young's counselor Daniel H. Wells and witnessed by Joseph F. Smith, Addison Pratt, and William H. Folsom.[35] In their family life, Alice Mary, who weighed a scant ninety-eight pounds, came to be known as "Little Alice" to distinguish her from her sister wife, Alice Ann, who was called "Big Alice."[36] Alice Mary stayed in the two-story stone house in Farmington for two years until she moved to Stoddard to reside with Julia.[37]

---

29. *Salt Lake Daily Herald*, in Journal History, February 20, 1872.

30. Journal History, April 15, 1872; Harold Schindler, *Orrin Porter Rockwell*, 355.

31. See Baskin, *Reminiscences of Early Utah*, 51–52.

32. Alice Ann Richards Smith, *The Living Words of Alice Ann Richards Smith*, 12.

33. Christensen, Minutes, June 16, 1872.

34. Christensen, Minutes, June 16, 1872.

35. Christensen, *Sealings of Couples*, Book H:127.

36. Mary Jean and Martha Schott, interview by Omer J. and Carmen R. Smith, Wyoming Lot Smith Reunion, June 1974.

37. Alice Baugh Smith, "Pioneer Personal History," 3.

Smith's wives lived together in the complex arrangement of polygamy. In the fall of 1872, Jane, Julia, and Laura complained to Brigham Young about their husband. Whatever the grievances, Young wrote a letter to Smith from Salt Lake City inviting him to visit with his disgruntled wives.[38] Their visit apparently reconciled the difficulty.

In 1875, Smith's wife Laura went again to Young. The matter involved two of Smith's daughters, Laura "Lollie" (Laura's daughter) and Nannie (Alice Ann's)—both about seven years old—and Smith's desire for reverence during family prayer. The carpeted parlor of Smith's Farmington home was kept for special occasions and as the gathering place for the Smiths' morning and evening family prayers. The parlor contained Smith's writing desk, a number of chairs arranged along the walls, and a table in the center. Large pictures of the Church presidency and the Twelve Apostles in beautifully carved frames hung in order high on the walls of the room.[39] Smith's daughter, Lollie, wrote that the family always held family prayer and devotion every morning and night in the parlor. One night, she and her sister Nannie knelt for prayers by a rocking chair. During the prayer, they discovered that the chair squeaked if it was rocked. They squeaked it once too many times, for after their father finished praying, he called them to him, knocked their heads together, and "warned [them] to never make a noise in prayers again."[40]

Perhaps this incident added fuel to the fire of Laura's mother's constant criticism of the Church and the practice of polygamy.[41] Laura asked President Young for a bill of divorcement from Smith in late May 1875.[42] Young wrote to Smith that he thought it proper to grant the divorce and told Smith to give Laura and her five children their portion of his property.[43] In a June 9 letter, Smith responded with an apology for again troubling Young. He explained how he wanted his children with him so that he could look after them, but would not tolerate anyone raising the devil at prayer time. He wrote, "I hope I do beleave the Gospel, notwithstanding all the folley I may have shown. I will comply with all you require in

38. Brigham Young, letter to Elder Lot Smith, September 13, 1872.

39. Laura Louisa Smith (Rice), "A Short Sketch of the Life of Laura Louisa Smith," 2–3.

40. Smith (Rice), "A Short Sketch," 1, 3.

41. Eva Augusta Rice, "Sketch of the Life of Laura Louisa Burdick [Smith]," 9.

42. Brigham Young, letter to John W. Hess, May 29, 1875.

43. Brigham Young, letter to Lot Smith, May 29, 1875.

your letter."[44] Smith gave all his farmland in Farmington to Laura as her share, and she moved out of the big stone house. After Smith later moved to Arizona, she hired William Messenger to help with the farm work. In 1878 Laura took her children, left Farmington, and went to the mines at Tintic to join Messenger.[45] In Tintic on July 2, 1879, Laura's twins Howard William and Charlotte Winifred were born. Laura soon felt she had made a mistake when she departed Farmington and the Smith fold. Laura left Messenger and courageously came back to the Farmington farm with her children, where she lived in a two-roomed log house and later a frame house owned by a son-in-law.[46] Smith would have one congenial visit with her after his move to Arizona.

Smith had spent his last years in Utah serving in the Legislature and facing the complexities involved in keeping his family together. He next accepted a daunting task given by Brigham Young when he committed the rest of his life to the establishment of a colony in desolate Arizona Territory.

---

44. Lot Smith, letter to Brigham Young, June 9, 1875.

45. No records have been discovered indicating whether there was a marriage between the two.

46. Smith (Rice), "A Short Sketch," 1; Eva Rice Howell, letter to Carmen Smith, April 13, 1969.

CHAPTER 9

Journey to Arizona

Brigham Young stood at the pulpit in the domed tabernacle on the temple block on Sunday, January 23, 1876. He spoke plainly, as usual, chafing at the vain attempts to peaceably expand the Kingdom of God into the Territory of Arizona. He expressed his pique at the failure of the one hundred missionary-colonists he had called in 1873. When they had found the Arizona country drear and barren with alkali soil and inadequate water, the colonists had trailed back to Utah.[1] Young said he was tired of sending colonists down to Arizona to have them come crawling back.[2] Yet Young remained determined. He had most recently sent James S. Brown with thirteen assistants to establish a fort and peace mission among the Hopi Indians at Moenkopi over a hundred miles into Arizona Territory.[3] As the fort at Moenkopi neared completion, Young had members of the Utah Legislature select additional missionaries to go to Arizona. Most had received their calls recently.[4] Now Young was concerned with whether or not the newly called missionaries would persevere. Young—still at the pulpit and suddenly inspired—announced that he knew a man who would stay if sent to Arizona: Lot Smith.[5] Smith's wife Julia was the only member of the family to hear the announcement.[6]

Immediately, a letter was sent calling Smith on a mission to settle the Arizona Territory.[7] Smith was to be one of four captains to lead approximately two hundred Saints to settle on the Little Colorado River.[8] He was to be ready to leave within ten days. Smith began preparations, purchasing

1. Christian L. Christensen, Minutes of the Ward Teachers Meeting; Kate B. Carter, *Heart Throbs of the West*, 7:473.

2. Paul Bailey, *Jacob Hamblin: Buckskin Apostle*, 349; Alvin "Mike" Steed, interview by Omer J. Smith and Carmen R. Smith, May 14, 1976.

3. *Deseret News*, July 13, 1872; January 21, 1876.

4. Journal History of the Church, February 5, 1876 (hereafter cited as Journal History); Henry Ballard, Private Journal, January 15, 1876.

5. Paul Bailey, *Jacob Hamblin*, 349; Helen Camp, "Sketch of the Life of Lot Smith," 3.

6. Steed, interview.

7. Alice Ann Richards Smith, *The Living Words*, 23.

8. Journal History, February 5, 1876.

supplies and equipment for the use of the colony. Smith kept his homes in Farmington and Morgan for his family members who were not going to Arizona. He left the care of his farm to his two sons: twenty-one-year-old William Lot and nineteen-year-old Jedediah. Alice Ann and their three small children planned to accompany Lot to Arizona; he took her to Salt Lake City where her mother and aunts helped sew new clothes.[9]

President Young was also resolved to establish the Mormon communitarian system of the law of consecration and stewardship, also called the United Order.[10] He had tirelessly promoted the United Order after implementing it in St. George in 1874.[11] He organized the United Order the following spring in Farmington, and Smith had been chosen as one of six directors.[12] A year later, all the acting priesthood in Farmington were re-baptized into the United Order, Smith included. He was re-baptized July 18, 1875, by George Q. Cannon in the creek near the meeting place and re-confirmed by Abraham O. Woodruff.[13] Shortly after General Conference on the evening of October 9, 1875, Young began chartering several United Order settlements throughout Utah and Arizona. However, most of these Orders were short-lived.[14] Now Young specifically charged Smith to initiate and maintain the United Order in Arizona as well as promote friendly relations with the Indians. Young handed Smith his small silver compass and said, "Take them, Lot, and find them homes in Arizona."[15]

On Saturday, January 29, at noon, Smith joined a large gathering of 250 in Salt Lake City. The next day the non-Mormon *Salt Lake Daily Tribune* reported the meeting under the title "The Arizona Tramps."[16]

---

9. Alice Ann Richards Smith, *The Living Words*, 14.

10. See Leonard J. Arrington, Faramorz Y. Fox, and Dean L. May, *Building the City of God*.

11. Nels Anderson, *Desert Saints*, 300–301.

12. Christensen, Minutes, May 14, 1874.

13. Farmington Ward membership records; Robert T. Burton, diaries, July 18, 1875.

14. Arrington, Fox, and May, *Building the City of God,* 408–11.

15. Philip Smith, *Lot Smith*. The compass was apparently taken to Canada by Mary Garn Smith and later returned to Arizona by son Al. It was given to Dr. D. W. Melick of Kingman, Arizona, and Salt River Valley to be deposited in the archives of the University of Arizona, but it was not accepted. Dr. Melick showed it to Glade M. Smith, a great-grandson of Lot. Melick died of cancer, and according to a casual acquaintance, his son moved somewhere to the south.

16. *Salt Lake Daily Tribune*, January 30, 1876.

The news item stated that the group would be under the leadership of Lot Smith and continued: "We think Brigham made an excellent choice in selecting Brother Smith, for if any of the boys get unruly, he will be just the man to blacksnake them." The report said that James Brown (who had recently returned from Arizona) almost ruined the meeting when he told "what a sand bank the promised land is, [but then] John Taylor pulled his coat tail in time to save all." The *Tribune* advised "the whole Church of Jesus Christ to follow on the march. . . . [T]he more of them the Prophet can induce to go there, the better. Send them along, Brother Brigham[;] we'll stand by you in the good work."[17]

Each of the four captains—Lot Smith, George Lake, William C. Allen, and Jesse O. Ballinger—were assigned approximately fifty colonists from four geographical divisions. Lake's company included those from Cache County, Box Elder, and Weber. Allen had charge of missionaries called from the south half of Salt Lake County and the counties of Tooele and Utah. Ballinger had charge of those from Sanpete and Juab Counties. Smith's fifty came from the northern Utah counties and from the northern half of Salt Lake County.[18] Those in Farmington who answered the call included Smith's nephew Hubert Burk, Elijah Jones and wife Malinda, Moroni Hess (a cousin of Elijah's wife), and a young Farmington bachelor, Andrew Lo'ce "Locy" Rogers (son of Thomas and Aurelia Spencer Rogers). Missionaries from Bountiful in company with Smith included Israel Call and wife Medora, Wilford Barlow and wife Laura, Parley B. Wiley, the Keppler Sessions family, and Joseph H. and Joseph J. Holbrook. The Peter and George C. Wood families and Daniel Moss would follow a few days later.[19] Frihoff G. Nielson from Morgan County also started out with Smith. Young gave specific instructions that the call to the Arizona mission was made for life. All were expected to put everything they had into the Order and work together.[20] To assure the permanence of the Arizona colonization, Young instructed the colonists to "[s]ell all that you have that you can't take with you. . . . Leave nothing to come back to."[21]

The day of departure arrived: Thursday, February 3, 1876. At three o'clock that morning, Smith took Alice Ann and their children to the train

17. *Salt Lake Daily Tribune*, January 30, 1876.

18. Brigham Young, letter to George Q. Cannon, February 3, 1876.

19. Israel Call, *A Life Sketch of Israel Call by His Own Dictation*, 5; Smith, *Living Words*, 30.

20. *Journal of Frihoff Godfrey Nielson 1851-1893*, vol. 1, 55–56.

21. Osmer Dennis Flake, *William J. Flake, Pioneer – Colonizer*, 56.

Alice Ann Richards Smith with children Willard, George Albert, and Nannie in 1876 before the journey to Arizona. Omer James and Carmen R. Smith Photo Collection.

depot so she could visit a few days with her sister in Nephi.[22] She planned to join Smith on his way down. A loose line of thirty or so Arizona-bound wagons extended southward along State Road and awaited the signal to roll. Smith's mule team was hitched to a light wagon loaded with food supplies, cooking equipment, and bedding for his family. Rag carpeting

22. Smith, *Living Words*, 13–14.

braided by Alice Ann's aunt draped the bows under the wagon cover.[23] Also in line stood two yoke of Smith's oxen chained to his new Studebaker, a sturdy freight wagon driven by Locy Rogers and loaded with the heavy farming equipment needed for the new colonies.[24]

Smith was the only one of the four captains present to lead the first contingent of Arizona missionaries who pulled out at about noon and began the trek south. Alice Ann wrote of the sadness on that day of departure: "You can imagine Lot's feelings in leaving his wives and children from whom he had previously been separated a great deal in performing his duties and answering the call of Church and State. Now it was for an indefinite period, but when duty called Lot Smith never hesitated."[25] The early February departure required the travelers to brave the late winter's severe weather, but it allowed the wagons to ford the watercourses before melting snow made them impassable. Most importantly, the colonists would arrive in the new location in time to plant and harvest crops.

Each morning the wagon train often traveled for several hours before stopping for breakfast. They drove past Draper, American Fork, Lehi, Pleasant Grove, through Provo to Springville, and on to Santaquin. When possible, they camped in the tithing yards of the towns.[26] At York, Smith sent the wagon train on to Nephi's tithing yard while he sidetracked to Grover's farm to pick up Alice Ann and their children: Nannie, almost seven, Willard, three-and-a-half, and George Albert, seventeen months. These three, along with the infant child of Israel and Medora Call, were the only children in the first company.[27] In contrast to the frozen roads out of Salt Lake City, the roads farther south were soft and muddy, which required doubled teams to pull out the bogged wagons.[28] Smith and his family arrived early Saturday morning, February 12, in Richfield and were guests of blacksmith Hans Christensen, an old friend from Morgan County. After the group was organized into smaller groups, the missionary-colonists paused in their journey on Sunday, and Smith spoke in the local stake conference.[29]

---

23. Smith, *Living Words*, 14.

24. Andrew Locy Rogers, *Reminiscences*, 6.

25. Smith, *Living Words*, 23.

26. Nielson, *Journal*, 1:57–58. Tithing yards were places where incoming converts or emigrants could temporarily stay to be fed and sheltered.

27. Call, *Life Sketch*, 5.

28. Carter, *Heart Throbs of the West*, 12:219–23.

29. Nielson, *Journal*, 1:58–59.

On Monday, Smith's original group of fifteen wagons (including Brigham Stowell, Rogers, and Nielson) drove to the Sevier River and forded it again. Alice Ann wrote:

> It was considerably swollen, and I was very much frightened. The bridges were all washed away. I had had no experience with anything of that kind, and every time we would go in the river it looked like we would never come out. Brother Smith was always in the lead, working with the shovel, pick, or axe, the minute he stopped. Some of the men seemed to prefer waiting in their wagons, but they were all pretty good.[30]

At Circleville, the group left the slower ox teams to recuperate while Smith led the horse and mule teams onward to break trail over the divide.[31] As the wagon train advanced through the southern communities, other missionaries called to Arizona joined the company and sympathy for the travelers increased from the outlying communities.[32] Along the way, they had hot suppers of meat, beans, rice, and hot bread. Alice Ann said Smith was a good cook. The children gathered wood, and holes were cut in the ice on the river for water.[33] On February 20, the group reached Panguitch. Alice Ann and Smith were put up with Meltair Hatch and his wife Permelia. Wrote Alice: "They had a nice home, and we had a chance to clean up. We ate with them, but we always slept in the wagon for fear of taking cold if we changed. Lot attended Sunday meetings, and I bathed the children."[34] At Panguitch, the company of about fifty wagons formally organized with Smith in charge of them all.[35] At this point, the group had to decide whether to take a shortcut over the snow-covered mountain to the south. The snow lay three feet deep at the lower level, and the people from Panguitch predicted that the wagons could never make it over the six-foot drifts on the rough mountainside. Smith called the company together. "Boys," he said, "they say there is so much snow we can't possibly get over the mountain. What about it?" Twenty-four-year-old Spence Raymond, with red hair and a face as ruddy as Smith's, said, "Send some of us redheaded cusses on ahead and we'll thaw it out." Smith laughed and said, "We'll make it boys."[36]

---

30. Smith, *Living Words*, 15.
31. Rogers, *Reminiscences*, 6; Nielson, *Journal of Frihoff Godfrey Nielson*, 1:59.
32. Smith, *Living Words*, 24.
33. Smith, *Living Words*, 14.
34. Smith, *Living Words*, 15.
35. Sullivan C. Richardson, "Brigham Stowell," in *Early Settlers of Arizona*, 10.
36. Brigham Stowell, *An Account of My First Trip Into Arizona*, 3–4.

With assistance from the Asay men of Asay's Ranch, the travelers tackled the mountain. All the spare men wrapped their feet and legs in gunnysacks and went ahead to tromp a route for the saddle horses. Then the men and saddle horses came, the light wagons hitched to the stoutest of the teams. Then everyone followed in line according to their ability to make the pull.[37] As the snow deepened to about four feet, two or three teams were hitched to a wagon to haul it a day's distance, and then the teams returned to haul another wagon. Thus, two nights were passed at each campground. Many of the men were untrained in handling a team, which made extra work for the more experienced.[38]

After they attained the summit (elevation 7,513 ft.), the company expected an easier downhill course. Not so. Many fallen timbers lay undetected under the snow until butted up against by the teams. They had to be cut out before moving onward.[39] It took one week for the horse teams to travel from the summit to Orderville, where they arrived on February 25.[40] While some of the teams rested at Orderville, Smith went back up the mountain with a few men and teams to help the other oncoming wagons.[41] The company left Orderville on March 3. After four days, the wagon train arrived in Kanab, situated midway on the trip.

The journey continued. Near the foot of the Buckskin Mountains, the wagons plunged for five days through deep snowdrifts before they reached the summit.[42] Alice Ann wrote: "We camped on the mountain in about a foot and one half of snow, and made huge camp fires. Many of the company were good singers. They sang Mormon hymns that were appropriate for the journey, 'Old Black Joe,' and the popular songs of that time."[43] On the downside of the mountains, the company endured a two-day storm of rain, hail, and sleet. Here and there, a spot in the downgrade route would be frozen hard, and then a few feet away so thawed that the wheels sank to the axle. The teams balked and had to be helped by men who held strong cross sticks tied in long ropes attached to the wagon tongue.[44]

---

37. Carter, *Heart Throbs of the West*, 12:219–23.

38. Richardson, "Brigham Stowell," in *Early Settlers*, 11.

39. Richardson, "Brigham Stowell," in *Early Settlers*, 11.

40. Carter, *Heart Throbs of the West*, 12:219–23; Stowell, *Trip Into Arizona*, 3–4; Richardson, "Brigham Stowell," in *Early Settlers*, 11.

41. Daniel Wood, Record Books, F 498.

42. Early Arizona settlers referred to the Kaibab Plateau as the Buckskin Mountain.

43. Smith, *Living Words*, 24.

44. Price W. Nelson, *Autobiography*, 24.

Next, they entered House Rock Valley, where heavy red sand so clogged the wagon wheels that ropes had to be used as much as ever. After leaving House Rock Springs, they traveled eastward along the foot of the Vermillion Cliffs through another long expanse of pink-red sand that continued to challenge the teams.[45] The trail continued past Jacob's Pools, Soap Creek, Badger Creek, and on to Lee's Ferry. Thirty outfits gathered with Captain Smith in early March at the ferry. The crossing of the Colorado River provided an enduring memory of the journey to Arizona. The wind, which was channeled through the narrow valley on the south by Echo Cliffs and on the north by the Vermillion Cliffs, sometimes had enough force to blow the loaded flatboat ferry upstream. [46]

Once across the river, teams were doubled to pull the wagons up the steep solid stone roadbed called Lee's Backbone that wound around the edge of the cliffs. At one place, perhaps where the roadway skirts the mountain a scant foot from the edge of a drop-off, Israel Call looked at the thread of river far below and concluded: "[I]f our wagons had turned over, they would have gone a thousand feet straight down and rolled another thousand feet into the river."[47] It took one day's travel from the ferry over Lee's Backbone and down the steep and narrow ridge to Navajo Springs. The journey then turned southward and paralleled the long range of Echo Cliffs on the east.

The trail continued to the scanty water at Willow Springs. On March 13 Smith and company reached Moen Ave eight miles past Willow Springs.[48] As they progressed five miles down Moen Ave Wash to Moenkopi Wash, the landscape became even more dusty and desolate. No more water would be available until they reached the Little Colorado River, so every barrel was filled to last the fourteen miles to the river. On March 14, Smith's missionaries pulled up at the muddy Little Colorado after dark, exhausted and famished.[49] The water was so thick with silt that the thirsty horses refused to drink, so the men dug holes on the sandy bank to let cleaner water seep in.[50] The people shut their eyes to allow

---

45. Sullivan C. Richardson, *Early Settlers*, 11.
46. Daniel Handley McAllister, *Reminiscences & Journal*, March 9, 1876.
47. Call, *Life Sketch*, 6.
48. McAllister, *Reminiscences*, March 14, 1876; Journal History, March 13, 1876.
49. Smith, *Living Words*, 25.
50. Nelson, *Autobiography*, 24; Kate B. Carter, *Heart Throbs of the West*, 12:219–23.

the muddy water to run down their throats.[51] Some of the river water was left to settle overnight in a seven gallon kettle, and in the morning there was only one inch of clear water on the top.[52] The route crossed the Little Colorado repeatedly. Ten miles upriver past Black Falls, they came to Grand Falls—a sight to behold. At Butterfield Road the pioneers were introduced to another Arizona problem: quicksand. They had to pull out their mired stock.[53]

On March 23, 1876, one month and twenty days after leaving Salt Lake City, the first thirty wagons under Smith's leadership reached Sunset Crossing on the Little Colorado, the place Young had specified the group to settle. The pioneers found the river very high and a challenge to cross.[54] Almost swimming across, "everybody got a soaking," according to one account.[55] Daniel McAllister looked over the gray, cheerless Little Colorado landscape and pronounced it a "hard looking country."[56] Some of the missionaries expressed resentment at being sent to such a forbidding place.[57] During their entire sojourn at this place, the colonists contended against constantly blowing wind and sand across the flats. Sand permeated their food and clothing and affected every aspect of their existence on the Little Colorado. Nevertheless, the Saints enjoyed a large pow-wow and stag dance that night around the campfire accompanied by the flute and violin, played by the Wood brothers. About sixty men danced in the dust—the first celebration of these pioneers on the Little Colorado.[58]

After the festivity, the entire company continued upriver about twenty-five miles, where they met the Latter-day Saint Indian missionaries James S. Brown, John Thompson, and Ira Hatch.[59] Although Brown had chosen town sites and farmlands for the newly arrived company, he had no authority over the new missionaries.[60] Captain Smith was committed to followingYoung's explicit instructions to settle at Sunset Crossing, stating, "If the servant of the Lord calls us to go and settle on a barren rock[,]

---

51. Sullivan C. Richardson, "Sketch by Joseph Richards," *Early Settlers*, 23.
52. McAllister, *Reminiscences*, March 17, 1876.
53. McAllister, *Reminiscences*, March 25–26, 1876.
54. *Arizona Republic*, June 26, 1976.
55. Nelson, *Autobiography*, 25.
56. McAllister, *Reminiscences*, April 1, 1876.
57. Sullivan C. Richardson, *Early Settlers*, 15.
58. Nelson, *Autobiography*, 25.
59. John Bushman, *The Life and Labors of John Bushman*, 32–33.
60. Brigham Young Jr., diaries, June 11, 1876.

it is our duty to go."[61] Smith went back downriver to Sunset Crossing and established a camp on the east side of the Little Colorado three miles below Sunset Crossing.[62] They were followed by Ballinger's group, who made a camp on the opposite side of the river from Smith. Both Allen and Lake established camps in areas Brown had indicated.[63]

The missionary-colonists created living quarters by lifting their wagon boxes off the running gears and settling them under the tall cottonwoods along the river. Scarcely two weeks later, the colonists of Smith's camp had erected a brush bowery for group dining and general gatherings, dug a well, cleared land of brush and planted a garden, and sown thirty-five acres with wheat to experiment with dryland farming. Captain Smith also explored the surroundings.[64] On April 28, Smith wrote a description of the Little Colorado country to the *Deseret News* in Salt Lake City. He described the country as dry and the Little Colorado River as high with snow melt, then quite small until the rains started in the summer, which made the river "a might rushing torrent" that looked twenty-five miles wide.[65] They had built a dam over two hundred yards long. He wrote, "The Indians tell us that if we intend to live where we are camped, we had better fix some scaffolding in the trees, for the river gets very mad sometimes." He described their relationship with the Navajos and Hopis as friendly. The country was suited to grazing, and in the mountains forty-five to fifty miles distant there appeared to be plenty of wild game. He added, "Now I hope all the old turkey hunters will not come at one time, unless they are prepared to stay and relieve some of those who are already homesick, for there are some in that fix. . . . All the brethren, as far as I am acquainted, who came to do their duty, are satisfied. Those impelled by other motives perhaps do not feel quite so much so."[66]

61. Rogers, *Reminiscences*, 3b.

62. Nielson, *Journal*, 1:182. This location is about one mile northwest of where the Sunset cemetery still remains.

63. Bushman, *Life and Labors*, 33–35. Jesse O. Ballinger arrived at the Little Colorado about April 17, 1876.

64. Lot Smith, letter to gentleman in Davis County, April 9, 1876, in Journal History, April 9, 1876, 3.

65. *Deseret News*, 25:324, in Journal History.

66. *Deseret News*, 25:324, in Journal History.

Young had instructed Captain Smith to cultivate friendship with the "Lamanites" and to proselytize to them.[67] Young wrote: "[O]ne of the great objects of planting the new settlements in Arizona is to incourage the Spirit of friendliness in the hearts of the Lamenites by our exampel."[68] Immediately after his arrival, Smith began to befriend the Navajos and Hopis or Oraibis (sometimes called Moquis). While building the dam and planting crops, Smith used every opportunity to establish amicable relations with the tribes. Smith's Hopi name was Pa-láh Sa-weéch-a-mee, which meant "Red Beard," as did his Navajo name, Da-gha-hi Chi.[69] J. C. Wood wrote a letter to Farmington on April 30 which told how the Moquis visited and asked to learn to work. He said, "It was better than a theator" to see them all sing and dance in perfect rhythm.[70]

President Wells, Brigham Young Jr. (the newest apostle), and Apostle Erastus Snow pulled into Smith's wagon camp on June 2, 1876.[71] They parked under the tall cottonwood trees and inspected the two-month-old camp. In front of the long, shed-type bowery with its canvas back, a neat line of settled wagon box living quarters faced east—their backs to the constant, sand-laden west wind.[72] The dam diverted water that flowed sluggishly to planted corn fields and watermelon vines. Most of the missionary-settlers in Smith's camp (forty-five men, fifteen women, and eighteen children) gathered the following Sunday on benches around the tables under the bowery, where the camp all ate together. President Wells remarked: "[A]ll he was afraid of was the country was to good and we would not be able to keep it from our enemies, that we should be united."[73] In fact, the Latter-day Saints had arrived on the Little Colorado in time to preempt a company from Boston who had planned to settle at Sunset Crossing. When the Bostonians arrived later in August, they reported that the country had been misrepresented to them. They noted

---

67. Early Mormons often referred to American Indians as Lamanites, based on teachings in the *Book of Mormon*. From the Church's organization, missionary work among American Indians was a primary focus. See Ronald W. Walker, "Seeking the 'Remnant': The Native American during the Joseph Smith Period."

68. Brigham Young, letter to Elder George Lake, July 13, 1877.

69. Smith's Navajo name is pronounced Da-ghá-hǐ [Beard] Chee [Red].

70. J. C. Wood, letter to Heber Wood, April 30, 1876.

71. Nielson, *Journal of Frihoff Godfrey Nielson*, 1:73.

72. Brigham Young Jr., diaries, June 2, 1876.

73. Nielson, *Journal*, 1:74.

the lack of water and timber and had no wish to settle on the spot.[74] The next day, the Church authorities left the Sunset camp and traveled upriver to Allen's camp and to Taylor farther up. Apostle Snow apparently did not favor the communal dining at Sunset, and while at Allen's camp he "said it was no more necessary for the saints to all eat together than it was for them all to sleep together."[75] At Taylor, he reiterated his dislike, declaring that "the Lord cared no more about the way we ate our food than He did how the squirrels ate their acorns."[76]

The colonists had come to Arizona Territory expecting to labor in the United Order.[77] An evening meeting was held in Sunset after the officials left, and the motion to establish the United Order passed by a large majority. However, "[s]ome ill feeling was manifested and some said they were not ready for the order."[78] At the next evening's meeting, they elected four directors: John Strock, Edward Jones, Nathan Cheney, and James T. Woods. Soon after, a proposed constitution and by-laws were read, and the directors approved the submission of a paper to be signed by the members.[79] The United Order was to be set up as a near total democracy. As a basis to make their own rules, Smith and the members used Young's Articles of Agreement:

> **Rule 1.** We will not take the name of Deity in vain nor speak lightly of His character or of sacred things.
>
> **Rule 2.** We will pray with our families morning and evening, and also attend to secret prayer.
>
> **Rule 3.** We will observe and keep the Word of Wisdom according to the Spirit and meaning thereof.
>
> **Rule 4.** We will treat our families with due kindness and affection, and set before them an example worthy of imitation; in our families and intercourse with all persons, we will refrain from being contentious or quarrelsome, and we will cease to speak evil of each other and will cultivate a spirit of charity towards all. We will consider it our duty to keep from acting selfishly or from covetous motives and will seek the interests of each other and the salvation of all mankind.

---

74. Nielson, *Journal*, 1:71.

75. John A. Blythe, diary, 11.

76. Kate B. Carter, *Our Pioneer History,* 6:349.

77. Rogers, *Reminiscences*, 4b; Levi Mathers Savage, *Family History Journal 1876–1935*, 22.

78. Nielson, *Journal*, 1:74–75.

79. Nielson, *Journal*, 1:75.

Rule 5. We will observe personal cleanliness, and preserve ourselves in all chastity, by refraining from adultery, whoredom and lust. We will also dis-countenance and refrain from all vulgar and obscene language or conduct.

Rule 6. We will observe the Sabbath day to keep it holy in accordance with the revelations.

Rule 7. That which is not committed to our care we will not appropriate to our own use.

Rule 8. That which we borrow, we will return according to promise, and that which we find we will not appropriate to our own use, but seek to return it to its proper owner.

Rule 9. We will, as soon as possible, cancel all individual indebtedness con-tracted prior to our uniting with the Order, and when once fully identified with said Order, will contract no debts contrary to the wishes of the board of directors.

Rule 10. We will patronize our brethren who are in the Order.

Rule 11. In our apparel and deportment, we will not pattern after nor en-courage foolish and extravagant fashions; and cease to import or buy from abroad any article which can be reasonably dispensed with or which can be produced by combination of home labor. We will foster and encourage the producing and manufacturing of all articles needed for our consumption as fast as our circumstances will permit.

Rule 12. We will be simple in our dress and manner of living, using proper economy and prudence in the management of all entrusted to our care.

Rule 13. We will combine our labor for mutual benefit; sustain, with our faith, prayers and works, those whom we have elected to take the manage-ment of the different departments of the Order, and be subject to them in their official capacity, refraining from a spirit of fault finding.

Rule 14. We will honestly and diligently labor, and devote ourselves and all we have, to the Order and the building up of the Kingdom of God.[80]

In a series of after-supper meetings, the missionaries began to organize the United Order. The proposed submission to community rules was still met with reluctance from some of the settlers. However, throughout the years of its existence, the Sunset United Order developed a remarkable democracy and was governed almost entirely by its Articles of Agreement. Through the years, the rules were amended at will after a discussion in a business meeting and voting by the membership. For any proposed proj-ect, complaints, or someone's desire to withdraw from the order, a com-mittee was appointed to resolve the matter.

---

80. Savage, *Family History Journal*, 17, rules copied in Coalville, Utah; also Kate B. Carter, *Heart Throbs of the West*, 1:70 (with slight variations).

The National Centennial on July 4, 1876, drew near and a committee of three—Dan Davis, William Hayes, and Henry Hobbs—planned and organized the celebration. The small group of Latter-day Saint colonists on the Little Colorado, who still lived in wagon boxes, commemorated the event. A salute fired at sunrise on the Fourth opened the celebration. A morning meeting featured music, an oration by Smith, an address by Hobbs, a historical address by J. T. Wood, recitations, and songs. They ate at noon and then danced in the evening.[81]

A devout spirit distinguished Smith's Sunset United Order. One of the Little Colorado residents, Henry F. Knowles, wrote: "Of the two camps [Ballinger's and Smith's], the Sunset Camp was by far the most religious. On the trip down [from Utah, Smith's camp] had prayers twice a day, while in [Ballinger's] camp there wasn't a public prayer offered on the entire journey."[82] On arrival at the river, Captain Smith had immediately held Church meetings. Although his group contained an average of only twenty-one to twenty-five families and a membership of 113 to 150, Smith organized the Church programs completely: Council Meeting, Sacrament Meeting, Sunday School, Mutual Improvement Association (MIA) for the young people, Elders Quorum for the men, and the Relief Society for the women.[83] The members fasted on Thursdays and held a testimony meeting in the evening.

Smith and his missionary colonists had begun to establish a tenuous toehold in the untamed territory of Arizona. Trials would come as they struggled with the flooding Little Colorado which devastated their crops. Relations with the Navajos and Hopis had to be stabilized before a fort could be built for protection. Yet amidst all the difficulties, the first stake in Arizona would be organized with Smith as its leader.

81. Nielson, *Journal*, 1:76–77.
82. Henry F. Knowles, *My Story*, 1.
83. Nielson, *Journal*, 1:226, 238.

CHAPTER 10

Arizona Stake President

A potentially serious dispute with Navajo Chief Comayazzie's tribe occurred shortly after the camp's decision to build a dam first rather than a fort for protection. In the summer of 1876, a Navajo chief and a warrior rode up to Smith's Sunset camp with a disturbing letter written by the Indian missionary of Moenkopi, James S. Brown, that accused the Mormons of stealing three head of their stock.[1] Chief Comayazzie and fifteen war-painted Navajos had ridden into the Moenkopi camp. In a talk with the missionaries, Comayazzie had demanded that the Mormons kill his two sons because these Navajo boys had killed Mormon cattle. Brown explained that he didn't want to kill the boys. Throughout the afternoon, Comayazzie became more frenzied as he repeated his demand, yet the missionaries remained firm. Near sundown, after a whole afternoon of agitated talk, the chief finally confessed that it was Mormon boys who had killed Navajo cattle and that the Navajos wanted to kill the Mormon boys. It was then apparent that Comayazzie had offered his sons as a ruse to provoke a judgment that could be served on the Mormons. The Navajo Chief was finally pacified when Brown promised to write Smith on the Little Colorado. Comayazzie then blew something like a conch shell, and a large band of war-painted Navajos came up from the wash where they had waited ready for warfare. Comayazzie made peace with the smoking of a pipe passed from hand to hand.[2] Bloodshed had been avoided.

Brown's letter caused a flurry in Smith's undefended site. Israel Call recalled, "Some of the boys wanted to pay for [the missing cattle] but Smith said, 'No we did not take them, and we will not pay for them.'"[3] Instead, he offered the Navajos dinner. After dinner, the two Navajos were furnished with fresh mounts from Smith's camp, and a few Mormon boys anxiously accompanied them to search for the cattle in the mile-wide dense cottonwood forest on the river.[4] The three head of cattle were found

---

1. Sullivan C. Richardson, *Early Settlers of Arizona*, 30.
2. Richardson, 31–32.
3. Richardson, 30.
4. Richardson, 30.

quickly and easily, winning the Navajos' confidence.[5] Nielson reported on November 7, 1876, "The Navajoes visited our camp this morning. They are very friendly."[6] Smith was concerned with treating the Navajos fairly and did not tolerate robbing the tribe. He later ordered a man to leave Sunset after he was accused of stealing from the Navajos.[7]

As the new colony struggled to establish itself in the harsh country, many who contemplated the unlikely prospect of raising enough crops for survival departed. By July 10, 1876, the board of directors of Smith's camp became alarmed by the drain of manpower.[8] The settlers also learned the volatile nature of the Little Colorado River. After it flowed serenely for three months from spring runoff, the river manifested its summer temperament. On July 17, a raging flood washed out a channel two rods wide above the dam.[9] The colonists decided the natives might have been right when they advised building scaffolding in the trees because "the river gets very mad."[10] For some settlers, the flood swept away any thought of a successful colonizing mission. The morning after the flood, twenty members of Smith's camp left to return to Utah.[11] Four days later, the river washed away three more rods of the dam.[12] No dam meant no food. More decided to return to Utah.[13] Only the strong devotion and stubborn determination of the stalwarts kept the mission alive. Those who remained had no option but to rebuild the dam as quickly as possible. At this critical point, an encouraging letter arrived from Brigham Young that gave support and expressed his wish for their success. He also remarked on those "whose mouths are full of murmuring and whose hearts incline to apostasy. We want none such to remain with you lest they poison the camp with the leaven of their ill-feeling."[14]

5. Sullivan C. Richardson, *Compilation Part 2*, 24.
6. Frihoff Godfrey Nielson, *Journal of Frihoff Godfrey Nielson 1851–1893*, 1:89.
7. Nielson, 1:139.
8. Nielson, 1:139.
9. Nielson, 1:78.
10. Lot Smith, letter to *Deseret News* editor, April 28, 1876, *Deseret News*, 25:324, in Journal History.
11. Nielson, *Journal*, 1:78.
12. Nielson, *Journal*, 1:78.
13. Nielson, *Journal*, 1:79.
14. Brigham Young, letter to Elders Smith, Lake, Ballinger, Allen and the Brethren encamped on the Little Colorado, July 15, 1876.

Food was never taken for granted by the Arizona settlers. In one afternoon meeting, Brother J. T. Wood arose to state he had heard "the women were all down on him for having said they had lunches when the men was away &c. and that they were going to have him hung and ducked for it."[15] Evidently, the women had been gathering for a midafternoon snack and perhaps some of the bachelors begrudged them. After discussion, the unanimous decision ruled that all eating thereafter would be at the Big Table, and "Pres Smith gave some counsel in relation to such things to not permit the devil to break up the camp."[16] Not long afterwards, Joanna Westover of Allen's camp came with her baby girl to visit Sunset and was invited to eat at the Big Table. As the meal finished, Sister Westover put a slice of bread in her satchel. The members of the Sunset United Order watched to see whether Smith would or would not abide by their unanimous decision. Smith toed the line. "Sister Westover," he said. "We eat our meals at the table." Rumors quickly spread in Allen's camp that Smith had denied her a crust of bread for her baby.[17]

By August 8, three-fourths of the men had left each company on the Little Colorado. Though some said that they were leaving only to retrieve their families and that they would return, few ever came back.[18] One later account stated that, out of the two hundred that formed the original companies, "not more than one out of ten remained."[19] At this point of discouragement, Smith made a remark that became legendary: "You may all go if you want and I will stay and keep tavern."[20] The statement had its effect—some stayed. Smith said about those who remained, "There is something in them besides the grit that is in the graham."[21] Floods on the Little Colorado became an oft-repeated occurrence. The small number of men likely did not completely repair the dam before another flood on August 26 ravaged it again. The work stopped. Smith called a meeting the following day at which the men decided to begin building a stockade instead.[22] Captain Smith wrote to President Young from Sunset

15. Nielson, *Journal*, 1:79.

16. Nielson, *Journal*, 1:79.

17. James M. Smith to J. Morris Richards, interview by Omer J. and Carmen R. Smith, March 27, 1976.

18. Richardson, *Early Settlers*, 24.

19. Andrew Locy Rogers, *Reminiscences*.

20. Rogers, *Reminiscences*, 4b.

21. Sullivan C. Richardson, Collections of Annie Burk.

22. Nielson, *Journal*, 1:82.

Crossing the following day. He reported that since the dam washed out, the group had decided to concentrate on building a stockade with housing and digging wells. He wrote that twenty-two men, fifteen women, and twenty children remained in the camp. Although Major Oglesby had been sent from Camp Apache to determine if the colonists could defend themselves against an attack from the native tribes, Smith reported that he had assured Oglesby that they were "on the most friendly terms with the Indians" and continued to Young, "We have no fears whatever that the Indians will trouble us, believing the Lord will preserve us."[23]

The men of Ballinger's camp located a better site for the dam: a rare strip of rock bottom in the river about two miles below the ruined dam. Without this discovery, Smith's camp and perhaps the entire Arizona mission might have failed. Smith's camp decided to build their stockade near the better dam location. A committee of twelve went to choose the new campsite.[24] The camps of both Ballinger and Smith had been existing on inadequate food—only bread and dried apples.[25] When the supply of apples gave out, Smith assessed the prospects and asked the members to "do with as little bread as possible."[26] He did not ration the food. Despite the troubles, Smith still felt optimistic about the mission. From an interview in the fall of 1876, a *San Bernardino* correspondent reported that the four settlements under the general direction of Smith expected their numbers to increase to two thousand within a couple of years.[27] The dam was eventually finished. It was 125 feet long, 18 feet wide, and 10 feet high with a middle section that could be opened in high water to allow driftwood to pass.[28]

Smith's camp harvested the wheat from their first location. Then, on September 17, another flood hit.[29] About mid-November, Smith's camp began to move downriver in hopes that the new location by the dam would be less vulnerable to flooding and to await completion of the fort.[30]

---

23. *Deseret News*, 25:528, in Journal History, August 28, 1876.

24. Nielson, *Journal*, 1:82.

25. Rogers, *Reminiscences*, 4b.

26. Rogers, *Reminiscences*, 4b.

27. "Sunset Crossing Yavapai County, November 5, 1876," *Latter-Day Saints' Millennial Star*, 12–13.

28. L. John Nuttall, letter, September 24, 1878, Journal History; Kate B. Carter, *Our Pioneer History*, 14.

29. Nielson, *Journal*, 1:84.

30. Nielson, *Journal*, 1:90.

The men laid out fields below the new campsite and began construction on the fort located about a mile and a half from the river on the flats east of the Little Colorado.[31] The abundant driftwood along the river was used to build the fort.[32] Ten-foot-long cottonwood logs were split and planted upright into the ground, pinned together, and then chinked with mud to form a stockade fourteen rods square. The colonists first built a dining room within the stockade. After the kitchen and commissary were ready for use, each family looked forward to moving from its wagon box dwelling into one of the 14 ft. x 16 ft. rooms that lined the inner sides of the fort square. The steam sawmill Young had promised was brought from Mount Trumbull and set up forty miles west of Smith's camp in the Mogollon Mountains to begin production.[33] It produced lumber for roofs and window frames in the fort. Even with boarded roofs, sand blown by the winds sifted down inside.[34]

The settlers continually worked on the fort. As each room was finished, families moved in. A fireplace in the inside masonry wall of each room provided warmth, a bit of light, and a place to cook. Until doors were available, some of the women hung Navajo blankets in the doorway and at the single inside window of each room.[35] On Christmas Eve, 1876, Smith's wife Alice Ann moved from her wagon box into one of the rooms in the new fort. On Christmas Day, her sister wife Alice Mary arrived from Utah to share the living space until her room next door was finished. The faithful little English wife had gathered her belongings, packed them into a wagon, and traveled the eight hundred miles from Farmington to the Sunset camp with Jane's nineteen-year-old son, Jedediah, as teamster as arranged by Smith. At Kanab she had been delayed a week by the illness and death from diphtheria of her first child, three-year-old Elizabeth Jane.[36] By mid-January 1877, all the camp members were housed in the fort.

Smith sought every opportunity to strengthen the self-sufficiency of the camps. He obtained an unused horse-powered gristmill from Kanab.[37]

31. Nielson, *Journal*, 1:82; Andrew Jenson, *Encyclopedic History*. The location is about four miles northeast of present-day Winslow.

32. Daniel Handley McAllister, *Reminiscences & Journal*, March 27, 1876.

33. Brigham Young, letter to Elder Lot Smith, July 29, 1876; Nielson, *Journal*, 1:86, 89.

34. Alice Baugh Smith, "Pioneer Personal History," 10.

35. Alice Ann Richards Smith, *The Living Words of Alice Ann Richards Smith*, 27.

36. Smith, "Pioneer Personal History," 3.

37. Lot Smith, letter to Brigham Young, November 6, 1876.

The settlers had been grinding wheat by hand in little coffee mills and making graham bread.[38] Next he acquired a sheep herd that numbered 2,025 for wool and soon obtained a carding machine to comb and clean the wool to spin and weave into fabric for clothing.[39] Smith also arranged to purchase a used thresher in Payson. Throughout the years, the Order provided education for the children with schoolteachers including Clara Rogers, Nielson, J. K. P. Pipkin, Levi M. Savage, and Smith's later wife Mary. Brother Brady taught singing lessons intermittently, and August Wilcken taught Spanish lessons. Smith's Yankee thrift was well-known. Recalled one account: "Lot would pick up a kernel of corn and give it to one of the animals, so that the kernel of corn would not be lost."[40]As leader, Smith made the work assignments at Sunset. The men worked the land—clearing, plowing, planting, irrigating, and harvesting. As wife of the Order president, Alice Ann made out the schedules for the women to work in the kitchen. Women took care of the wool without being assigned: washing, carding, spinning, and weaving. Seven women spun and one woman wove.

Smith expected all in the Sunset United Order—including himself— to be righteous and perform their duties. C. L. Christensen said of Smith that despite his kindness, his quick temper brought sharp rebukes which "were generally kindly received as all knew they were intended to elevate and better mankind."[41]

President Young scheduled the April 1877 General Conference of the Church in St. George. In conjunction with conference, the St. George Temple would be dedicated. Smith had never missed a general conference since he had come to Utah from California until he moved to Arizona. Smith and Ballinger attended the conference. Smith called on President Young, who was suffering from rheumatism in his legs and feet, and gave him a progress report of the Little Colorado camps.[42] When Smith related the Arizona colonists' mass desertion of the mission and return to Utah, "Young raised up and shook himself like a lion and said, 'When will the elders of Israel have any backbone in them[?]'"[43]

---

38. Richardson, *Early Settlers*, 15.

39. Nielson, *Journal*, 1:140; Levi Mathers Savage, *Family History Journal, 1876–1935*, 28–29.

40. Claridell DeWitt, interview by Carmen R. Smith, July 4, 1977.

41. C. L. Christensen, "Lot Smith in Life and Death," 230.

42. Brigham Young Jr., diaries, December 13 and 20, 1876; Nielson, *Journal*, 1:94.

43. Christian L. Christensen, Minutes of the Little Colorado Stake, August 29, 1880.

On April 6, Smith attended the dedication of the St. George Temple, where two thousand people were present.[44] Aside from the dedication, the conference focused on Young's effort to establish the United Order. In the afternoon conference session of the second day, Smith and Ballinger were the first speakers. Young followed and again urged Church-wide acceptance of the United Order.[45] This was the last time Smith saw the leader for whom he felt such loyalty. Brigham Young passed away five months later in August 1877.

From the beginning in Arizona, Smith had routinely convened all the Little Colorado colonists in quarterly conference meetings in the mission. Total membership was always less than six hundred. The conferences were held in various localities and were conducted as in larger congregations of the Church. More distant settlements that attended the conferences included Moenkopi, Mogollon Mills/Millville, Tonto Basin, and Tuba City. In December 1877, John Taylor wrote to Smith:

> The Council of the Apostles have had under consideration the question of the advisability of forming the settlements south of the Utah line into a Stake of Zion. . . . [I]f it is felt that the numbers of Saints are at present too small to warrant a full organization as a Stake of Zion, the brethren will probably grant you a partial organization.[46]

In late January, 1878, Smith welcomed Brigham Young's son Apostle John W. Young with his large party to Sunset Fort and fed them all at the Big Table. Two days later at a 10:00 a.m. meeting on Sunday, January 27, held at Sunset, Apostle Young wanted to know if the people wished to be organized as a Stake of Zion. The leaders Lot Smith, J. O. Ballinger, George Lake, and John Bushman, along with several other men, felt it would be an advantage to be organized. The Saints moved, seconded, and voted unanimously to be organized as a stake.[47]

The meeting was adjourned and the Saints reconvened later in the afternoon to organize Arizona's first stake and the Church's twenty-first stake. The membership sustained Lot Smith as stake president with Jacob Hamblin as first counselor and Lorenzo H. Hatch as second counselor. The stake high councils, priesthood quorums, and bishoprics of Sunset, Brigham City, Taylor, and Saint Joseph were also organized. After remarks

---

44. Brigham Young Jr., diaries, April 6, 1877.

45. Brigham Young Jr., diaries, April 7 and 8, 1877.

46. John Taylor, letter to Elder Lot Smith and the Elders and Saints in Arizona and New Mexico, December 13, 1877.

47. Arizona Stake Minutes, January 27, 1878.

from John W. Young, the Saints joined in singing "We Thank Thee O God for a Prophet" and dismissed after prayer. During a meeting the next day, the camps were officially renamed. Smith's camp continued as Sunset, Ballinger's camp as Brigham City, Allen's camp as Joseph City, and the place where William J. Flake resided as Taylor.[48] Apparently, Smith's second counselor Hatch had been unable to attend the conference. A week later on February 3, Apostle Young met Hatch "two miles below San Francisco wash on the Little Colorado River" and ordained him "as a second counselor to president Lot Smith of the Arizona Stake of Zion."[49]

At first, the Arizona Stake held quarterly conferences for three days on Fridays, Saturdays, and Sundays, with a morning and afternoon meeting each day. Bishops and Saints from Sunset, Brigham City, St. Joseph, Taylor, Woodruff, and Moenkopi attended the first stake conference presided over by Smith in May 1878, which convened at Brigham City. A report was given from each ward and settlement of the stake on Friday and Saturday. Sunday was reserved for sermons by the leaders. Smith had recently visited the Navajo and Hopi villages, and the minutes of the meeting recorded that Smith spoke his gratitude that the Saints had good feelings towards the Lamanites.[50] He pointed out that although the colonists had many wants, their true wants were but few. Recorded in the meeting minutes: "[Smith] felt anxious to straighten up everything as he went along, and not have any of his weaknesses follow after."[51] He explained that because of weaknesses, people oftentimes fail to fulfill the requirements of the Lord. However, if the requirements were understood and then not followed, "we would be beaten with many stripes."[52]

Soon after Smith's camp had set up on the river, Pleasant Valley (later known as Mormon Lake) began to be the economic focus of Smith's Arizona mission.[53] Only forty miles from Sunset, the marshy meadow with excellent springs was in a five-by-six-mile-wide depression set in the midst of a thick growth of oak and tall pine. Shortly after the organiza-

---

48. Arizona Stake Minutes, January 27–28, 1878.

49. Arizona Stake Minutes, February 3, 1878. This is the only reference in the stake minutes to the actual name of the new stake.

50. Nielson, *Journal,* 1:125–26.

51. Arizona Stake Minutes, May 26, 1878.

52. Arizona Stake Minutes, May 26, 1878.

53. This Pleasant Valley is not to be confused with another Pleasant Valley in Arizona in the Tonto Basin below the Mogollon Rim which later figured in the notorious Pleasant Valley War.

tion of the Arizona Stake, Sunset's council discussed the idea of a dairy at Pleasant Valley.[54] The Saints of Sunset and Brigham City built an access road west from Sunset to the spring they named Dairy Spring. The colonists built the dairy's main building near the spring—a double log cabin above a basement. Three log cabins to house five dairy families were built at the edge of the lake bed nearby. An early report numbered the dairy herd at 115 cows with 75 being milked.[55] The dairy produced cheese and butter in abundance. Some of the big horns of cheese weighed as much as a hundred pounds. The three Latter-day Saint colonies—Sunset, Brigham City, and Joseph City—received a percentage of butter and cheese according to the manpower they furnished. Sunset's share of the 1879 summer produce was 4,500 pounds of cheese and about 700 pounds of butter.[56]

Everyone, including Smith and his family, enjoyed the summer climate at Mormon Lake. Smith constructed a double log cabin a little over a mile south of Dairy Spring.[57] The 40 ft. x 20 ft. cabin stood in a thinning forest on the west side of the lake about eighty steps above Smith Spring (so named on present-day maps). Farther downslope at the edge of the lake, Smith placed an extra-long hollowed-out log. This log was filled from the spring to water the cattle.[58] Near his cabin Smith built a smaller log structure to store hay, grain, and tools. A short distance to the south, a corral in a thick stand of pine sheltered his horses. During the cold months, the dairy herd wintered on the river along with the majority of the workers. Personnel at the dairy varied, and the numbers fluctuated. The June 1880 census of the dairy district counted twenty-nine people living in seven cabins.[59] Each "milker" milked twenty-five cows both night

---

54. Nielson, *Journal,* 1:124.

55. L. John Nuttall, letter to John Taylor, November 4, 1878; Journal History.

56. Levi Mathers Savage, *Family History Journal,* 30.

57. Bob Lockett, interview by Omer J. and Carmen R. Smith, October 1978. Lockett, who was a later cattle rancher in Mormon Lake area, said that Earl Spearman later paneled the inside of the cabin and operated a store from 1926 to 1940. There were two rooms in the "living end" and a larger room for the "store end." The only door was in the "store end." Coordinates for Smith's cabin site: N 34° 56'212", and W 111° 29'151"; for the spring N 34° 56'206", and W 111° 29'178".

58. Karl Smith, interview by Omer J. and Carmen R. Smith, June 22, 1974, Rock Springs, WY.

59. Arizona Supreme Court, District 28 Census, June 19, 1880. Henry Rogers, stage driving; Andrew Locy Rogers, herding sheep; Hiram Judd (56) with Mary (18), Daniel (14), and Lyman P. (11); James McNeil, farming, wife Phoebe and

Long log trough below (east) of Lot Smith's cabin at Mormon Lake in 1880s. Courtesy Bob Carlock.

and morning.[60] The workers also tended garden plots and raised an abundance of potatoes and grain.

Smith made acquaintance with his nearest non-Mormon neighbor, William "Bill" H. Ashurst, a sheepman with whom he enjoyed a long-lasting friendship. Ashurst, his wife Sarah, and their family lived in a cabin about ten miles to the northeast of Smith at Ashurst Run. Smith invited the Ashursts to participate in the Mormon Lake religious activities held regularly in the summer. The Ashursts' oldest son Henry said, "When I was a boy I saw [Lot Smith] at Mormon Lake, Arizona, emerge from the wilderness, preach eloquently to his people, mount his trusty mule, and then disappear into the forest."[61]

daughter; Mason [Marius] Porter (25), farming; Jerome Adams (45), wife Mary, and six children; Edwin Whiting (22); Sarah Garn (17); Annie Porter (21); Charles Whiting (27), wife Verona and two children; Hubert Burk, herding, wife Laura and baby; Hiram Judd (30), herding. (Spelling of names is corrected in some instances and may include persons not connected with the dairy.)

60. Samuel Uriah Porter, *Life Sketch of Samuel Uriah Porter.*

61. Henry Fountain Ashurst, *A Many-Colored Toga, the Diary of Henry F. Ashurst*, 299. As Senator Henry Fountain Ashurst in the United States Congress, Henry's speeches earned him the title, "the silver tongued orator from Arizona." He told a number of people that "while in his youth he received his inspiration to become a good speaker while listening to Lot Smith hold his hearers spellbound in the pine forests of Northern Arizona."

Brigham Young's choice of the seemingly unpromising site of Sunset Crossing proved to be advantageous. Smith's Sunset United Order became essential to the colonization of the Arizona territory, parts of New Mexico, and northern Old Mexico, as it served as a continual way station for trail-worn Saints before they headed to more favorable sites. It was written of Smith: "[M]any a humble Saint has found in him a sincere friend in need when they came by Sunset, exhausted by the terrible trials and privations of that sandy desert between Utah and Lot's domicile."[62] If families were unable to continue their journey due to poverty or loss of animals, only a word to Smith brought assistance.[63] As Sunset shared its funds, food, and accommodations unavailable elsewhere on the Little Colorado, some members of Smith's United Order objected to the drain on their provisions caused by hosting so many passing parties. Smith, nevertheless, remained generous to those who traveled through. Smith wrote to the *Deseret News* on February 24, 1878:

> This mission has a strange history so far, most who came having got weak in the back or knees and gone home. Some, I believe have felt somewhat exercised about the way we were getting along, and mode in which we conducted our culinary affairs. Now I always had a preference for eating with my family, and I have striven to show that I was willing to enlarge [invite additional diners] as often as circumstances required. . . . We have enlarged ours to the amount of 40 in one day.
>
> We have noticed that most people that pass the road are willing to stop and board with us a week or more, notwithstanding our poor provisions and the queer style it was served up. But, without joking, I believe most of the Saints who have remained wish to carry out the counsel of the servants of God who sent us on this, as we think, important mission.[64]

Romance began to bloom between Smith and twenty-five-year-old Mary Merinda Garn, the daughter of Samuel Garn and Paralee Harmon Garn. Smith asked for and received permission in John Taylor's letter of April 17, 1878, to take another wife.[65] Smith and Mary left Sunset on May 28.[66]

62. Sullivan C. Richardson, *Richardson Family*, 36.

63. Sullivan C. Richardson, *Remembrances of Lot Smith*, 1.

64. *Deseret News*, 27:123, in Journal History, February 24, 1878.

65. Lot Smith, letter to John Taylor, February 26, 1878.

66. Nielson, *Journal*, 1:135.

They were one of the earliest couples—if not the first—to journey over the Honeymoon Trail to be married in the St. George Temple on June 13, 1878.[67]

Each member of the Sunset United Order added his or her influence to the colony's daily life. Joe James was one who helped make life in the Order enjoyable. For one Christmas celebration, the sisters prepared gifts for the children almost all night. "Joe James dressed up as Santa Claus, got a stick horse and jingled around the Fort and delivered presents to the children . . . of molasses candy, paper baskets, animals, paper dolls with paper dresses."[68] James, like Smith, could find humor in hardships. When food was short, he would say, "We'll feed the children dried apples for breakfast, give them water for dinner, and let them swell for supper."[69]

The very thick yellow or red flood waters of the Little Colorado were devastating for Smith and the Little Colorado colonists.[70] Serious flooding began in April and May of 1878. The most ravaging flood of the Sunset colonization mission occurred three or four months later. The rain began on Sunday, August 18. One member of the colony, Frihoff Godfrey Nielson, reported that it was one of the heaviest rain showers he had witnessed there. He wrote: "The inside of the fort was nearly all one sheet of water."[71] The rain continued through Thursday night, and the men built levees to protect the fort. The overwhelming floodwaters floated much of the bundled shocked wheat off the field and into the river—a disastrous loss of Sunset's food supply. When the water receded off the fields, the men tried to salvage the remaining wheat. They tossed bundles down from the soaked stacks that hadn't washed away and set them up to dry.[72] The Little Colorado continued to roll one to three miles wide and one to three feet deep. The men of the fort built a boat, which was used for several weeks. Alice Ann wrote: "We were in a modern Venice, and traveled from the fort in a boat. However, our boat was drawn by oxen."[73]

Despite the flood, the faithful Saints still held a quarterly conference the following weekend on August 31 and September 1 at Brigham City. Oxen drew the boat through the river between Sunset and Brigham City,

---

67. Mary's Bible mistakenly listed her marriage date as June 13, 1879. Nielson's diary confirms the year 1878.

68. Kate B. Carter, "United Order," *Our Pioneer Heritage,* vol. 15, 361.

69. Edmund W. Richardson, interview by Carmen R. Smith, August 21, 1974.

70. Rogers, *Reminiscences,* 6a.

71. Nielson, *Journal,* 1:142.

72. Nielson, *Journal,* 1:142.

73. Smith, *Living Words,* 29.

loaded with passengers. Unfortunately, when it was nearly to the opposite shore, the boat sank. The Saints wrung out their sodden skirts and trouser legs to attend the meetings.[74] The speeches of that conference acknowledged the flood but reflected a willingness to endure.[75] Over and over again the Little Colorado River tested the faith and courage of the missionary settlers.

One month after the destructive flood, apostle Erastus Snow pulled into the Little Colorado settlements[76] He was accompanied by eight other men including two Utah stake presidents, L. John Nuttall of Kanab and Ira N. Hinckley of Millard. The others were Jesse N. Smith, Bateman H. Wilhelm, John Hunt, C. H. Oliphant, Edward A. Noble, and John J. Starley.[77] Two years had elapsed since Snow had first visited the Arizona camps, and the mission had progressed significantly. Sunset now had a fort of thirty-one dwellings, a dining hall-schoolroom, two store rooms, and a granary. Nearby stockyards and corrals enclosed three acres. The land under cultivation exceeded two hundred acres planted to wheat, corn, barley, oats, sugar cane, an orchard, and garden produce. Furniture came from the production of the sawmill, flour came from a water-powered grist mill, and harvesting was more efficient with a Champion Reaper. Sunset's population now totaled 102: nineteen men, eighteen women, forty-three boys, and twenty-two girls.[78]

By the time of Snow's arrival, the floodplain's sandy surface had dried out. Even so, the boat still had to be used to cross the flooding river to attend Saturday's conference meetings held in Brigham City.[79] Snow presided, conducted, and spoke at the meetings. Nielson observed that although "[g]ood instructions were given," many of the people were "disappointed" and did not feel fully sustained in their labors when Snow did not seem to "understand just how fine the margin between life and death had actually been" on the Little Colorado.[80] During the Monday evening meeting at Sunset, "Pres. Snow reprimanded Pres. L. Smith for the coarse [*sic*] he had

---

74. Nielson, *Journal,* 1:143.

75. Arizona Stake Minutes, August 31–September 1, 1878.

76. Nielson, *Journal,* 1:145.

77. *Journal of Jesse Nathaniel Smith,* 221.

78. L. John Nuttal, letter to John Taylor, September 26, 1878, in Journal History.

79. L. John Nuttal, letter to John Taylor, September 26, 1878, in Journal History.

80. Nielson, *Journal,* 1:145–46; Minutes of the Little Colorado Stake, September 21, 1878; Arizona Stake Minutes, Charles S. Peterson, note #17.

taken in regards to his temper."[81] It was true that at times Smith had a hot blaze of temper. When cooled, however, Smith returned to his hearty and good-natured temperament.

Snow planned to continue upriver to the Silver Creek settlements and then southward to visit more distant Arizona settlements. Experienced as a guard for several of Brigham Young's tours, Smith accompanied Snow's group for the trip. His friend Nuttall enjoyed his company, and Hinckley welcomed his captain of Civil War days. With the addition of Jesse N. Smith, Lorenzo H. Hatch, George Lake, and Bateman Wilhelm, Snow's party left Sunset on Tuesday, September 24. Snow visited settlements, chose town sites, and installed officers at Show Low, Bagley (later Taylor), Cluffs, and Forest Dale. At Forest Dale, Lot Smith spoke at an afternoon meeting with Snow, Jesse N. Smith, Hinckley, and Nuttall.[82] They rode through the pine forests to the log fort built by the military at Fort Apache and then followed the military road currently known as the Yellow Jacket Trail southward. Lot Smith's expertise was invaluable as the wagons inched down into the canyon of Black River; he had considerable experience in holding wagons to prevent their tipping off the road into a canyon. The next morning, they climbed out over "a most extraordinary bad rocky hill."[83] After they exited Rocky Canyon, the group continued to the north fork of Ash Creek and descended to the Gila River.

The company camped on the Gila and on October 4 traveled by Camp Goodwin, an abandoned military camp. The tour then left the Gila River and drove south through a pass in the west end of Mount Graham in the Pinaleño mountain range and southwest to the San Pedro River.[84] They arrived on October 6 at the camp of Philemon C. Merrill, Lot Smith's friend from Farmington and Morgan County. Snow's party left Merrill's Camp to follow the San Pedro River. Only a few miles north of Benson, they came to the Tres Alamos Stage Station, a shanty with a fence of ocotillo poles. There they took the road toward Tucson some sixty miles distant and followed Pantano Wash into Tucson, the same route the Mormon Battalion had taken in 1846. Lot Smith pointed out the place where the Battalion had camped thirty years previously.[85]

---

81. Nielson, *Journal*, 1:146.
82. Nuttall, letter to John Taylor, September 29, 1878.
83. Smith, *Journal*, 224.
84. *Ogden Daily Herald*, in Journal History, February 24, 1882.
85. Smith, *Journal*, 225–26.

Snow's party left Tucson and, like Colonel Cooke, cut down a valley directly for the Gila River. In contrast to the Mormon Battalion, Snow's party watered at wells which had been dug at Desert Station and Picacho. They traveled to the Mormon settlements on the Salt River, which had been organized into United Orders. The Snow party left the camps on October 15 to return north. They passed abandoned Camp Reno and continued past Tonto Creek to arrive at the camp of Price Nelson on Rye Creek. Lot Smith was back within the borders of his Arizona Stake. They visited the John B. Freeman family on the East Verde River and climbed onto the Mogollon Rim. After they reached the United Order's sawmill south of Mormon Lake, Hubert R. Burk guided them cross-country through a cedar forest. The rest of the party then headed for Grand Falls on the Little Colorado while Smith took the Beale Road toward Sunset. He returned to Sunset on October 26 after a month-long tour.[86]

President Smith gave the opening address at the November 1878 Arizona Stake Conference held at Brigham City. He said that the congregation could bear testimony that they were engaged in the work of the Lord and that gathering together could strengthen their faith. He spoke of being united to overcome their obstacles and of keeping a firm trust in the Lord. His timely advice was that the group needed to "not look so much to our neighbor's faults" but to "watch ourselves."[87]

The ravages of the flooding Little Colorado River had made it difficult for the settlements to carry on. Many became discouraged and returned to Utah. Those who remained changed their location to a less vulnerable place and built a fort where Sunset became an important way station as Smith and the residents gave succor to those traveling to settle elsewhere. Smith extended the settlements to include a dairy established in the mountains at Mormon Lake, forty miles away. The Saints were favored to be organized into the first stake in Arizona with Smith as president. The stake would soon be divided, and the Saints would be blessed with an extended visit of the senior apostle, Wilford Woodruff. As they strove to strengthen their friendship with the Navajos, the colonists would face the reality of near starvation.

86. Smith, *Journal*, 227–28.
87. Arizona Stake Minutes, November 29, 1878.

CHAPTER 11

Sunset's Succor

Eleven months after the Arizona Stake of Zion had been organized in 1878, President Smith received a letter from President John Taylor that gave notice to divide the Arizona Stake at Barados Ranch (Holbrook) on the Little Colorado River. President Lot Smith's stake was named the Little Colorado Stake of Zion and contained all the settlements and scattered Saints west of the dividing line and extended northward to include all the settlements between the Little Colorado and Kanab.[1] The other stake, with Jesse N. Smith as president, was named the Eastern Arizona Stake of Zion. The Little Colorado Stake included the lower (northern) Little Colorado settlements and land that was hardly suitable for colonization, while the value of the land upriver included in the Eastern Arizona Stake continued to increase. Historian Charles S. Peterson assessed the division: "[In] [t]his decision . . . to insulate Lot Smith and the Little Colorado Stake . . . in a shrinking stake of their own, the United Orders were, in effect, gut shot, left to suffer a lingering and tortured death."[2] Smith's response was characteristically optimistic: "I believe the division of [by] the Presidency of the settlements in this widely scattered section will result in good as it is quite inconvenient to get a union of action when so far removed from each other."[3]

Taylor's November 27 letter continued on with the subject of the United Order. He felt anxious that people might be persuaded to join the Order unwillingly. If they were dissatisfied, he was concerned that when they left they would simply take what "they brought in (if it can be found)" and receive no credit for their labors.[4] Smith replied: "With regards to the persons leaving here and getting what they put into the company, if it can be found, if you have been informed that is the way business is transacted here, I beg leave to state that you have been misinformed to put it in the mildest language I can think of."[5] Smith felt that all who had

---

1. Arizona Stake Minutes in *Little Colorado Stake Minutes*, L. M. Savage, December 7, 1878.

2. Arizona Stake Minutes in *Little Colorado Stake Minutes*, Charles S. Peterson, notes 14 and 15.

3. Lot Smith, letter to John Taylor, December 10, 1878.

4. John Taylor, letter to Lot Smith, November 27, 1878.

5. Smith, letter to John Taylor, December 10, 1878.

withdrawn from the company had been treated fairly. He further stated that they did not recruit members in hopes of gaining wealth but rather discouraged those who were not sincere and likely to withdraw. On the other hand, he said there were "some regular land sharks" who seemed to plan to bring in their poor and worn out stock, have the Order feed them all winter, then leave in the spring with fattened stock and let the Order make good any losses. Smith wrote: "While I hold any position, I will use my influence to prevent such trickery. On the other hand I will do all in my power to succor the poor and carry out the spirit of the United Order."[6] Taylor had been given the impression that the Order members were compelled to eat at the same table, to which Smith replied that it was certainly not the situation but just the opposite. He wrote, "[I]n fact, we have thought sometimes we should have to ask some to eat somewhere else," and expressed his willingness to comply with all Taylor requested.[7]

Not long afterwards, the Sunset leaders received a letter from Erastus Snow concerning the United Order. The leaders (stake president Lot Smith, Sunset bishop Levi M. Savage, counselors John Bloomfield and Hiram Judd, and stake clerk F. G. Nielson) wrote to Taylor on behalf of the Sunset Saints in a January 10, 1879, letter:

> Brother Snow says many do not like the workings of the Order as we have it. . . . Now, which shall we do, seek to please those who withdraw or never were connected with us, or those whose whole desires seem to be to do the will of our Father in Heaven? If there are those who can show we have wronged them, we will not stop at fourfold, but we will restore tenfold. [8]

The letter from the Sunset Saints explained that in the beginning, the Little Colorado companies had made Articles of Association to suit the minds of the people. When some did not agree, they were changed so all could agree. The leaders also detailed that even if a family with no assets joined and another family with $10,000 joined, "[i]t does not make any difference here—the child's feet that is nearest naked gets the shoes, whether its father fetches one dollar into the Order or not."[9]

The first conference of the Little Colorado Stake of Zion convened at Sunset from February 28 to March 2, 1879. In the Saturday meeting, two new counselors were sustained in the Stake Presidency: William C. Allen as Smith's first counselor and John Bushman as second counselor.

---

6. Smith, letter to John Taylor, December 10, 1878.
7. Taylor, letter to Lot Smith, November 27, 1878.
8. Smith et al, letter to John Taylor, January 10, 1879.
9. Smith et al, letter to John Taylor, January 10, 1879.

After remarks on March 1 by Allen, President Smith mentioned that when Brother Allen first came to the settlements, "[H]e could hardly get him up to speak, but we all changed some, and those who are workers could learn to speak, and they were more apt to preach what they practice." [10] On March 8, 1879, Smith wrote to Taylor that he hoped to speak plainly to him as he had spoken to Brigham Young. Smith had heard that "many strange reports" had been given to Taylor and the presiding authorities of himself and his handling of the United Order. Smith thought the brethren may have believed the stories, or partially believed them, enough to question if all was right, but he stated that the Lord knew he had only sought to do his duty and he had not overstepped it. Smith assured Taylor he was more than willing to listen to his counsel. He reported the good health of the Saints and then lamented that he had lost some of his strength—he couldn't hold a bull by the tail—but hoped to soon regain his health. [11]

Smith encouraged hundreds of Hopis to visit Sunset and showed them how to plant and harvest wheat. [12] The Hopis also gleaned wheat in Sunset's fields. Several incidents occurred during the time they came to glean in the fall of 1879. Lightning was an especially well-liked Hopi who often came to the settlements. He was friendly and personable, and the Mormons enjoyed his dancing. It was said that Lightning in his younger days would run to his farm thirty-five miles distant from his mesa-top home, hoe his corn, and run back home the same day. [13] Lightning had been one of the fleetest Hopis, but he was growing old. When he didn't come to the Little Colorado for an extended time, Smith inquired of his whereabouts. He learned that Lightning, too old to maintain himself, had been crowded into a hole in a sitting position with his knees up to his chin and buried. The sad fate of the elderly was the Hopis's way to ensure survival of the villages where food was often short. [14] The old and feeble Hopis knew what to expect.

In early August 1879, one ancient Hopi grandmother came with the others to glean in the fields around Sunset. [15] She knew that what she collected meant her life for the coming winter. When Smith came up from the lower fields, he found the elderly lady crying because someone had stolen some of her wheat. She showed Smith how she had tied the small

---

10. Little Colorado Stake Minutes, March 1, 1879.

11. Lot Smith, letter to John Taylor, March 8, 1879.

12. Andrew Jenson, *Latter-day Saint Biographical Encyclopedia*, 1:803.

13. Sullivan C. Richardson, *Compilation, Part 2*, 24.

14. Richardson, *Compilation, Part 2*, 24.

15. Nielson, *Journal of Frihoff Godfrey Nielson, 1851–1893*, 1:179.

bundles she had gleaned in a certain way. Smith searched and found that a big Hopi boy had stolen her gleanings and hidden them under his own gleanings. The boy tried to deny it until the theft was proven. Smith, sympathetic for the older lady and indignant at her treatment, whipped the thief without mercy. A member of Brigham City said: "Though truly too severe . . . Lot's chastisement brought good will."[16]

A welcome addition to life in the Latter-day Saint settlements on the Little Colorado was the extended stay of senior apostle Wilford Woodruff, who came from St. George where he had presided at the temple. As the anti-polygamy campaign increased in Utah, Woodruff escaped to Arizona to avoid arrest. Smith and Woodruff renewed their friendship. On his way to Moenkopi—the first Latter-day Saint refuge south of the Utah line—Woodruff recorded April 26, 1879: "We drove untill we met Lot Smith and Camped to gether for the night and talked untill midnight."[17] Woodruff spent several days in Moenkopi before he came to Sunset.[18] The apostle came incognito as Lewis Allen and made Sunset his headquarters from May 1879 to March 1880. The first day of his stay in Sunset, Woodruff commented: "All eat at one Common Table. . . . Each head of family had his place with his wives & Children the same as He would in his own house and all I talked to seemed to prefer this manner of living."[19] Woodruff's positive assessment of the Big Table contrasted with Apostle Snow's view.

Smith and Woodruff rode out four miles to see ruins of an old Indian village of stone houses. Smith then took Woodruff to the mountains to visit the sheep camp and afterwards traveled the rough and rocky mountain road to Pleasant Valley and the dairy where the apostle remained a week or more to hunt in the forest.[20] Woodruff was an asset to the Sunset United Order and the other settlements. Wherever he visited, the members were gratified by his sermons. Woodruff was better known—especially among the children—as Brother Allen. On December 6, 1879, Woodruff moved into a one-room log cabin that was built for him in the center of Sunset Fort. He wrote, "The room that I am occupying Br Lot Smith Built for me is the Best room I have been in in Arizona 18 x 16 well Carpeted Chimney & Mantle peace 2 good windows and Curtains and

---

16. Sullivan C. Richardson, *Remembrances of Lot Smith*, 3.

17. Wilford Woodruff, journal, April 26, 1879.

18. Nielson, *Journal*, 1:172.

19. Wilford Woodruff, journal, May 17, 1879.

20. Wilford Woodruff, journal, May 20–27, 1879.

cealing and all vary Comfortable."[21] After Woodruff returned to Utah, the room was used as an office and council house.

Perhaps the most significant contribution of the Sunset United Order to the Arizona mission was the rescue of the upper river settlements from starvation. Smith was alert to the scant food supply in Jesse N. Smith's new Eastern Arizona Stake. At a business meeting of the Sunset United Order on February 1, 1879, the residents voted to assist destitute Saints at Silver Creek with provisions as much as possible.[22] Before the end of the month, they had "assisted the brethren at Snowflake and other places with both breadstuff and seed wheat."[23] Before and after Eastern Arizona's first conference on June 28–29, 1879, Woodruff, Lot Smith, and his wife Mary toured the outlying settlements. They confirmed the scarcity of food. Woodruff noted that Snowflake's sixty-two families had only one hundred fifty acres of wheat planted.[24] This contrasted with Sunset's twenty-five families who had planted two hundred acres of wheat. When the company returned to Sunset from the tour, Smith wrote President Taylor: "[N]one of the Mormon settlements as far as I am informed, in Arizona have raised sufficient bread to last until this harvest with the exception of this place and St. Joseph and having no word from you, I have loaned some graine to the settlements."[25]

During the next three months, the threat of famine intensified. Smith and Woodruff together wrote President Taylor about how those who were called to Arizona customarily deposited their wheat in the tithing offices of Utah and then arrived empty-handed in Arizona expecting to acquire wheat in Sunset. Taylor answered on August 14: "[W]e will endeavor to adopt such measures that exchanges of this kind shall be limited; and only so far as known, to those who are poor and actually need such assistance as an exchange would give them."[26] Despite the shortage of grain, President Smith pointed out the positive progress the Saints had made on August 30 at the Little Colorado Stake Conference. He "[c]ontrasted the difference in the looks of this country now from when we first came here, when we did not know an ear of corn or a head of wheat would grow here."[27]

---

21. Wilford Woodruff, journal, December 6, 1879.
22. Nielson, *Journal*, 1:162.
23. Minutes of Little Colorado Stake, March 1, 1879.
24. Wilford Woodruff, journal, June 24–July 2, 1879.
25. Lot Smith, letter to John Taylor, July 12, 1879.
26. John Taylor, letter, August 14, 1879.
27. Minutes of the Little Colorado Stake, August 30, 1879.

Woodruff was as interested in the "Lamanites" as he was in the welfare of the Saints. Smith took Woodruff on a tour north to the Hopis beginning October 20. The company included Woodruff, Smith with his young son Willard, Indian missionary Ira Hatch as interpreter, and Thomas W. Brookbank. After several days, the group arrived and camped at the Oraibi well at the foot of a steep-walled mesa. The village had been built out of stone on top of the mesa for protection. The Hopis carried all their supplies up steep stone trails.[28] The group held meetings with most of the Hopi and Moqui groups, and arrived back at Sunset several days later.[29]

Ten days after the return from Oraibi, two US Marshals tracked Woodruff to the remote settlements on the Little Colorado. On an unusually cold November 11 afternoon, the marshals found Woodruff preaching in a meeting in Brigham City's dining hall. The two federal officers first made sure of their quarry, then stationed themselves one at each of the two side doors that opened into the common yard of the fort and waited for the meeting to conclude. Woodruff finished his sermon, and the choir sang a closing song which was followed by the usual benediction. The meeting ended and the room began to empty. The two officers closely scrutinized every person who exited through the two doors. Yet when the hall was empty, the officers did not have their man. When Smith had first seen the marshals, he had quickly made arrangements while Woodruff still spoke. The apostle took his seat when he finished speaking. While the choir sang the closing anthem, Smith arose and caught Woodruff's eye. They sauntered together down the aisle through the seated congregation to the back door that led to the kitchen and exited out to saddled horses. An eyewitness said, "It seemed strange as [we] saw Bro. Woodruff and Lot Smith walk down through the audience and out of this back door, which the officers seem not to have seen."[30] Smith and Woodruff rode to the river, crossed to Sunset, and took a wagon to the dairy in the mountains. From there they drove to McNeal's Spring and then through five miles of snow to Pine Hill, where they camped in a grove of pine trees. The wind was so fierce that they cut down limbs for a shield and built a large fire to keep warm. After fixing supper, they went to bed, but Smith arose at midnight to bring his horses to the fire.[31]

---

28. Wilford Woodruff, letter to Bishops Hunter and Hardy, October 29, 1879, LDS Church History Library.

29. Wilford Woodruff, journal, October 20–November 26, 1879.

30. Andrew Christian Peterson, "An Account Related."

31. Wilford Woodruff, journal, November 12, 1879.

They kept the fire ablaze most of the night.[32] The next day, Smith and Woodruff drove farther up the mountain in a storm, breaking through a foot of snow over the rocks. Two feet of snow lay on the ground at the dairy. Smith took Woodruff to Hubert Burk's secluded cabin where he sat before a warm fire, quite safe from any US Marshals, and Smith returned to Sunset.[33]

Woodruff continued to be watchful for marshals. Once, when he had finished preaching for days in Sunset, he fled with Smith to the mountains to elude the officers. Woodruff hid behind the carriage of the United Order's sawmill in a space under the floor. The place was large enough to back a wheelbarrow in to remove the sawdust. Lined with sawdust, it was a pleasant place for Woodruff to stay. The marshals thoroughly searched the houses and the mill—and even emptied a lady's trunk—yet they failed to discover the hiding place.[34]

The colonists' provisions continued to be limited. During December 1879, Sunset's grain and shelter was threatened in an unusual way. Marintha, wife of Sunset's Bishop, Levi Savage, had reluctantly come to live at the settlement. Her husband was to take another wife, and when he arrived in Sunset with the fiancé, Marintha's feelings exploded. In an outrage she seized a burning firebrand and threatened to set fire to everything, including the grain storage. An account recalls: "She was not considered safe as she had threatened to burn up everything. . . . She was watched by two men [that] night."[35] The next day, Smith sent her with her two children unwillingly back to Utah in the wagon of Lyman Mecham.[36]

Woodruff recorded in his journal on January 8, 1880, that while he and Smith visited St. Joseph they administered to Sister Martha Jane Richards. She had given birth to twins and was thought to be doing well, but:

> After getting our dinner we were informed that she was having a sinking spell and wished us to Call in and see her. We went in 10 minuts to 3 oclock and I saw that she was dying and at 3 oclok she breathed her last. . . . Her death was quite unexpected to all. We Blessed the two babes. Lot Smith was mouth. The youngest [child] was dead an hour afterwards.[37]

---

32. Matthias F. Cowley, *Wilford Woodruff, History of His Life and Labors*, 529.

33. Nielson, *Journal*, 1:127.

34. Sullivan C. Richardson, *Early Settlers of Arizona*, 10.

35. Nielson, *Journal*, 1:196.

36. Charles S. Peterson, "'A Mighty Man was Brother Lot': A Portrait of Lot Smith—Mormon Frontiersman," 403–4.

37. Wilford Woodruff, journal, January 8, 1880.

One of Smith's children, born December 27 to Alice Ann, was less than two weeks old at the time. Smith asked his children if they would like to name their baby brother after Brother Allen since they admired him so much. They gladly agreed. Woodruff recorded January 11, 1880:

> I find quite a large Number of fine Children among the Saints in Arizona named Wilford. But I am not the father of any of them but am what may be Called the God Father of some of them if blessing them would make me so. And to day I was Called upon to Bless a son of Lot and Allice Ann Richards Smith and He was named Wilford Woodruff Smith.[38]

When the Smith children heard the baby named as Wilford Woodruff, they cried in disappointment that the baby was not named after Brother Allen.[39]

Conditions in the upper settlements of Eastern Arizona Stake worsened in 1880 as the year advanced. The heaviest snowstorm known for years hit at the end of January. Livestock, especially those newly arrived and weakened from the journey from Utah, nearly all perished.[40] Smith's contemporary, Joseph Fish, wrote: "The winter of 1880 was severe followed by famine. It was all they could do to survive."[41] Since the fall of 1879, President Jesse N. Smith had been in Salt Lake City serving in Utah's Territorial Legislature. Before Jesse's return, his first counselor Lorenzo H. Hatch wrote him:

> My sympathies are drawn out in behalf of the many poor and destitute of this stake of Zion. Many have consumed the last of their scanty supplies and are in want. How and in what manner to get aid for a large majority of the old, and last year's emigration are all destitute before they reach Brigham City, and supplies have to be sent to aid them to reach that point. Could the tithing be had, it would be but a tithe of what is wanted to supply the wants of the people. [42]

Most of Sunset's assistance to the upper settlements occurred during February 1880. Woodruff recorded that Lot Smith furnished John W. Young and Morten P. Mortensen with 4,500 pounds of flour and meal to take to Moenkopi, and wrote, "There is a Cry for bread in the land." [43] President Lot Smith expressed his feelings in the February stake confer-

---

38. Wilford Woodruff, journal, January 11, 1880.
39. Alice Ann Richards Smith, *The Living Words of Alice Ann Richards Smith*, 50.
40. John H. Krenkel, ed., *The Life & Times of Joseph Fish, Mormon Pioneer*, 205.
41. Krenkel, *Joseph Fish*, 208.
42. Lorenzo H. Hatch, letter to Jesse N. Smith, February 2, 1880.
43. Wilford Woodruff, journal, February 11, 1880.

ence at Sunset: "[I] [n]ever felt to complain with the providences of God in planting us in this land. This land had been blessed for us."[44]

Woodruff received counsel to return to Salt Lake City.[45] When the Saints learned that Woodruff would be leaving, they came from Brigham City and St. Joseph to Sunset on March 1, 1880, to celebrate the seventy-third birthday of their beloved Lewis Allen. Despite the scarcity of food, "the saints here gave him many presents and tokens of regard and partook of a well prepared dinner of chickens, geese, preserves, custard pies &c."[46] Levi Savage wrote: "[Woodruff's] kind and fatherly counsel; his many wise and interesting discourses to us; his forbearance, encouragement, and appreciation of our struggles in this land have all secured to him the warmest friendship, and highest esteem of the Saints all through this land."[47] Two days later, Woodruff left Sunset with Lot Smith and Smith's seven-year-old son Willard for St. George. In Kanab, Smith's best horse collapsed from eating too much grain without grass. David K. Udall lent his best team to Smith to continue transporting Woodruff to St. George.[48] Traveling in Utah, Woodruff recorded that they met "the coldest most terrific snow storms I was ever in."[49] Their cask of water was frozen solid so they and the horses had no water until they found some on the road. In St. George on Sunday, March 14, both Woodruff and Smith spoke in the tabernacle.[50]

Smith and his son returned to Sunset and the famine persisted. In the settlement of Woodruff, Lorenzo Hatch recorded in April 1880 that he had never seen food so scarce; all his neighbors had no milk and bread was scarce.[51] That summer Smith furnished the destitute St. Johns Saints with barley to sustain them until their menfolk working on the railroad could send flour.[52] In June, Joseph Fish recorded that Smith was "very generous and divided with the people all that he could spare." Smith gave him flour,

---

44. Minutes of the Little Colorado Stake, February 29, 1880.

45. John Taylor, letter to Wilford Woodruff, February 20, 1880.

46. Nielson, *Journal,* 1:207.

47. Levi Mathers Savage, *Family History Journal, 1876–1935,* 31.

48. Wilford Woodruff, journal, March 12, 1880; David King Udall and Pearl Udall Nelson, *Arizona Pioneer Mormon: David King Udall, His Story and His Family, 1851–1938,* 199.

49. Wilford Woodruff, journal, March 12, 1880.

50. Wilford Woodruff, journal, March 14, 1880.

51. Lorenzo Hill Hatch, *Lorenzo Hill Hatch Journal, Copied from Original Journals by Ruth Savage Hilton,* April 18, 1880.

52. Udall and Nelson, *Arizona Pioneer Mormon,* 199–200.

shorts, and bran. Fish wrote that most paid Smith back at the next harvest, but Smith "lost considerable by his liberality." [53] By the slimmest margin, the Little Colorado settlements finally survived the famine.

In early 1880, President Smith wrote to Morten P. Mortensen of Moenkopi to come to Conference and bring his daughter.[54] The daughter of Mortensen was Dorthea (Dorothy) "Diantha" Elizabeth. She was a well-mannered young lady who was schooled in old-fashioned Danish courtesy. Smith, Alice Ann, and two of their sons then visited the Mortensen family in Moenkopi that summer for two weeks.[55] After Smith received permission from President Taylor to take another wife in September, he again traveled the Honeymoon Trail to St. George, this time via Moenkopi.[56] He and Diantha were married and sealed on October 21, 1880. [57] Diantha was nineteen and Smith was fifty. That day Smith also stood proxy for his deceased brother Hyrum's temple endowments. The newlyweds returned to Sunset on November 25.[58] Two years after their marriage, Diantha traveled to Parowan, Utah, with her father to visit relatives. In Parowan, opinion of Smith was divided. Her aunts were so concerned over her marrying that "awful Lot Smith" about whom such wild tales circulated that they wept over her. According to family descendants, her reply was, "Oh, I'd much rather be an old man's darling than a young man's slave."[59] Diantha was skilled in an unusually wide variety of homemaking arts and headed the sewing room of the Order.[60]

The day to begin threshing came on December 1, 1880. The thermometer registered only twelve degrees above zero that morning.[61] The crew assembled and the Buffalo Pitts thresher was set up. Smith worked the most dangerous of the threshing operations: riding the horsepower. To drive the horses, Smith stood atop the cast iron master wheel on a

---

53. Krenkel, *Joseph Fish,* 208.

54. Diantha M. Smith to Nephi Lot Smith, interview by Omer J. and Carmen R. Smith, June 10, 1972.

55. Nielson, *Journal,* 1:222, 224.

56. Wilford Woodruff, letter to Lot Smith, September 15, 1880.

57. Nielson, *Journal,* 1:229.

58. Nielson, *Journal,* 1:236.

59. Amelia Topham, interview by Omer J. and Carmen R. Smith, circa 1950s.

60. Diantha Smith Craig to Alberta Craig Rider, interview by Carmen R. Smith.

61. Nielson, *Journal,* 1:238.

small two-foot-wide wooden platform in the center.[62] Around the center platform turned the radiating spokes which were attached to the center master wheel cogs under his feet. As Smith stood on the horsepower, he cracked the whip over the horses to start the machine. Clouds of dust and chaff immediately billowed up. In the cold weather, his foot slipped off the small platform and caught in the revolving spokes of the horsepower. The horses were quickly stopped, but not before Smith's foot was badly torn and severely bruised.[63]

The Sunset Saints completed a new dining hall on March 15, 1881, in the center of the fort. Adobes lined the inside of the new framed building and the attached kitchen was built over a cellar.[64] Eating together at the "Big Table" (often two or three rows of tables) was the focal point of life for the people in the Sunset United Order. Of all the features of Arizona's United Order, none evoked more interest and varied reaction than Sunset's Big Table. The members met together and knelt by the long benches to join in prayer before both supper and breakfast. Each family sat together in a place they had chosen—father and mother with their children. Smith sat at the south end of the center row with his wives and children.[65]

An incident at the Big Table showed one of Smith's quirks. He insisted on eating from a particular plate with a certain knife, fork, and spoon, although his place setting was of no better quality than that of the other diners.[66] Once, when Diantha was helping to prepare dinner for some visitors from Utah, she set the table with the china reserved for special occasions. When the guests were seated at the table, Smith looked down at his place setting and asked, "Where is my plate?" Diantha answered, "I thought that since we had company today, you would like to have the table set with nicer dishes." He picked up the plate and slammed it down on the table and said, "Well, I want my plate." Diantha, of even temperament, walked alongside the table, gathered up the plates, stacked them in the shelves, turned to her husband, and said, "Now you may find dishes and food for your company yourself. You shall not see me any more today." Later that evening when Smith and the visitors returned, Diantha apolo-

62. Ronald V. Jensen, Living Historical Farm, located six miles south of Logan, Utah.

63. Nielson, *Journal,* 1:238.

64. Nielson, *Journal,* 1:251.

65. George A. McClellan, "My Family," 7.

66. Mr. and Mrs. Owen Bloomfield from Elva Leavitt Bond, interview by Carmen R. Smith, February 24, 1979.

gized. "I guess I never should have done what I did today," she began. She was cut short by a visitor, who declared, "Not at all, Diantha. You did just right, and I glory in your spunk. Brother Lot got just what he deserved."[67]

Stories about the Big Table proliferated—some wild and ridiculous. A traveling trader named Don Maguire arrived at Sunset in late November 1881 from the Atlantic and Pacific Railway, which had recently completed a stop at Winslow four miles from Sunset.[68] Maguire gave a detailed description of Sunset's Big Table. He remarked that Sunset "bore an intensely religious and formal air."[69] He described that a bell rang to signal that supper was ready. After a presiding authority offered a long prayer before the meal, all began to eat without speaking. (Apparently the hubbub at mealtime had brought a decision to eat in silence.) The menu included beans and pork fat, molasses, cornbread, and water. After the meal, the presiding authority again arose and thanked God for their supper, asked for protection, requested strength for the youth to resist falsehoods, and that their enemies be laid low. At the prayer's conclusion, the group vocalized amen and a hymn was sung. The tables were then moved to the sides for dancing by both young and old. A prayer again ended the activity and all retired to their own rooms for the night.[70]

One evening in November 1881, the Sunset Order members were all seated to eat at the Big Table. Relations with the Navajos had progressed from uncertainty to tentative friendship, and the Navajos decided to test and perhaps solidify the relationship. The Navajo chief Comayazzie came to visit Da-gha-hi Chi. Smith's wife Alice Ann recorded that the Navajos and their ladies were all beautifully dressed and their horses, as well, were adorned with beautiful blankets and silver brides. To communicate, both Smith and Comayazzie spoke Spanish. Smith invited them to eat and requested that tables in the kitchen be quickly set for their guests. However, with one glance into the kitchen quarters, the Navajos gave a dark look and mounted their horses to leave. Lot stood by Comayazzie's horse to ask why they were leaving. The chief would not answer. At last Comayazzie

67. Emma Mortensen Skousen, interview by Omer J. and Carmen R. Smith.

68. Nielson, *Journal*, 1:277; William C. McClellan, diary, November 28, 1881. Maguire was a former teamster for Russell, Majors & Wadell who spent the winter of 1857–58 at Fort Bridger with short rations caused by Smith's burning of the wagons.

69. Don Maguire, "Don Maguire's Trading Expedition in Northern Arizona, 1879," 380–95.

70. Maguire, "Trading Expedition," 380–95.

expressed his displeasure of not being seated with Smith and his family. Smith vigorously professed friendship and offered flour, meat, and blankets—all to no avail. He then called for the ladies, including Alice Ann, to bring their brass buckets. Alice Ann protested. Her bucket had belonged to her grandmother and was the most prized possession in her trousseau. Smith knew that the Navajos must not leave until they were pacified. She brought it out and Smith gave it to the chief's wife, who was dazzled by its gleaming exterior. The other women followed suit, and, to everyone's relief, the Navajos happily strapped the treasures onto their horses. The Navajos were then willing to eat. The dining room was vacated, and the Navajos sat down to eat the best the camp could offer. Smith sat and ate with them, told stories, and laughed with them. They were in good humor when they left and, from then on, the Navajos were friendly.[71]

At least some progress was made in proselyting to the Navajos and Hopis over the years. Smith wrote a letter on October 21, 1882, to John Taylor to inform him that a number of the "Lamanites" who had been baptized wished to be endowed. He inquired whether Taylor would consider it proper to send the converted natives to the temple in St. George.[72] Indian Missionary C. L. Christensen summed up Smith's relationship with the tribes in Arizona: Smith followed Brigham Young's counsel to feed rather than fight them, and he often visited the tribes, always asking if the settlers were welcome in their land. The Navajo chiefs esteemed him highly. Smith gave them good advice, and Christensen heard him say, "All who feel like cursing an Indian and saying that the only good Indian is a dead one, are released to go home."[73]

As Smith presided over the Little Colorado Stake, the senior apostle Wilford Woodruff blessed the lives of the settlers as he stayed for an extended time. During this time, Smith's Sunset United Order helped many of the starving Saints by giving them food until more could be harvested. Although Smith's leg was severely injured while threshing, he would yet suffer an even more painful injury on the same leg. Many trials would beset the colonists; Smith would personally experience some of the hardest, and the United Order would end.

---

71. Smith, *Living Words*, 26–27; Miss Nona Smith (Rhead) in Philip Smith, *Lot Smith*, 7.

72. Lot Smith, letter to John Taylor, October 21, 1882.

73. Andrew Jenson, "Lot Smith," *Biographical Encyclopedia*, 1:805.

CHAPTER 12

Circle S Ranch

In the 1881 winter threshing, Smith worked the same hazardous horse power as the season before. On December 15, he slipped again and badly mangled the same leg far worse than he had the year before.[1] Much of the flesh between the ankle and knee was torn off his calf, and the bone itself was crushed and splintered. Smith went to his wife Mary for treatment. As he sat in the chair, he expressed his disgust with himself.[2] Mary began to gingerly cleanse the lacerated flesh around the slivers of bone with hot water. Smith snapped, "Come on, scrub it, or I am going to kick you right into the tub! This shouldn't hurt anybody." Then, with his injured foot, he kicked at her. He allowed no sign of weakness.[3] Smith reported the details of his mishap only three days after the accident in a letter to the *Deseret News*, which was reported by Nielson:

> You will perhaps recollect that about a year ago, Brother Lot Smith met with an accident in getting his foot caught in the horse power of a threshing machine while in motion. Strange as it may seem, a similar accident occurred to him on the 15th.
>
> After having driven the horse power a number of days, his ankle that had not fully recovered from the other hurt, having become benumbed with cold, and stepping from the power while in motion, in an instant, his ankle gave way. Rolling over, he was caught, this time the foot escaping but the ankle and leg suffered severely.
>
> The brethren, with great presence of mind, caught the horse very quickly, not soon enough, however, to prevent the left leg from being severely lacerated from the ankle up to the calf of the leg on the left side, and with appearance that the ankle was injured.
>
> He wishes to say this much for fear his friends would think he is doing this for effect (and it had its effect). He thinks with a couple more attempts and a little greasing, he will be able to go clear through. He does not think the injury will prove permanent at all, but that he will fully recover."[4]

---

1. *Journal of Frihoff Godfrey Nielson 1851–1893*, vol. 1, 278.
2. Alden B. Smith II, interview by Carmen R. Smith, January 9, 1983.
3. Alden B. Smith II, interview.
4. Lot Smith, letter to *Deseret News,* December 18, 1881.

Woodruff wrote January 16, 1882 to Smith to inquire of health after the accident. He also gave some counsel, "[P]ut some young man onto that machine next year [so as] not to kill yourself at that kind of work."[5] Since Woodruff had heard that he was very sick, he wanted someone to answer back for him if Smith was unable to write. In a January 31 letter, Woodruff expressed his pleasure that Smith had written him a reply. He wanted to share with Smith a remedy that he felt had saved his life when he was poisoned through a cut he received while skinning a poisoned ox. With onions, he had drawn the poison from his body into his arm until it was dangerously inflamed. Fearing for his life, an impression flashed into his mind to make a poultice of charcoal and wild sage. He covered his arm with the poultice, which took the inflammation out. He urged Smith to try it. He wrote, "I would recommend you to wrap up your leg with cloths wet with strong hot sage tea besides the charcoal poultice. Again, if it becomes inflamed, make a smoke of woolen rags on wood & hold your bare leg over that."[6]

Six weeks after the accident, Smith wrote to Jesse N. Smith that his leg had become inflamed a second time and was much more painful than at first. He had not yet attempted to walk, even with crutches. He continued, "They have carried me around to meetings a little. They seemed to be the first thing that induced sleep."[7] Smith slowly began to recover and attended the February 1882 stake conference at Sunset.[8] The lengthy, painful healing process tested him. His leg would appear to heal and then would repeatedly break open and suppurate as bits of bone worked their way to the outer skin; the sordid flesh sloughed off. These complications were more painful than the original injury. The unending excruciating pain and weeks of sleepless nights tended to impair Smith's strong memory. He suffered for more than a year.[9]

Smith had not attended the General Conference of the Church in five years. Determined to attend, and ignoring the suppuration on his leg, he started a journey to Salt Lake City with Brigham Young Jr. on March 31, 1882, boarding the Atlantic & Pacific Railroad.[10] In Albuquerque, they met John W. Young, and the three put up at a hotel in Old Town. The

---

5. Wilford Woodruff, letter to Lot Smith, January 16, 1882.
6. Wilford Woodruff, letter to Lot Smith, January 31, 1882.
7. Lot Smith, letter to Jesse N. Smith, January 31, 1882.
8. John Bushman, diaries, February 25, 1882.
9. Andrew Jenson, *Latter-day Saint Biographical Encyclopedia*, 1:804.
10. Nielson, *Journal*, 1:288.

Albuquerque Weekly printed an article under the title "DISTINGUISHED VISITORS" which included the following assessments of Lot Smith: "Mr. Smith is an entertaining talker and will always be welcome at this office, regardless of what may be his peculiar religious ideas"; "He is one of the most energetic of the Mormon elders, having for a generation been closely connected with the history of his people"; and "Mr. Smith is a bluff, hale old man and abounds in witty jokes about men and things connected with the history of Utah."[11]

In Albuquerque, the three men boarded the Denver & Rio Grande train and traveled into Salt Lake City. Smith spent the night at the home of Robert T. Burton.[12] Salt Lake City had changed in the last six years. Large homes and impressive meetinghouses built in the Gothic style lined the streets. After six years in the crude log cubicles of Sunset Fort, Smith—to his discomfort—found the large and beautiful new buildings, the elegant, stylish dress of the people, and the sophistication of the city an utter contrast. The *Deseret News* published Smith's report on the Arizona colonization:

LITTLE COLORADO COUNTRY

We learn from President Lot Smith of Little Colorado Stake, that the settlements on the stream of that name—Sunset, Brigham City, St. Joseph and Woodruff, are as prosperous as could be expected considering the character of the country.

One of the principal difficulties the settlers have to contend with is the treacherous character of the river, which is filled with quicksand, rendering the construction and maintainance [*sic*] of dams no easy task.

The Atlantic & Pacific R. R. has reached Diablo Canyon, about twenty-five miles from Sunset. The company will find considerable difficulty in constructing the line through that defile, owing to the ruggedness of the ground and the heavy character of the grade.

Brother Smith, it will be remembered, met with an accident some time since, by which he had a large portion of the flesh of his left leg, between the ankle and the knee, torn away by a threshing machine. He has almost entirely recovered from the effects of the injury, the limb being now nearly as sound as ever.[13]

---

11. *Albuquerque Weekly*, April 7, 1882.

12. Robert T. Burton, diaries, 1856–1907, April 6, 1882.

13. Journal History of the Church of Jesus Christ of Latter-day Saints, April 11, 1882 (hereafter cited as Journal History).

The day after conference, Smith borrowed a horse from Burton and rode into Farmington in the midst of a snowstorm.[14] He called on Jane at his big stone house and rode over the mountain to Stoddard to visit his wife Julia, where he saw his seven-year-old daughter Julia playing with her small dog. Little Julia, of course, did not recognize who to her was a stranger. Back in Farmington, Smith reined in his horse in front of Laura's small, back-frame house. In the street, a now thirteen-year-old Lollie tended the Messenger twins who were almost three years old. Smith dismounted and asked Lollie her name. She answered, "I am Lollie, Laura Smith's daughter." Lot then asked who the little ones were. "They are my brother and sister, Howard and Lottie." Lollie followed her father into the house where Laura was tailoring a dress. Smith took Laura in his arms and kissed her and said, "Laura, I love you very much. If having my right arm severed to right everything that had gone wrong between us, I'd gladly have it done."[15] Smith kissed the twins and asked, "Laura, why didn't you have twins for me?"[16] Smith expressed his desire to take eleven-year-old Alden with him back to Arizona. "Oh, he's much too young," objected Laura. "He's just right," Smith insisted. "I want them while they're still in the pink."[17]

Soon, father and son began to get acquainted on the long wagon trip to Arizona. Along the way in some larger town, they stopped and went into a gentile shoe shop. The shoe merchant was aghast when Smith bought over thirty pairs of shoes. Smith enjoyed the merchant's amazement and said, "If these give good service, I'll come back and buy shoes for the rest of my family."[18] After a six-week absence, Smith pulled his wagon into Sunset's fort on Sunday, May 14.[19] Perhaps it was during Smith's visit to Utah that the editor of the *Contributor*, Junius F. Wells, asked Smith to write his account of the 1857 Echo Canyon War. On his arrival home, he promptly dictated his recollections, most likely to his wife Mary. Less than two weeks later, his stake clerk Nielson sent the manuscript to Utah.[20]

The Little Colorado Stake Quarterly Conference was scheduled in St. Joseph on May 27 and 28. On Saturday, Smith gave an account of his

---

14. Eva Rice Howell, letter to Carmen R. Smith, April 13, 1969. The sequence of Smith's visits is not known.

15. Howell, letter to Carmen R. Smith, April 22, 1972.

16. Eva Rice Howell, letter to Carmen R. Smith, June 29, 1972.

17. Alden Rice, interview by Carmen R. Smith, June 2, 1971.

18. Alden Rice, interview by Sterling J. Smith, September 1979.

19. Nielson, *Journal*, 1:292.

20. Nielson, *Journal*, 1:293.

visit to Utah. He said that he had been away from Utah too long to belong there anymore. He was unhappy with the "indifference manifested by many of the Saints, [the] style in dress, high living and disregard for the rights of others." Still, he "did not believe the wicked would have power to trample the Saints down, but that they would be chastened."[21] An announcement by President Smith in Sunday morning's conference meeting was unexpected. Either during Smith's absence or during the two weeks before the conference convened, a notice had arrived from missionary Ernest A. Tietjen. The message called five members of the Sunset United Order on a colonizing mission to Savoia, located northeast of St. Johns and thirty miles into New Mexico Territory.[22] During the Sunday morning meeting, Smith complied with Tietjen's request, even though it hit hard where Sunset was most vulnerable—membership. He announced the Savoia mission calls to the families named by Tietjen: Brothers John Bloomfield, Samuel Garn, Peter Nielson, Aser Pipkin, and James Knox Polk Pipkin.[23] President Smith closed the final session of conference with his customary gracious comments and the conference ended. Those who had been called as colonists to Savoia left in shock.

The next day, Frihoff Nielson talked with his father, who had been called to Savoia, and some of the other men, noting that a "very unsettled feeling pervades the community. The 5 bre. were believed to be called out of spite by Lot Smith."[24] Those called to Savoia soon left to look over their new location. By June 28, most returned to Sunset to make arrangements to leave and settle their accounts. Smith named a committee of Samuel Garn, Frihoff Nielson, J. R. McNeil, and himself to settle accounts with those who were leaving. Although Nielson wrote that Smith was "a very disagreeable man to do business [with]," he concluded that "[a] fair settlement [was] given those who [were] going away, most of them, taking considerable more than they brought in."[25]

The call of five families from Sunset to Savoia signaled the beginning of the end of the Sunset United Order. More settlers left and some sent complaints to authorities in Salt Lake City.[26] Lot refuted the charges, beg-

21. Christian Christensen, Minutes of the Little Colorado Stake, May 27, 1882.

22. Gary L. Tietjen, *Encounter with the Frontier,* 31.

23. Nielson, *Journal,* 1:293; Christensen, Minutes of the Little Colorado Stake, May 28, 1882.

24. Nielson, *Journal,* 1:293.

25. Nielson, *Journal,* 1:298.

26. Wilford Woodruff, letter to Lot Smith, October 23, 1882.

ging the question: "Was the Order to be run for the benefit of malcontents who pulled out or for those with the gumption and faith to stay and make it a success?"[27] During this time, Woodruff wrote Smith a supportive letter from Salt Lake City: "I consider that I am somewhat acquainted with you and I have been satisfied a good while that many things have been said about Br. Lot Smith that are not true."[28]

With the loss of half of the twenty families in 1882, Sunset could no longer function as a self-sustaining community. A few stalwarts continued to stay but, by late June, 1882, there were only three men, a few small boys, women, children, and babies.[29] There were not enough men to service the dam when it broke later in 1882, so farming at Sunset had to be abandoned. Sunset, however, remained as headquarters of the Little Colorado Stake, and the fort continued to be occupied. Despite these setbacks, Smith retained a positive outlook.[30]

Smith began to focus more on his livestock. At this time, the boundaries of ranches were not proscribed by law; ranchers simply claimed the areas they actively used. The Order's Circle S Ranch holdings were located in the mountains around Mormon Lake, and did not include any of the Little Colorado Basin. Smith oversaw improvements on the ranch, built fences and corrals, and cleaned out springs for watering holes. He placed great value on fine cattle and horses. As soon as the Mormon Dairy was established, Smith purchased and upgraded the stock. All cattle and horses were branded with the Circle S brand (an *s* inside a circle) of the Sunset United Order.[31]

Smith was one of the earlier stockmen to import blooded animals, and the Circle S horses soon acquired a reputation for quality.[32] Smith's Circle S horses were admired and envied throughout all northern Arizona. According to northern Arizona rancher-historian Earle Forrest, "No better horses ever roamed the Arizona ranges than Lot Smith's Circle S.

---

27. Samuel W. Taylor, *The Kingdom or Nothing, The Life of John Taylor, Militant Mormon*, 315.

28. Wilford Woodruff, letter to Lot Smith, November 10, 1882.

29. Nielson, *Journal*, 1:295.

30. Jesse Nathaniel Smith, *Journal of Jesse Nathaniel Smith, The Life Story of a Mormon Pioneer, 1834–1906*, 268.

31. *Arizona Champion*, February 21, 1885, 4/2. The horses were branded on the right thigh; cattle were branded on the right hip with a swallow notched in the right ear.

32. The term *blooded* refers to any pedigreed animal.

They were as tough as horses come."[33] Smith had outstanding stallions—Manitou (purchased in Kentucky), Brown Dick (purchased from Saxon S. Aker), and Red Cloud. The purchase of Red Cloud as a colt in May 1881 caused anything but a mild reaction within the Order. Stated one source: "There were some of the United Order people that darn near died over him . . . buying that expensive thoroughbred horse."[34] Some members felt that Smith had unwisely used United Order funds to pay an exorbitant price for a mere colt—particularly one for his personal transportation. In exasperation at the uproar, Smith presented himself astride the rear quarters of a small burro—a ridiculous figure. He said that if the people of the United Order didn't care to have their leader properly mounted, they might be better satisfied to have him riding on a burro.[35] The agitation eventually subsided as other stockmen in Northern Arizona began to acquire blooded stock. This colt grew to become one of the loves of Smith's life.

On Friday, January 5, 1883, Smith boarded the train for Wayne, Illinois, and the Oaklawn Stables, which was boasted as "the largest importing and breeding establishment in the world."[36] He was accompanied by a Dane, James Mortensen of Snowflake.[37] Both planned to purchase Percherons. The cross of a Percheron with a range horse produced very desirable colts. In a story that Smith enjoyed retelling about this trip, early one morning, about three o'clock, a knock sounded at the door of their hotel room.

> "Come in," Smith called out. The hotel keeper, who carried a lamp, begged their forgiveness and explained that a stranger wished to speak to them. The stranger also begged their pardon and asked permission to step in.
>
> "Gentlemen," he said, "I am going away on the train in a few minutes. But I have just been told there is a Mormon here who has five wives. I have never seen one of them yet and I would like to see a real Mormon. May I come in and talk just a minute?"
>
> "Yes sir," Smith replied. "Come right along."
>
> "Have I been correctly informed?" he asked. "And which of you is it?"

33. Earle R. Forrest, "Riding for the Old CO Bar," 3.

34. Willard and Karl Smith, interview by Omer J. Smith and Carmen R. Smith, October 2, 1975.

35. Charles E. Richardson to Edmund W. Richardson, interview by Carmen R. Smith, n.d.

36. Nielson, *Journal*, 1:315; Original bill of sale, University of Arizona Special Collections.

37. *Pinckney Dispatch*, April 6, 1885.

"As to the first question," Smith replied, "You certainly have. As to the second, see if you can guess which it is." The visitor stared at Smith's receding hairline and bushy red beard.

Uncertain, he turned his gaze to Smith's companion, twenty-nine-year-old Mortensen.

"It's him," said the visitor as he indicated the younger Danish man.

"Good guess," said Smith. The stranger stood a long moment and stared intently. Then he thanked them, closed the door, and was gone.[38]

The two men returned home from Illinois on February 6, bringing a two-year-old highbred Percheron mare Smith had purchased for eight hundred dollars.[39] The mare, named Penelope, had been imported from France the year before and had been bred to an imported Brilliant in November 1882.[40] The big, black-gray heavy draft mare was treasured by Smith. Mortensen brought back a four-year-old Percheron stallion.[41]

At the time he purchased Penelope, Smith also brought home a Durham bull and upgraded the breeds of the base stock at the dairy ranch to prize beef cattle. By 1888, Smith's cattle were known as "the finest steers ever marketed in Arizona."[42] Smith's cattle and horses received his close attention and care.

While Smith ran the Circle S Ranch, a grizzly bear began to kill the stock. Smith gathered a few of his brethren to help hunt the slayer, and they found its trail north of Mormon Lake. Since they were near Ashurst Run, Smith stopped at the home of his friend Ashurst to invite him along. When Smith noticed that Mrs. Ashurst was in delicate health, he asked Ashurst if he should leave his wife since she was nearing the time to deliver her baby. Ashurst, who was eager to join the hunt replied, "She's had seven before, and she knows just how to do it." He pointed to the big fireplace and said, "Five of her children were born on the hearth of that fireplace." As he started to leave with the men, Ashurst grabbed his wife's new gun. She objected, "You don't take my gun. I earned the money for that gun, and you're not taking it." Mrs. Ashurst then told the men they were foolish for hunting a grizzly on horseback and declared that the bear would always be two miles ahead of them. Ashurst left with Smith and the hunters with his own gun. While the men were gone, Mrs. Ashurst

---

38. Sullivan C. Richardson, *"In Desert Arizona,"* 78–79.
39. Nielson, *Journal*, 1:318.
40. Original bill of sale.
41. Nielson, *Journal*, 1:318; *Pinkney Dispatch*, April 6, 1885.
42. *Weekly Champion*, June 21, 1890.

gave birth to a little boy (Edward). The children bathed the newborn in the dishpan and put him to sleep on the hearth. Soon after, Mrs. Ashurst heard something shake just outside. She looked out, saw a big grizzly, grabbed her gun, shot it dead, and returned to bed. Smith and the hunting party returned that afternoon about four o'clock; they had tracked the bear to the Ashurst cabin.[43]

Ashurst's son, Henry, who grew up to be a US Senator from Arizona, told how Smith played a part in his life when he was nine or ten. Henry was captured, tied up, and taken to a small cabin at Pine Breaks fifteen miles from the Mormon Dairy by four men of the Daggs camp. Tightly bound, they dumped him onto the dirt floor. The kidnappers built a fire on the bare floor and sat down to drink and play cards. Between laughter and yarns, they discussed whether or not to brand Henry. After what seemed to Henry an interminable time, he distinctly heard hoof beats approaching and was afraid his captors could hear them also. However, they were oblivious. Smith strode into the cabin, kicked the fire onto the troublemakers, and demanded, "What are you sunnzabitches doing here?"[44] The men scrambled to avoid the hot cinders and escape. Smith turned to Henry, cut his bonds, and said, "Henry! What are you doing here? You had better get up and get out of here!"[45]

In February 1883, Apostles Brigham Young Jr. and Heber J. Grant visited the colonists in northern Arizona Territory. Smith guided the apostles on a trip around the settlements and to the Navajo and Hopi villages. They started out from Sunset and crossed the Little Colorado to Brigham City. A mile and a half out, the team became mired in quicksand. Grant and Young Jr., who had been riding in the carriage, rode horses out of the mess. For an hour and a half, Smith waded in the mire and finally extracted the carriage onto solid ground. Smith returned to Sunset to obtain doubletrees to replace the broken ones, and they continued on.[46] The

---

43. Edward B. Ashurst, audio recording, Lot Smith Reunion, Flagstaff, AZ, July 11–12, 1969.

44. Henry F. Ashurst to Alden B. Smith, Alden B. Smith II, interview by Carmen R. Smith, January 9, 1984.

45. Henry F. Ashurst to Alden B. Smith, Alden B. Smith II, interview by Carmen R. Smith, January 9, 1984.

46. Brigham Young Jr., diaries, February 20, 1883.

group traveled on to visit the seven villages of the Oraibis, where Grant, Young Jr., and Smith each spoke.[47]

The day after Smith and the two apostles arrived back in Sunset, a tragic accident occurred at the fort. Smith's wife Mary was minding the children and decided to make soap. In the afternoon, Mary had built a hot fire under the big iron pot set up in front of her room.[48] When the lye water was about to boil, Mary stepped into her room to get the fat to combine with the hot lye water. As she did so, she heard screams. Alice Ann's fifteen-month-old toddler Wilford Woodruff had somehow fallen into the big iron pot of hot lye water. Karen Mortensen carried the child to Alice Ann's room.[49] Little Wilford endured excruciating pain that night and the next day until his death in the afternoon about five o'clock.[50]

The funeral was held the following day in the dining room. Both Apostles Grant and Young Jr. spoke comforting words to the grief-stricken parents. The small casket was carried to the sand hill cemetery about a mile southeast of the fort and buried with two other children who had recently died of measles.[51] Two days after the funeral, Young Jr. and Grant attended the quarterly conference of the Little Colorado Stake held at Sunset. The stake minutes noted "President Lot Smith believed . . . that the spirit of revelation should be in every family and member. The sisters were consulted if they wished to be in any important measure."[52]

After conference, President Smith and his wife Alice Ann with his counselors, Allen and Bushman, made a tour to outlying settlements of the stake. They visited Chevelon on March 27 where a few Saints resided. The weather was cold and the roads were muddy. They ran out of provisions and would have gone hungry if not for a large turkey that Bushman captured and killed.[53] They visited the Saints in Adams Valley, where they had breakfast with the Jerome J. Adams family and traveled

---

47. Heber J. Grant, letter to Lucy Grant, March 12, 1883; Young Jr., diaries, March 12, 1883. On this trip Grant received a personal confirmation of his apostolic calling.

48. Karen Katrina Olsen Mortensen, *Life Story*; Brigham Young Jr., diaries, March 13, 1883.

49. Mortensen, *Life Story*.

50. Nielson, *Journal*, 1:322.

51. Young Jr., diaries, March 15, 1883; Christensen, Minutes of the Little Colorado Stake, March 17, 1883.

52. Christensen, Minutes of the Little Colorado Stake, March 17, 1883.

53. John Bushman, *John Bushman Journal Abbreviated*, 19.

to Joseph City for a meeting. "President Smith gave good counsel to not destroy the timber near the settlements & not kill the game only when their circumstances required."[54]

Smith and Alice Ann received a letter from Woodruff dated March 23 in which he expressed his sympathy at the death of little Wilford. Woodruff wrote that he also had a son named Wilford who had almost died after drinking lye when he was a child and who still struggled with choking at age forty-three. He consoled the Smiths with these words: "Truly the loss of children in that way is painful but there is one consolation in the matter— you will have him again in the morning of the first resurrection in your family organization, of the same age and size that you laid him away." [55] Woodruff closed with an expression of love and comfort. Almost a month after the death of little Wilford, Mary wrote to her father in Savoia and asked him to come and get her. Perhaps the circumstances of the tragedy were too painful for her to bear. Her father did not come immediately, but instead consulted Apostle Young Jr.[56] When her father did not respond, Mary loaded her two young sons into her husband's light wagon and left on a nearly two-week journey to where her father lived in New Mexico.

Later in the spring of 1883, Bishop Levi Savage contemplated a withdrawal from the United Order Company at Sunset. He noted that Sunset's soil was losing production. With only twelve families remaining, they had all agreed (Smith included) to leave Sunset for the mountains where crops grew without irrigation. Their intention was to keep the United Order intact, and the visiting apostles Grant and Young concurred. However, Savage stated that if President Smith counseled him to remain with the United Order, he would do so, but Smith did not. Thus, Savage gave notice on May 22 that he wished to withdraw and left five days later.[57]

About two weeks after Savage left, calamity struck again. The Little Colorado River claimed the life of another child of Smith and Alice Ann: eight-year-old George Albert. Alice Ann wrote: "Dear little George A. was drowned while herding sheep about 4 miles from home. He left us cheerful & happy on Sunday afternoon. We little thought when we watched him go & he looked up and smiled at us that we would not see him again alive."[58] Alice Ann could not be consoled and mourned unceasingly.

54. John Bushman, *Diaries*, April 1, 1883.
55. Wilford Woodruff, letter to Lot Smith, March 23, 1883.
56. Young Jr., diaries, April 8, 1883.
57. Bushman, *Diaries*, May 27, 1883.
58. Alice Ann Richards Smith, journal extracts, 7.

Though a few residents still maintained the fort at Sunset, most of the Order moved to the Mormon Dairy to make a living. During the cold winter months, Smith's family and most of the United Order personnel returned to live at Sunset Fort. Smith carried on his responsibilities as president of the Little Colorado Stake. When thirteen Mormon families (some from Sunset) moved to Adams Valley, Smith scheduled a stake quarterly conference on August 25, 1883, at the little mountain community.[59] There, he organized the Adams Valley membership into a ward with Joe H. James as bishop and changed the name to Wilford in honor of Woodruff. The minutes report: "President Lot Smith said . . . the settlement at Sunset had been nearly vacated this season, but what remained held their meetings, and a good feeling prevailed."[60]

That fall, Alice Ann and her children drove a span of mules on a four-week journey to Utah to visit her folks, arriving in Farmington in late October.[61] Since both Alice Ann and Mary had left him, perhaps Smith reflected on a letter Woodruff had written to him on January 31, 1882. Woodruff praised Smith's wives, who had always been true to him and never found fault with him. He counseled, "And the woman righteously demands at your hands love, affection and kind treatment, and it is not a weakness in a good man to manifest these principles to his wives & children. . . . [O]ur wives have a great deal of sorrow, affliction, care and labor to pass through in raising a family of children . . . and we should help bear their burdens." [62]

Smith had suffered many personal afflictions—his painful leg injury, the deaths of two children, and the departure of two wives. Most of the residents of Sunset had withdrawn from the United Order and Smith turned his focus to raising stock. He would face more stressful times ahead in defending his range rights and avoiding arrest.

---

59. The settlement of Adamsville was named for Jerome J. Adams who, with his son-in-law Charles Edmund Richardson, discovered and settled the site.

60. Christensen, Minutes of the Little Colorado Stake, August 25, 1883.

61. Smith, *Living Words*, 16; Bushman, *Diaries*, October 30, 1883.

62. Woodruff, letter to Lot Smith, January 31, 1882.

CHAPTER 13

A Wanted Man

In the spring of 1884, stake presidents and bishops were requested to attend the April General Conference of the Church in Salt Lake City. Mary had returned, and Smith hoped to also bring Alice Ann back with him to Arizona. Lot Smith, Brigham Young Jr., Lorenzo H. Hatch, and others rode the train to Salt Lake City. When Smith asked Alice Ann to return with him to Sunset, she sought advice from Franklin D. Richards, her father figure. Richards advised her, "Lot is a special spirit. One day you will be very proud and honored to be connected with him."[1] Alice Ann returned to Arizona on the train with Smith and arrived on May 21. She said Sunset was partially deserted and the polygamy raids had begun.[2] The Edmunds Act had passed in February 1882.[3] Anyone who had a living husband or wife and then married another was guilty of polygamy and could be sentenced to a five hundred dollar fine and five years in prison.

According to one family legend, in order to evade the officers, Smith and Alice Ann once exchanged clothes: she put on his coat, and he donned a skirt. Then the officers followed her instead of him. Another story tells of the sheriff and his deputy thinking they had captured Lot Smith. When the officers announced he was under arrest, Smith offered them a welcome meal before the long ride back. As they all came into the house, Smith gave a nod to his son who went out and saddled his horse. He picked up the wash basin and announced that he was going to wash his hands. Stepping out the back door, he set down the wash basin, jumped into the saddle, and galloped away.[4]

By August 1884, it was obvious that Sunset's United Order was finished, and Smith called together the remaining Saints to disband.[5] He

1. Eva Rice Hamson Howell, letter to Carmen R. Smith, April 13, 1969; James L. Kimball from his father LeRoy Kimball, interview by Carmen R. Smith, n.d.

2. Alice Ann Richards Smith, *Living Words of Alice Ann Richards Smith, Selected Writings of a Great Lady*, 16.

3. For further reading, see Sarah Barringer Gordon, *The Mormon Question: Polygamy and Constitutional Conflict in Nineteenth-Century America*.

4. Alden B. Smith II, interview by Carmen R. Smith, January 9, 1983; Sullivan C. Richardson, *Remembrances of Lot Smith*, 5; Karl Smith, interview by Omer J. and Carmen R. Smith, October 3, 1975.

5. Israel Call, *A Life Sketch of Israel Call by His Own Dictation*.

told them, "Take what you want and go."[6] Some members took considerably more than they had turned in. True to his commitment, Smith stayed when everyone else left. Sunset's fort was deserted except for his own families. He had successfully established and maintained the United Order on the Little Colorado for eight years. One reminiscence stated: "While Lot was not a success in leading by kindness, gentleness, long suffering, and persuasion, he did stand as a monument of determination when men of his caliber were sorely needed to keep those colonies there."[7] At Woodruff the month following the dissolution of the United Order, President Smith said, "I have always blessed this country. It has been cursed enough by others."[8]

The threat of arrest for polygamous men always loomed. However, as a rancher, Smith had additional concerns. Stockmen on the western frontier had to defend their range rights. They either submitted to the loss of their stock by theft or they battled the rustlers. Smith chose to contest the lawbreakers and acquired a solid reputation as a dangerous gunman who was never seen without a gun. According to Earle Forrest:

> Lot Smith's reputation as a killer is second to none in all Arizona, even to this day [1935], and yet when the matter is sifted down, it is impossible to find the name of one man whom he is supposed to have slain. For years this reputation was the talk of the range, but as a matter of history, he never killed. In fact, his record shows that he had a high respect for human life.[9]

Not all of the residents in the Mormon Lake area welcomed the Mormons. A group of ten or twelve cattlemen were envious of the choice Mormon ranch holdings around Mormon Lake. They gathered to consult how to rid the area of Lot Smith and the Mormons. They pitched a good-sized tent out in the forest for the meeting. Since it was raining and chilly, they had the flaps down. In the midst of their discussion, they heard the approach of a horse, and one man raised the flap to peer out. He exclaimed, "Oh my Lord! Here is Lot Smith now!" All the men bolted to the back of the tent to escape. They quickly slit an opening in the back with a knife and dashed into the timber. Smith dismounted his horse, walked to the

---

6. Kate B. Carter, "United Order by Leonora S. Rogers," *Our Pioneer Heritage*, 15:360–61.

7. Gary Tietjen, letter to Carmen R. Smith, August 1976.

8. *Journal of Jesse Nathaniel Smith*, 295.

9. Earle R. Forrest, "Riding for the Old CO Bar," *Journal of Arizona History*, 3; See also Earle R. Forrest, "Fort Rickerson, Greatest Old-Time Cattle Ranch."

tent, and raised the flap just in time to see the last man disappear out the back into the rain. He had heard of the meeting and wanted to attend.[10]

Almost from the beginning of his Arizona residency, the greatest threat to Smith's peaceful existence came from the Daggs family.[11] The Daggs Brothers—the largest sheep owners in Arizona by 1887—were the chief contenders for the superior ranges held by the Mormons. Their large flock of Merino sheep had been in northern Arizona only a short time before friction developed with the Mormon settlers—Smith, in particular. Other northern Arizona stockmen had ranges that were more or less defined, but the Daggs herded their sheep where they pleased.[12] When the Daggs began to herd sheep at Pine Breaks, the Order moved its entire sheep herd far away from the Daggs's sheep to the opposite (west) side of Pleasant Valley.[13] Since the Daggs raised only sheep, Smith left the United Order cattle on the Pine Breaks range. As the Daggs brothers moved their sheep to Chaves Pass, they took one look at what Smith had considered the ideal sheep camp with the finest grazing country in Arizona and immediately coveted it. The Daggs Brothers did not cease their efforts to force Smith off the choice range. Shortly after Smith returned to northern Arizona from the April 1884 General Conference, he read an item in the *Arizona Champion* insinuating that Smith's employees were responsible for the death of a man.[14] Smith did not let this blatant attempt to turn public opinion against himself and the Mormons pass. He made a personal call upon the "men in the vicinity" before he wrote to the editor on July 14. Under the heading "A Correction Demanded," his letter was published on the front page of the *Arizona Champion*:

> In your paper of May 31st I find an article headed "Found Dead," in which you charge me or my employees of being the cause of the death of Elmont W. Parker. I now ask a retraction of the charge or an investigation of the matter.
>
> You say at first it was supposed he was killed by lightning, but further investigation since burial leads his friends to believe he met with foul play. Now it is an easy matter to make a charge, but the proof is what I demand.

---

10. Charlie Ashurst to Nephi Lot Smith, interview by Omer J. Smith and Carmen R. Smith, June 1, 1972.

11. Hubert H. Bancroft, "Arizona Dictations."

12. George H. Tinker, *A Land of Sunshine, Flagstaff and its Surroundings*, 19.

13. Pine Breaks, located in Sec 2 T18N R 10E, could also qualify as the "Gulch," referred to in various diaries.

14. *Arizona Champion*, May 31, 1884, 2.

You say Parker had located on a range which had been contended for by the Mormons a long time, which had caused considerable trouble. Now this is news to me. I located the ranch called Duck's Nest years before Parker came into the country and have never been informed by him that he made any claim to it.

You say it is supposed that Parker, after being informed of the attempt to set fire to the building, went over to investigate the matter, and being taken unawares, was killed. Not a close investigation, truly. Please inform your readers that Duck's Nest and Jaycox's Tanks are ten or twelve miles apart.

You call on the Coroner to investigate. So do I. So I have been informed, a hole was dug and his body dumped in without any investigation.

You say that the men in the vicinity are strongly of the opinion that the lightning story was bosh. Please inform me who the men are in the vicinity who think the lightning story all bosh. Daggs Bros. is the only ranch within miles of the place where Parker was found dead, and Daggs Bros. and Clark inform me that there is not the slightest doubt but what Parker was killed by lightning.

By giving this a place in your paper, you will oblige
Lot Smith[15]

Editor George H. Tinker printed an addendum:

We cheerfully give the above a place in our columns, hoping to set matters right. The coroner ought, even now, make an investigation, and if there are no signs of foul play on the body, it would forever set at rest any doubts on the question. Lot Smith is one of the most esteemed citizens of Yavapai County, and we never intended to cast any reflection upon his good name. He, too, wants an investigation into the cause of Parker's death. –Ed.[16]

Despite Smith's successful rebuttal, harassment from the Daggs continued, but they were not the only threats to his range. The Aztec Land and Cattle Company (locally named "Hash Knife," derived from their brand) had brought in forty thousand head of Texas cattle in 1885 with headquarters in Holbrook. When the Hash Knife outfit came to Arizona, they "were very hostile at first. They kept sending notices to the Sunset authorities to abandon certain ranges and watering places, but Lot Smith paid no attention to their threats."[17] As was typical of the early West, some of the Hash Knife cowboys and other latecomers started their own herds from cattle they simply took from neighbors. Cattle rustling became such a problem in northern Arizona that twenty-seven cattlemen

---

15. *Arizona Champion*, August 2, 1884, 1.
16. *Arizona Champion*, August 2, 1884, 1.
17. Asahel Burk, "Biographical Sketch of Hubert Rosell Burk and Family," 44.

(including Smith) formed the Mogollon Livestock Protective Association and offered a five-hundred-dollar reward for anyone who was convicted of illegally taking any stock of the association's members.[18] Despite widespread lawlessness, Smith carried on his stock business successfully. The son of Bill Ashurst, Edward, told that Smith always came to the defense of Bill against gunmen of the Hash Knife ranchers, the Daggs brothers, and cattle thieves. Once, the Daggs brothers sent men to ambush the Ashurst cabin and kill Ashurst. When Ashurst was warned of the planned attack, he sent for Smith. That night, the two men hid in the boulders a short distance from the cabin to watch the road from Flagstaff. According to oral account, when the hired killers rode up to the spot, Lot and Bill Ashurst stepped out from the rocks with cocked guns and required the gunmen to unsaddle their horses and turn them loose."[19] The would-be-killers no doubt grumbled as they stumbled in the darkness down the rough mountain carrying their saddles.[20]

The expansion of the railroad altered the environment of northern Arizona. The Atlantic & Pacific (later Santa Fe) Railroad had entered northern Arizona on July 21, 1881. The railroad spur built in 1886 and 1887 from Flagstaff to Mormon Lake offered easy access to the Mormon Lake resort, and scores of people flocked to the area. Prior to the construction of the railroad spur, the forty miles of primitive road from Flagstaff to Mormon Lake had offered Smith and other polygamous men refuge from arrest by the U.S. Marshals. As his safety at the ranch became more precarious, Smith no longer slept in his bed in the cabin. He climbed the steep bluff on the west side of the lake and slept amid the dry leaves under a thick stand of scrub oak and, according to one account, "in the daytime he took his chances with the rest of the men."[21]

A resident of Mormon Lake, Asahel Burk, told that soon after the railroad spur entered Pleasant Valley, two strangers arrived on horseback at the lake. It was rumored that they were US Marshals who sought the arrest of Smith. When Smith saw them, he galloped up to them and stated that he understood that they were after Lot Smith. The men denied it. "Well, that's strange," said Smith, "I am informed that you have authority from the government and are here to take Lot Smith! I'm Lot Smith! Now's your chance." The men rejected the claim again and the threesome rode

18. *Arizona Champion*, February 21, 1885, 4.
19. Edward B. Ashurst, audio recording, July 11–12, 1969.
20. Ashurst, audio recording.
21. Burk, "Biographical Sketch," 46.

on in friendly chitchat until Smith bid them goodbye and rode off. When Smith was forced to leave Mormon Lake due to threats of arrest, he left the ranch to be managed by his sons. Whenever he visited the Mormon Lake ranch again, it was only with the greatest caution.

Apache County became a hot seat of corrupt politics that threatened the Mormon colonists. As far back as the fall of 1879, "[a] number of office seekers came electioneering and offered President Lot Smith considerable money for his influence, but he said his people had never taken bribes and he was too old to commence."[22] The five thousand Mormons who had settled in Apache County comprised a majority, usually voted as a bloc, and could swing any election. A group of non-Mormon political leaders called the St. Johns Ring proposed to the Mormons in September 1880 that if they voted to retain the county seat in St. Johns in the coming election, they would divide the political offices with the Mormons.[23] Among other offices, Smith was chosen as a candidate for the House of Representatives. Though nominated, none of the Saints campaigned for office. The St. Johns Ring reneged. The county seat remained in St. Johns, but no Mormons were elected to office.[24] The political tension in Apache County against the Mormons deepened. The Ring attempted to drive the Mormons out of the county and started to prosecute polygamists. During this time of tumult, Smith spoke at a quarterly conference held at Taylor on March 8, 1884, where he admonished the Saints to maintain their commitment, saying, "We should rejoice when the wicked ridicule us for keeping the commandments of God."[25]

Apostles Francis M. Lyman and Brigham Young Jr. visited Arizona to assess and try to improve the relationship between the Mormons and the territorial government of Arizona. After the Little Colorado Stake Conference, Lyman, Young Jr., and Smith boarded the train at Winslow to call on Territorial Governor Frederick A. Tritle at Prescott, the territorial capitol. The conciliatory efforts of the Mormons were in vain. The leaders and prominent men of the Church continued to be singled out for prosecution, and Smith was among those targeted.

---

22. Martin Walderfen Mills, journal, 15; *Journal of Frihoff Godfrey Nielson*, vol. 1, 145.

23. Smith, *Journal*, 248.

24. Nielson, *Journal*, 1:237; Wilford Woodruff, letter to Lot Smith, December 14, 1880.

25. Smith, *Journal*, 285.

The reminiscence account of Sunset resident Lauritz Mortensen tells of a cool December day in 1884 when a wary Smith went out to greet two men who had ridden into the enclosure of the fort. Smith offered the men a drink from the well.

"'Is this Lot Smith?' one of the men asked. Smith had red whiskers that came down on his chest [and] always carried a gun, even to meetings. 'Yes,' he nodded. 'Well, we have come to take you . . .' the officer began, but stopped as he stared at the black hole in the muzzle of a pistol drawn by Smith. 'Go ahead and take me,' said Smith."[26] The officers from the Apache County seat may have taken a quick breath, but they did not take Smith or his dare. Smith had foiled arrest for the moment. Yet the warrant they carried plagued him the rest of his life.

Smith strode to the council room near the center of the fort and wrote a short note to President Jesse N. Smith, who was also a polygamist. He urged a hasty departure and offered to furnish supplies and conveyance to Utah.[27] It looked as if the federal officers planned to arrest all violators simultaneously to prevent any escape. Four other men, on the advice of Lot Smith, also decided to flee to Utah to avoid arrest.[28] On December 6, Jesse N. Smith, Eastern Arizona Stake president; Lorenzo H. Hatch, stake patriarch; Joseph Fish, stake clerk; and Henry Standifird headed for Sunset. With a wagon and team of horses, John L. Bushman conveyed the four men from Joseph City to Sunset, where they arrived the next evening.[29] That evening, Smith reorganized his counselors in the Little Colorado Stake Presidency. His first counselor, William C. Allen, had been absent for an extended time, so second counselor, John L. Bushman, was advanced to first counselor. Thomas W. Brookbank was then ordained a High Priest and set apart as second counselor in the stake presidency.[30]

Lot Smith then tackled the logistics of a journey to Utah. In the fort was an old carriage or light wagon that Lot could hurriedly repair. Then, if Bushman could be convinced to join the group with his team and wagon, they could all go, although they would be crowded. Jesse helped Lot persuade Bushman to join the flight. With a lookout posted, Lot repaired

26. Lauritz F. Mortensen, *Life Sketch*, 1–2.

27. Smith, *Journal*, 296.

28. John H. Krenkel, ed., *The Life & Times of Joseph Fish, Mormon Pioneer*, 259.

29. Lorenzo H. Hatch, *Lorenzo Hill Hatch Journal, Copied from original Journals by Ruth Savage*, 145; John L. Bushman, *Diaries*, December 7, 1884.

30. Christian Christensen, Minutes of the Little Colorado Stake, December 7, 1884.

the old carriage. The others assembled and packed bedrolls and provisions for man and beast into Bushman's wagon. By ten o'clock in the morning, all was ready for a speedy departure. The group quickly left the fort and headed north over the barren landscape.

The journey was bone-chilling; the men often trudged in the mud and snow to keep warm and to lighten the load for the teams. Not the least of their trials, two of the men had to sleep under the wagons on muddy or snow-covered ground. Bushman and Fish were allotted the less desirable sleeping quarters because they were "the youngest."[31] The other four slept two apiece in the wagons. Despite the discomfort and constant watch for federal officers, they were a jolly crowd. They sat around the evening campfires and related entertaining experiences.[32] To pass the long hours of the drive, Lot turned to his old friend Standifird, an admirer from the Civil War expedition, and "joked him very hard, always calling him Chilblain Henry."[33] The company offered prayers regularly at night, in the morning, and at mealtime the entire journey.[34] It was Lot's turn to pray when they camped for a meal by the cliffs either at Willow Springs or House Rock Springs. As he finished praying, Lot looked up to see men whom he feared could be federal officers coming on the road. As he stared at the approaching horsemen, he intoned a postscript to his prayer: "And, oh, Lord, spare thy pure eyes the sight of the blood and guts of those sunnzabiches scattered over these canyon walls; cause them to take the other fork."[35] The men did take the turn at the fork, sparing bloodshed.

As they traveled from Willow Springs, the cold increased. North of Limestone Tanks they were forced to camp in snow eight inches deep. There was no wood to make a fire, so they crawled into bed to try to keep warm. Hatch wrote: "Some serious thoughts passed through our minds as to our persecutions and the cause thereof. But the voice of the good spirit said, 'Fear not, the Kingdom is yours.'"[36] The snow decreased as they neared Lee's Ferry. As they descended to the river in the shelter of the cliffs, the men found the climate comparatively pleasant.

---

31. Krenkel, *Joseph Fish*, 260.

32. Bushman, *Diary,* December 10, 12, 1884.

33. Krenkel, *Joseph Fish*, 262.

34. Krenkel, 260.

35. Charles S. Peterson, "'A Mighty Man was Brother Lot': A Portrait of Lot Smith—Mormon Frontiersman," 411.

36. Hatch, *Journal,* 146.

The Little Colorado men crossed the river about dark and discovered six men who were camped at the ferry. The six arriving polygamists immediately assumed to be six non-Mormon travelers. To maintain their anonymity, they used fake names as follows: Lot as John Brown, Jesse as George Washington Jones, Fish as Mr. Johnson, Hatch as Mr. Hill (his middle name), Standifird as Mr. Henry (his middle name), Bushman as Mr. Lewis (his middle name).[37] The six Mormon men remained at the ferry the next day and enjoyed the warmer climate and good food. C. L. Christensen, who had been at Sunset, was temporarily assisting at the ferry. Christensen's diary that day recorded: "Bro. L[ot] S[mith] gave me one pear shoes. . . . Until this time I had Suffered very much with Cold Wet feet my Shoes being very old[.] [T]hem Shoes was thankfully Received."[38]

The men left the ferry and traveled the road that hugged the north side of the valley along the Vermillion Cliffs, passed the Pools, and turned north up House Rock Valley. They met Henry M. Tanner, who joined the party. He had unsuccessfully tried to cross the Buckskin Mountains on horseback. The group started over the Buckskins where the snow piled up in front of the dragging axles and quickly drained the strength of the teams. To relieve them, all but the drivers got out of the wagons and waded in the snow nearly all day.[39] The teams took turns breaking trail and, at one point, the men dug through a huge drift of snow in a hollow. When they topped the mountain, they met four wagons from St. Johns that had broken the trail ahead. They learned that three St. Johns polygamists had been sentenced in Prescott on December 5 to three years and fined five hundred dollars each.[40] The fleeing men knew they had barely escaped the same fate. They drove toward Kanab through mud and snow under a deluge of rain and sleet. Before they reached Upper Kanab, Lot's wagon broke. They repaired the damage and continued to toil through snow over the divide.[41]

The two Smiths stopped to rest in Hillsdale, where Jesse had relatives. In Hillsdale, a horse that belonged to George D. Wilson caught Lot's eye. Wilson was a former member of Lot's Company E of the Mormon Battalion and was as hard-headed a Yankee bargainer as Lot himself. The two horse-lovers bickered, and Wilson finally named his price. Smith said it was too high and left but then came back. Wilson raised the price ten

---

37. Bushman, *Diary*, December 15, 1884.
38. Christian L. Christensen, *Journal*, 63.
39. Krenkel, *Joseph Fish*, 261.
40. Krenkel, 261.
41. Krenkel, 262.

dollars, and Smith again said it was too much. When he came back the third time, Wilson raised the price another ten dollars. Smith didn't leave that time until he had bought the horse.[42]

Lot and Jesse arrived in Panguitch about 11:00 a.m. on Christmas Eve. They attended an evening meeting and addressed the assembled congregation about the persecution in Arizona.[43] Lot and Stake President James Henrie had been old acquaintances in Utah—Lot in Farmington and Henrie ten miles away in Bountiful. Fish reported that the two men had many jokes to tell on each other in their speeches that evening.[44]

At Panguitch, Fish left the group and the five others continued on to Richfield, where they all spoke in a meeting on the 29th. Lot's friend A. K. Thurber entertained the group. Lot had known him in the Utah Legislature, and Thurber was now the acting stake president in the Sevier Stake.[45] At Sandy, Lot, Jesse, and Hatch boarded the northbound Utah Southern railroad. Bushman and Standifird continued to drive the teams. Hatch got off in Provo, and the train arrived in Salt Lake City at 7:00 on January 1, 1885.[46] The two Arizona stake presidents, Smith and Smith, detrained and walked to the Gardo House, the home of President John Taylor. Brigham Young Jr. and Taylor's first counselor, George Q. Cannon, had arrived earlier to discuss with Taylor the train trip he had planned to arrange the purchase of Mexican land as a refuge for polygamous Church men. The plans were held in secrecy because of arrest threats. Lot and Jesse were invited to join the group.[47]

Three days after they arrived in Salt Lake City, Lot and Jesse boarded Railway Superintendent James Sharp's luxuriously furnished private railway car early in the morning. Others who assembled in the car included President John Taylor; Taylor's counselor, Joseph F. Smith; three apostles: Brigham Young Jr., Moses Thatcher, and Francis M. Lyman; and others.[48] The train headed for Denver, Colorado, as the leaders discussed find-

---

42. Philip Smith, *Lot Smith*, 10–11.

43. Bushman, *Diary*, December 24, 1884.

44. Krenkel, *Joseph Fish*, 262.

45. In about 1886 Albert King Thurber sent Smith a leather-bound copy of *The Compiled Laws of the Territory of Arizona, 1864–1871* with Smith's name stamped in gold on the backbone. Inside Smith wrote: "Lot Smith, presented by his friend A. K. Thurber."

46. Smith, *Journal*, 298.

47. Smith, 299.

48. Smith, 299.

ing a place of refuge. From Denver, the rail car rolled to Pueblo, then to Albuquerque, New Mexico, where the Atlantic & Pacific took them westward toward the Little Colorado settlements. The train was twice delayed on this leg of the journey. At Sanders, a freight train smashup had demolished four freight cars, which forced a wait of seven hours.[49] The other delay was shorter. After they had waited for some time, Lot and Jesse went forward to ascertain the cause. According to a descendent of Jesse Smith, the men found the engineer and several trainmen standing around looking at a cow that had walked out on the trestle and whose legs now dangled beneath the bridge. Lot walked out on the trestle, grabbed the cow by the tail, jerked it out of the railroad ties, and tossed it off into the streambed below. Impressed, the engineer wanted to know Lot's identity. To have betrayed his identity might have led to his arrest as well as that of his companions and Church leaders. Lot, however, spoke only the truth. He replied, "My name is Smith. I came from the East, and I am travelling for my health."[50]

The group had expected to arrive in Joseph City on January 7 at 2:00 p.m., but with the delays, they did not arrive until 11:00 p.m. The president and apostles toured some of the Little Colorado communities. Then the entire party reunited at Holbrook on the 11th and rode east on the passenger train. On the 14th, some of the group, including Lot, took the Sonora railroad and crossed into Mexico at Nogales. At 2:00 a.m. the next morning, Lot, Jesse, James H. Martineau, and Meliton G. Trejo, led by Apostle Thatcher, got off the train at Magdalena. For two or three days, the five men, with Trejo as interpreter, made inquiries in town about possible sites to purchase. On January 18, the group returned to St. David. While there, President Taylor met with his counselor, six apostles, and three of the four Arizona stake presidents to discuss the urgent need of refuge.[51] St. Joseph's stake president, Christopher Layton, presented a flattering report of Casas Grandes in Mexico where he had left Maricopa's stake president Alexander F. Macdonald. Taylor then appointed the four Arizona stake presidents, Layton, Macdonald, and the two Smiths, to a committee led by Thatcher to purchase lands for the Latter-day Saints in Mexico.[52] Then he directed

---

49. Smith, 299.

50. Son of "Pen" Smith, interview by Carmen R. Smith.

51. James H. McClintock, *Mormon Settlement in Arizona: A Record of Peaceful Conquest of the Desert*, 237.

52. Smith, *Journal*, 303.

Lot and Jesse to first warn the polygamous men of northern Arizona to immediately seek refuge with others already in Chihuahua, Mexico.

The two President Smiths embarked on the journey back to the Little Colorado. Since the roads would be blocked with snow, the two decided to ride on horseback. On January 20, they joined Albert Martineau, William B. Maxwell, and George C. "Parson" Williams to make a five-man party. In the San Simon Valley, the group followed a direct route northward along the Arizona-New Mexico line, a trip of approximately three hundred miles from St. David to Snowflake. They arrived at Luna Valley and Williams's ranch.[53] At that time, Luna Valley was one of the wildest places in the West.[54] J. David Lee, a rancher of the area, told of an incident that occurred about January 28. Lee was the only Mormon in a group of Luna Valley ranchers who were gathered around their early morning campfire for breakfast. As they looked south through the pine forest, the cattlemen saw Lot and his companions push their horses up The Blue toward their camp. Young Bill Jackson, known for his practical jokes, said to the group, "That's likely some Mormon polygamists running from the federal officers. Invite them to stay to breakfast, and we'll have some fun." Lot, at ease with cowmen, accepted the invitation. The approximately twenty men gathered around the warmth of the fire to visit in friendly fashion and eat breakfast. In the lull following the meal, the time for fun arrived. Jackson placed himself directly opposite Lot and cleared his throat for attention. "Mr. Smith," Jackson announced, "I'm a federal officer." No sooner had the words left his mouth than Jackson was staring into the muzzle of Lot's .45. "Mister," Lot declared, "I don't know who you are, but if you're a federal officer there's room in this camp for only one of us, and it's your move." Jackson quickly confessed that it was all a big joke.[55]

Lot and Jesse arrived at Snowflake on January 31. By February 5, Lot was ready to begin the journey to Mexico with his wife Diantha and their children. Twenty wagons with men, women, and children headed south toward Chihuahua, Mexico.[56] Bishop John Hunt from Snowflake caught up with the Mexico-bound group at Luna Valley on Sunday, February 15, with a telegram from Apostle Thatcher. The message, dated February 12 in

---

53. Smith, *Journal*, 303–304.

54. Evans Coleman, "Nesters, Rustlers, and Outlaws," 17.

55. J. David Lee to James M. Smith, interview by Omer J. Smith and Carmen R. Smith.

56. Nephi Lot Smith, interview by Omer J. Smith and Carmen R. Smith, June 28, 1974.

San Francisco, asked Lot and Jesse to meet him either in St. David or on the Gila on the 22nd or earlier. Jesse wrote to Thatcher that they hoped to reach Smithville on the Gila on the 21st.[57] Lot, Jesse, and Williams hurried onward in Lot's carriage with James's team and Hiram Clark as driver. The men made good time. On February 18, they entered the Gila Valley where they passed the Hispanic town of Solomonville, the gentile town of Safford, and continued down the valley by the recently established Latter-day Saint settlements on the south side of the Gila River—Layton, Thatcher, and Central. They arrived at Smithville (later renamed Pima) to be entertained by Bishop John Taylor. When no word came from the apostle after four days, the four men continued on into Mexico.

Smith had vowed to never spend time in prison for polygamy. So far, Smith had successfully avoided arrest. The Sunset United Order had been settled and disbanded and most of the settlers had established themselves elsewhere. However, during Smith's stay in Mexico, the distressing resettlement of the Order would begin.

---

57. Smith, *Journal*, 305.

CHAPTER 14

Resettlement of United Order

In the afternoon of March 4, 1885, Lot, Jesse, and Williams reached Corralitos, the seat of a large mining and cattle company. At an old grist mill about a mile downriver, they found a small group of Latter-day Saints planting crops on land rented from the Corralitos Company.[1] Apostle Thatcher immediately met with both Smiths and Macdonald, the stake presidents who were authorized to purchase land. With the approach of spring, the necessity to begin plowing and planting was urgent. Lot, Thatcher, and Macdonald drove to El Paso in Lot's carriage to try to buy the Garcia Ranch above and close to La Ascensión but were unsuccessful.[2]

The Latter-day Saints soon began to congregate in a camp about ninety miles from the US border on the bank of the Casas Grandes River three miles north of La Ascensión.[3] The Mexicans in surrounding towns became suspicious as more Mormons arrived. The acting governor of Chihuahua wrote a letter that asked for an explanation of the mass immigration. The letter was delivered to Lot Smith on April 4 by a delegation headed by La Ascensión's president. According to historian Annie R. Johnson, "Lot Smith and others accompanied the delegation back to the office at La Ascensión to explain that they were merely seeking to raise a crop until they could buy land upon which to settle."[4]

Since the Saints' camp was only temporary until land could be purchased, comfort and convenience received little consideration. The families lived in dugouts, tents, and wagon boxes.[5] In the summer, the dugouts—with no doors or windows, dirt floors, and loose board roofs—offered no protection against heat or flies. Snakes hid in the dugouts to escape the temperature extremes. In winter, the dugouts could not be kept warm. In early spring, the winds turned the dugouts into dust holes.[6] In the grueling conditions, leaders did not always concur on matters, and conflicts arose. Smith was not exempt. On April 7, 1885,

---

1. *Journal of Jesse Nathaniel Smith*, 306–7.
2. Smith, *Journal*, 307.
3. Thomas Cottam Romney, *Life History of Miles P. Romney*, 181.
4. Annie R. Johnson, *Heartbeats of Colonia Diaz*, 40.
5. Levi Mathers Savage, *Family History Journal, 1876–1935*, 40.
6. Sullivan C. Richardson, *Compilation*, 68.

Apostle George Teasdale appointed Sixtus E. Johnson and Samuel H. Rogers to investigate a dispute between two strong-minded men: Lot Smith and Alexander Macdonald.[7]

Though Lot Smith was strong-willed, he was also sympathetic and charitable. Daughters of the Utah Pioneers wrote: "With his rough exterior he was thought by many to be a tyrant . . . but with all his rough ways he had a heart within him that beat with human sympathy and an appeal to him for help was never made in vain."[8] Miles P. Romney remembered the humble circumstances of his first home in Mexico and Smith's compassion. He had come by rail partway with his wife and three children and had not brought a full supply of camping equipment. On April 11, he and his family joined Smith in the Camp of the Saints. For shelter, Romney planted four poles in the ground, placed a wagon box and brush to form two sides of the living quarters, and sewed burlap sacks together to form the other two sides. Having no decent shoes, Romney had strapped sandals to his feet with strands of rawhide. Smith provided Romney with a wagon cover and a pair of boots. He said, "Use these to protect yourselves from the weather."[9] Alma Millet also had cause to be grateful for Smith's bigheartedness. One of Millet's horses died, and Millet was unable to continue to farm his rented ground. When Smith heard of Millet's plight, he sent a boy on a workhorse to replace Millet's animal.[10]

Latter-day Saints were still arriving in Mexico when a crisis developed. Levi M. Savage recorded on Saturday April 11:

> Early this morning Prest. Lot Smith rec[eive]d a letter from A. F. McDonald containing the following language. 'We have just received an order to leave the State in 15 days [on April 15].[11] Some of us must visit the Governor in Chihuahua where we hope to have the order changed.' This has had quite a depressing and discouraging effect upon the camp.[12]

Smith and Edward Noble started for Corralitos that morning to confer with Macdonald and returned that evening.[13] Savage reported a fast and testimony meeting: "Said mtg. held, good spirit. Lot Smith said he was

7. Samuel Hollister Rogers, *Journal (1819–1886)*, April 8, 1885.

8. Helen Mar Miller Camp, "Sketch of the Life of Lot Smith," 3.

9. Thomas Cottam Romney, *Life History of Miles P. Romney*, 181–82.

10. Sullivan C. Richardson, *Remembrances of Lot Smith*, 7–8.

11. Smith, *Journal*, 309.

12. *Levi M. Savage Journal March 1, 1885 to April 10, 1886*, Folio 2:58.

13. Rogers, *Journal*, 272.

not surprised that we had created a little suspicion in the land. His faith was that the Lord would overrule this order for the good of the Saints." [14]

It was probably during the agitation of the expulsion order that a mob of Mexicans came to the Camp of the Saints where Lot Smith was staying, determined to get rid of the Mormons. The incident was told by eyewitness Edward J. Wood. The Mexicans proposed that they would spare the lives of the colonists if any Mormon could ride a particular wild mule that no one had ever ridden. Smith stepped forward to volunteer. The Mexicans scornfully asked if he was going to try to ride the mule. Smith replied, "No, I'm not going to try, I'll ride him." When Smith mounted, the mule tried all his tricks to throw his load. Unable to loosen Smith, the mule streaked across the desert with Smith on its back, tight as a burr with his red beard parted in the breeze. [15]

General Pacheco overruled the Chihuahua governor's Order of Expulsion. The situation calmed, and the Saints continued to try to purchase land. Savage recorded:

> 19 Apr (Sun) Prest. Lot Smith spoke of the necessity of asking a blessing upon everything we did, whether it be poor or good. . . . He felt that there is room for a reformation. Referred to his experience in the United Order. He would go into it again upon his own volition only, and not because somebody else wished to push him in. [16]

Lot Smith's addresses give insights into how he felt about the circumstances of the Saints in Mexico; this is seen in particular in his remarks on July 5, 1885, when he related that "there has never been a time when there was such a concentrated action taken against the Saints. . . . If we know we are right, then we should tenaciously hold to our convictions, but if not, then yield." [17] He was chosen as the orator of the day for the 24th of July celebration. [18]

The Saints gradually acquired some Mexican land, but not enough. Land obtained by the close of 1885 included fifty thousand acres at Colonia Juarez, fifty thousand acres at Colonia Pacheco, and seven thou-

---

14. Savage, *Journal*, Folio 2:62.

15. Sally Smith, "A Choice Memory." Cardston Alberta Temple President Edward J. Wood told the incident to Melissa Packer Smith and daughter Sally Smith in June 1946 in Canada.

16. Savage, *Journal*, Folio 2:69–70.

17. Savage, *Journal*, Folio 4:130.

18. John H. Krenkel, ed., *Life and Times of Joseph Fish, Mormon Pioneer*, 287.

sand acres at Colonia Díaz.[19] A group under the leadership of Lot Smith chose to settle at the site that became Colonia Díaz, which was located three miles north of La Ascención.[20] Among those who moved to the site in July 1885 were Lot Smith, Joseph H. James, Hubert Burk, the Edwin and Charles Whiting families, the C. Edmund and Sullivan Richardson families, John Kartchner, Jesse N. Smith Jr., and Levi M. Savage.[21] All were members of Lot Smith's Little Colorado Stake.

Jesse N. Smith received a letter in August 1885 that gave "a doleful account of the condition of the A.C.M.I."[22] Lot wrote of the circumstances. To try to remedy the Arizona Co-op Store's financial failure, apostle Teasdale called in the co-op president Jesse N. Smith, vice president Lot Smith, and directors G. C. Williams and Joseph H. James. When Teasdale reprimanded Jesse for trying to build a large store while paying a full dividend, Jesse pointed to Lot and the other two men and said that he had done nothing without their advice and consent. Shocked at the statement, Lot wrote, "I sat Stupified for a few moments" before stating that he had no knowledge of the building's construction until after it had commenced. Both Williams and James also testified that Jesse did not have their consent and that they would not have given it. To the regret of both Lot and Jesse, this incident caused a cooling of their friendship.[23]

Apostle Erastus Snow instigated an examination of the settlement of the Sunset United Order. The investigation was to begin with a review of the Sunset United Order records, so Lot set out the next day for Sunset to retrieve them.[24] When Smith arrived in northern Arizona to pick up the United Order books, someone asked how he liked Mexico. He replied, "Too many bellwethers."[25] Smith's pithy observation aptly described the conditions among the Saints in Mexico. In the vernacular of the sheepmen, there were too many leaders in Mexico with nothing worthwhile to do. Smith returned to Mexico with the books on October 14.[26] For a year, former Order members were notified of a new basis of settlement and that

---

19. Thomas F. Peterson, *A. C. Peterson: Citizen of Three Nations,* chap. 7.
20. Johnson, *Heartbeats,* 38.
21. Johnson, 39.
22. Smith, *Journal,* 316.
23. Lot Smith, letter to Wilford Woodruff, March 17, 1890.
24. Smith, *Journal,* 317.
25. Burton Smith, interview by Omer J. Smith and Carmen R. Smith, n.d.
26. Krenkel, *Joseph Fish,* 291; Savage, *Journal,* Folio 6:187.

additional distribution might be expected. Many came forward and only a few refused to submit claims for additional money.

Efforts to purchase suitable Mexican land continued, but without much success. Savage recorded on April 4, 1886: "This eve. Lot Smith who went up to Piedres Verdes with Bro. Snow returned bringing the sad . . . news . . . of their finding that the purchase recently made there does not contain the land they expected and had settled on."[27] Theft of stock was also a problem.[28] Smith's sorrel horse was stolen during the first days of June 1886. His horse (along with two mules stolen from Martin Sanders) was recovered but soon died—apparently poisoned.[29]

During the spring of 1886, one of Smith's seven dairy cows sparked his quick temper. One evening as Smith milked, the cow continually switched Smith with her tail. Smith became annoyed and told his son Hyrum—not quite three years old—to hold the cow's tail. Hyrum tried to clutch the cow's tail as his father instructed, but he could not. When the cow's tail switched him one too many times, Smith's temper flared and he disciplined Hyrum. Diantha was indignant. She knew their little son had not deserved it.[30] She gathered up their three children, Charlotte (four), Hyrum (almost three), and Nephi (one), and drove her team and wagon out of Mexico.[31] Near the end of May 1886, she arrived near Joseph City where her mother was living on a small piece of land managed by Diantha's brother Martin.[32] Diantha had only lived in Joseph City a month when her baby Nephi died.[33] Devastated, Diantha believed that her baby might have died as punishment for leaving her husband.

Back in Mexico, a preliminary investigation of Smith's settlement of the Sunset United Order began in July 1886 by the three apostles Young Jr., Snow, and Teasdale. With some recrimination, some of the former residents of Sunset had signed complaints and felt they were entitled to reimbursement. [34] Smith was shown a letter written to President Taylor stating that Smith had "swindled" some members of about one third of their property. Smith called it "a Damed lie" and felt like resigning as stake

---

27. Savage, *Journal*, Folio 8:281.

28. Johnson, *Heartbeats*, 145.

29. Richardson, *Compilation*, 74.

30. Alberta Craig Rider, interview by Carmen R. Smith.

31. Savage, *Journal*, Folio 2:67.

32. Krenkel, *Joseph Fish, 308*.

33. John Bushman, *Diaries*, June 27, 1886.

34. Brigham Young Jr., *Diaries*, July 9, 1886.

president.[35] As the investigation continued, Young Jr. reported, "Bro. Smith acts and feels like he had lost faith in humanity."[36] A committee was chosen to settle the Sunset affairs: Lot Smith, John Bushman, Hubert R. Burk, Frihoff G. Nielson, and Thomas W. Brookbank. Smith declined, and David K. Udall was chosen in his stead.[37] Smith wrote from La Ascención to President Taylor on July 19, 1886, about the complaints of the Sunset United Order settlement. Smith reported that the Order books showed that members had received from one to three times the capital turned in and also what Smith had received. Although Snow believed that Smith had received "the lion's share" of Sunset's property, Smith wrote Taylor, "If ever I was honest[,] I was with that Company and when I am dead I do not want my children told to the contrary. To congregate a few of a man's enemies, filled with malise, hatred and greed, hear their say and theirs only and make up a man's character from such testimony, I cannot conceive to be Just."[38] This was a trying time for Smith. The committee found that no funds had been misappropriated, and when Snow tried to smooth things over with Smith, Smith threatened to leave the room. Smith later wrote to Woodruff: "I have often laughed to myself since I did not Laugh then & wondered what they would have done if I had have walked away. . . . Would there not have been a noise if the Charge had been proven true."[39]

When Diantha left Mexico in the spring, Smith had no wife with him. That summer, Alice Mary and her five children (the youngest age two) with Julia's eighteen-year-old Hyrum as her teamster left Sunset for Mexico alone in a covered wagon, undaunted by the threat of Geronimo's raids and Apaches on the warpath. Alice Mary told of their arrival: "We reached Diaz the last of July '86 to find the town suffering from Scarlet Fever and to begin a miserable existence in a dugout."[40] Shortly after her arrival, Alice Mary contracted the fever, and Smith tended their toddler, Jesse Nathaniel. Then little Jesse also caught the fever. Only a month after Alice Mary's arrival, Smith was summoned to return to Arizona to help with the Order resettlement. Smith gave the child back to his mother for care when he left for Arizona in August 1886. Sadly, Jesse Nathaniel

---

35. Smith, letter to Wilford Woodruff, March 11, 1890.
36. Young Jr., *Diaries*, July 11, 1886.
37. Young Jr., *Diaries*, July 13, 1886.
38. Lot Smith, letter to John Taylor, July 19, 1886.
39. Smith, letter to Wilford Woodruff, March 11, 1890.
40. Alice Baugh Smith, "Pioneer Personal History," 26:9.

passed away.[41] Alice Mary did not travel out of Mexico until the next spring. Smith's sojourn in Mexico had not changed the fact that a warrant for his arrest on a charge of polygamy was still serviceable. Although Smith remained president of the Little Colorado Stake while in Mexico, when he had left the Little Colorado settlements, Snow installed Joseph H. Richards as *pro tem* president of the stake in April.[42] Because of arrest threats, Smith did not preside over any stake meetings after his return, and he was released December 18, 1887, when the Snowflake Stake was organized, absorbing the Little Colorado Stake.

While Smith traveled out of Mexico, the resettlement of the Sunset United Order began in Arizona.[43] A subcommittee of Bushman, Burk, and Nielson traveled to Sunset on August 15 to list and appraise all the Order property. Smith's wives Alice Ann and Mary were "willing to render all the aid they could."[44] The subcommittee then proceeded to the dairy ranch and began its appraisal there. Smith arrived at Mormon Lake on August 27 in the midst of the assessment. Chairman Bushman wrote:

> [W]e met Bro. Lot Smith at the field. He did not speak when we saluted him. We went west of the field & got some cattle. Bro. Smith camped in the field. We met Bro. Smith there and had a long talk with him. He said he felt slited because we had not waited until he had arrived.[45]

The next morning, Smith called on the committee as they sat to breakfast.[46] Bushman wrote that Smith made a proposition of distribution. However, the subcommittee could not accept the proposal until it was presented to the whole committee. "Bro. L. Smith . . . thought that the property should go to the church. We gave him to understand that we would [still] have to do as our instructions directed, & we would have to list all the property & appraise it."[47] The resettlement committee offered Smith the first option on the Sunset United Order herd of sheep in a September 15, 1886, letter. They also asked Smith for a statement of all expenses that he incurred in taking care of the United Order stock and

---

41. Smith, 26:6.

42. Savage, *Journal*, Folio 5:154, 155; Andrew Jenson, *Encyclopedic History of the Church of Jesus Christ of Latter-day Saints*, 438.

43. Christian Christensen, Dates of Resettlement of the Sunset United Order Meetings, LDS Church History Library.

44. Bushman, *Diaries*, August 15, 1886.

45. Bushman, *Diaries*, August 27, 1886.

46. Frihoff Godfrey Nielson, *Minutes of Frihoff Nielson for the Sunset Committee*.

47. Bushman, *Diaries*, August 28, 1886.

any other expenses in conjunction with the company. All the renegotiating upset Smith. His temper flared, and he wrote Snow a letter which Young Jr. described as "altogether unbrotherly in relation to Sunset U.O. affairs."[48] Smith then tried to make amends, and he wrote a letter to Young Jr. asking forgiveness for all past offenses. Young Jr. wrote in his diary that Smith's "unfortunate situation [was] brot on I think by his ungoverned temper."[49] Smith also attempted to reconcile with others, including Bishop John Hunt of Snowflake who had received wheat from the Sunset United Order during the famine. Smith wrote Hunt from Sunset on October 8, 1886: "I have been told you did not feel well about some of our transactions or deal. I understood when I sent an order to you for wheat and your Family honored it you felt very much agreaved or put out and other little matters. Now if there is a things on earth that needs straightening tell me and I will fix it too your satisfaction." He continued, "I would like to get straight before I leave this earth. I don't want any of my sins following after. . . . I have not knowingly done wrong to any mortal but have willingly [illegible] to think otherwise of fellows."[50]

The challenging task of resettling the Sunset United Order was not Smith's only concern. He still had to maintain his range rights and avoid arrest. Smith drew his gun on a number of men in northern Arizona. He pulled the trigger only once, and that was at the sheep camp at Sunset on the last day of November 1886.[51] The event was recounted by Smith's two sons Lorenzo and Willard, who were present, to their younger brothers and sons. Smith sat at his desk that morning in the office-council house in the fort when Mary's seven-year-old Lorenzo "Ren" burst into the room. Ren and his older brother, Alice Ann's fifteen-year-old Willard, were supposed to be out herding the sheep. Ren told his father that the sheep were mixed. During the last several days, the Daggs brothers' sheep had been herded presumptuously close to the Sunset fort. When the United Order companies of both Brigham City and Sunset were breaking up, the Daggs brothers—as well as other ranchers—hoped that the Mormons' ranges would be up for grabs and tried to take over some of them. Smith and those who claimed the ranges had serious differences.[52]

48. Young Jr., *Diaries*, September 20, 1886.
49. Young Jr., *Diaries*, October 16, 1886.
50. Lot Smith, letter to Bishop J. Hunt, October 8, 1886.
51. Bushman, *Diaries*, November 30, 1886.
52. Richardson, *Remembrances of Lot Smith*, 4.

And now the Daggs' sheep were mixed with Smith's. Smith told his son that it was probably accidental. Ren insisted it was done on purpose. Smith calmly told him that he'd take care of it.[53] If the Daggs were picking a quarrel to set a trap to kill him, Smith would prevent any potential gun battle by leaving his gun in the house. The code of the West condemned shooting an unarmed man. He stepped out of the fort toward the corrals and the three-acre sheep camp. There, Smith saw three men: a cowboy on his horse, a Basque sheepherder, and Mr. William A. Daggs, who was seated in a long-tailed buggy.[54] Daggs, unarmed to avoid his own personal risk, had hired a gun and came to enjoy the kill. Smith, determined not to have a quarrel, tended the dodge gate as they separated the Daggs from the Smith sheep according to their earmarks. As the cutting progressed, one sheep went through whose earmark appeared somewhat damaged. The stranger was alert to the opportunity. "That sheep belongs to Daggs, and he has had his earmark changed."[55] He got off his horse.

"No, that sheep does not belong to Daggs; it belongs to me. And it has not had its earmark changed." Smith shut the dodge gate and climbed down. "There will be no more sheep pass this gate today until they can go through peaceably."[56] The rest of the herd went through with no disagreement. Smith had foiled the plan to pick a quarrel to excuse a killing. However, as he bent over to pick something up, the hired gunman tossed frozen cow dung onto Smith's arm as an insult. As he straightened, Smith's eyes burned with rage.[57] He looked the stranger full in the face, and then, without a word, he turned and strode toward the front gate of the fort.

---

53. Lorenzo Smith to James M. Smith, interview by Omer J. and Carmen R. Smith, December 25, 1964.

54. A long-tailed buggy was used for hauling as well as for transportation. The buggy could carry a heavier load because it had stronger shafts between the front and back wheels. Edmund W. Richardson, interview by Carmen R. Smith, August 21, 1974. Ren, who disagreed with Willard, said Daggs arrived after the sheep had started to be cut.

55. Lorenzo Smith to James M. Smith, interview by Omer J. and Carmen R. Smith, December 25, 1964.

56. Karl Smith, interview, October 2, 1975.

57. Lorenzo "Ren" Smith to his brother James M. Smith: "'Jim, you are in the cow business, aren't you?' Jim agreed and Ren continued, 'This is the best way that I can explain to you the look on father's face. You have seen an old wild bull throwed into a roundup for the first time in his life, and he looks up and sees cowboys sitting all around him on horses. He throws up his head and with that glare in his eyes says, 'Look out, cowboys, I'm coming out.' That's the look

As soon as Smith was out of hearing, young Ren, still at the sheep camp, heard Daggs say in a low voice, "You had better kill him." Daggs's man hesitated. "You had better kill him *now*," Daggs urged. "He's going to the house to get his gun and kill us all."[58]

"F'gawdsake, man," cried the gunman. "I will kill him if he'll turn around so I can shoot him from the front."[59] He called to Smith, "You take another step and I'll shoot you, even if I have to shoot you in the back!"[60]

Smith said, "I'll be back in a few minutes."[61] He passed his son Willard, who had retreated to a spot nearer the front gate of the fort. He knew that his father faced death in the next few minutes and had turned white as a sheet. Smith broke his stride. "What's the matter, boy? Are you scared?"[62] Willard knew better than to confess fear. He quickly denied any fright. As Smith disappeared through the fort's gate, the hired killer looked around for cover and ran behind the 10 ft. x 32 ft. corncrib. When Smith entered his room to get his .45-70 rifle, he encountered opposition from his wives. He brushed them aside and stepped out the door with his rifle at his hip.[63] This time instead of coming out the front gate on the south side of the fort, Smith passed through the small east alley gate and dropped down into the creek bed that ran almost parallel with the side of the fort. Now much less visible, he walked from the north toward the sheep camp corrals. From his lower elevation in the creek bed, Smith could see under the corncrib, which was built on stilts to keep out rats. On the far side, he saw the gunman scurry from one corner of the granary to the other. At each end of the corncrib, Daggs's gunslinger peered cautiously around the corner, his pistol raised to fire. Then, at the same moment the gunman came to one of the corners, Smith rose up in full figure out of the creek bed. Crack! The hired killer yelped and ran from cover with both hands in the air. His little finger dangled by the skin and spurted blood—a sight Smith's son Ren would never forget. One instant of surprise and Smith's ability to shoot from the

---

that was in father's eyes when he raised up.'" Lorenzo Smith to James M. Smith, interview, December 25, 1964.

58. Karl Smith, interview, October 2, 1975.

59. Lorenzo Smith to James M. Smith, interview, December 25, 1964.

60. Willard R. Smith to Nephi L. Smith, interview, June 28, 1974.

61. Karl Smith, interview, October 2, 1975.

62. Willard R. Smith to Nephi L. Smith, interview, June 28, 1974.

63. Lorenzo Smith to James M. Smith, interview, December 25, 1964. Whether Smith carried a short .45-70 rifle or a long .45-70 that day has not been ascertained.

hip had given him the advantage. Smith had not aimed to kill; he had aimed only to shoot the pistol out of the gunman's hand.

The gunman fell whining to the ground and begged for his life. Smith looked at him and said, "You don't need to be afraid. I would not even kick a yellow dog when he is down."[64] Then Smith said, "Go on to the house, and I'll dress your hand." Daggs's man objected; he said he would go to a doctor in Flagstaff. Flagstaff was over sixty miles distant, and the cowboy risked infection if he made the trip before he received attention to his hand. Smith said more firmly, "I said, go on to the house, and I'll dress your hand."[65] The subdued gunman walked with Smith to the fort to Mary's room, where Smith removed the dangling finger with his pocket knife and Mary dressed the hand with bandages and turpentine.[66] The two men walked back to the sheep camp. As Smith passed by the corncrib, he picked up the gunman's pistol and found his bullet lodged in the handle of the pistol.[67]

Smith walked to the buggy where Daggs sat. He tossed the other man's gun into the back of the buggy and faced Daggs. Smith said clearly, "I'll give you ten days to be out of this country with all of your sheepherders and pack animals and anything else that belongs to you. And if any of them are here after ten days, I'll kill you and all your gunmen."[68] He then said, "We need this buggy to take this man to the doctor." Without a word, Daggs got out of the buggy and mounted the cowboy's horse. Smith turned to Willard, who had followed his father and the gunman back to the sheep corrals, and said, "Take this man to Flagstaff and get his hand dressed by the doctor. Keep your eyes open. If it looks like any officers are going to come back, you get in the buggy and beat them back here. This team looks like they could give a pretty good run."[69] Obediently Willard got into the buggy. He did not relish a long, cold drive to Flagstaff with

64. Willard R. Smith to Nephi L. Smith, interview by Carmen R. Smith, June 1, 1977.

65. Lorenzo Smith to James M. Smith, interview by Omer J. and Carmen R. Smith, December 25, 1964.

66. Lorenzo Smith to James M. Smith, interview, December 25, 1964; Gary L. Tietjen, *Encounter with the Frontier*, 32.

67. Karl Smith, interview, October 2, 1975.

68. Lorenzo Smith to James M. Smith, interview, December 25, 1964.

69. Willard Smith and Karl Smith, interview, October 2, 1975.

a gunman who had been hired to kill his father.[70] Daggs and the Basque herder started off with the sheep.[71]

J. F. Daggs, a brother of William, left northern Arizona for Phoenix and reported the shooting at Sunset to the *Phoenix Gazette*. The item was copied in the Flagstaff *Weekly Champion* in the December 4, 1886, issue:

> A shooting scrape took place at Brigham City [Sunset] last Tuesday be-tween Lot P. Smith and John Thistle, which grew out of a dispute over some sheep which, it appears, had got mixed.[72] Angry words passed between the men and Smith ran into his house, obtained his gun and fired two shots at Thistle, shooting off his little finger. Thistle had no arms. Smith then pulled his gun on W. A. Daggs, who was present, but did not shoot. A warrant has been issued for his arrest. This is the Mormon Bishop who left here some two years ago for Sonora at the time the U.S. marshals were arresting the prominent polygamists.[73]

Smith wrote his friend Thomas Abbott in Farmington about the difficulty he had with Daggs, and that, soon after, the sheriff came to arrest him "but he gave him the slip and is now a fugitive."[74] In December 1887, about a year after the Thistle shooting, Smith met Thistle and confirmed that the Hash Knife cowboy had been hired by Mr. Daggs to kill him for $1000.[75] The meeting was printed in the December 21, 1887, issue of the *Weekly Champion*: "It is reported that Mr. Thistle, who had some trouble a few months ago with Lot Smith, has offered the olive branch. Himself and Smith met the other day near the old Knight's Ranch where they shook hands, talked about old, unpleasant feelings, and buried the hatchet."[76]

---

70. Willard Smith and Karl Smith, interview, October 2, 1975; Apache County Court Records; Cora Creswell Kahl, interview by Carmen R. Smith, March 31, 1978.

71. After Smith's ultimatum, Daggs leased the sheep to the Tewksburys in Pleasant Valley on Cherry Creek in the Tonto Basin below the Mogollon Rim (not to be confused with the Pleasant Valley of Mormon Lake). That band of sheep has been popularly credited as the cause of the Pleasant Valley feud between the Tewksburys and the Grahams. The bloody five-year Pleasant Valley War ensued.

72. Lot P. Smith (no relation) was a clerk for one of the lumber companies and is mentioned occasionally in the Flagstaff newspapers. He is here confused with Lot Smith.

73. *Weekly Champion*, December 4, 1886, 3.

74. Young Jr., *Diaries*, January 17, 1887.

75. Everett E. Ellinwood to James M. Smith, interview by Omer J. Smith and Carmen R. Smith, December 25, 1964.

76. *Weekly Champion*, December 21, 1887, 3.

Cowboys of the Old Hash Knife Ranch 1886 posed in front of a barber shop on First Street where Rufus Creswell (Cora Kahl's father) has just been shaved. *Left to right seated*: "Black Pete" Schwartz or William Swank (of whom the Creswell family was afraid of at night and was glad when he soon left), unknown man (John Thistle or possibly Jeff Lefford) whose right hand appears to be missing the little finger and must have left soon after the picture was taken; Pete Pemberton with a pipe; *back*: Rufus Creswell, Pruitt or Henry Prusser, Charlie Moss. Courtesy Cora Creswell Kahl, 1978.

Smith now had to avoid being murdered as well as evade arrest for unlawful cohabitation. Immediately after the Thistle shooting, Smith prepared to go to Woodruff to meet the resettlement committee.[77] Minutes of the December 7, 1886, committee meeting showed that Smith, Udall, and Burk appraised Smith's blooded horses: one bay male at $116.00, one bay mare at $78.33, and one brown stallion at $125.00.[78] Among other items in the business of the meeting, David K. Udall moved that Smith be allowed $1,500 per annum for services rendered from March 1876 to July 1884. It

77. Bushman, *Diaries*, December 7, 1886.
78. Sunset United Order (SUO) Committee Letterpress Copybook, December 7, 1886.

was moved by Brother Burk that Smith have the entire sheep herd at two dollars per head. Brother Udall moved that the committee let Brother Smith have all of the horses belonging to the Company for $8,500 (175 horses at $50 apiece). The motion carried unanimously. Five thousand dollars of ACMI stock was transferred to the general account of Lot Smith.[79]

In December 1886, Smith took Alice Ann to look over the prospects of moving to Tuba City. It was located over 130 miles from Flagstaff—far from the fringes of civilization—where Smith would be less susceptible to arrest from both Flagstaff and St. Johns. Tuba City had a two hundred-member congregation of the Church and was an oasis in the desert with green fields and tree-lined streets. Smith and his wife traveled at night and rested in the day.[80] Near Tuba City, in the small Hopi village of Moenkopi (meaning "running water"), traders occupied the twelve-foot-high stone fort built by early Mormon missionaries.[81] The Latter-day Saints had allowed use of the building subject to ten days' notice to vacate. For more than a year, the traders Ed Stone and Sam Dittenhoffer had refused to leave.[82] Smith asked the owner, Ashton Nebeker, if he might have the fort if he could remove the traders.[83] Nebeker agreed. Smith went alone to the fort early on the morning of January 31, 1887, told the traders they had twenty-four hours to vacate the premises, and walked out.[84] The traders' account of what followed appeared in the February 12 issue of Flagstaff's *Arizona Champion*:

> On Monday, January 31st, Lot Smith, a well known Mormon, (the same man that had trouble with Mr. Daggs about two months ago and shot one of his men) made his appearance at the settlement of Moen Copie with about 20 armed men and demanded possession of the property, which was at first refused, but those present at the time, Dittenhapper, Narney Williams, Ed Stone and Mrs. Stone had to succumb to a superior force. Smith and his myrmidons broke in the doors, took possession of the place, and made the occupants prisoners.[85]

79. SUO Letterpress, December 7, 1886.

80. Alice Ann Richards Smith, *The Living Words of Alice Ann Richards Smith: Selected Writings of a Great Lady, With Other Articles of Interest*, 16.

81. Helen Bay Gibbons, *Saint and Savage*, 185.

82. Bushman, *Diaries*, February 1, 1886.

83. John Quentin Ressler, "1937 Moenkopi, Sequent occupance, landscape change & view of the environment in an oasis in the Western Navajo Reservation."

84. Karl Smith, interview by Omer J. Smith and Carmen R. Smith, June 22, 1974.

85. *Arizona Champion*, February 12, 1887, 3. Dittenhapper was probably written as "Dittenhoffer" and Narney Williams as "Varney Williams."

Perhaps the traders' fear of Smith caused them to falsely report that he had others with him. After the traders heard Smith's ultimatum, all three men had immediately saddled their horses, deserted the store, and left it to feisty Mrs. Stone. Smith took possession of the store, held Mrs. Stone hostage, piled up the traders' possessions outside, and waited for their return.[86] The garbled newspaper account continued:

> Thos. S. Hubbell, who resides at Tuvasita, a few miles east of Moen Copie, where he has a store and ranch, hearing of the trouble went to their rescue with nine men. On approaching the place they were warned off by Smith's men, who were all armed with revolvers and Winchesters. The rescuing party demanded the release of the prisoners, Mrs. Stone especially. This was refused, but Smith calling Hubbell by name, said if he would lay down his weapons, he might advance and he (Smith) would talk to him.[87]

The news of Smith's repossession of the fort raced through the small communities of Tuba City and Moenkopi. Fifteen-year-old Melissa Packer (who later married Smith's son Willard) left school in the afternoon to observe the unfolding events. With her four-year-old niece, Melissa lay in the sand behind a scrubby clump of low sagebrush on the wind-whipped hill where the fort was situated. She saw Smith watch the approach of a group of men who came up the dugway that led to the fort. Smith drove his buckboard to meet them as the horsemen topped the hill. He pulled up his team some distance from the approaching traders and stood on the seat of the buckboard—with no gun or hat. As he stood tall, he held up his hand and shouted, "Halt!" Though he was alone, he shouted, "I don't want you to turn to the east; I don't want you to turn to the west; I don't want you to turn to the north, or to the south. If you do, we will shoot you. I have men positioned all around who are armed and ready. Drop your guns."

Frightened, they called, "You won't shoot us, will you?"

Smith shouted back, "Not if you act peaceably." The traders dismounted and laid down their arms. Smith then negotiated with Hubbell. Melissa could not hear the peace terms.[88] The traders' version continued in the newspaper:

> After a parley, the Mormons agreed to let their prisoners go, but retained possession of the place with the contents of the store and the personal property of the residents.

---

86. Karl Smith, interview, June 22, 1974.

87. *Arizona Champion*, February 12, 1887, 3.

88. Karl Smith, interview, June 22, 1974; Willard Smith and Karl Smith, interview, October 2, 1975.

Mrs. Stone and the rest of the party took refuge at Mr. Hubbell's ranch while [Sam] Dittenhapper, T. S. Hubbell and Narney Williams immediately left for Flagstaff to obtain the aid of the law. Smith and his Mormon followers were left in possession of the property.[89]

Smith quickly made arrangements with Austin M. Farnsworth and Robert E. Sainsbury to hold the fort and fled to Utah.[90] When Dittenhoffer, Hubbell, and Williams arrived in Flagstaff, they telegraphed Apache County Sheriff Commodore Perry Owens, who rode the train to Flagstaff. However, Owens did not go to Tuba City.[91] He sent deputies John W. Francis and James L. Black to aid the traders with warrants for Smith's arrest. According to the newspaper, they expected to "muster a force of about eighteen men." The article continued: "The sheriff of Apache county has a warrant in his possession for the arrest of Lot Smith that was issued two years ago, charging him with unlawful co-habitation, under the anti-polygamy law. Smith was arrested once on this charge by T. D. Hubbell, who was then a deputy sheriff, but he presented a pistol at the sheriff's head and managed to escape."[92] The following week the February 19 issue of the *Arizona Champion* printed:

The party that went out to arrest the Mormons under the leadership of Lot Smith, who took forcible possession of property, and arrested the settlers at Moen Copie, as related in the CHAMPION of last week, returned on Thursday, bringing with them three Mormon prisoners named Brinkerdorf [David Brinkerhoff, Tuba City's new bishop], Sanesbury, and Farnsworth. The first named was arrested before reaching the settlement. On arriving at the scene of the outrage about 134 miles north of here, it was found that Lot Smith, the chief culprit, had flown and no trace of whereabouts could be found. Sanesbury and Farnsworth who seemed to be in charge of the place were taken into custody and Mr. and Mrs. Stone replaced in possession of their property. The three prisoners had a preliminary examination before the justice of the peace, Crothers yesterday.[93]

Evidently, Deputies Francis and Black discovered the details of Smith's bluff, for following events portrayed them as staunch friends and admirers of Smith. Smith returned shortly to Arizona when he realized he would

89. *Arizona Champion*, February 12, 1887, 3.
90. Mahonri M. Steele, letter to his parents in Arizona, February 17, 1887.
91. Joe Lee, "My Wonderful Country," 11.
92. *Arizona Champion*, February 12, 1887, 3.
93. *Arizona Champion*, February 19, 1887, 3.

likely be arrested for polygamy in Utah.[94] The newspaper story caused re-
percussions. William A. Daggs, who had hired Mr. Thistle to shoot Smith,
took advantage of the public outcry against Smith. The same issue of the
Arizona Champion printed:

> Lot Smith is accused by the grand jury of the County of Apache, Territory of
> Arizona, by this indictment of the crime of an assault with intent to commit
> murder committed as follows:
>
> The said Lot Smith on or about the first day of June [December] in the
> year 1886, and before the finding of this indictment, did at the county of
> Apache, Territory of Arizona, in and upon the body of one—Thistle, whose
> further name is to the grand jury unknown, unlawfully, wilfully, feloniously,
> premeditatedly and of his malice aforethought, make and commit an assault
> . . . with the intent to, the said—Thistle to then and there kill and murder,
> contrary to the statutes of the Territory of Arizona in such case made and
> provided and against the peace and dignity of the same.[95]

A warrant was duly issued. On February 26 the jury, with Daggs as the
sole witness, found a True Bill of Indictment. Sheriff Owens now had
an additional warrant to arrest Smith for the more serious crime of attempted murder.

Smith had now avoided arrest for a couple of years by moving to
Mexico, where more troublesome times began when questions arose
concerning Smith's settlement of the Sunset United Order. When he returned to Arizona, he still had to avoid arrest and deal with the distasteful
Order resettlement. These two struggles would continue as he moved
north from Sunset and Mormon Lake to safer, more remote locations in
Yavapai County.

---

94. Steele, letter, February 17, 1887.
95. Steele, letter, February 17, 1887.

CHAPTER 15

To Yavapai County

Smith's wife Diantha returned to Sunset from Joseph City, likely shortly after Smith's return from Mexico. Their daughter Diantha was born in Sunset on October 20, 1886. Alice Mary returned from Mexico the following March.[1] Smith bought orchards, alfalfa fields, and two houses and lots in Tuba City in Yavapai County from Alonzo L. Farnsworth. During the last of March and early April 1887, Smith's families moved north to Tuba City.[2] The families had settled in the new location before the beginning of May when Alice Mary gave birth to Martha. After the move to Tuba City, Smith hurt his back and was unable to walk for a while. He wrote to the resettlement committee that he preferred not to meet them in Woodruff because of attempted arrests by officers. He informed the committee that since his sheep had been losing wool, he had sheared early, which caused a great loss when the winter storms came. He didn't ask to trade the sheep back but wished the committee had them.[3]

For the next committee meeting in June, Smith and Brookbank "sent word they wished to meet at E. Greer's place" instead of St. Johns to elude arrest.[4] Greer's ranch was located near the Meadows, a cienaga located only about six or seven miles northwest of St. Johns on the Little Colorado.[5] St. Johns was headquarters of Apache County Sheriff Commodore Perry Owens who held warrants for Smith's arrest and whose reputation extended throughout northern Arizona and beyond. The committee met at a vacant house on Gilbert Greer's ranch on June 2 and 3 to consider all the debtors to the Sunset United Order.[6] At this meeting, the committee found "all but one had drawn more than their capital stock."[7] Smith's generosity in his settlement of the Order was confirmed.

1. Alice Baugh Smith, "Pioneer Personal History," 7.

2. Alice Ann Richards Smith, *The Living Words: Selected Writings of a Great Lady, With Other Articles of Interest*, 16.

3. Lot Smith, letter to SUO Committee, n.d.

4. John L. Bushman, *Diaries*, June 1, 1887.

5. Thomas W. Brookbank, *Religious Experiences of Thomas Walter Brookbank*, 23.

6. Bushman, *Diaries*, June 1–3, 1887; Sunset United Order (SUO) Committee Letterpress Copybook, June 2–3, 1887.

7. Bushman, *Diaries*, June 3, 1887.

Smith left the meeting as he had arrived: hidden in a wagonload of cornstalks. When safely away, he mounted his horse and headed for Tuba City, still on the alert for Sheriff Owens and other officers. Unexpectedly, Smith and Owens met on the Little Colorado. Sheriff Owens was coming from Holbrook or points westward. He knew that Smith had returned from Mexico and may have been hunting him. Smith easily recognized the thirty-four-year-old sheriff by his long blonde hair and the sombrero-type hat he wore. Smith dismounted, laid his rifle across the saddle, and waited as he stood behind his horse. When the sheriff drew near enough to hear, Smith called, "You have come close enough. Don't come any closer." The sheriff knew Smith had him in the sights of his rifle. Unaccustomed to such a reversal, Owens complied with the order. As Smith continued to turn his horse for protection against the oncoming lawman, Owens detoured in a wide circle around Smith before he hit the trail on the far side of the Little Colorado. Back in St. Johns, one of the townspeople who knew that Smith had just left the vicinity asked the sheriff, "Didn't you meet Lot Smith?"

"Yes," he answered.

"Don't you have a warrant of arrest for him in your pocket?"

"Yes," he answered again.

"Well, why didn't you bring him in?"

"It looked to me," replied the sheriff, "like one of two damn good men might get killed, and I was not sure which one it would be."[8]

The next committee meeting was held July 13–15, 1887, at Mormon Dairy. The minutes recorded the stock at the dairy: 525 cows at $25; 300 calves at $6; 250 yearlings at $13; 75 two-year-old steers at $20; 80 three-year-old steers at $27; 140 steers three years and older at $34; and 40 bulls at $25. The total value equaled $27,596.[9] At this meeting, Smith told the committee that they could reconsider their settlement with him.[10] The committee argued on both sides. Burk and Nielson voted to reconsider; Udall, Brookbank, and Bushman voted no. Nielson wrote: "Bushman would have voted for, only he did not appear to have the courage to."[11] A week later Bushman wrote: "Met Bro. Smith early. He seemed to be out of humor & accused me of mistreating him, & became very harsh

---

8. James M. Smith, interview by Omer J. Smith and Carmen R. Smith, n.d.

9. SUO Committee Letterpress Copybook, July 13–15, 1887.

10. *Journal of Frihoff Godfrey Nielson*, vol. 1, 453.

11. Nielson, *Journal*, 1:453.

insulting." He noted that he had "walked off & left [Smith]," but that they had later reconciled.[12]

Smith attended the next committee meeting held the first three days of August in Woodruff in the upper room of the co-op store.[13] Smith was allotted the Dairy Ranch, which did not include the Grapevine and Kinnikinick ranches.[14] On August 30, the committee told Smith that they were willing to settle with him and would vent (void ownership by marking across the brand with a hot iron) the Circle S brand. Smith would not agree to venting the brand, and he forbade the committee the use of the corrals.[15] Woodruff addressed the situation in similar letters written September 17 to both President Udall and Bushman. Woodruff felt Smith should be allowed to keep the brand with which his cattle were branded and that it was wrong for a man to vent the brand on his own cattle. He urged both men that since the committee had settled with Smith once, that it should be sufficient. He also wrote, "I think Lot has been roughly handled. If there has been any property made in that Institution, he has been the man most interested in making it. I was there for two years with him, and he did more work than any two men in the order. He cut the Hay, Wheat and Lucerne. He was as well on the water ditches, and the raggedest man in Camp." Woodruff continued, "There has been a great deal of prejudice against him from quarters where it ought not to be expected. He has got his imperfections and some of them strange ones; but he should not be persecuted."[16]

Udall recorded that at the last committee meeting at Mormon Dairy, he had slept on the kitchen floor and was awakened before daylight by Smith, who wrote him a note "expressing his deep appreciation for my disinterested efforts in the committee work." Smith included in the note that Udall could have his choice of any span of mares that Smith owned. When Udall asked why he offered the mares, Smith replied, "I have done this because you have eyes that can see and a heart that can feel."[17]

On September 18, Woodruff wrote to Smith and asked him about what stock he owned after the settlement of the Order. He also wrote: "Brother Lot, you have some friends left—George Q. Cannon, Joseph F. Smith and

---

12. Bushman, *Diary*, July 21, 1887.
13. Nielson, *Journal*, 1:455.
14. SUO Committee Letterpress Copybook, August 1–3, 1887.
15. Bushman, *Diaries*, August 30, 1887.
16. Wilford Woodruff, letter to David K. Udall, September 17, 1887.
17. David King Udall and Pearl Udall Nelson, *Arizona Pioneer Mormon*, 200–201.

W. Woodruff and many others are your friends and don't feel disposed to kill you yet and all wish to be remembered."[18] He signed the letter Lewis Allen. The September 26 minutes of the committee recorded the Articles of Agreement drawn up with Smith. Lot agreed to pay the ACMI $2,000 for all the horses and cattle branded Circle S.[19] Two months later Woodruff wrote again to Bushman urging him to make a final settlement with Smith. Since Smith seemed to cultivate few friends, Woodruff had befriended him as a matter of principle, "for I know there has been great prejudice against him from persons in high places. All I want is justice done, but I am anxious to have this matter settled for good and get through with it."[20]

The last committee meeting Smith attended was held on December 20, 1887, in Woodruff, at which Bushman recorded that Smith did not speak to three members of the committee: Burk, Nielson, or Bushman.[21] The committee followed the counsel of Woodruff and worked until 2 a.m. to transact the final settlement with Smith as well as several others.[22] The committee finally closed its business in meetings held on March, 1888, in St. Johns, although it did resurface.[23] Smith wrote a March 11, 1890, letter to Woodruff that Erastus Snow had insisted that Smith meet with the committee once again about unsettled Sunset affairs. Smith told Woodruff that he had once known more about Sunset matters than anyone, but not anymore. Smith attended the meeting, at which the committee almost completely ignored him.[24] The United Order resettlement had been a great strain to Smith. In addition, he was constantly on guard against arrest.

As Smith lived in Tuba City, he continued his friendly relations with the Hopis and Navajos and routinely visited the Hopis on the mesas to help with their farming. However, conflicts arose between the tribes and the Mormons over water and land, and relationships deteriorated. Young Jr. directed Bishop Brinkerhoff to call meetings in February 1888 to help resolve the difficulties.[25] In addition to the bishop, those present at the first meeting included Smith, Indian missionaries Ernest Tietjen and Seth

---

18. Wilford Woodruff, letter to Lot Smith, September 18, 1887.
19. SUO Committee Letterpress Copybook, September 26, 1887.
20. Wilford Woodruff, letter to John Bushman, November 25, 1887.
21. Nielson, *Journal*, 1:464.
22. Bushman, *Diaries*, December 19–20, 1887.
23. SUO Committee Letterpress Copybook, March 19, 1888.
24. Lot Smith, letter to Wilford Woodruff, March 11, 1890.
25. R. E. Sainsbury, Official Minutes Tuba meetings, February 1888.

Tanner, R. E. Sainsbury, Joseph H. Lee, and possibly others. Smith's remarks were recorded: "[H]e did not want to root the Indians out nor have
any trouble with them. [H]e was to[o] old to stand the anoyance and could
could [sic] afford to give it up and we could give it all to the Indians."[26]
The same personnel met the following week and included Smith's thirty-
year-old son, Jed. As the discussion continued during the meeting, one
attendee remarked that he had heard from Qua-chequa that "Bro. Smith
had beaten him and driven him off his own land. Bro. Smith said he had
abused this Indian and was sorry for it, said he would make it right with
him, and if he wanted any pay, he would satisfy him."[27] Either the same
person, or another, then accused Smith and his son of killing five sheep,
shooting four shots at a herd boy, and whipping him. Smith replied, "I
deny killing any. I shot over them, [and] did not strike or touch the boy." [28]
Someone then either called Smith a liar or implied it. A blazing Lot stood.
"Jed, hold the door," he commanded his son. The men stumbled over the
chairs as they escaped out the low windows.[29]

Water was a major issue in Tuba City. The distribution of water caused
problems not only with the Hopis but also among the Saints themselves.
The limited water of Musha's Springs watered all the Tuba City farms, and
each owner received his turn once in eight days.[30]

Even after his release as stake president, Smith was still dominant as
"the strongest man in the area."[31] He helped the families obtain supplies
to help with the farming and ranching, including a During Grain Binder
and a Buffalo Pits Thrasher. [32]

Smith's residence in Tuba City was short-lived—only about a year. He
obtained the four-mile Big Canyon (also known as Pasture Canyon and
Reservoir Canyon) east of Tuba City from Joseph H. Lee and moved there
early in 1889.[33] The box canyon provided a hideaway as secluded as any
livable spot in northern Arizona. The white- and coral-colored sandstone
walls of Big Canyon had been carved into strange and wonderful forms by
wind and water. Springs up and down the canyon created a marsh that the

26. Sainsbury, Tuba Minutes, February 1, 1888.
27. Sainsbury, Tuba Minutes, February 9, 1888.
28. Sainsbury, Tuba Minutes, February 9, 1888.
29. Al Smith to Omer J. Smith, June 11, 1972.
30. Christian L. Christensen, *Journal*, June 14, 1885.
31. Minutes of the Little Colorado Stake, 1878–1887, fn86.
32. Price W. Allen, typescript, June 16, 1958.
33. Joe Lee, "My Wonderful Country," 14.

Latter-day Saints drained into three reservoirs. The place was so verdant and peaceful that Smith requested to be buried there. Smith used the lush growth of Big Canyon as pasture for his stock. He planted an orchard below the present-day reservoir, possibly south of current US Highway 60. His grain field was above the current reservoir. With the first water right at the head of Big Canyon, Smith had no hassles. He needed only to use his allotted water time before he relinquished the stream to farmland lower in Moenkopi Wash.

Smith's wife Mary and her children occupied the cottonwood log cabin with an established orchard located at the north end of the canyon on the west side just south of a cave.[34] The cabin could be accessed only with difficulty from any route other than the canyon road and was probably built by Lee's father, John D. Lee, who had used it as a hideout. Smith built an adobe home—mud plastered, whitewashed, and with flagstone floors— for his wife Diantha by the northern edge of the middle reservoir near a flowing spring in the meadow. The house sat fairly close to Big Canyon's east side where a large, unusual sandstone formation, red with a white stripe, formed part of the family's calf corral. He still owned the mission fort in Moenkopi. The stone fort stood near the edge of a cliff about a half mile above the Hopi village. The fort and two rows of log houses formed three sides of a square.[35] From early 1889, the two Alices lived in the log house that adjoined the fort. Smith used the fort itself as a barn.[36] Alice Ann's son Joseph wrote, "Father never would have a hog or a dog on the place. . . . Father said, 'Only poor people could afford dogs and the more they had, the poorer they were.'"[37]

The farmland of Smith and his fellow Latter-day Saints lay below the Hopi farms in Moenkopi Wash. Smith had another orchard there, a garden, a melon patch, an alfalfa patch, and fields of grain and corn. One midday, while Smith was in his cornfield cultivating with a pair of mules,

---

34. Nephi L. Smith, interview by Omer J. Smith and Carmen R. Smith, September 1975.

35. L. John Nuttall, letter to John Taylor, *Deseret News,* 27:599,.

36. Lot Smith, letter to Wilford Woodruff, July 31, 1890. Big John Adams [son of Jerome J. Adams] flailed the wheat, and the boys rode their horses round and round the big room. After Smith's death the Navajos kept sheep there. The Methodist missionary Philip Johnston lived in the fort after Smith's death. Johnston initiated the Navajo Code Talkers, whose Navajo language thoroughly defied cracking by the Japanese in World War II.

37. Joseph H. Smith, Autobiography, 4.

two federal officers rode up before they were observed. Smith quickly un-hooked one of the mules, mounted it—harness and all—and went up a slope about as "steep as the side of a barn." The tugs flopped all the way. The officer said afterward, "Of course, we couldn't catch him. He went out of a canyon that a bird could hardly have flown out of."[38] Another time, when Smith was shocking corn in the same field, he saw a US Marshal on the road fairly close at hand. Smith quickly called to his sons, "Shock me up, boys." The boys did and continued to work. When the marshal rode up, the boys cordially greeted him. The officer returned to Flagstaff and wondered how Smith had escaped the area.[39] Another close encounter with officers was recorded by Smith's son Al. Since Smith knew that no deceit could enter the Kingdom of God, he demanded the truth even in the face of danger. Al was traveling with his father in their wagon when Lot looked up the road to see a man on horseback. He said to Al that it looked like a US Marshal coming down the road. He told Al to stay in the wagon and not to lie or he'd skin him alive. Smith took his gun and hid behind a bush. The officer approached and asked Al if he was Lot Smith's son. Al acknowledged the relationship. When the officer asked where his father was, Al answered, "Right behind that bush beside you." The officer didn't look; he only said to wish his father a good day and rode on.[40]

Despite the influence of the anti-Mormon Indian agents and trad-ers, Smith continued his friendly relations with the Navajos when he moved to Moenkopi and Big Canyon. He invited the Navajos to store their hides in the attic of Diantha's house in Big Canyon. In about 1889, Smith cooled his relationship with the Navajos for a time.[41] It began as a joke. With a rope tied to his horse, Smith had dragged a large barrel to a different location. As he looked back at the smoothed ground, he noticed its resemblance to a big snake track. About then, a Navajo came by. Smith quipped that a huge, ravenous snake had crawled into the canyon and that his sheepherder had barely escaped with his life. The herder had jumped

---

38. Degen Bushman, "Charles S. Peterson."

39. Charles S. Peterson, "'A Mighty Man was Brother Lot': A Portrait of Lot Smith—Mormon Frontiersman," 411; Philip Smith, *Lot Smith*, 9.

40. "Relics and Interesting Historical Data, in the possession of Lot Smith, That Are Now in the Possession of Al Smith," September 16, 1938, 1.

41. This date is uncertain. The source, Gary L. Tietjen, cited the journal of his father, Ernest A. Tietjen, with the date 1892 and wrote "just a few weeks later Lot was shot." Yet Smith's daughter Nannie, who is included in the story, left Moenkopi to be married on February 10, 1889.

off his horse and fled while the snake swallowed the horse. As a clincher, Smith showed the Navajo the snake's huge track. The Navajos believed the story and immediately removed their stock from the vicinity.[42] Later, when they discovered that there had never been a big snake, they were aggrieved. They reasoned that when forage had been insufficient for both their sheep and Smith's fine horses, Da-gha-hi Chi (Smith's Navajo name) had contrived the tremendous big snake and its track to save all the good grass for his own use. The Navajos complained to the Indian missionaries Ernest Tietjen and Luther Burnham. The missionaries brought the Navajo chiefs to Smith's home at the fort to settle the dispute. Hospitably, Smith showed the chiefs his horses. In the corral a fractious colt caught Smith off guard, kicked him in the ribs, and knocked him to the ground, where he lay unconscious for a few moments. When he revived, Smith somehow made it to the house. After a short time, he came out the door leaning on his wife Alice Ann. He sat in his rocking chair and "promised to be more fair with his Navajo neighbors."[43] The Navajos felt that the Great White Spirit had punished Smith for his misdeed when the colt kicked him, and they forgave Da-gha-hi Chi then and there.[44] Only when Mormon-Indian relationships deteriorated to a new low did Smith confine the Navajos' freedom to visit him at any time to three trusted Navajo friends.[45]

Throughout his life, Smith had been optimistic. Yet, in Arizona, his tribulations were many. His close associate C. L. Christensen wrote: "Brother Lot was tried sorely in the latter part of his life, and none but the angels can tell his story correctly."[46] In addition to the resettlement of the United Order, avoiding arrest and murder, the tragic loss of two children, and two severe leg injuries, another difficulty stemmed from a business matter. Smith considered his word sufficient for his business deals. He had purchased his Tuba City property from Alonzo L. Farnsworth with five hundred sheep at $2.50 per head ($1,250.00), one pair of mules at $225.00, and promised a pair of colts for the balance.

Through a series of events, misunderstandings arose between Smith and Farnsworth. Since members of the Church had been advised by President John Taylor not to settle their differences with Church broth-

---

42. Gary L. Tietjen, *Encounter with the Frontier*, 126.

43. Tietjen, 126.

44. Tietjen, 126; Gary L. Tietjen, interview by Carmen R. Smith, August 1976.

45. Kee W. Dougi, interviews by Omer J. Smith and Carmen R. Smith, July 20, 1976 and October 16, 1977.

46. Andrew Jenson, *Latter-day Saint Biographical Encyclopedia*, 1:804.

ers in "gentile" courts, these troubling matters were taken to Bishop Brinkerhoff for mediation.[47] Smith's anguish and frustration are evident from letters penned to Wilford Woodruff during these trying times. Smith wrote Woodruff from Tuba on January 23, 1889, explaining how he had made fair offers that Farnsworth would not accept and that the bishop advised him to take the matter to the high council in Snowflake. However, Smith did not want to risk arrest from federal authorities by going to Snowflake. He wanted Woodruff to settle the matter, but Farnsworth would not agree.[48] Woodruff wrote Brinkerhoff on January 24 that he had taken time to find out Smith's circumstances since moving to the Tuba Ward. Woodruff stated that for the past few years Smith "had had much to contend with; in fact, enough to break down the most staunch, and as I look at it, he should not now be crowded by his brethren but taken hold of and treated kindly." He urged Bishop Brinkerhoff to take care of this matter in the spirit of the gospel so that peace and joy could abound.[49] On the same date, Woodruff wrote Lot Smith: "I have fully considered your case, as you have stated it, and being so well acquainted with you as I am, I have not lost faith in you, but feel that you are yet disposed to do every thing in your power to have peace and treat everybody right."[50]

Feelings escalated between Smith and Farnsworth. Smith wrote Woodruff in February 1889, stating that he felt he had complied with the bishop's decision. According to Smith, he had made several reasonable offers to Farnsworth, but Farnsworth would not accept them. Smith wanted a rehearing or to have Woodruff arbitrate. He wrote to Woodruff: "Farnsworth and the Bishop said they would do neither. . . . One objection they made to leave it to you was that *you were a personal friend of mine.*"[51] Shortly before being sustained as president of the Church in April 1889, Woodruff suggested in a March 14 letter to Smith that he appeal to the High Council:

> This is my counsel to you. I trust you will divest yourself of any or all personal feelings toward your brethren, and seek for the guidance of a good spirit, that you may control your temper, your feelings and words in prudence and wisdom and if you will do these things and be humble before the Lord and

47. Samuel W. Taylor, *The Kingdom or Nothing: The Life of John Taylor, Militant Mormon*, 273, 280.

48. Lot Smith, letter to Wilford Woodruff, January 23, 1889.

49. Wilford Woodruff, letter to David Brinkerhoff, January 24, 1889.

50. Wilford Woodruff, letter to Lot Smith, January 24, 1889.

51. Lot Smith, letter to Wilford Woodruff, February 1889.

your brethren, I will assure you that impartial justice will be done, and these difficulties, so long pending will come to an end.[52]

Smith wrote and expressed his gratitude to Woodruff for his "good council" and appealed the case in Snowflake on May 31 and June 1.[53] Although Smith did not attend, he sent a statement. On the second day, statements were read from Smith's wife, Diantha, and his sons, Jed and Hyrum. The dealings between Smith and Farnsworth were discussed in detail. The council decided that Smith owed Farnsworth. Smith disagreed. He wrote about the proceedings to Woodruff on June 10: "Now I want advice to pay him or I want an appeal & I don't care which it is. I don't want [gentile] litigation & I hope I don't want anything but my own. . . . [Written on the side of the letter:] My son Jed and Bro. Lamb have just come from the Dairy & say the officers are on the way to arrest me. Quite a possey."[54]

Fifteen days later, Smith wrote President Woodruff that the posse was not after him and in a post script: "There were a few words in one of your letters I must answer a little. You advise me to make friends with all good men. I acknowledge the wisdom of the Council. Show me the man I have not done so with and I will ask his forgiveness more than Seventy times seven."[55] Woodruff replied to Smith that he thought it best for Smith to "abide by the decision of the High Council and let the matter rest."[56] Smith responded and told Woodruff that he had followed his advice—he had even paid Farnsworth an extra seventy-five cents and felt good about it. It cost him twenty horses, twelve cows, twelve calves, and forty-two fat steers.[57]

Smith had increased his odds to avoid arrest when he moved to Tuba City, Moenkopi, and Big Canyon. The Sunset United Order resettlement finally ended, but the wrangling with Farnsworth would continue. To further avoid arrest, Smith would travel to Utah and Idaho only to return home to be arrested twice.

---

52. Wilford Woodruff, letter to Lot Smith, March 14, 1889.
53. Lot Smith, letter to Wilford Woodruff, April 2, 1889.
54. Lot Smith, letter to Wilford Woodruff, June 10, 1889.
55. Lot Smith, letter to Wilford Woodruff, June 25, 1889.
56. Wilford Woodruff, letter to Lot Smith, June 27, 1889.
57. Lot Smith, letter to Wilford Woodruff, December 9, 1889.

CHAPTER 16

Under Arrest

When Smith was forced off the mountain by persistent law officers, he had first assigned the management of the Circle S Ranch to his oldest son in Arizona, Jedediah.[1] Upon his return from Mexico, he discharged Jed and appointed Laura's son, Alden, to manage the ranch. In 1889, he shipped horses under Jed's care to Los Angeles, only to find that horses were so cheap it was difficult to find buyers at any price. He then decided to sell cattle in the Los Angeles market. Around the first of November, Smith left Moenkopi to help his sons round up steers from the Mormon Lake Ranch.[2] He had avoided arrest for a long time and, when the deputy sheriffs of Flagstaff learned that Smith was at the Circle S Ranch, they immediately set out to take him. Smith and his sons were busily engaged in and around the pole corral at Nob Hill. As the lawmen rode closer to the corral to make what seemed a certain arrest, they heard a warning call: "Don't come any closer." Careful scrutiny revealed a number of guns aimed in their direction from between the corral's poles. The lawmen left without Smith. He and his sons finished gathering the cattle and loaded two railcars at the railroad terminal at Mormon Lake. This time Smith rode the train with the cattle to Los Angeles.

Smith wrote to Woodruff of an incident on his trip home. On the train at Peach Springs 150 miles from Flagstaff, Smith was fast asleep when he thought someone shook him. When he opened his eyes, a man was looking down into his face and laughingly asked how he was doing. Smith answered that he was well and asked the gentleman his identity. The man answered that he was deputy sheriff James Black and that he had come for his man. Smith asked if he had found his man. Black answered in the affirmative and pointed to a large Mexican man who had committed murder. Smith asked if Black was sleepy and if so, he volunteered to guard the prisoner while Black rested.[3] Smith did not want to handcuff himself to the prisoner as the deputy had done. He loosed the criminal, sat him in a seat opposite,

---

1. *Arizona Champion*, April 17, 1886, 3.

2. Alice Ann Richards Smith, *The Living Words of Alice Ann Richards Smith: Selected Writings of a Great Lady, With Other Articles of Interest*, 18.

3. Lot Smith, letter to Wilford Woodruff, December 9, 1889.

and told him not to make any suspicious move or he'd be blown to bits. Smith then seemed to fall asleep, and the prisoner made a cautious move. Instantly alert, Smith warned him sternly. Thereafter, the prisoner sat perfectly still until he and Black got off the train.[4] When Smith arrived in Flagstaff, John Marshall hurried to him and asked if he had seen Jim Black. When Smith said he had seen him, Marshall asked if Black did not want him. Smith said that he did not, apparently. Then Marshall said there was another man who might arrest him, so he checked and came back laughing to tell Smith that the coast was clear and if he could help it, he would not be arrested. Smith stammered his best thanks, "Much Obliged."[5]

Smith and Woodruff continued to correspond. In an April 14, 1890, letter, Smith expressed his appreciative thoughts of Woodruff, even though he did not believe in flattery. "I am sure you will be known in the long years to come as Wilford the Good." He wished he could see Woodruff and wrote, "Do not forget me if you ever find a place I can do any good in our Father's kingdom." Smith's health had not been good, and he signed, "A Poor Lot."[6]

Smith dismissed his son Alden as manager of the Mormon Lake Ranch and in May 1890 designated Julia's son Hyrum to replace him.[7] The next month, he sold 250 head of steers to the Honorable Saxon S. Aker. The newspaper said of Smith's livestock: "[W]e will gamble that these will be the finest steers ever marketed in Arizona."[8] That summer, Isaac Duffin filed a complaint against Smith that charged him with burning him out of his house. At Woodruff's request, Smith wrote him the circumstances. When Smith had returned from Mexico in 1886, he had found the Duffins on the Mormon Lake Ranch by permission of his son Jed, which did not please Smith because Duffin had a bad record in Utah. Later, Smith hired Duffin's brother-in-law William Lamb, who brought with him his brother Preston. Lamb and Duffin built a one-room log house south of the dairy with building materials that Duffin had stolen from the dairy. When Smith learned of Duffin's conduct, he asked Lamb to get Duffin off the ranch. At the time, Smith did not know that both Duffin and Lamb were stealing cattle and horses. Duffin's family left. Even though Smith had allowed William Lamb

---

4. Sullivan C. Richardson, *Remembrances of Lot Smith*, 7; Willard Smith to Nephi Lot Smith, interview by Omer J. Smith and Carmen R. Smith, June 28, 1974.

5. Lot Smith, letter to Wilford Woodruff, December 9, 1889.

6. Lot Smith, letter to Wilford Woodruff, April 14, 1890.

7. Lot Smith, letter to Hyrum Smith [son of Lot], May 20, 1890.

8. *Weekly Champion*, June 21, 1890.

Lydia Smith's cabin in Rockland, Idaho, where she lived until she died. Omer James and Carmen R. Smith Photo Collection, c. 1970s.

to use "all the land he wanted to plant and all the cows he choose to milk" and other amenities, he fired Lamb when he learned that Lamb was increasing his own herd by killing Smith's and other ranchers' cows and taking their calves. (Dead cows cannot bawl for their calves.)[9] Lamb left for the winter but said he would return in the spring to take possession of the dairy property because Smith had more holdings than he could manage. Early in the spring, Smith sent young Adams to take possession of the ranch and burn the little log cabin before Lamb returned. Adams "became timid" and sought Smith. Smith accompanied him to the dairy, where they found that all the tools at the dairy had been stolen and most were found in the Lamb cabin. After removing the valuables, Smith set the cabin on fire. When the Lamb brothers arrived, Preston announced that he planned to take over the dairy. William said that "*he* would not assist in jumping the property, but if [Smith] would allow him to gather his stock he would go." Smith offered to have his cowhands help him gather his stock. However, instead of gathering stock, Lamb gathered four officers. Luckily, Smith "mistrusted him and left that night. The officers came but their bird had flown."[10]

In late June, Smith wrote his son Hyrum from his hideout in Big Canyon that the officers were hunting him (Smith) and gave his son instructions on

9. Lot Smith, letter to Wilford Woodruff, August 20, 1890.
10. Lot Smith, letter to Wilford Woodruff, August 20, 1890.

the cattle and horses. "You can ride my horse if you will be very careful of him but no one else. Don't use the young mules at all. I want to breake them myself & have them get their full growth." He continued, "Hyrum, I am Determined to have all the stock treated better than they have been before. God is not pleased when we are unkind with his Creations." [11]

To avoid arrest, Smith left for Utah and Idaho. He visited Jane and Laura in Farmington and also an old comrade Thomas M. Abbott, his second-in-command in the Echo Canyon War. [12] Then Smith took Jane with him to Smithfield to see his brother Bill and to visit Alice Ann at Poverty Flats, located east of Fielding (ten miles south of the Utah-Idaho border). [13] Smith tried to persuade Alice Ann to return with him, but she declined. [14] Jane continued to ride with Smith to Rockland in southern Idaho to visit Lydia. She lived in a one-room log cabin near Rock Creek. Alone in southeastern Idaho in July, Smith called on his friend Sol Hale in Gentile Valley (Thatcher). The two made plans to meet later in Salt Lake City. From Gentile Valley, Smith continued to his children's families who lived farther north in Idaho where they had moved in the early 1880s.

Harassment in Arizona did not cease in Smith's absence. Smith wrote to Woodruff from Cassia Creek, Idaho:

> I had a little scrap of news that I thought might interest you, the folks at home in Arizona write me that when the officers failed to find me they got an old Squaw to slip up behind the barn and set it on fire and burned the barn, a stack of wheat of 176 bushels and all the things in the barn, burning mill, hampers, tools, hay in loft, all the barn contained. I think you will recollect the large stone building the Missionaries built with port holes in it. That was what I call the barn & it joined the dwelling house & it must have kept the folks pretty busy to keep the houses from burning. [15]

Smith wrote to Hyrum from Cassia Creek in August that he was leaving for Utah and then possibly Mexico. He warned him to tell no one of his plans and asked him to take the mules to Big Canyon without letting the people of Tuba City know because they would suspect his coming. He wrote, "I can't tell you how I will come. I want the *Lord to direct that* for I want to *come safe.*" He was very anxious for good feelings on the ranch

---

11. Lot Smith, letter to Hyrum Smith, June 24, 1890.

12. Fred Abbott, interview by Omer J. Smith and Carmen R. Smith, June 25, 1960.

13. Nona Smith Rhead, *Lot Smith: Captain-Colonizer-Churchman, 1830–1892*, 18.

14. Nona Smith Rhead to Carmen R. Smith, February 29, 1984.

15. Lot Smith, letter to Wilford Woodruff, July 31, 1890.

with no greed and covetousness. He emphasized that he "would rather not have one dollar than that my children should grow up *Dishonest.*"[16]

Smith went to Salt Lake City, where he was joined by Hale, and they prepared to travel south together. When he went to Robert T. Burton's place to buy a horse to ride home, he did not find him home. Smith selected a pony and left a signed blank check written out to Burton with his folks. As Hale and Smith traveled south, the two men joked and laughed all the way to the Colorado River, where they reportedly performed a blood brothers ceremony. The last evening at their riverside campsite, the kindred spirits enjoyed one last wild wrestle before they parted. The camaraderie refreshed Smith's spirit. He hoped to arrive home undetected, so he rode cross-country to the north end of Big Canyon. However, as a local resident Joseph (also Joe or Jode) Lee wrote, "We always knew when [Smith] came back to Tuba City from hiding because watchers were posted on the south mesa rims."[17] Smith received a letter from Burton that returned Smith's blank check. He presented the pony to Smith as a gift. [18]

Smith reported to Woodruff more details he had learned about the barn burning. His Navajo friends had warned his families that the officers were out to get him. The Navajos also told that A. L. Farnsworth had said that they were going to have Smith if it took burning him out; ten minutes later the barn was on fire. Smith's adversaries were urging the Navajos to join them, and he figured it would not be long until all he had would be taken.[19]

After filing the complaint of the cabin burning, Duffin had continued to steal from Smith's ranch. Shortly after his return from Utah, Smith wrote to Hyrum from the Reservoir: "Dear Hyrum. . . . If one of you would get behind a tree as Ike Duffin comes from Flag & fill his ass with fine shot, he would get away from there in quick time & if he did not, I would increase the size of the shot."[20] Two days later Smith wrote to Hyrum of an encounter with Adair, Duffin's associate in theft: "[I] had a race with Adair. He came out second best and I did not strik[e] nor shoot him but I scared him and it amounts to the same thing. All is well that ends well."[21]

---

16. Lot Smith, letter to Hyrum Smith, August 1890.

17. Joseph Lee, "My Wonderful Country," 14.

18. Robert T. Burton, letter to Lot Smith (with blank check), September 6, 1890.

19. Lot Smith, letter to Wilford Woodruff, September 10, 1890.

20. Lot Smith, letter to Hyrum Smith, September 17, 1890.

21. Lot Smith, letter to Hyrum Smith, September 19, 1890.

Smith strove to follow the counsel of Woodruff to make friends with all good men. Earlier, Smith had considered himself and Brother Jesse N. Smith "on the best of terms."[22] Lot had even named one of his children Jesse Nathaniel after his friend. However, their relationship had deteriorated following their rift in Mexico. After he attended ward conference in Tuba on September 21, 1890, Lot had a lengthy conversation with Jesse. Jesse reported in his journal that Lot "almost seemed like himself again."[23] Two days later, Jesse recorded: "Lot Smith asked Bro. Hatch and self to hear a grievance between himself and R. Sainsbury and Cyrus Farnsworth. These parties met accordingly. The dispute at first seemed very grave, but was finally settled to the satisfaction of all parties."[24] Hatch wrote that Sainsbury and Farnsworth "had jumped some of Brother Lot's land. Brother Lot acted with some dignity, and did a good part in the way of dealing liberally."[25] Jesse continued his journal entry of that day: "Went over to Moen Copie accompanied by the Bishop, Lot Smith and many others. Held evening meeting in the beautiful moonlight. . . . After meeting[,] Lot Smith came and offered his hand for the first time since returning from Mexico, emotion checked his utterance."[26]

Difficulties continued with A. L. Farnsworth. While in Farmington, Lot had written Jesse Smith in Snowflake: "I have been informed, not officially, that A. L. Farnsworth has entered suit against me for Two-thousand Dollars."[27] Knowing that Lot could not publicly appear in court in Flagstaff because of arrest threats, Farnsworth nevertheless engaged an attorney for one third of the proceeds, if the attorney would agree to carry the case on at his own expense.[28] On December 16, 1890, Farnsworth took judgment by default (since Smith did not show) in the amount of $1,036.75.[29] Not two weeks later, Farnsworth won another judgment of $995.25 against

---

22. Lot Smith, letter to Wilford Woodruff, March 17, 1890.

23. Jesse Nathaniel Smith, *Journal of Jesse Nathaniel Smith, The Life Story of a Mormon Pioneer, 1834–1906*, 380.

24. Smith, *Journal*, 380.

25. *Lorenzo Hill Hatch Journal, Copied from original sources by Ruth Savage Hilton*, September 23, 1890.

26. Smith, *Journal*, 380.

27. Lot Smith, letter to Jesse N. Smith, August 19, 1890.

28. A. L. Farnsworth, letter to First Presidency, December 22, 1890.

29. Arizona Supreme Court, Abstract Judgment in the District Court of the Third Judicial District of The Territory of Arizona in and for the County of Yavapai, Book 1, 170.

Smith—again by default.[30] In Smith's opinion, Farnsworth had "stolen" nearly two thousand dollars from him when he was forced to pay both judgments.[31] The large amounts of money paid to Farnsworth contributed to breaking Smith financially. And Smith's stock continued to be stolen, including his blooded Percheron mare Penelope and a prized stallion.[32]

Smith continued to avoid arrest in Moenkopi and Big Canyon with several narrow escapes. He had trained his horse Cloud to jump a fence at the snap of his fingers. At other times, he kept Cloud saddled. When his children ran in to say that the officers were coming, Smith would leap onto Cloud's back, jump the fence, and disappear before the officers arrived.[33] Two officers once rode from St. Johns to Smith's home at the fort. Smith was enjoying the cool of the evening in his rocking chair and had not seen their approach. "You are under arrest," they announced. "All right," he said as he rose. "I'll get my hat and coat." He stepped inside the house and soon came back with his coat held in front of him. He walked to his rocking chair and again seated himself. He lifted his coat off his lap, and there lay his trusty old Long Tom, his rifle. "I've changed my mind," he said. "I don't think I'll go with you today."[34]

Smith firmly stated that he would not rot in jail for a crime he had not committed. Accordingly, he told the sheriff that he would submit to arrest on the Duffin complaint; he was taken into custody on January 5, 1891. Smith wrote Woodruff:

> Dear Brother, three weeks since 3 officers came from Flagstaff and arrested me. They were very much afraid least I should get into the house. I told them they need have no fear as I had all ready sent the Sheriff word that I would meet him at any place he should mention for if I had broken any Law, I was Ignorant of it. Well they compelled me to go with them a mile & I went 100. They treated me verry kindly.[35]

---

30. Arizona Supreme Court, Abstract Judgment, Book 1, 242.

31. Lot Smith, letter to Elder George Reynolds, December 28, 1891.

32. Lot Smith, letter to Hyrum Smith, December 1890.

33. Alden Rice, interview by Sterling J. Smith, September 1979.

34. See Charles S. Peterson's version from Earle Forrest's file. See also: Ralph Pierson, "What the Hell Do You Want Two Guns For?," 120.

35. Lot Smith, letter to Wilford Woodruff, January 26, 1891. Another tale may refer to this arrest. According to the legend, Smith asked if he might first take a bath before going to town. The request may have been reasonable, but the officers replied, "Only if we can come in and watch you." Smith replied, "No man watches me while I take a bath." In that instance he went to town without the bath.

Additional details of the trip to Flagstaff were furnished by Smith's son, Willard. In the wind and cold of the journey, Lot convinced the officers to get off the wagon and run to keep warm while he drove the wagon. When Smith left them behind, they wondered if he had given them the slip. However, when the officers reached a little draw sheltered from the wind, they found Smith had built a bonfire and started supper.[36] That night, one of the officers, B. M. Spencer, shackled himself to Smith to sleep. In the morning, Smith helped fix breakfast. When the group was ready to travel on, "Smith politely handed Spencer his .45 Colt revolver, saying 'I was afraid you might forget it, so I was keeping it for you.' Spencer had not missed it."[37] Smith continued his account to Woodruff:

> [W]hen we neared Flagstaff one of the horses came near giving out on account of the snow[;] they thought someone would have to take the best horse & go for another. I said[,] if anyone goes, I insist on going[.] [T]hey said they did not care a Dam if I did go for I would be turned loose in 5 minutes after we arrived, but we got through with the tired one[.] [W]e went to the hotell & got dinner & then to the courtroom.[38]

The news of Smith's arrival in town on January 15 spread quickly. Smith wrote: "[A] number of the Prominent men of Flag came & offerd any assistance they could give. I thanked them and told them it was the other fellows that needed the help not *Me*."[39] Flagstaff's newspaper reported the outcome of the case. Duffin had "skipped the country," and the principle witness, William Lamb, was in a Utah prison for stealing cattle. Smith was dismissed because no one appeared against him.[40] Smith continued to Woodruff:

> I told the Judge I wanted him to put me back where he found me[.] [H]e said it was just outside the door. I told them that was best for them as that would make nothing out of *me*. It seemed to turn out as a joke and I took the traine for Canon Diablo and found Bro. Foutz & came home with him.[41]

More troubles arose from the conflict with Farnsworth. When Farnsworth was suing Smith in December 1890, both Smith and

---

36. Karl Smith, interview by Omer J. Smith and Carmen R. Smith, June 1973.

37. George E. F. J. Hochderffer, *Flagstaff, Whoa! The Autobiography of a Western Pioneer*, 112.

38. Lot Smith, letter to Wilford Woodruff, January 26, 1891.

39. Lot Smith, letter to Wilford Woodruff, January 26, 1891.

40. *Arizona Champion*, January 17, 1891.

41. Lot Smith, letter to Wilford Woodruff, January 26, 1891. Joseph H. Foutz lived a few miles from Moenkopi at Moen Ave.

Farnsworth exchanged negative feelings in letters that contained unrestrained language. Unknown to Smith, Farnsworth sent Smith's letters to Woodruff and threatened to use them to file a suit of slander against Smith for twenty-five thousand dollars.[42] In a letter dated May 16, 1891, to George Reynolds of the First Seven Presidents of the Seventy, Smith asked Reynolds why he seemed to have lost the confidence of President Woodruff. "If it is as it look[s], it is one of the worst blunders of my life," Smith wrote.[43] Smith prized his relationship with Woodruff "far more than money."[44] Reynolds replied: "There is . . . one thing which, I think, has hurt the feelings of President Woodruff—some letters written by you were sent to him which were pretty rough, and as he considered, contained expressions beneath the dignity of a servant of the Lord. Other than this, I know of nothing."[45]

Earlier, Smith had written President Jesse N. Smith from the Reservoir on February 24, 1891, that he felt it was the president's duty to stop Farnsworth's swindling. It wasn't easy for Lot to scrape together two or three thousand dollars. Lot felt that he had abided by the council's decision and Farnsworth had not.[46] The matter with Farnsworth was never resolved; Farnsworth left to Mexico where he was not under the jurisdiction of the council.[47] Lot received a letter from Jesse which stated that, as stake president, he had been advised against collecting debts from a high council decision, and suggested that Lot seek recourse from "gentile" law. Lot responded that he would not.[48]

Years of stress, constant threats of arrest, and lack of rest began to destroy Smith's typically good-natured frame of mind. No record has been found of who filed a complaint, but on June 10, 1891, Smith was required to "be held or bound under the sum of one thousand dollars to keep the peace for six months."[49] A thousand-dollar peace bond was exorbitant. That same day Thomas W. Brookbank posted bond for him.

---

42. A. L. Farnsworth, letter to First Presidency, December 22, 1890.

43. Lot Smith, letter to George Reynolds, May 16, 1891.

44. Lot Smith, letter to Wilford Woodruff, March 17, 1890.

45. George Reynolds, letter to Lot Smith, June 20, 1891.

46. Lot Smith, letter to Jesse N. Smith, February 24, 1891.

47. Lot Smith, letter to High Council of the Snowflake Stake, September 2, 1891.

48. Lot Smith, letter to Jesse N. Smith, September 2, 1891, February 29, 1892, May 10, 1892.

49. Coconino County Court Records, Records of Clerk, 1891–1940.

Smith's son, Alden, recalled a scene from his childhood standing with his father before the Tuba bulletin board where news was posted. Lot read one of the bulletins. He turned to Alden, pointed at the item, and said, "What does that say?"

Alden said, "It says Lot Smith is a slave driver."

Smith replied, "I thought that's what it said." He just stood there and let tears roll down his cheeks, according to his son.[50]

No doubt Smith felt further alienated when the Church's local authorities did not accept his offering of twenty head of big steers as tithing in kind (tithing paid in commodities). Smith wrote to Presiding Bishop W. B. Preston on January 17, 1892, to explain the situation. Although the bishop had said it was Smith's best property, the stake said they could not use it. Smith even offered a carload of steers and horses if needed, but it was likewise not accepted. All the agitating events combined to ruin not only Smith's peace of mind but also his health. Smith wrote to Preston, "My Dijestion [*sic*] is not good & I used to think I had one equal to a Dog."[51]

A warrant for the arrest of Smith on the charge of attempted murder for the shooting of John Thistle had been issued four years earlier on May 9, 1887.[52] Deputy Fletcher Fairchild finally arrested Smith in June 1891. Fairchild recounted the details to Everett E. Ellinwood, Smith's attorney in the suit. When Fairchild knocked on Smith's door, Smith answered it. Fairchild said, "Lot, I have a warrant for your arrest for the shooting of Thistle." Smith replied, "And suppose I do not submit to arrest?" Before Fairchild could answer, Smith smiled and said, "But I will, under two conditions. . . . I will go to town unarmed, but you take my horse and my gun; and when I have either come clear or served my time for this offense of which I have been accused, you will give me the bridle reins of my horse and hand me my gun." Fairchild agreed. Fairchild, his undersheriff Martin, and Smith started to Flagstaff. While cooking a meal on the way, Martin was cooking over the fire when in a flash Smith drew Martin's .45 six-shooter out of its holster. Smith spun it once on his finger and said, "'Martin, you've got a fine gun here, but you're awful careless with it,' and jabbed it back down in the holster." Fairchild walked to the fire and

50. Alden B. Smith II, interview by Carmen R. Smith, January 9, 1984.
51. Lot Smith, letter to Presiding Bishop W. B. Preston, January 17, 1892.
52. Apache County Court Records, Holograph, No. 11, District Court of Apache County.

said to Martin, "Unbuckle your gun and throw it into the buckboard." Fairchild did likewise, and they all went into Flagstaff unarmed.[53]

Attorney Ellinwood said that at the trial, Daggs and the Mexican herder were the only witnesses against Smith and both testified that Smith was the aggressor. Since Smith's two boys were the only witness for Smith, Ellinwood and Smith decided to have only Lot testify in his own defense. Ellinwood put Smith on the witness stand, asked only a few mundane questions, and turned him over to the prosecutor. The prosecutor started out very roughly. "Smith, didn't you willfully shoot at Thistle to try to take his life?" Lot Smith, as casually as if he were giving instructions to some of the boys on the ranch, said, "Thistle came to my ranch to take *my* life. He was offered a thousand dollars by the owner of these sheep, Mr. Daggs, to come out and pick a row with me and take *my* life. He came out to the ranch and picked a row, and when the going got rough, Mr. Thistle ran for the granary. When he put his gun around the corner of the granary to take *my* life, I shot the gun out of his hand and one of the thorns off the thistle. I am not sure, Mr. Prosecutor, what would have happened had there been more of Mr. Thistle sticking around the granary."[54]

Within five or ten minutes, the jury returned with an acquittal. Ellinwood saw Fairchild send a deputy to get Smith's horse, saw it saddled, and saw Fairchild hand Smith the reins and his six-shooter. Sheriff John W. Francis told Smith, "Lot, you lived up to your part of the agreement, and now I am living up to mine." Even though the whole town knew a federal officer was there to arrest him on charges of polygamy, Smith mounted and rode out of town unmolested.[55] Smith's daughter, Francis Mary, who was born three months later to Mary, was named for Sheriff Francis.

Smith had delayed his arrest by traveling to Utah and Idaho, but on his return, he succumbed to arrest twice and was acquitted both times. He would never serve in prison but would meet an untimely death by gunshot only a year later.

---

53. Everett E. Ellinwood to James M. Smith, interview by Omer J. Smith and Carmen R. Smith, December 25, 1964. Other sources include Hochderffer in *Flagstaff*.

54. Everett E. Ellinwood to James M. Smith, interview, December 25, 1964.

55. Everett E. Ellinwood to James M. Smith, interview, December 25, 1964.

CHAPTER 17

Marked Man

By the year 1892, Smith's son-in-law George W. Palmer observed that only occasionally did Smith rise above his troubles to revert to his former joyous self. In some instances, Smith was "greatly excited at intervals over small affairs, being very irritable at the slightest provocation and much disturbed over some of his financial complications. However, at other times he was unusually kind and communicative to his family."[1]

At the end of May 1892, Smith went up to the Oraibi Village to help them in their farming operations.[2] He returned home to prepare to harvest his own crops. On the morning of Monday, June 20, sixty-two-year-old Smith bent over his Osborn twine binder to install the new gear wheels he had ordered.[3] The past week had been busy. He had made a trip to Flagstaff to get an older model Champion mower and returned to cut his hay. While it dried, he prepared to harvest his grain to feed his eighteen children in Arizona.[4] For some weeks past, several Navajos—not locally known—had entered Big Canyon and established camp in the low sand hills and scrub brush west of the meadow Smith used as a cow pasture.[5] They built a crude enclosure for the flock of sheep they brought and had turned Smith's cows out of his pasture, allowing their sheep into his field of grain. During Smith's absence, his young sons—Mary's thirteen-year-old Ren and Diantha's nine-year-old Hyrum—had tried to keep the sheep out of the grain by shooting in the air, but were not successful.[6]

The possibility of a conspiracy behind the weeks of harassment from the unknown Navajos apparently never entered the mind of Smith. Yet a young Navajo horseman named Pat Shortfingers—also known as Stubbs—menaced Smith's life.[7] The flock of sheep that trampled Smith's

---

1. George W. Palmer, "Lot Smith in Life and Death," 230.

2. Alice Baugh Smith, "Pioneer Personal History," 7.

3. Lot Smith, letter to Brother Fish, March 14, 1892, April 12, 1892, May 4, 1892.

4. Smith, "Pioneer Personal History," 7; David Brinkerhoff, letter to *Deseret News,* June 23, 1892.

5. "Bishop Lot Smith Dead, No further trouble Anticipated with the Navajoes," *Coconino Weekly Sun* [as reported by Jode Lee], June 23, 1892.

6. Alden B. Smith II, interview by Carmen R. Smith, January 9, 1984.

7. He also had other names according to the Indian custom of changing names.

grain field belonged to Stubbs and had been trailed twenty to forty miles from Stubbs's hogan above The Gap to Big Canyon. Astride an unusually fine horse, Stubbs had reached the height of a young Navajo's aspirations. He rode toward the Navajo camp near Smith's grain field.[8] In the camp were five Navajo men from the northern part of Navajo Land inhabited by several hundred renegade Navajos who were only loosely controlled by Chief Hoskinini. Among the five Navajos, one was unidentified, and the others were Chachos/Catchose and his brother (otherwise unnamed), and Dinet-tsosi and his brother Dinetcloth.[9] The latter two were both Hoskinini-begay—sons of the chief of northern Navajo Land. Dinet-tsosi was already notorious as a murderer.[10]

Noon neared. Smith rode Old Jim at his habitual slow gallop northward along the bluffs on the east to Diantha's home.[11] While Smith ate, Stubbs rode into the Navajo camp in the sand hills west of the cow pasture. Ten minutes later, Stubbs turned his sheep again into Smith's grain field. He then crossed the dale and crouched with loaded pistol behind a lone, large shoulder-high boulder which lay at the side of the roadway at the foot of the bluffs east of the grain field.[12] The weeks of pestering had been calculated to erode Smith's patience. If he could be provoked into firing the first shot, the Navajos could then shoot him and claim self-defense—or at least retaliation—in a quarrel.

Smith ate and sat to write a letter to his son Alden. Before he had written a page, his son Hyrum ran into the house to announce that the Navajo sheep were back in the grain. Smith wrote one more sentence, that the sheep were in the grain field again and that he would have to go get them out, and then left the unfinished letter.[13] He went out the door, remount-

---

8. Afterwards, Shortfingers said that the purpose of his ride was "to exercise his horse." Kee W. Dougi [Shortfingers's grandson], interviews by Omer J. and Carmen R. Smith, July 20, 1976 and October 16, 1977.

9. Samuel E. Shoemaker, "Interview with the Navajo, Cat-chose, on the Death of Lot Smith, February 17, 1985."

10. Frank McNitt, *The Indian Traders*, 182–83; Charles Kelly, "Chief Hoskaninni," 223.

11. Diantha Smith Craig, interview, June 1966.

12. Kee W. Dougi, interviews, July 20, 1976 and October 16, 1977.

13. Laura Smith Jones, interview by Carmen R. Smith, July 19, 1984; Diantha Smith Craig, interview, June 1966. This half-written letter, which advised in a different handwriting the death of Lot Smith, was received by Alden and kept by him until his death. It was stored by his daughter Laura in her granary but was "thrown out with the trash" when a hired man was making

ed his horse, and returned to the field. Without dismounting, Smith let down the two top bars of the gate, jumped his horse into the grain field, and tried to move the sheep. But the sheep bunched and refused to move. Smith needed his gun. He galloped back to Diantha's house and called to Diantha to bring his pistol. Since she felt that he would be killed if he took his gun, she tried to persuade him otherwise. When he again asked for his gun, the command was not to be ignored. She knew that when his mind was fixed, no one told him differently. She handed him his .45 Colt.[14] Smith buckled on his gun, turned, jumped his horse over the gate, and started back down the road.

When Smith came to the grain field, he found that the Navajo shepherdess and her two children had driven the sheep eastward toward the gate and also toward the big boulder beside the roadway. Smith entered the field and again crowded the sheep. Again, they refused to move. He began to fire his gun both in the air and at the sheep. The five Navajos who watched from their camp with loaded rifles immediately shot six of Smith's milk cows in the pasture.[15] The cows bellowed and started toward the house.[16]

Smith did not intend to engage in a shooting battle. He knew his pistol was no match against rifles. He turned his back to the Navajos, jumped the gate, and started again at a slow gallop back to Diantha's house only about a half mile north. He had barely gained the roadway when the first rifle bullet whined past Old Jim's nose. The horse, wise to bullets, whirled, but steadied under Smith's firm hand.[17] More rifle shots followed. Apparently at the same time that Stubbs shot at Smith from his crouch behind the rock, one of the Navajos who shot from the encampment across the meadow scored a lucky hit. Smith pitched forward in the saddle but straightened up. Stubbs thought that one of the shots from his pistol had hit his mark.[18] But only a rifle shot in a more horizontal trajectory could have entered Smith's left side just below the shoulder blade and

---

room to store grain. Laura recalled the contents. Laura Smith Jones, interview, July 19, 1984.

14. Diantha M. Smith to Eliza Coombs Cluff as remembered by daughter Vera Cluff Norton, interview by Carmen R. Smith, March 28, 1975.

15. Coroner's Report, *Coconino Sun*, June 23, 1892.

16. Brinkerhoff, letter to *Deseret News* June 23, 1892.

17. Joseph "Jode" Hyrum Lee Jr., interview by P. T. Reilly, n.d. Lee's close association with the Navajos enabled him to obtain from them details of the shooting.

18. Kee W. Dougi, interviews by Omer J. and Carmen R. Smith, July 20, 1976 and October 16, 1977.

then exited out about three inches below the right nipple.[19] The bullet nicked his right thumb where he held the reins close to his chest. The deed now done, the Navajos helped themselves to the best cuts of meat from Smith's dead cows, and Stubbs started his sheep northward toward his hogan above The Gap.[20]

As Smith rode northward—wounded badly—he called to the men who were working at the head gate of the middle reservoir: Bishop David Brinkerhoff, Ernest Lee, Alexander Allen, and Stephen Heward. The men had heard the shots. Diantha had also heard the shots and watched her husband jump Old Jim over the gate without stopping to remove any poles. She thought all was well until she saw bright red blood covering the bay horse's back. He rode up to the plum tree by the dining room door to dismount, and it was then that she saw that blood streamed all the way down Old Jim's hind leg and crimsoned his white fetlock.[21] Smith called to his son Hyrum to take the horse. He entered the door and said to Diantha, "I'm afraid . . ." She thought he was going to say "they've got me this time." He paused, however, as if he had heard himself, and then continued, "No, I'm not a damn bit afraid."[22] Diantha's first impulse was to rush her husband to a doctor in Flagstaff, but he refused. He pointed out that he would never survive half the distance.[23]

Smith unbuckled his gun belt, laid it on the table, and turned to the bedroom. "Bring me my pillows," he said.[24] He sat down on the edge of the bed and began to take off his clothes. Fifteen-year-old Stephen Heward, more fleet of foot than his older companions, arrived from the head gate of the Middle Reservoir. "Here, boy," Smith said to Heward, "Pull off my boots."[25] A neighbor, Jode Lee, was immediately dispatched

19. David Brinkerhoff, letter to Jesse N. Smith, June 23, 1892.

20. "Bishop Lot Smith Dead," *Coconino Weekly Sun*, June 23, 1892; Kee W. Dougi, interviews, July 20, 1976 and October 16, 1977.

21. Diantha Smith Craig, interview by Carmen R. Smith, June 1966.

22. Price W. Nelson, *Autobiography*; Diantha Smith Craig, interview, June 1966; Zina Brinkerhoff Hatch, interview by Carmen R. Smith, February 9, 1977.

23. Nephi L. Smith, interview by Omer J. Smith and Carmen R. Smith, December 16, 1980.

24. Alice Ann Richards Smith, *The Living Words of Alice Ann Richards Smith: Selected Writings of a Great Lady, With Other Articles of Interest*, 51.

25. A number of stories tell of Smith's boots at the time of his death. The plausible version had Heward pulling off the boots. Yet Lydia Nelson Brinkerhoff said that Diantha pulled off his boots before Heward arrived. Also, either Brigham Young or Heber C. Kimball supposedly warned Smith that if he didn't curb his

to inform Smith's sons at Mormon Dairy. Messages were sent to Alice Mary at Moenkopi and Mary up the canyon. The family began the vigil over their dying husband and father. Bishop Brinkerhoff sat in a chair at the side of the bed. The news of the shooting spread rapidly among the local Navajos who were Smith's friends. "They all felt so bad because they thought so much of him."[26] As evening drew near, they gathered in the yard in significant numbers. Some of them dismounted and came to the open window to keep vigil for their friend Da-gha-hi Chi.[27]

According to Diantha, her husband spent the next five or six hours more peacefully than she had ever seen him. He was meek and submissive during the long afternoon and evening of his suffering.[28] His regret was deep. "I never should have turned my back, but I thought the Indians would not shoot. I should have come away when they began shooting the cows."[29] In the yard outside, the mourning Navajos' soft, eerie, off-key wailing rose and fell like the wind that so often howled around the house and up over the barren cliffs. These were the Navajos who had laughingly cautioned that Smith's red beard could set the *jacale* (Indian brush shelter) on fire. His name Da-gha-hi Chi would be remembered long after his Christian name was forgotten.

Smith asked for a looking glass, "saying, when he looked at the glass, 'Well, I am not dead yet.' And in an hour after looking again, he said, '[S]till alive but rather pale.'"[30] Smith begged for a drink of cool water. His wives feared that cool water would cause further hemorrhage, so they gave him only warm water. At about nine o'clock he insisted on a drink of cold water from the spring, and they complied.[31] He half arose to drink long and deeply, then he sank back on the pillows and seemed almost immediately to worsen.

---

temper, he would die with his boots on. See Charles S. Peterson, "'A Mighty Man was Brother Lot': A Portrait of Lot Smith—Mormon Frontiersman," 413. Smith, as he turned to lie on the bed, is supposed to have told Heward to put them back on.

26. Alice Baugh Smith, "Pioneer Personal History," 7.

27. Sally Smith Peterson, letter to Carmen R. Smith, August 23, 1978.

28. Emma Mortensen Skousen, interview by Omer J. Smith and Carmen R. Smith, c. 1950s.

29. Coroner's Report, *Coconino Weekly Sun*, June 23, 1892.

30. Lenora S. Rogers, *Sketch of the Life of Andrew Locy Rogers*, 16.

31. William J. Hunt, *History Extracts*, 1.

Alice Mary arrived from Moenkopi and came into the bedroom with her almost seven-month-old baby girl Kate in her arms. The baby saw her father and cooed. Smith, who was already blind from his approaching death, still responded. "Yes. Da Da," he returned. "I hear you. I wish I could live to raise you."[32] His baby girl was the last person he addressed. He exhaled a few more breaths while his thoughts continued along the same line. "I hope none of my children ever go hungry."[33] He sensed his helplessness to further care for his family, and he appealed to the heavens. "God bless the wives and children."[34] That prayer was his last utterance. Consciousness faded. His life's fire burned lower and lower until the flame flickered out shortly before ten o'clock. Smith's "mighty spirit fled."[35] The date was June 20, 1892—not June 21, as has been commonly recorded.[36] Brinkerhoff arose from his chair at the bedside and turned to the two wives who stood at the foot of the bed. As he did so, the Navajos at the window suddenly wailed louder—to a nerve-shattering pitch. Their Da-gha-hi Chi was dead. The news spread rapidly. The Hopis who had not joined the Navajos at the house learned almost immediately that Pa-lah Sa-weech-a-mee was dead.

Lee must have ridden hard to inform Smith's sons, and so had the sons, for they "arrived in time for breakfast the next morning"—too late to see their father alive.[37] The warm June weather dictated a burial without delay. The Relief Society ladies of Tuba City arrived at Diantha's house early the next morning to help sew the burial clothes.[38] They found that

---

32. Smith, "Pioneer Personal History," 9; Smith, *Living Words*, 51; Sue Bateman, "Sketch of the Life of Alice Baugh Smith (as related to Sue Bateman)," 2.

33. Smith, *Living Words*, 51.

34. Smith, "Pioneer Personal History," 9; Palmer, "Lot Smith in Life and Death," 230.

35. Rogers, *Sketch*, 16.

36. The date was clearly Monday, June 20, 1892. The published coroner's report was dated 21st and listed death the previous day. Jode Lee, who gave notice to the Flagstaff newspaper, said death occurred on Monday [20th]. A telegram received by Woodruff in Salt Lake City at 2:52 p.m. on June 25 from Jesse N. Smith in Snowflake read: "Reported that Lot Smith was killed by Navajo Indians at Tuba June twentieth." The *Deseret News* incorrectly printed that Smith was killed June 21, as reported by David Brinkerhoff (*Deseret News*, June 23, 1892). This most widely disseminated report with the mistaken date accounts for the confusion.

37. Alden B. Smith II, interview by Carmen R. Smith, February 9, 1984.

38. Lydia Ann Nelson Brinkerhoff, *Autobiography*.

none of Smith's wives had any white cloth that was necessary for temple burial clothes. A search among the neighbors began. Susannah (Mrs. Lehi) Heward offered what seemed to be the only white cloth in Tuba City or Moenkopi. She also had an unusual tale to tell. Just a day or so previously, she had unfolded and laid her bleached muslin on the bed to be cut for bed linens. At that moment, a large spot of blood appeared to drop on the cloth. She was so unnerved that she folded the fabric and put it away uncut. The next day, Smith was shot and her fabric was the only white cloth available.[39] As the sisters sewed the burial clothes, an inquest into Smith's death by coroner Joseph H. Lee was held. A jury of Orville E. Bates, Thomas W. Brookbank, Seth B. Tanner, and Edward Kelly assembled at ten o'clock, the witnesses testified, and the jury reached a verdict as to the cause of death:

> We, the undersigned, a jury empaneled to hold an inquest upon the body of Lot Smith, lying before us dead, do find from the evidence that said Lot Smith came to his death on the 20th day of June, from a gun or pistol shot fired by some Indian to us unknown.[40]

On June 22, Bishop Brinkerhoff conducted funeral services in Diantha's house in the canyon. Afterward, a long cortege of wagons wended up the deep-sanded canyon road towards Mary's cabin in the upper canyon. "It took four good animals to take [Smith's remains] to the spot."[41] The body of Smith was laid in a grave located thirty or forty feet in front (east) of Mary's cabin near a plum tree in the orchard. They marked the grave with a board and built a fence of small poles for protection.[42]

Brinkerhoff reported the death to the *Deseret News* in Salt Lake City.[43] Stories of Smith—whether contemptuous, adulatory, or exaggerated—escalated after his death. Tales were repeated around campfires for many years, often more garbled with each telling. Newspapers at the time of his death mistakenly gave him credit for notorious exploits. The *Coconino Weekly* published in the same issue with the Coroner's Report:

---

39. Kate B. Carter, *Heart Throbs of the West*, 3:340.

40. Coroner's Report, *Coconino Weekly Champion*, June 23, 1892, 3/3 and 3/4.

41. Rogers, *Sketch*, 16.

42. Nephi L. Smith, interview by Omer J. Smith and Carmen R. Smith, September 1975; Diantha Smith Craig, interview, June 1966; *Lorenzo Hill Hatch Journal, Copied from original Journals by Ruth Savage,* September 15, 1894.

43. *Deseret News*, June 23, 1892.

Lot Smith was one of the prominent characters that marked the early history of Utah. He accompanied the Mormons in their exodus from Nauvoo, and was always an admirer of the prophet Brigham Young, one of whose "destroying angels" he was reputed to be.

There were four companies of these destroying angels, each of whom worked in ignorance of the duties of the others, and their duties varied with the character of the men. The leaders of these four gangs were Porter Rockwell, Bill Hickman, Lot Huntington and Lot Smith. The work of the two former was usually from ambush, but Lot Smith's was done openly and with a dash that won him admirers even from his opponents, and had his efforts been directed in a worthy cause might have made him famous.

Smith's chief notoriety was achieved during the Mormon war in 1857, when the United States forces, 3000 strong, were marching to Utah. Lot Smith, with his gang, was detailed to annoy and rob the army on its march. He had a thorough knowledge of the country, which gave him great advantage over the troops, and with his handful of men was enabled to harass the soldiers at every turn.

On the 4th of October of the year mentioned Lot Smith and his party suddenly appeared at Simpson's Hollow, near Green river, where a government supply train was corraled, dashed into the camp, took possession of it and fired every wagon before the troops realized his presence. Afterwards he burned two trains on the Sweetwater in the same manner, destroying seventy-five loaded wagons with their loads of provisions, tents, tools and clothing.

Large quantities of horses, mules and cattle were also run off by this gang, none of which was ever recovered and most of which became church property. Smith's instructions were to shed no blood except in the extremity of self defense, but to waste away the army by robbery, by cutting their supplies and by burning the country around them, and these instructions he obeyed in a manner characteristic of the man. Whether he was ever engaged in 'private enterprises' is not known, but as Hickman and Rockwell were retained for these, it is generally supposed that Smith's hands were comparatively free from 'dirty work.' He was settled for many years a few miles north of Salt Lake City, where he had a large farm, but when the Gentile domination became too great for his comfort he removed to Arizona, where he met his death as stated.[44]

The *Arizona Enterprise* of June 30, 1892, also published an obituary, copied from the *Prescott Journal Miner*:

Lot Smith led a checkered life. He was, by common report and on apparently good authority, credited with being a member of the Danite society or destroying angels of the Mormon Church, and was a Lieutenant of John D.

---

44. *Coconino Weekly Sun,* June 23, 1892.

Lee at the time of the Mountain Meadow Massacre; he was also charged with
the burning of the baggage train of Albert Sidney Johnson. He figured before
the courts of this [Arizona] country to some extent prior to the division of
the county, but escaped conviction. He was a warm hearted though passion-
ate man. He was a good friend but a relentless enemy. The circumstances
under which he met his death illustrates the impetuous character of the man,
as one with his temper and greater discretion would have realized the suicidal
policy of declaring war singlehanded on a lot of Indians.[45]

Historians have not erred when they report that Smith was shot by
Navajo Indians in a quarrel over sheep that invaded his grain field.
However, forces other than gunpowder were behind the bullets directed
at Smith. The Mormons did not know that the death of Smith had been
only the first step in a plot to massacre all the Mormons in the area.
Before the shooting of Smith, Navajos from the vicinity had gathered
and pow-wowed for two days.[46] Since their only avenue to glory was
in warfare, the younger braves had clamored for an all-out massacre of
the Mormon villages of Tuba City and Moenkopi. The older Navajos
were adamantly opposed. They remembered all too keenly the misery
of the long walk to Bosque Redondo/Fort Sumter where they had been
held prisoners in poverty, filth, and hunger from 1864 to 1868.[47] The
Navajo fathers assured their young sons that any unprovoked massacre
would bring annihilation. Back and forth for two days the two sides argued their views in fiery oratory. In the end, the wisdom of the ancients
prevailed, but the young Navajos did not give up hope of warfare.[48]
They reasoned that if one big Mormon could be killed, the Mormons
would surely retaliate. Who would be the big Mormon? Lot Smith,
"Da-gha-hi Chi."

After Smith's death, hundreds of Navajos swarmed the surrounding
hills. Five hundred braves, armed and painted for war, paraded through
the town as an open challenge to fight.[49] Although the people were frightened, Bishop Brinkerhoff wisely urged calmness among the Saints. He
asked them to continue to gather their crops, repair fences, clean ditches, convene on Sunday, and even to gather on the banks of the Lower
Reservoir to hold prayer meeting—all unarmed. Brinkerhoff trusted that

45. *Arizona Enterprise* 12, no. 12 (June 30, 1892): 3/3.
46. Palmer, "Lot Smith in Life and Death," 230.
47. Frank McNitt, *Indian Traders*, 47.
48. Brinkerhoff, *Autobiography*, 7.
49. Hunt, *History Extracts*, 2.

judicious behavior and courteous treatment of the Navajos would prevent further difficulty.[50]

The investigation of the murder began. Lieutenant Robert E. L. Michie of Fort Wingate rode into Tuba on July 8 with a detachment of cavalry to find the Navajos greatly excited. Only through Michie's fact-finding did the Tuba City residents learn the chilling truth of why the Navajos still roamed the hills and villages. The morning of Smith's death, a Navajo had leaked the subject of the Navajo council to a small group of men including L. DeCloss. The Navajo said, "Maybe pretty soon Navajos kill and clear out some White men."[51] When DeCloss laughed at him, the Navajo bragged that "[w]e kill one White man, anyhow," and that they had "talked about it two days."[52]

Factions opposed to Smith and the Mormons likely used the clash of the Indian and White cultures to create a rift. Bishop Brinkerhoff's counsel to the Saints to say and do nothing out of the ordinary combined with Michie's diplomatic investigation and the influence of some of the older Navajos calmed the open hostilities. The young braves' hopes for the glory of warfare in a massacre slowly subsided. The Navajos themselves did not know who had fired the fatal shot that killed Smith. When Navajo justice dictated that a life would be demanded for the life taken, the Navajos settled on Chachos (meaning syphilis), who would likely have the shortest life span. However, Chachos was never officially punished.[53] Nor did the Navajo Stubbs, who thought his pistol fired the fatal shot, receive official punishment, though he later suffered anguish and remorse from his guilty feelings.[54]

Smith's grave lay waterlogged for years, but he was not forgotten. Lorenzo H. Hatch came to meetings at Tuba City two years after the burial of Smith and wrote that he and others went to visit Smith's grave at the north end of Big Canyon. They arrived at Mary's cottonwood log cabin near a high cliff, where she welcomed them with a treat of melon. In

---

50. David L. Brinkerhoff, letter to Jesse N. Smith, July 5, 1892.

51. Andrew Jenson, *Latter-day Saint Biographical Encyclopedia*, 1:805; Robert E. L. Michie, *Report on Lot Smith Killing, July 13, 1892*, 3; Palmer, "Lot Smith in Life and Death," 230.

52. Michie, *Lot Smith Killing*, 3

53. Philip Johnston, letter to Omer Smith and Carmen Smith, April 11, 1976; Joseph "Jode" Hyrum Lee Jr., interview by P. T. Reilly, n.d., 3.

54. S. Eugene Flake, interview by Carmen R. Smith, March 26, 1976; Hunt, *History*, 2.

the orchard of peaches, apples, and plums, Smith's grave lay near the plum trees, marked only with small scraps of board. Hatch was troubled by the sorrow and loneliness of the spot. He wrote, "A mighty man was Brother Lot, a brave, daring pioneer and soldier. History cannot say too much of this great man."[55]

---

55. Hatch, *Journal*, 187. Hatch attended the memorial service for Lot Smith held in 1902 in Farmington. Hatch, *Journal*, 252.

EPILOGUE:

Reinterment

In Utah in October 1899, more than seven years after Smith's death, Smith's friend Sam Bateman had spoken to President Joseph F. Smith about reinterring Lot Smith in Farmington.[1] Two years later, Bateman wrote in his diary on January 24, 1902:

> I went to the president's office and had a talk with him [Joseph F. Smith] and his councilors about bringing up the body of my old friend & soldier from Arizona & burying him in the graveyard at Farmington, this place being his old home. It was granted & they said they would have him brought up. I had been asking for this for the last 18 months.[2]

Five days later, a letter was written to Bishop Brinkerhoff in Tuba City with instructions that the First Presidency of the Church was "desirous of removing the body of Elder Lot Smith from where it is now buried, to Farmington, his old home."[3] The First Presidency appropriated forty dollars for expenses to exhume Smith's body and transport it to the railway station in Flagstaff and fifty dollars more to pay transportation costs to Farmington, Utah.[4] Brinkerhoff rode up Big Canyon to Mary's abandoned cabin to locate the grave.[5] However, almost ten years and rising water had wiped away any sign of the gravesite. The bishop sent a message to Mary in Flagstaff, who sent her thirteen-year-old son Al to Tuba City. With Al, the bishop and his son James drove their wagon up the canyon. Al showed them the spot beneath a winter-bare plum tree. The men thrust their shovels into the coral-colored sand and dug until they struck the wooden box. As they wrestled the casket from its depths, water that carried long red hairs from Smith's beard dribbled out of the corners of the coffin.[6] They set the box down and pried

1. Samuel Bateman, *Diary*, 169.

2. Bateman, 251.

3. Joseph F. Smith, John A. Winder, and Anthon H. Lund, letter to Bishop David Brinkerhoff, January 29, 1902, LDS Church History Library.

4. Journal History of the Church of Jesus Christ of Latter-day Saints, March 10, 1902 (hereafter cited as Journal History); Joseph F. Smith, John R. Winder, and Anthon H. Lund, letter to Bishop David Brinkerhoff, March 10, 1902.

5. Warren Brinkerhoff, interview by Carmen R. Smith, May 15, 1977.

6. Mrs. Louis Gardner, June 1968, as quoted in Charles S. Peterson, "'A Mighty Man was Brother Lot,'" *Western Historical Quarterly* 1, no. 4 (October 1970): 414.

up the lid to see the remains. The draining water had slipped the long red beard from Smith's face to his upper chest.[7] They replaced the lid and carried the dripping box to a nearby sand bank, buried it, and left it to drain.[8] The bishop then stored the box in the basement of his house.[9]

Brinkerhoff transported the body to Flagstaff in his wagon in a zinc-lined wooden box sent from Salt Lake City by undertaker Joseph E. Taylor.[10] At the Santa Fe railroad station, the bishop delivered his charge to Snowflake Stake President Jesse N. Smith, who was traveling to Salt Lake City for the Church's general conference.[11] Smith's remains arrived in Salt Lake City late Tuesday the first of April and were taken to Taylor's morgue. On the front page of the April 5, 1902, *Deseret News*, Lot's picture and obituary appeared in two-column width:

> More than passing interest has been aroused by the bringing home of the body of the late Lot Smith, whose name is encountered in nearly all the critical junctures in the history of Utah
>
> Many years of his life were spent in camp and on marches after Indians and other foes, surrounded by conditions that generally harden men, but under the gruff surface, which to those who did not understand him, was fierce and forbidding, there beat a heart filled to overflowing with human sympathy.
>
> An appeal to Lot Smith for help was never made in vain, but on the contrary, he often sought out those who needed assistance, and rendered whatever he could.
>
> The transaction in which his name comes up most prominently is the service rendered by him at the time Johnston's army was endeavoring to enter Salt Lake. In no period of his life did his noble qualities show to more advantage. As the head of that expedition he was wise and patient, carrying out to the very letter the instructions given him by Prest. Young, one of which was that he was to shed no blood.

---

7. Warren Brinkerhoff [son of David] and Lydia Ann Nelson Brinkerhoff, interview by Carmen R. Smith, March 1977; Al Smith to Kent N. Smith, interview by Carmen R. Smith, October 21, 1974.

8. Mrs. Louis Gardner, June 1968, as quoted in Charles S. Peterson, "A Portrait of Lot Smith," *Western Historical Quarterly* 1, no. 4 (October 1970): 414.

9. Leona Brinkerhoff Graves Colvin Bolinger, interview by Carmen R. Smith, August 30, 1976; Warren Brinkerhoff and Lydia Ann Nelson Brinkerhoff, interview by Carmen R. Smith, March 1977; Zina Brinkerhoff Hatch, interview by Carmen R. Smith, February 9, 1977.

10. *Deseret News*, April 2, 1902; Joseph F. Smith, John R. Winder, and Anthon H. Lund, letter to Bishop D. Brinkerhoff, February 28, 1902; Joseph F. Smith, John R. Winder, and Anthon H. Lund, letter to Jesse N. Smith, March 10, 1902.

11. *Journal of Jesse Nathaniel Smith*, 440.

His skirmishes with the red men, were invariably preluded by a prayer to heaven, that the necessity for the shedding of human blood might never come. . . . During the Johnston army epoch, but he was to the last degree a protector of his friends and people and it was their only safety, and immunity from further suffering, that he sought, and his life he would have given up on the instant if it had been necessary.

He died at the hands of a renegade Navajo, incited against him by an unscrupulous white man who had gone into that country to beat the Indians.[12]

The April 8, 1902, *Deseret News* reported that over a hundred people from Salt Lake City rode the Oregon Short Line to attend the funeral of Lot Smith in Farmington that afternoon. The train made a special stop at Farmington to accommodate those attending the services.[13] Included were the President of The Church of Jesus Christ of Latter-day Saints, Joseph F. Smith, and his First Counselor, John R. Winder, accompanied by four apostles (John H. Smith, Heber J. Grant, Mathias F. Cowley, and A. O. Woodruff). At the Farmington depot, the flag-draped casket was met by twenty or more carriages; the stores were closed in Smith's honor; and it looked as if the whole town was there to pay their last respects. The casket bearers were Samuel Bateman, James Sharp, Charles H. Wilcken, Orson P. Arnold, Joseph H. Felt, and Samuel Hill.[14]

The crowd overflowed Farmington's rock chapel.[15] Three of Smith's wives attended the memorial services: Jane, Alice Ann, and Alice Mary.[16] Twenty-five of Smith's fifty-two children and nine grandchildren also attended.[17] Presidents Joseph F. Smith and Winder sat in carved, velvet-covered chairs on the podium, and Bishop J. M. Secrist of Farmington conducted.[18] At 2:00 p.m. the memorial service began. The opening hymn by the Farmington choir was "Gates Ajar," followed by the invocation offered by Elder Seymour B. Young. The choir then sang "God is Just."[19] Men who had joined Smith in his military campaigns paid tribute

---

12. *Deseret News*, in Journal History April 5, 1902, front page.

13. *Deseret News*, in Journal History, April 8, 1902.

14. Seymour B. Young of the First Council of the Seventy, "Lest We Forget, Captain Lot Smith (Concluded)," *Improvement Era* 25, no. 11 (1922): 1006; Bateman, *Diary*, 259.

15. Bateman, *Diary*, 259.

16. Mary was in Flagstaff (shortly to join her son in Canada); Diantha was in southern Arizona; Lydia was in Idaho; Julia was in California; and Laura was deceased.

17. Alice Ann Richards Smith, Lot Smith family reunion, June 20, 1929.

18. Margaret S. Hess, *My Farmington*, 258.

19. Seymour B. Young, "Captain Lot Smith (Concluded)," 1006–8.

to their leader. The *Deseret News* reported: "[A]s the speakers would relate one after the other the noble acts of their captain, tears would suffuse the eyes of the members of his household, and not only they, but many others wept, including many of the grey-haired veterans who had not wiped tears from their eyes for years."[20]

Among others, Heber J. Grant took detailed notes of the proceedings. President John R. Winder was the first speaker, followed by Samuel Bateman (Utah War 1857), Solomon H. Hale (Civil War 1862), President Seymour B. Young (Civil War 1862), James Sharp (Civil War 1862 and mission in Scotland 1869), Orson P. Arnold (Utah War 1857), Joseph H. Felt (Civil War 1862), Samuel H. Hill (Civil War 1862), President Ira N. Hinckley (Civil War 1862), James P. Terry (Utah War 1857), Thomas Abbott (Utah War 1857 and Provo War 1850), Joseph Parry (Utah War 1857), President John W. Hess (Smith's Farmington Bishop and School of Prophets 1867), President Anthony W. Ivins (Mexico), and President Joseph F. Smith.[21]

George W. Palmer (Smith's son-in-law) expressed the family's appreciation. The services closed with the hymn "Nearer, my God to Thee," followed by the benediction by President Jesse N. Smith. A large cortege of carriages followed the remains to the family plot in Farmington's cemetery, where President Joseph E. Taylor dedicated the grave and a closing prayer was offered by Joseph H. Felt.[22] In the words of Civil War soldier Alley S. Rose: "[At the services, we h]ad a glorious time together. One never to be forgotten."[23] *The Deseret News* reported:

> In all the eulogies pronounced . . . the conclusion would be forced upon one, that for care and forethought exercised in behalf of his men, Lot Smith never had a superior. The master impulse of his nature was fidelity to duty, self-sacrificing and all un-remitting thought for the comfort and safety of those who followed him.[24]

---

20. *Deseret News,* April 9, 1902.

21. Seymour B. Young, "Captain Lot Smith (Concluded)," 1006-1008; Heber J. Grant, journal, April 8, 1902, LDS Church History Library; Anthony W. Ivins, journal, April 8, 1892, LDS Church History Library.

22. Samuel Bateman, *Diary,* April 8, 1902.

23. Alley S. Rose, *Journal, 1896-1910,* April 8, 1902.

24. *Deseret News,* April 9, 1902.

Utah War Participants
With Lot Smith

The personnel who participated with Lot Smith in the Echo Canyon War fluctuated. At least four men are reported to have served with Smith during the entire Utah War Campaign: Lieutenant Thomas Marsh Abbott (25) of Farmington who had also participated with Smith in the Provo War; Thomas Rogers (30) also of Farmington; Philo (Phil) Dibble (44) of Bountiful, Davis County; and Lieutenant John Vance (62) of Salt Lake City.

Eight of the ten men from Draper, Utah, include Orson P. Arnold (18), with whom Smith had played as a child in Williamstown; Sam Bateman (25) (both Arnold and Bateman remained close friends with Smith the rest of their lives); Edwin Booth; Norman Brown (26), who spent fifty-two days with Smith[1]; Henry Day (33); James Kilfoyle (52), born in Ireland; lst Lieutenant Joseph S. Rawlins (34), also Smith's Lieutenant in the Civil War campaign; and James Parshall Terry (27).

Other men of the original forty-four include John Bagley; Henry Beckstead (30), formerly of Farmington who "was also a member of Lot Smith's company at the time the government wagons were burned and the cattle stampeded"[2]; Mark Bigler son of original Jacob; William Butler (32) of Kaysville, Davis County;[3] George W. Cleveland (20), probably of Centerville who "was with Lot Smith during the Johnston army trouble . . . and many nights was in the saddle all night," which indicates participation in burning the wagons[4]; Albert D. Dickson (17); Paul Gourley (44) of Lehi who was "one of the men that assisted Lot Smith in burning some of the soldier's supply wagons in October"[5]; Captain Horton D. Haight (25) of Farmington;[6] Mark Hall (33) of

1. Norman Brown, "Old Homes and Buildings," in *An Enduring Legacy,* 241.

2. Andrew Jenson, *Latter-day Saint Biographical Encyclopedia,* 2:747.

3. Norma B. Winn, "The Texas Expedition," 80.

4. *Portrait, Genealogical and Biographical Record of the State of Utah,* 433.

5. Raymond W. Madsen, "Scottish Convert Made Long Ocean Journey to Join Ill-Fated Handcart Group," 6.

6. Jenson, *Latter-day Saint Biographical Encyclopedia,* 1:302.

Ogden who narrowly escaped being killed when a bullet shot through his hat[7]; Henry W. Jackson (30) who also served in the Mormon Battalion; Charles McMurry; James Pickard, Adjutant to Sam Bateman and the first platoon; Lyman W. Porter (24) who scooped up melting soap that streamed from the burning wagons;[8] John Henry Standifird (26) of Bountiful, Davis County who also served under Smith in 1862 and later went to Arizona;[9] and James Stevenson of Farmington (27).[10]

In Smith's company, period unknown: Paul Cardon (18) of Ogden[11]; Isaiah Cox (19)[12]; George Patten (29) of Payson ("During the winter of 1857-8 I participated in the Echo canyon campaign, part of the time under the command of Captain Lot Smith")[13]; John Rigby of Farmington[14]; Andrus Roos/Andrew Ross; William B. Smith (44) from Kaysville, Davis County, served "mostly under the command of Lot Smith"[15]; and Samuel Stowe of Ogden, later in Arizona.[16]

Those in Smith's company after he burned the wagons and who may have been in the original forty-four include Harvey Bliss with Abbott at ambush; William H. Hill (17) with Abbott at ambush[17]; James R. Miller (19) with Abbott at ambush[18]; William Kelsey Rice (35) of Farmington who ate beef after stampede[19]; and Thomas Rich (39) at stampede.[20]

Others with Smith: George Frederick Hamson, Henry Cahoon, Benjamin F. Knowlton, Joseph Parry, Stephen Taylor, Newton Tuttle, John Woolley, Brigham Young Jr.

7. *Contributor*, 4:169.

8. Joseph Grant Stevenson, ed., *Porter Family History*, 1:100.

9. John Henry Standifird, *Diary*.

10. Margaret Steed Hess, *My Farmington: A History of Farmington, Utah, 1847–1976*, 122.

11. Jenson, *Latter-day Saint Biographical Encyclopedia*, 2:76.

12. Wayne Stout, *Hosea Stout, Utah's Pioneer Statesman*, 218.

13. Jenson, *Latter-day Saint Biographical Encyclopedia*, 2:158.

14. Annie C. Carr, *East of Antelope Island: History of the First Fifty Years of Davis County*, 237.

15. Jenson, *Latter-day Saint Biographical Encyclopedia*, 3:244.

16. Obituary, *Graham County Guardian*, February 1919.

17. Jenson, *Latter-day Saint Biographical Encyclopedia*, 1:791, 792.

18. Jenson, 1:563.

19. William Kelsey Rice, *History of William Kelsey Rice*.

20. Jenson, *Latter-day Saint Biographical Encyclopedia*, 3:212.

Members Of Lot Smith's
1862 Civil War Company

Moroni Woodruff Alexander (1837–1901), private; William Coleman Allen (b. 1843), private; John Taylor Arrowsmith (1841–1910), private; James Isaac Atkinson (1841–1933), private; Richard Attwood, 1st sergeant; William Henry Bagley (1841–1923), teamster; James Madison Barlow (1812–1893), 2nd sergeant; Lachon Barnard (b. 1834), teamster; John Rowland Bennion (1840–1899), private; Samuel Roberts Bennion (1842–1915), private; William Bess, private; Andrew Bigler (1836–1893), corporal; Henry Bird, teamster; William A. Bringhurst (1839–1912), corporal; Edwin Brown, private; Charles Carrol Burnham (1838–1926), private; John Farrington Cahoon (1839–1910), private; Thomas S. Caldwell, private; Theodore J. Calkin, private; Francis Robert Cantwell (b.1841), private; Jesse Yelton Cherry (1840–1865), private; Hiram B. Clawson, corporal; Hyrum B. Clemons, corporal; Peter/Pierre Cornia/Cournoyer (1829–1887), private; George Cottrell (1840–1909), private; Everett Covert (d. 1913), private; James H. Cragun, private; Charles Crismon Jr. (1844–1916), private; Henry L. Dalton, teamster; George W. Davison, teamster; Albert Wesley Davis (1841–1928), private; Parley Pine Draper (1843–1924), private; Josiah H. Eardley (1842–1931), musician; Charles M. Evans (1831–1902), musician; Joseph Henry Felt (1840–1907), corporal; Joseph Armstrong Fisher (1841–1922), private; Will Fuller, teamster; Jonathon Gibson, private; Moses Washington Gibson (1840–1912), private; Joseph Goddard (1841–1911), private; William Grant, private; James Green (1837–1924), private; Edward Francis Mailon Guest (1828–1896), private; Solomon Henry Hale (b. 1839), wagoner; Thomas H. Harris (1841–1924), private; John Helm, farrier; James Hickson, private; Samuel Hill, private; Ira Nathaniel Hinckley (1828–1904), farrier; John Hoagland (1833–1893), corporal; Richard Howe (1839–1927), private; Lewis Albert Huffaker (1841–1918), private; Harvey Coe Hullinger (1824–1926), private; James Havens Imlay (1815–1890), private; Lars Jensen (b. 1814), private; Powell Johnson (1840–1927), private; Hiram Kimball Jr. (1841–1863);

John Quincy Knowlton (1835–1886), 2nd lieutenant; James H. Larkins (1843–1922), private; Thurston Larson (1830–1907), teamster; Leander Lemmon (1839–1940), private; William Longstroth (1840–1911), private; Thomas Jefferson Lutz (1837–1884), private; William Wharton Lutz (1839–1893), private; William Lynch, private; Elijah H. Maxfield (b. 1832), teamster; Donald/Daniel McNichol (d. 1862); Edwin de Lafayette Merrill (b. 1836), private; Reuban Parley Miller (1844–1901), private; Mark Murphy (1837–1918), teamster; Merrick Myrick (1838–1911), corporal; Benjamin Barr Neff (1834–1883), private; John Neff (1837–1918), corporal; Edward Alvah Noble (1841–1909), private; Hyrum Bennett North (b. 1840); Lewis Osborn, private; Hugh D. Park (1840–1908), private; Francis Platt Jr. (1824–1886), saddler; Lewis L. Polmantur, private; Francis Prince (1840–1929), private; Alfred Randall (1811–1891), teamster; Joseph Sharp Rawlings (1839–1903), 1st lieutenant; Adelbert Rice (b. 1839), private; Landon Rich (1840–1908), private; Samuel Harvey Wollerton Riter (1835–1908), sergeant; William Henry Rhodes (1842–1914), private; Alley Stephen Rose (b. 1841), private; James Sharp (1843–1904), private; Emerson Davis Shurtleff (1839–1868), private; Daniel C. Sill, private; Harlan Edward Simmons (1841–1893), private; Lot Smith (1830–1892), captain; Howard Orson Spencer (1838–1918), sergeant; John Henry Standifird (1831–1924), private; James Henry Steed (1844–1885), private; Joseph James Taylor (1838–1908), private; Joseph Terry (b. 1842), private; William Terry, private; Moses Thurston (1817–1873), private; John H. Walker (1843–1915), private; William Harrison Walton (1822–1907), teamster; Elijah M. Weiler (b. 1839), private; James H. Wells, private; Bateman Haight Williams (1843–1903); Ephraim Henry Williams (1842–1919), private; John Peter Wimer (1835–1904), sergeant; Seymour Bicknell Young (1837–1924), corporal.[1]

---

1. Craig L. Foster, "The Men of the Lot Smith Company of 1862," 150–62. Reprinted with permission. See article for more information on each member.

Wives and Children of Lot Smith

1. Lydia Minerva McBride (February 9, 1832–April 4, 1908). Born in Villenovia, Chautauqua, New York. (Photograph unavailable.) Children: Lot Samuel (1852), Robert Taylor Burton (1862).

2. Jane Walker (August 2, 1832–March 23, 1912). Born in Peacham, Caledonia, Vermont. Children: Rhoda Jane (Hutchinson) (1853), William Lot (1855), Jedediah Heber (1857), Emily Abigail (Hess) (1859), Annetta (Udy) (1863), Alice (Robinson) (1865), Margaret Agnes (Palmer) (1868), Lucy Effie (Palmer) (1874).

3. Julia Ann Pence Smith (March 6, 1837–May 21, 1923). Born in Van Buren County, Missouri. Children: Phoebe Vilate (Steed, Smith) (1859), Louise Marie "Tude" (Stoddard, Krumperman) (1861), Julia Adelaide (1863), Sarah Theresa (1866), Hyrum Burton (1869), Julia Amanda (Zion, West, Latimer, Wilson, Beamish) (1875).

4. Laura Louisa Burdick (November 8, 1838–December 19, 1895). Born in Quincy, Hancock, Illinois. Children: Helen Mar "Nell" (France) (1861), Lydia May "Lillian" (Stoddard) (1863), Abiah Ann "Bide" (Nelson) (1866), Laura Louisa "Lollie" (Rice) (1868), Alden Burdick (1872), Howard William Messenger (1879), Charlotte Winifred Messenger (Kaberry) (1879).

5. Alice Ann Richards (March 24, 1849–June 17, 1940). Born in Salt Lake City, Salt Lake, Utah. Children: Nannie Amelia (Ashcroft) (1869), Willard Richards (1872), George Albert (1875), Lot Jr. (1877), Wilford Woodruff (1879), Joseph Howe (1882), Rhoda Minerva (1885), Alice Roxey (1887), George Albert (1889).

6. Alice Mary Baugh (December 28, 1853–November 9, 1947). Born in Birmingham, Warwick, England. Children: Elizabeth Jane (1873), Mary Melissa (Carr) (1875), Brigham (1878), Diantha "Dora" (Wilson) (1880), Franklin Dewey (1882), Jesse Nathaniel (1884), Martha (Schott) (1887), Charles Rich (1889), Kate "Katherine" (Fleischmann, Freeman) (1891).

7. Mary Merinda Garn (November 5, 1852–March 17, 1916). Born in Placerville, Placer, California. Children: Lorenzo Lot "Ren" (1880), Samuel (1881), Emily (1884), Alma "Al" (1888), Helaman "Jim" (1889), Francis Mary (Short) (1891).

8. Dorthea "Diantha" Elizabeth Mortensen (March 18, 1861–December 6, 1922). Born in Ephraim, San Pete, Utah. Children: Charlotte Elizabeth "Lottie" (Moody) (1881), Hyrum (1883), Nephi (1885), Diantha (Craig, Bratcher) (1886), Nephi Lot (1889), Edwin Dilworth (1891), James Martin "Jim" (1892), Julius Peter "Pete" Christensen (1896), Victor "Vic" Christensen (1898).

Lot Smith Timeline

May 15, 1830	Birth in Williamstown, Oswego County, New York, to William Orville Smith and Rhoda Hough Smith
1839–1841	Baptisms of William O. Smith family into The Church of Jesus Christ of Latter-day Saints
June 10, 1841	William O. Smith family left New York with Elder Joseph L. Robinson to gather with Saints
August 1841	William O. Smith family settled on Sugar Creek in Hawley Settlement (renamed Ambrosia), Iowa, across Mississippi River from Nauvoo
January 16, 1845	Death of mother Rhoda Hough Smith
July 1846	Volunteered for Mormon Battalion as "Luther"
November 24, 1846	Traveled to Las Playas and took water back to thirsty comrades
January 29, 1847	Arrived at Mission of San Diego de Alcala, California
February 3– March 19, 1847	Stationed at San Luis Rey, California
July 16, 1847	Discharged in Los Angeles, California
July 20, 1847– March 14, 1848	Extended military service as a California "Mormon" Volunteer
March 14, 1848	Discharged at San Diego, California
July 7, 1849	Death of father William O. Smith in North Cottonwood (modern-day Farmington), Utah Territory
November 1849	Arrived in Great Salt Lake Valley, Utah Territory
February 5–19, 1850	Appointed private under General George D. Grant on expedition to fight Utes at Provo Fort
Spring 1850	Bought Thomas Grover's farm in Farmington, Utah Territory

September 17–22, 1850	Expedition #3427 as private, traveled north to Shoshonis
September 25–October 5, 1850	Expedition #3428 as private, returned to Shoshonis
January 26, 1851	Baptized by John W. Young of Fourth Quorum of the Seventy, age 20
February 19–27, 1851	Expedition #3432 as private, traveled to Tooele to Gosiutes in Skull Valley
April 20–May 1, 1851	Expedition #3430 as acting sergeant under Ferguson
May 31, 1851	Appointed Color Bearer General of Nauvoo Legion
June 3, 1851	Married to Lydia Minerva McBride in Brigham Young's home
September 27, 1851	Elected sergeant
February 14, 1852	Married to Jane Walker in Council House
April 26, 1852	Ordained an Elder by George D. Grant
June 8–17, 1852	Explored for lead and silver
August 9, 1852	Endowed in Council House with wife Lydia
April 1853	Walker War began
April 25–May 2, 1853	Expedition #3503B as 2nd Lieutenant to southern Utah settlements
August 21–September 9, 1853	Expedition #3035B as 1st Lieutenant to Green River
April 22, 1854	Elected Captain of Company B, Life Guards Cavalry
May 4–June 1, 1854	Acted as guard while escorting Young south to Utah settlements and to make formal peace with Wakara
September 5, 1854	Elected sheriff of Davis County; death of sister Abiah Ann Smith McBride
October 27, 1854	Death of brother Hyrum Smith
March 4, 1855	Ordained a Seventy

1855–1867	Served as one of seven presidents of the 40th Quorum of the Seventy located in Farmington
February 6–7, 1855	Mormon Battalion celebration in Great Salt Lake City
September 14, 1855	Traveled to Salmon River with B. F. Cummings to search for gold
November 25, 1855	Married to Julia Ann Pence Smith in Beehive House
March 3, 1856	Appointed Road Supervisor of District #5
September 20, 1856	Rebaptized in Reformation
October 1856	Rescued Martin Handcart Company
April 24– May 26, 1857	Acted as guard while escorting Brigham Young to Fort Limhi
June 27, 1857	Elected Major of 1st Battalion of Cavalry
September 27, 1857	Traveled to Fort Bridger in beginning of Utah War
October 5, 1857	Burned wagon trains of John Dawson and R. W. Barrett in pre-dawn hours; burned wagon train of Lew Simpson in daylight
October 12, 1857	Stampeded Simpson's cattle
October 16, 1857	Almost captured by Captain Randolph B. Marcy
November 14, 1857	Began duty on Bridger Butte
December 5, 1857	Traveled to Great Salt Lake City
January 3, 1858	Married to Laura Louisa Burdick by Brigham Young
March 1, 1858	Sealed to wives Jane, Julia, and Laura
March 1858	Indicted for treason for burning US Army wagons
April 4, 1858	Traveled to Echo Canyon station above Weber station
April 1858	$1,000 reward offered for Smith's capture
April 20, 1858	Returned with part of cavalry to Great Salt Lake City at end of service in Utah War
1858–1859	Purchased Stoddard land in Weber Valley, Morgan County

January 16, 1859	Joined Deseret Agricultural and Manufacturing Society (July 31, 1864, acquired life membership)
August 28, 1859	Court publicly dropped prosecution of Smith for treason
October 19, 1859	Antelope Island outing and roundup with Brigham Young party
August 5–6, 1860	Appointed as Davis County Commissioner
October 19, 1860	Elected Representative to the Legislative Assembly from Davis County (did not serve)
February 14, 1861	Appointed as Davis County Assessor and Collector of Taxes
May 15– June 8, 1861	Acted as guard while escorting Young through southern Utah; brought wife Lydia to Farmington from Fillmore
July 1861	Retrieved wife Julia from US Army traveling east
March 10, 1862	Appointed to help reserve Farmington's Big Range for winter grazing
April 30, 1862	Appointed captain in US Army and called for ninety days to guard telegraph lines and mail routes in the American Civil War
May 1862	Traveled to Green River with twenty men to recover four animals stolen from Big Sandy
July 19– August 8, 1862	Expedition #3664 Snake River Expedition (total of nine expeditions throughout career)
February 6, 1863	Appointed to Davis County board to issue licenses for brewers and liquor merchants
July 5, 1863	Appointed as Davis County fair horse racing judge
August 17, 1863	Fined $300 for contempt of court in Newton Austin trial
May 1864	Acted as guard while escorting Brigham Young to Bear Lake
September 27, 1864	Death of daughter Julia Adelaide Smith
April 9, 1865	Black Hawk War began
August 11, 1865	Led Brigham Young's procession from Farmington to Salt Lake City

August 27, September 3, September 10, 1865	Reported to have "Gone South" (Farmington Ward Teachers' roll)
May 19, 1866	Elected Brigadier General of the Davis County Militia
September 22, 1866	Led Brigham Young's procession from Centerville into Farmington
May 11, 1867	Death of daughter Sarah Theresa Smith
December 9, 1867 through 1872	Attended School of the Prophets (excluding time on mission)
March 29, 1868 through 1876	Served as Senior President of 74th Quorum of the Seventy in Farmington
May 30, 1868	Married to Alice Ann Richards in the Council House
August 9, 1868	Black Hawk War ended
May 25, 1869	Received call to serve in British Mission
May 29, 1869	Set apart as missionary to British Mission by Wilford Woodruff
June 21, 1869	Began trip east across continent via railway
June 29, 1869	Embarked on SS City of Washington to cross Atlantic Ocean
July 11, 1869	Arrived at British Mission office in England
July 23, 1869	Appointed as Traveling Elder to the Glasgow Conference in Scotland
September–December 1869	Served as Traveling Elder on east coast of Scotland
January–April 1870	Served as Traveling Elder on west coast of Scotland
June 8, 1870	Appointed as Birmingham England Conference President
July 26, 1871	Left England aboard SS Nevada bringing ninety-three immigrant Saints
August 17, 1871	Arrived home in Utah
January 8–February 16, 1872	Served in Twentieth Session of Utah Territorial Legislature
February 19–March 3, 1872	Attended Constitutional Convention in Salt Lake City

April 29, 1872	Married to Alice Mary Baugh in Endowment House
February 3, 1876	Left Salt Lake City as leader to colonize Arizona Territory
March 24, 1876	Arrived at Sunset Crossing on Little Colorado River
December 1876	Death of daughter Elizabeth Jane Smith due to diphtheria in Kanab
April 1877	Attended General Conference and temple dedication in Saint George
January 27, 1878	Sustained as Stake President of Arizona Stake of Zion
June 13, 1878	Married to Mary Merinda Garn in Saint George Temple
September 24–October 26, 1878	Accompanied tour through settlements in southern Arizona with Apostle Erastus Snow
February 28–March 2, 1879	Arizona Stake divided into Little Colorado Stake and Eastern Arizona Stake; began service as president of Little Colorado Stake
May 17, 1879	Apostle Wilford Woodruff arrived at Sunset
March 3, 1880	Took Woodruff back to Saint George
October 21, 1880	Married to Dorthea "Diantha" Elizabeth Mortensen in Saint George Temple
December 1, 1880	Injured left foot on horsepower
June 2–16, 1881	Made annual tour of stake with wife Diantha, Margaret Mortensen, Levi M. Savage, John Bushman, and William C. Allen
December 15, 1881	Injured left leg second time on horsepower
March–April 1882	Attended General Conference in Salt Lake City
March 14, 1883	Death of son Wilford Woodruff Smith by scalding in lye at Sunset
June 19, 1883	Death of son George Albert Smith by drowning in Little Colorado
January 1, 1884–November 23, 1887	Appointed Sunset's postmaster

April 1884	Attended General Conference in Salt Lake City
June 4, 1884	Visited Governor F. A. Tritle in Prescott with Brigham Young Jr. and Francis M. Lyman
August 1884	End of Sunset United Order
December 7, 1884	Left Sunset for Utah with five other men to avoid arrest
January 3, 1885	Left Salt Lake City by train for Mexico
January 18, 1885	Met in Saint David, Arizona, with President John Taylor and Arizona stake presidents
January 20, 1885	Returned to Little Colorado on horseback to warn polygamist men
February 5, 1885	Started to Mexico in wagons with family
February 28, 1885	Arrived in La Ascensión, Mexico
August 29, 1885	Left Mexico to retrieve Sunset United Order books in Arizona
October 14, 1885	Arrived back in Mexico
June 1886	Death of son Jesse Nathaniel Smith in Mexico
June 27, 1886	Death of son Nephi Smith in Joseph City, Arizona
July 12, 1886	Death of daughter Rhoda Minerva Smith in Sunset
August 1886	Left Mexico for Arizona
November 30, 1886	Shot finger off hired gunman, Mr. Thistle
1886–1887	Sunset United Order Resettlement Meetings
January 31, 1887	Obtained Fort Moenkopi
March to April 1887	Moved families to Tuba City
December 18, 1887	Released as stake president when Snowflake Stake was organized from the Little Colorado and Eastern Arizona Stakes
March 1888	Moved to Moenkopi

June 20, 1888	Death of daughter Alice Roxey Smith due to diphtheria in Tuba City
Between January 3 and March 5, 1889	Moved to the reservoir in Big Canyon
May 31, 1889	Chose not to attend High Council hearing due to threat of arrest
Early December 1889	Traveled with cattle on train to sell in Los Angeles
June or July 1890	Received summons in newspaper for burning of Duffin cabin
After June 24, 1890	Boarded train in Flagstaff for Salt Lake City
July 1890	Visited wife Lydia and friend Sol Hale in Idaho; also visited in Parker and Basalt, Idaho
July 31, 1890	Traveled to Cassia Creek, Idaho, and helped son-in-law Joseph Udy
August 28, 1890	Left Salt Lake City for Arizona with Sol Hale
January 15, 1891	Acquitted at trial for burning Duffin cabin
June 19, 1891	Arrested for shooting Thistle; acquitted at trial
June 20, 1892	Shot by Navajos and died
June 22, 1892	Buried at north end of Big Canyon, east of Tuba City, Arizona Territory
April 8, 1902	Memorial Service and re-interment in Farmington, Utah

Bibliography

Albuquerque Weekly. December 18, 1881–December 24, 1882.

Allen, Andrew Jackson. "Andrew Jackson Allen Diary, 1848–1884," Typescript. Vol. 1. Joel E. Ricks Collection of Transcriptions. Salt Lake City: Utah State University Library, 1955.

Allen, Elijah. Autobiography. Manuscript, LDS Church History Library, Salt Lake City.

Allen, Price W. Typescript, June 16, 1958. In possession of authors.

Alter, J. Cecil. *Utah: The Storied Domain—A Documentary History of Utah's Eventful Career, Comprising the Thrilling Story of Her People from the Indians of Yesterday to the Industrialists of Today.* Chicago: American Historical Society, 1932.

Anderson, Devery S. *Salt Lake School of the Prophets, 1867–1883.* Salt Lake City: Signature Books, 2018.

Anderson, Nels. *Desert Saints: the Mormon Frontier in Utah.* Chicago: University of Chicago, 1966.

Apache County Court Records. Holograph, No. 11, District Court of Apache County. Saint Johns, AZ.

Arizona Supreme Court. Abstract Judgment in the District Court of the Third Judicial District of The Territory of Arizona in and for the County of Yavapai in *Reports of Cases Argued and Determined in the Supreme Court of the Territory of Arizona, 1884–1911.*

Arrington, Leonard J., Feramorz Y. Fox, and Dean L. May. *Building the City of God: Community and Cooperation Among the Mormons, 2nd ed.* University of Illinois Press, 1992.

Attwood, R. H. *Journal of the Utah Volunteers.* Utah State Archives and Records Service No. 709.

Ashcroft, Nannie Smith [daughter of Lot Smith]. "Lot Smith," 1925. Typescript in possession of authors.

Ashurst, Edward B. Audio recording at Lot Smith Reunion, Flagstaff, AZ, July 11–12, 1969. In author's possession.

Ashurst, Henry Fountain. *A Many-Colored Toga, the Diary of Henry F. Ashurst.* Edited by George F. Sparks. (Tucson, AZ: University of Arizona Press, 1962).

Bailey, Belle. "Severe Winters." Iowa City, IA: Iowa State Historical Department.

Bailey, Paul Dayton. *Jacob Hamblin, Buckskin Apostle.* Tucson, AZ: Westernlore Press, 1966.

Ballard, Henry. *Private Journal (1852-1904), Typescript.* Provo, UT: Brigham Young University Library, 1956.

Bancroft, Hubert Howe. *History of Utah 1540-1886.* Las Vegas, NV: Nevada Publications, 1982.

———. "Arizona Dictations." Bancroft Library, Berkley, CA.

Bartholomew, Rebecca and Leonard Arrington. *Rescue of the 1856 Handcart Companies.*

Provo, Utah: Brigham Young University Press, 1981. Distributed by Signature Books.

Barton, George. Diary. Manuscript, LDS Church History Library, Salt Lake City.

Bateman, Samuel. *Diary*. Samuel Bateman Papers, 1886–1907. University of Utah Libraries, Special Collections, Salt Lake City.

Bateman, Sue. "Sketch of the Life of Alice Baugh Smith (as related to Sue Bateman)," 1935. Typescript in possession of authors.

Baskin, R. N. *Reminiscences of Early Utah*. Salt Lake City: Utah Lighthouse Ministry, 1914.

Bean, George W. *Autobiography of George Washington Bean, A Utah Pioneer of 1847, and His Family Records*. Compiled by Flora Diana Bean Horne. Salt Lake City: Flora D. B. Horne, 1945.

Beem, Lucille Satterfield. "My Grandfather—Alexander Morrison Spence." Typescript. June 1980. Courtesy Lucille S. Beem.

Bigler, Henry William. *Diary of a Mormon in California. Discovery of Gold, 1848 By Henry William Bigler*. Berkeley: University of California Berkeley, 1872.

———. "Extracts from the Journal of Henry W. Bigler." *Utah Historical Quarterly* 5 (April 1932).

Bliss, Robert S. "Journal of Robert S. Bliss with the Mormon Battalion." *Utah Historical Quarterly* 4 (July 1932, October 1931): 67–97, 110–28.

Blythe, John A. Journal, Typescript. Arizona Diaries, Northern Arizona University; Manuscript, LDS Church History Library, Salt Lake City.

Boyle, Henry G. Diary. Manuscript, LDS Church History Library, Salt Lake City.

Bringhurst, William A. Item to *Deseret News*, April 1902.

Brinkerhoff, David. Letter to *Deseret News*, June 23, 1892. Copy in author's possession.

———. Letter to Jesse N. Smith, June 23, 1892. Holograph courtesy of Jesse Smith. Copy in author's possession.

———. Letter to Jesse N. Smith, July 5, 1892. Holograph courtesy of Jesse Smith. Copy in author's possession.

Brinkerhoff, Lydia Ann Nelson. *Autobiography*. Manuscript. Flagstaff:, Special Collections Division, Northern Arizona University, n.d.

Brookbank, Thomas Walter. *Religious Experiences of Thomas Walter Brookbank*. Flagstaff: Special Collections Divisions, Northern Arizona University Library.

Brooks, Juanita. *John Doyle Lee, Zealot-Pioneer Builder-Scapegoat*. Glendale, CA: Arthur H. Clark, 1979.

Brooks, Juanita, ed. *On the Mormon Frontier, The Diary of Hosea Stout 1844-1861*. University of Utah Press, Utah State Historical Society, 1964.

Brown, Benjamin. "Antelope Island Mountain." In Annie Call Carr, *East of Antelope Island*. 3rd ed. Farmington: Daughters of the Utah Pioneers, 1969.

Brown, James S. *Giant of the Lord*. Salt Lake City: Bookcraft, 1960.

Brown, Lorenzo. Journal, 1823–1862. Copied by Brigham Young University, Provo, Utah, 1960.

Brown, Norman. "Old Homes and Buildings," in *An Enduring Legacy*. Vol. 2. Salt Lake City: Utah Printing, 1979.

Buchanan, Frederick S. ed. *A Good Time Coming: Mormon Letters to Scotland*. Salt Lake City: University of Utah Press, 1988.

Burk, Asahel Woodruff. "Biographical Sketch of Hubert Rosell Burk and Family." In *Burk Family History*, edited by Karl W. Burk. Mesa, AZ: Lofgreen Printing & Office Supply, 1980.

Burton, Alma P. and Clea M. Barton. *Stories From Mormon History*. Salt Lake City: Deseret Book, 1960.

Burton, Robert Taylor. *Autobiography*. LDS Church History Library, Salt Lake City.

———. Diaries, 1856–1907. Manuscript, LDS Church History Library, Salt Lake City, 1857, 1862, 1872, 1876.

———. Letter to Lot Smith (with blank check), September 6, 1890. First Presidency Letterpress Copybooks, 1877–1949, LDS Church History Library.

Bushman, John. *Diaries*. Typescript by George S. Tanner. Flagstaff: Special Collections, Cline Library, 1876, 1883–1887.

———. *The Life and Labors of John Bushman, Son of Martin and Elizabeth Dagen Bushman. Copy of edited diary copied by himself, Typescript.* LDS Church History Library, Salt Lake City.

———. *John Bushman Journal Abbreviated.* Copy by George S. Tanner, 1965.

Call, Israel. *A Life Sketch of Israel Call by His Own Dictation, Typescript.* Flagstaff: Special Collections, Northern Arizona University Library, n.d.

Camp, Helen Mar. "Sketch of the Life of Lot Smith." Farmington, UT: Daughters of the Utah Pioneers.

Carr, Annie Call. *East of Antelope Island: History of the First Fifty Years of Davis County.* 3rd ed. Salt Lake City: Publishers Press, Daughters of the Utah Pioneers of South Davis County Company, 1969.

Carrington, Albert. *Diary of Albert Carrington.* Msf 317, LDS Church History Library.

Carter, Kate B. *Treasures of Pioneer History.* 6 Vols. LDS Church History Library.

———. *Heart Throbs of the West, "A Unique Volume Treating Definite Subjects of Western History."* 2nd ed. Salt Lake City: Daughters of the Utah Pioneers, 1939.

———. *Our Pioneer Heritage.* Salt Lake City: Daughters of the Utah Pioneers, 1972. 2:449–451; 8:593; 12:336; 15:396.

———. *The Mormon Battalion.* USA: Daughters of Utah Pioneers, Utah Printing, 1957.

Carvalho, Solomon Nunes. *Incidents of Travel and Adventure in the Far West; With Col. Fremont's Last Expedition Across the Rocky Mountains; Including Three Months' Residence in Utah and a Perilous Trip Across the Great American Desert to the Pacific.* New York: Derby & Jackson, 1859.

Cheney, Thomas E. *Mormon Songs from the Rocky Mountains: A Compilation of Mormon Folksong.* Salt Lake City: University of Utah Press, 1981.

Christensen, Christian L. British Mission Statistics Records. LDS Church History Library, Salt Lake City.

———. Dates of Resettlement of the Sunset United Order Meetings. LDS Church History Library, Salt Lake City.

———. Endowment House, Endowments of the Living, 1851–1884. Microfilm of holograph, LDS Family History Library, Salt Lake City.

———. *Journal, Typescript.* Flagstaff: Special Collections, Northern Arizona University Library, n.d.

———. Minutes of the Ward Teachers Meeting of the Farmington Ward 1 (1862–

68), 2 (1868–73), LDS Church Historian's Office.

———. Minutes of the Little Colorado Stake, 1878–1887. LDS Church History Library, Salt Lake City.

———. Missionary Register 1860-1959. Microfilm of holograph, LDS Church History Library, Salt Lake City.

———. Record of members collection 1836–1970. Microfilm of holograph, LDS Church History Library, Salt Lake City.

———. Sealings of couples, living and by proxy 1851–1889. Microfilm of holograph, LDS Family History Library, Salt Lake City.

———. *State of the Edinburgh Conference, Scotland May 1878.* Microfilm of holograph, LDS Church History Library, Salt Lake City.

Clark, William. "A Trip Across the Plains in 1857." *Iowa Journal of History & Politics* 20 (April 1922): 163–223. See http://hickmansfamily.homestead.com/files/clark.htm.

Cleland, Robert Glass. *This Reckless Breed of Men: The Trappers and Fur Traders of the Southwest.* New York: Knopf, 1963.

Coconino County Court Records, Records of Clerk, 1891–1940. Flagstaff, Ariz.

Coconino Weekly Sun. June 23, 1892; "Bishop Lot Smith Dead, No further trouble Anticipated with the Navajoes," June 30, 1892.

Cody, William F. *Story of the Wild West and Campfire Chats by Buffalo Bill, (Hon. W. F. Cody.).* Philadelphia: Historical Publishing, 1888.

Coleman, Evans. "Nesters, Rustlers, and Outlaws." *Journal of Arizona History* 14, no. 3 (August 1973).

Coleman, W. C. Journal. Special Collections, Arizona State University, Tempe.

Contributor, 1882–1883, LDS Church History Library, Salt Lake City.

Cooke, Philip St. George. "Cooke's Journal," *Exploring Southwestern Trails 1846–1854.* Edited by Bieber, Ralph P. The Southwestern Historical Series. (Philadelphia: Porcupine Press, 1974), 7:63–240.

———. *The Conquest of New Mexico and California: An Historical and Personal Narrative (1878).* Albuquerque, NM: Horn and Wallace, 1964.

Cowley, Matthias. *Wilford Woodruff, History of His Life and Labors.* Salt Lake City: Bookcraft, 1974.

Crawley, Peter. *A Descriptive Bibliography of the Mormon Church, Vol. 3.* Provo, UT: BYU Religious Studies Center, 2012.

Cross, Whitney R. *The Burned-Over District: the Social & Intellectual History of Enthusiastic Religion in Western New York 1800–1850.* New York: Harper & Row, Cornell University Press, 1965.

Davis County. *Minutes of the Davis County Court.* Vol. 1 (1852–69) and vol. 2 (1869–84). County Clerk's Office, Farmington, Utah.

Dewey, Albert P. British Mission Journal (1869–1871). Microfilm of holograph, LDS Church History Library, Salt Lake City.Dibble, Philo (Phil). Journal (1869–1871). Manuscript, LDS Church History Library, Salt Lake City.

Douglas, William Machrie. Diary (1869–1871). Microfilm, LDS Family History Library, Salt Lake City.

Earl, Ada Arvilla Burk. Autobiography. N.p, n.d. Typescript in author's possession.

Eldredge, Alma. Diary (1869–70). LDS Church History Library, Salt Lake City.

Eldredge, Horace Sunderlin. Diary 1869–71. Manuscript, LDS Church History Library, Salt Lake City.

Elmer, Elijah. *Elijah Elmer's Journal April 19, 1846, Typescript.* Mormon Battalion Diary. Copy in possession of authors.

Farnsworth, A. L. Letter to First Presidency, December 22, 1890. Utah State Historical Society, Salt Lake City.

Fife, Austin and Alta Fife. *Saints of Sage & Saddle, Folklore Among the Mormons.* Bloomington: Indiana University Press, 1956.

Fisher, Margaret M. *Utah and the Civil War; Being the Story of the Part Played by the People of Utah in That Great Conflict with special reference to Lot Smith Expedition and the Robert T. Burton Expedition.* Salt Lake City: Deseret Book, 1929.

Flake, Osmer Dennis. *William J. Flake, Pioneer – Colonizer.* Published by the author, 1954.

Forrest, Earle R. Earle Forrest File. Arizona Pioneer Historical Society, Tucson, AZ.

———. "Riding for the Old CO Bar." *Arizonian: The Journal of Arizona History* 5, no. 1 (1963): 3.

———. "Fort Rickerson, Greatest Old-Time Cattle Ranch." *Frontier Times* 12, no. 4 (January 1935).

Foster, Craig L. "The Men of the Lot Smith Company of 1862." *Genealogical Journal* 26, no. 4 (1998): 150–162.

Gardner, Hamilton, Colonel AUS (Ret). *Pioneer Military Leaders of Utah.* Salt Lake City: N.p., 1952.

Gardner, Hamilton, ed. "A Territorial Militiaman in the Utah War, Journal of Newton Tuttle." *Utah Historical Quarterly* 22 (1954): 305–311.

Gibbons, Helen Bay. *Saint and Savage.* Salt Lake City: Deseret Book, 1965.

Golder, Frank Alfred, Thomas A. Bailey and J. Lyman Smith. *The March of the Mormon Battalion From Council Bluffs to California, Taken from the Journal of Henry Standage.* New York: The Century Company, 1928.

Gordon, Sarah Barringer. *The Mormon Question: Polygamy and Constitutional Conflict in Nineteenth-Century America.* Chapel Hill: The University of North Carolina Press, 2003.

Gottfredson, Peter. *History of Indian Depredations in Utah.* (Salt Lake City: printed by the author, 1919, 2nd ed., 1969).

Gove, Captain Jesse A. *The Utah Expedition, 1857–1858, Letters of Capt. Jesse A. Gove, 10ᵗʰ Inf., U.S.A., of Concord, N.H., to Mrs. Gove, and special correspondence of the New York Herald.* New Hampshire Historical Society Collections 12. Edited by Otis G. Hammond. Concord, NH: New Hampshire Historical Society, 1928.

Grant, Heber J. Journal. Manuscript, LDS Church History Library, Salt Lake City.

———. Letter to Lucy Grant, March 12, 1883. LDS Church History Library.

Grover, Stephen E. and Dean R. Grover. *Thomas Grover, His Ancestors and Descendants.* Phoenix: W. A. Krueger, 1966.

Hafen, LeRoy R. and Ann W. Hafen. *Handcarts to Zion, The Story of a Unique Western*

Migration 1856-1860 with contemporary journals, accounts, reports; and rosters of members of the ten Handcart Companies. Glendale, CA: Arthur H. Clark, 1960.

Hale, Heber Q. *Biography of J. H. Hale.* Section on Solomon H. Hale. Salt Lake City: N.p., 1938.

Hales, Brian C. *Joseph Smith's Polygamy, Vol. 3: Theology.* Salt Lake City: Greg Kofford Books, 2015.

Hamilton, Henry S. *Reminiscences of a Veteran.* Concord, NH: Republican Press, 1897.

Hammond, William Wallace. Biography. Works Progress Administration, 2:157.

Hansen, Klaus J. *Quest for Empire: The Political Kingdom of God and the Council of Fifty in Mormon History.* Lincoln: University of Nebraska Press, 1974.

Harper's New Monthly Magazine 16 (December 1857–May 1858): 258.

Hatch, Lorenzo Hill. *Lorenzo Hill Hatch Journal, Copied from original Journals by Ruth Savage Hilton, Typescript.* Mimeographed by Brigham Young University Adult Education and Extension Services Extension Publications, March 1958.

Hatch, Lorenzo H. Letter to Jesse N. Smith, February 2, 1880. Utah State University Special Collections.

Hess, Margaret Steed. *My Farmington: A History of Farmington, Utah, 1847–1976.* Farmington: Daughters of the Utah Pioneers, 1976.

Hilton, Hope A. *"Wild Bill" Hickman and the Mormon Frontier.* Salt Lake City: Signature Books, 1988.

Hinckley, Bryant S. *Daniel Hanmer Wells and Events of His Time.* Salt Lake City: Deseret News Press, 1942.

Historical Department Journal. LDS Church History Library, Salt Lake City.

Hochderffer, George E. F. J. *Flagstaff Whoa! The Autobiography of a Western Pioneer.* Flagstaff, AZ: Northern Arizona Society of Science & Aft, Northland Press, 1965.

Howell, Eva Rice. Letter to Carmen R. Smith, April 13, 1969. In author's possession.

———. Letter to Carmen R. Smith, April 22, 1972. In author's possession.

———. Letter to Carmen R. Smith, June 29, 1972. In author's possession.

Hubbard, Lester A. *Ballads and Songs from Utah.* Edited by Kenly W. Whitelock. Salt Lake City: University of Utah Press, 1961

Hullinger, Harvey Coe. Diary (1862). LDS Church History Library, Salt Lake City.

Hunt, William J. *History Extracts.* Courtesy of Mrs. LaRoy Saline. Copy in author's possession.

Hyde, William. *The Private Journal of William Hyde.* Manuscript. LDS Church History Library, Salt Lake City.

Ivins, Anthony Woodward. Journal. LDS Church History Library, Salt Lake City.

Jacobs, Henry Chariton. Diary (1867-1870). Manuscript, LDS Church History Library, Salt Lake City.

Jacobus, Donald Lines. *Families of Ancient New Haven.* Vol. 4. Baltimore: Genealogical Publishing, 1981.

Jensen, J. Marinus. *History of Provo, Utah.* (Provo, UT: New Century, 1924).

Jenson, Andrew. *Chronology of the Church of Jesus Christ of Latter-day Saints, 1805-1884.* Vol. 1, LDS Church History Library, Salt Lake City.

———, ed. *Documentary History of the Church.* LDS Church History Department, Salt Lake City.

———. *Encyclopedic History of the Church of Jesus Christ of Latter-day Saints.* Salt Lake City: Deseret News Publishing, 1941.

———. *History of Seventy Quorums.* LDS Church History Library, Salt Lake City.

———. *Latter-day Saint Biographical Encyclopedia, A Compilation of Biographical Sketches of Prominent Men and Women in the Church of Jesus Christ of Latter-day Saints.* Salt Lake City: Andrew Jenson History Company, 1914.

Johnson, Annie R. *Heartbeats of Colonia Diaz.* Mesa, AZ: Published by the author, 1972.

Johnston, Philip. Letter to Omer Smith and Carmen Smith, April 11, 1976. In author's possession.

Johnson, Rolla Virgil. *The Life Review of a Mormon.* Edited by Miles Edgar Johnson. Brigham Young University Library.

Jones, Daniel W. *Forty Years Among the Indians.* Tucson, AZ: Western Lore Press, 1960.

Jones, Nathaniel V. Diary, 1846–1847. Special Collections and Archives, J. Willard Marriott Library, University of Utah, Salt Lake City.

Journal History of the Church of Jesus Christ of Latter-day Saints. LDS Church History Library, Salt Lake City.

Journal of Discourses, 26 vols.London and Liverpool: LDS Booksellers Depot, 1854-86.

Journals of the Legislative Assembly of the Territory of Utah. Twentieth Session For the Year 1872., Salt Lake City,: Deseret New Book and Job Office, 1872.

Journals of US Volunteers. Utah State Archives & Records, Service No. 1507.

Judd, Zodak Knapp. Reminiscences, Typescript. Utah State Historical Society.

Kane, Elizabeth W. *Twelve Mormon Homes Visited in Succession on a Journey Through Utah to Arizona.* Dallas, TX: L. K. Taylor Publishing Company , 1973).

Kelly, Charles S. "Chief Hoskaninni." *Utah Historical Quarterly* 21, no. 3 (July 1953).

Keysor, Guy Messiah. Battalion Journal (1846). Manuscript. Salt Lake City: Utah State Historical Society, n.d.

Kimball, Solomon F. "Thrilling Experiences." In *Stories from Mormon History,* ed. Alma P. Burton and Clea M. Burton, 241–44. Salt Lake City: Deseret Book, 1960.

———. "Our Pioneer Boys." *Improvement Era* 11, no. 9 (July 1908): 668-680.

Kimball, Stanley B. "Nauvoo West: The Mormons of the Iowa Shore." *BYU Studies Quarterly* 18 (Winter 1978): 132–42.

Kirkham, Francis W., Ph. D. and Harold Lundstrom, eds. *Tales of a Triumphant People, A History of Salt Lake County, Utah 1847-1900.* Salt Lake City: Stevens and Wallis Press, 1947.

Knowlton, George Quincy. *History of Farmington, Utah. 1956, As Compiled and Edited by His Daughter Jannetta K. Robinson.* N.p.: Inland, 1965.

Knowlton, Minerva Richards. "History of Nanny Longstroth Richards." Typescript in possession of authors.

Krenkel, John H., ed. *The Life & Times of Joseph Fish, Mormon Pioneer.* Danville, IL: Interstate Printers & Publishers, 1970.

Larson, Gustive O. "The Mormon Reformation." *Utah Historical Quarterly* 26 (January 1958): 45–63.

Latter-Day Saints' Millennial Star (England), 1869–71.

Lee, Joseph "Jode" Hyrum Jr. Interview by P. T. Reilly, n.d. Typescript. Cline Library, Northern Arizona University, Flagstaff, AZ.

Lee, Joseph. "My Wonderful Country." *The True West Frontier Times* 48, no. 2 (February–March 1974).

Leonard, Glen M. *A History of Farmington, Utah, to 1890, A Thesis submitted to the Faculty of the University of Utah in partial fulfillment of the requirements for the degree of Mater of Arts, Department of History, University of Utah, June 1966.* Typescript in possession of authors.

Lincoln, Abraham. Telegram from President Abraham Lincoln to President of The Church of Jesus Christ of Latter-day Saints, April 26, 1862. Brigham Young Collection, Box 16, F 219, LDS Church History Archives.

Little Colorado Stake Quarterly Conference Minutes. Typescript. Special Collections, Northern Arizona University, Flagstaff, AZ.

Madsen, Raymond W. "Scottish Convert Made Long Ocean Journey to Join Ill-Fated Handcart Group." *Pioneer* (City Creek Chapter, Sons of the Utah Pioneers) (May–June 1984): 5–6.

Maguire, Don. "Don Maguire's Trading Expedition in Northern Arizona, 1879." Edited by Gary Topping. *Utah Historical Quarterly*, 53 (Fall 1985): 380–95.

Majors, Alexander. *Seventy Years on the Frontier. Alexander Major's Memoirs of Lifetime on the Border.* New York: Rand McNally, 1893.

Martineau, James Henry. Autobiography and journal. LDS Church History Library, Salt Lake City.

McAllister, Daniel Handley. *Reminiscences & Journal.* Manuscript, LDS Church History Library, Salt Lake City.

McAllister, John Daniel Thompson. Diary, Typescript. Provo, UT: Brigham Young University, n.d.

McClellan, George A. "My Family." LDS Church History Library, Salt Lake City. Typescript courtesy of Mrs. Leland Hicks.

McClellan, William Carroll. Diary. Manuscript, LDS Church History Library, Salt Lake City.

McClintock, James H. *Mormon Settlement in Arizona: A Record of Peaceful Conquest of the Desert.* (Phoenix, AZ: Manufacturing Stationers, 1921.

McFarland, James C. *A Warrior for His People, Lot Smith and the Civil War.* Kaysville, UT: 1982).

McNitt, Frank. *The Indian Traders.* Norman: University of Oklahoma Press, 1962).

Michie, Robert E. L. *Report on Lot Smith Killing, July 13, 1892.* National Archives, Records of the War Department, Record Group 98, Department of Arizona.

Miller, Marilyn McMeen, and John Cafton Moffitt. *Provo, A Story of People In Motion.* Provo, UT: Brigham Young University Press, 1974).

Mills, Martin Walderfen. Journal of Martin Walderfen Mills. Typescript. Courtesy of Karma Smith. In author's possession.

Mortensen, Karen Katrina Olsen. *Life Story.* N.p.: n.d. Typescript in possession of authors.

Mortensen, Lauritz F. *Life Sketch.* N.p: 1955. Typescript in possession of authors.

Nauvoo Legion, Utah Territory. LDS Church History Library, Salt Lake City.

Nauvoo Legion (Utah) records. The Church of Jesus Christ of Latter-day Saints. Church History Library, Salt Lake City.

Nelson, Price W. *Autobiography.* Manuscript, Utah State Historical Society.

"Interesting From Utah." *New York Times*, July 8, 1858.

Nibley, Preston. *Brigham Young the Man and His Work*. Salt Lake City: Deseret News Press, 1937.

Nielson, Frihoff Godfrey. *Journal of Frihoff Godfrey Nielson 1851–1893*. 3 vols. (Published by the Nielson family, n.d.)

———. *Minutes of Frihoff Nielson for the Sunset Committee*. LDS Church History Library, Salt Lake City.

Nuttall, Leonard John. Letter, September 24, 1878. *Deseret News* 27:599; Letter to John Taylor, September 26, 1878, *Deseret News* 27:603; Letter to John Taylor, September 29, 1878, *Deseret News* 27:615; *Deseret News* 27:622, 658.

———. Letter to John Taylor, November 4, 1878. Journal History, November 4, 1878. LDS Church History Library, Salt Lake City.

Oliver, James A. *Biography of Samuel Bateman, 1832–1881*. Provo, UT: Brigham Young University Press, 1945.

Pace, William Byram. Journal (1832-1880), Typescript. Brigham Young University, Provo, UT.

Palmer, George W. "Lot Smith in Life and Death." *Deseret Weekly*, August 3, 1892.

Park, Hamilton G. Letter to Brigham Young, October 15, 1869. LDS Church History Library, Salt Lake City.

Parry, Joseph. Journal. Holograph duplicate. LDS Church History Library, Salt Lake City.

Patrick, John R. "The School of the Prophets: Its Development and Influence in the Utah Territory." Master's thesis, Brigham Young University, 1970.

Peterson, Andrew Christian. "An Account Related," Letter to Carmen R. Smith, October 20, 1979. In author's possession. Courtesy of Dale Peterson.

Peterson, Charles S. "'A Mighty Man was Brother Lot': A Portrait of Lot Smith— Mormon Frontiersman." *The Western Historical Quarterly* 1, no. 4 (October 1970): 393–414.

Peterson, Sally Smith. Letter to Carmen R. Smith, August 23, 1978. In author's possession.

Peterson, Thomas F. *A. C. Peterson: Citizen of Three Nations*. Thomas F. Peterson and Ruthie P. Skousen, 2003.

Pettigrew, David. Journal. Manuscript, MSS 473. Provo, UT: Utah State Historical Society, Brigham Young University..

Petree, Sandra Ailey. *Recollections of Past Days: The Autobiography of Patience Loader Rozsa Archer*, Logan, UT: USU Press, 2006).

Pinckney (MI) Dispatch. Vol. 3, 1885.

Pierson, Ralph. "What the Hell Do You Want Two Guns For?" *Complete Novel Magazine* 27 (July 1927).

Porter, Samuel Uriah. *Life Sketch of Samuel Uriah Porter*. Typescript courtesy Elma Bigler Richards Price. In author's possession.

Portrait, Genealogical and Bibliographical Record of the State of Utah. Chicago: National Historical Record Company, 1902.

"Relics and Interesting Historical Data, in the possession of Lot Smith, That Are Now in the Possession of Al Smith." September 16, 1938, Special Collections, University of Arizona.

Ressler, John Quentin. "1937 Moenkopi, Sequent occupance, landscape change &

view of the environment in an oasis in the Western Navajo Reservation." Master's thesis, University of Oregon, 1972.

Reynolds, George. Letter to Lot Smith, June 20, 1891. First Presidency Reel 20, vol. 23, September 1890–August 1891. LDS Church History Library, Salt Lake City.

———. Letter to Carmen R. Smith, June 25, 1960. In author's possession.

Rhead, Nona Smith. *Lot Smith: Captain-Colonizer-Churchman, 1830–1892.* Manuscript, n.d. LDS Church History Library, Salt Lake City.

Rice, Eva Augusta. "Sketch of the Life of Laura Louisa Burdick [Smith], Daughter of Alden Burdick and Jerusha Park. Wife of Lot Smith, and William Messenger." Typescript, 1962.

Rice, William Kelsey. *History of William Kelsey Rice.* N.p., n.d. Courtesy of Mrs. Owen F. Bloomfield.

Richardson, Sullivan C. *Compilation, Parts 1 and 2.* Self-published, n.d. Copy in possession of authors.

———. (Mesa, Arizona: 1931), Collections of Annie Burk.

———. *Early Settlers of Arizona.* Typescript, n.d., LDS Church History Library, Salt Lake City, Utah.

———. *In Desert Arizona.* Independence, MO: Press of Zion's Printing and Publishing, 1938).

———. *Remembrances of Lot Smith.* Typescript. Mesa, Arizona: N.p., 1936 In possession of authors.

———. *Richardson Family.* LDS Church History Library.

Riverton Wyoming Stake. *Remember, The Willie and Martin Handcart Companies and Their Rescuers—Past and Present.* Provo, UT: Centaur Print Partners, 1997.

Roberts, B. H. *The Mormon Battalion: Its History and Achievements.* University of Michigan Library: January 1, 1919.

Robison, Lewis. Journal. Microfilm. LDS Church History Library, Salt Lake City.

Robinson, Joseph Lee. *History of Joseph Lee Robinson.* Provo, UT: Brigham Young University, n.d.; LDS Church History Library, Salt Lake City.

———. *Book of Joseph L. Robinson, Bishop of North Cottonwood Ward.* Manuscript, LDS Church History Library, Salt Lake City.

Rockwood, Albert Perry. Diary. Manuscript, LDS Church History Library, Salt Lake City.

Rogers, Andrew Locy. *Reminiscences, Typescript.* Flagstaff: Special Collections, Northern Arizona University Library, n.d.

Rogers, Lenora S. *Sketch of the Life of Andrew Locy Rogers.* Flagstaff: Special Collections, Northern Arizona University, October 23, 1946.

Rogers, Samuel Hollister. Journal (1819-1886), Typescript. Copied at Provo, UT: Brigham Young University, 1954); Manuscript, msd 883 883, LDS Church History Library, Salt Lake City.

Romney, Thomas Cottam. *Life History of Miles P. Romney.* Independence, MO: Zion's Printing & Publishing, 1948.

Rose, Alley S. *Journal, 1896–1910.* LDS Church History Library, Salt Lake City.

Sainsbury, R. E., clerk. Official minutes Tuba meetings February 1888 sent to Brigham Young Jr. Manuscript 3897, LDS Church History Library, Salt Lake City.

Salmon River Mission Journal, 1855–1858. LDS Church History Library, Salt Lake City.

Savage, Levi Mathers. *Family History Journal 1876-1935.* Manuscript. Provo, UT: Brigham Young University Press, 1955.

———. *Levi M. Savage Journal March 1, 1885 to April 10, 1886.* Manuscript, LDS Church History Library, Salt Lake City.

Schindler, Harold. *Orrin Porter Rockwell, Man of God, Son of Thunder.* Salt Lake City: University of Utah Press, 1966.

Seegmiller, Janet Burton. *"Be Kind to the Poor": The Life Story of Robert Taylor Burton.* (USA: Robert Taylor Burton Family Organization, 1988.)

Settle, Raymond W. and Mary Lund Settle. *War Drums and Wagon Wheels, The Story of Russell, Majors and Waddell.* Lincoln: University of Nebraska Press, 1966).

Shirts, Morris A. and Kathryn H. Shirts. *A Trial Furnace, Southern Utah's Iron Mission.* Provo, Utah: Brigham Young University Press, 2001.

Shoemaker, Samuel E. "Interview with the Navajo, Cat-chose, on the Death of Lot Smith, February 17, 1895." Manuscript. Los Angeles, CA: Braun Research Library, n.d.

Smith, Al. Letter to Omer J. Smith, June 11, 1972. Kingsman, AZ. In author's possession.

Smith, Alice Ann Richards. Letter to Lula Greene Richards, July 21, 1921. Louise Lula Greene Richards Papers, circa 1860-1935. Manuscript, LDS Church History Library, Salt Lake City.

———. Journal extracts. Manuscript, LDS Church History Library, Salt Lake City.

———. *The Living Words of Alice Ann Richards Smith: Selected Writings of a Great Lady, With Other Articles of Interest.* Logan, UT: N.p., 1968.

Smith, Alice Baugh. "Pioneer Personal History." Federal Writers' Project, UTAH HRS 314, Revised March 9, 1937. *Utah Pioneer Biographies.* Vol 26. Salt Lake City: Genealogical Society Library, n.d.

Smith, Azariah. Journal (1828-1912). Manuscript, LDS Church History Library, Salt Lake City.

Smith, Carmen R. Al Smith to Kent M. Smith, interview by Carmen R. Smith, October 21, 1974. In author's possession.

———. Alden Rice, interview by Carmen R. Smith, June 2, 1971. In author's possession.

———. Alden B. Smith II, interview by Carmen R. Smith, January 9, 1984. In author's possession.

———. Alden B. Smith II, interview by Carmen R. Smith, February 9, 1984. In author's possession.

———. Charles E. Richardson to Edmund W. Richardson, interview by Carmen R. Smith, n.d. In author's possession.

———. Claridell DeWitt, interview by Carmen R. Smith, July 14, 1977. Utah. In author's possession.

———. Cora Creswell Kahl, interview by Carmen R. Smith, March 31, 1978, Sun City, AZ. In author's possession.

———. Diantha M. Smith to Alberta Craig Rider, interview by Carmen R. Smith, June 10, 1972. In author's possession.

———. Diantha M. Smith to Eliza Coombs Cluff as remembered by daughter Vera Cluff Norton, interview by Carmen R. Smith, March 28, 1975. Copy in author's possession.

———. Edmund W. Richardson, interview by Carmen R. Smith, August 21, 1974. In author's possession.

———. Gary L. Tietjen, interview by Carmen R. Smith, August 1976, Los Alamos, NM. In author's possession.

———. James L. Kimball from his father LeRoy Kimball, interview by Carmen R. Smith, n.d. In author's possession.

———. Laura Smith Jones, interview by Carmen R. Smith, July 19, 1984, Shouldice, Alberta. In author's possession.

———. Leona Brinkerhoff Graves Colvin Bolinger, interview by Carmen R. Smith, August 30, 1976, Safford, AZ. In author's possession.

———. Leonard Valgene Hamson, interview by Carmen R. Smith, n.d. In author's possession.

———. Mr. and Mrs. Owen Bloomfield from Elva Leavitt Bond, interview by Carmen R. Smith, February 24, 1979, Salt Lake City. In author's possession.

———. "The Lost Well of the Mormon Battalion Rediscovered." *Utah Historical Quarterly* 57, no. 3 (N.d.): 277–286.

———. S. Eugene Flake, interview by Carmen R. Smith, March 26, 1976. In author's possession.

———. Son of "Pen" Smith, interview by Carmen R. Smith, n.d., Pintura, AZ. In author's possession.

———. Warren Brinkerhoff and Lydia Ann Nelson Brinkerhoff, interview by Carmen R. Smith, March 1977, Mesa, AZ. In author's possession.

———. Warren Brinkerhoff, interview by Carmen R. Smith, May 15, 1977, Mesa, AZ. In author's possession.

———. Willard R. Smith to Nephi L. Smith, interview by Carmen R. Smith, June 1, 1977. In author's possession.

———. Zina Brinkerhoff Hatch, interview by Carmen R. Smith, February 9, 1977, Mesa, AZ. In author's possession.

Smith, Celia. *The Story of Eliza Ann Dibble and Her Three Husbands, Orson Spencer, Henry W. Jackson, and Julius A. C. Austin.* N.p.: M. A. Smith, 1994.

Smith, Elias, ed. "The Expedition After Indians." *Deseret News.* August 13, 1862.

Smith, Jesse Nathaniel. *Journal of Jesse Nathaniel Smith, The Life Story of a Mormon Pioneer, 1834-1906.* Salt Lake City: Jesse N. Smith Family Association, Deseret News Publishing, 1953.

Smith, Joseph F., John A. Winder, and Anthon H. Lund. Letter to Bishop David Brinkerhoff, January 29, 1902. First Presidency Joseph F. Smith Letterbooks, August 1901–September 1902, LDS Church History Library, Salt Lake City.

Smith, Joseph F., John A. Winder, and Anthon H. Lund. Letter to Bishop David Brinkerhoff, February 28, 1902. First Presidency Joseph F. Smith Letterbooks, August 1901–September 1902, LDS Church History Library, Salt Lake City.

Smith, Joseph F., John A. Winder, and Anthon H. Lund. Letter to Jesse N. Smith, March 10, 1902. First Presidency Joseph F. Smith Letterbooks, August 1901–September 1902, LDS Church History Library, Salt Lake City.

Smith, Joseph H. Autobiography, Typescript. Utah State Historical Society.

Smith (Rice), Laura Louisa. "A Short Sketch of the Life of Laura Louisa Smith Born December 21, 1868 at Farmington, Davis Co., Utah." Ogden, UT: N.p., September 7, 1932, Holograph copy in possession of authors.

Smith, Lot. Letter to Brigham Young, June 16, 1862. University of Utah Special Collections.

———. Letter to Brigham Young, June 27, 1862. Utah State Archives, No. 712. Salt Lake City.

———. Letter to Brigham Young, June 9, 1875. LDS Church History Library, Salt Lake City.

———. Letter to Brigham Young, November 6, 1876. University of Utah Library, Salt Lake City.

———. Letter to John Taylor, December 10, 1878. LDS Church History Library, Salt Lake City.

———. Letter to John Taylor, February 26, 1878. LDS Church History Library, Salt Lake City.

——— et al. Letter to John Taylor, January 10, 1879. Utah State Historical Society Collection, Salt Lake City.

———. Letter to John Taylor, March 8, 1879. LDS Church History Library, Salt Lake City.

———. Letter to John Taylor, July 12, 1879. John Taylor 1808–1887 Collection, LDS Church History Library, Salt Lake City.

———. Letter to *Deseret News*, December 18, 1881. Lot Smith Personal papers and correspondence, Special Collections, University of Arizona, Tucson.

———. Letter to Jesse N. Smith, January 31, 1882. Courtesy of Mrs. Burton (Jessie) Smith. Copy in author's possession.

———. Letter to John Taylor, October 21, 1882. John Taylor 1808–1887 Collection, LDS Church History Library, Salt Lake City.

———. Letter to Bishop J. Hunt. Holograph. LDS Church History Library, Salt Lake City.

———. Letter to John Taylor, July 19, 1886. John Taylor 1808–1887 Collection, LDS Church History Library, Salt Lake City.

———. Letter to Wilford Woodruff, February 1889. First Presidency Letterpress Copybooks, 1877–1949, LDS Church History Library, Salt Lake City.

———. Letter to Wilford Woodruff, April 2, 1889. First Presidency Letterpress Copybook, 1877–1949, LDS Church History Library, Salt Lake City.

———. Letter to Wilford Woodruff, June 10, 1889. First Presidency Letterpress Copybook, 1877–1949, LDS Church History Library, Salt Lake City.

———. Letter to Wilford Woodruff, June 25, 1889. First Presidency Letterpress Copybook, 1877–1949, LDS Church History Library, Salt Lake City.

———. Letter to Wilford Woodruff, December 9,1889. First Presidency Letterpress Copybook, 1877–1949, LDS Church History Library, Salt Lake City.

———. Letter to Wilford Woodruff, March 11, 1890. First Presidency Letterpress Copybooks, 1877–1949, CR 1 20 #17, LDS Church History Library, Salt Lake City.

———. Letter to Wilford Woodruff, March 17, 1890. First Presidency Letterpress

Copybooks, 1877–1949, LDS Church History Library, Salt Lake City.

———. Letter to Wilford Woodruff, April 14, 1890. First Presidency Letterpress Copybooks, 1877–1949, LDS Church History Library, Salt Lake City.

———. Letter to Hyrum Smith (son of Lot), May 20, 1890. Courtesy of Kenneth B. Smith. Copies in author's possession.

———. Letter to Hyrum Smith (son of Lot), June 24, 1890. Courtesy of Kenneth B. Smith. Copies in author's possession.

———. Letter to Wilford Woodruff, July 31, 1890. First Presidency Letterpress Copybooks, 1877–1949, LDS Church History Library, Salt Lake City.

———. Letter to Hyrum Smith (son of Lot), August 1890. Courtesy of Kenneth B. Smith. Copies in author's possession.

———. Letter to Jesse N. Smith, August 19, 1890. Handwritten by scribe, signed by Lot Smith, copy in author's possession. Courtesy of Jesse N. Smith.

———. Letter to Wilford Woodruff, August 20, 1890. First Presidency Letterpress Copybooks, 1877–1949, LDS Church History Library, Salt Lake City.

———. Letter to Wilford Woodruff, September 10, 1890. First Presidency Letterpress Copybooks, 1877–1949, LDS Church History Library, Salt Lake City.

———. Letter to Hyrum Smith (son of Lot), September 17, 1890. Courtesy of Kenneth B. Smith. Copies in author's possession.

———. Letter to Hyrum Smith (son of Lot), September 19, 1890. Courtesy of Kenneth B. Smith. Copies in author's possession.

———. Letter to Hyrum Smith (son of Lot), December 1890. Courtesy of Kenneth B. Smith. Copies in author's possession.

———. Letter to Wilford Woodruff, January 26, 1891. First Presidency Letterpress Copybooks, 1877–1949, LDS Church History Library, Salt Lake City.

———. Letter to Jesse N. Smith, February 24, 1891. Holograph courtesy of Jessie Smith. Copy in author's possession.

———. Letter to George Reynolds, May 16, 1891. First Presidency Letterpress Copybooks, 1877–1949, LDS Church History Library, Salt Lake City.

———. Letter to High Council of the Snowflake Stake, September 2, 1891. Holograph courtesy of Jessie Smith. Copy in author's possession.

———. Letter to Jessie N. Smith, September 2, 1891. Holograph courtesy of Jessie Smith. Copy in author's possession.

———. Letter to George Reynolds, December 28, 1891. First Presidency Letterpress Copybooks, 1877–1949, LDS Church History Library, Salt Lake City.

———. Letter to Presiding Bishop W. B. Preston, January 17, 1892. First Presidency Letterpress Copybooks, 1877–1949, LDS Church History Library, Salt Lake City.

———. Letter to Jessie N. Smith, February 29, 1892. Holograph courtesy of Jessie Smith. Copy in author's possession.

———. Letter to Brother Fish, March 14, 1892. Holograph courtesy Ed Karges, ACMI Records.

———. Letter to Brother Fish, April 12, 1892. Holograph courtesy Ed Karges, ACMI Records.

———. Letter to Brother Fish, May 4, 1892. Holograph courtesy Ed Karges, ACMI

Records.

———. Letter to Jessie N. Smith, May 10, 1892. Holograph courtesy of Jessie Smith. Copy in author's possession.

———. Letter to SUO Committee, n.d. LDS Church History Library, Salt Lake City.

Smith, Lydia M. Pension Records, Deposition A, Case of Lydia M. Smith, No. 15411, September 17, 1900, Military Service Records, National Archives, Washington, D.C.

Smith, Omer J. and Carmen R. Smith. Interview of Alvin "Mike" Steed. Audio recording. May 14, 1976. In author's possession.

———. Amelia Topham, interview by Omer J. Smith and Carmen R. Smith, circa 1950s, Parowan, UT. In author's possession.

———. Bob Lockett, interview by Omer J. Smith and Carmen R. Smith, October 1978. In author's possession.

———. Burton Smith, interview by Omer J. Smith and Carmen R. Smith, n.d., Flagstaff, AZ. In author's possession.

———. Charlie Ashurst to Nephi Lot Smith, interview by Omer J. Smith and Carmen R. Smith, June 1, 1972, Central, AZ. In author's possession.

———. Chloe Knowlton Hess, interview by Omer J. and Carmen Smith, May 1979. In author's possession.

———. Diantha M. Smith to Nephi Lot Smith, interview by Omer J. and Carmen R. Smith, June 1966. In author's possession.

———. Diantha M. Smith to Nephi Lot Smith, interview by Omer J. and Carmen R. Smith, June 10, 1972. In author's possession.

———. Emma Mortensen Skousen, interview by Omer J. Smith and Carmen R. Smith, c. 1950s. In author's possession.

———. Everett. E. Ellinwood to James M. Smith, interview by Omer J. Smith and Carmen R. Smith, December 25, 1964. In author's possession.

———. Fred Abbott, interview by Omer J. Smith and Carmen R. Smith, June 25, 1960. In author's possession.

———. J. David Lee to James M. Smith, interview by Omer J. Smith and Carmen R. Smith, n.d., Central, AZ. In author's possession.

———. James M. Smith, interview by Omer J. Smith and Carmen R. Smith, n.d., Central, AZ. In author's possession.

———. Karl Smith, interview by Omer J. Smith and Carmen R. Smith, June 1973. In author's possession.

———. Karl Smith, interview by Omer J. Smith and Carmen R. Smith, June 22, 1974, Rock Springs, WY. In author's possession.

———. Karl Smith, interview by Omer J. Smith and Carmen R. Smith, October 2–3, 1975. In author's possession.

———. Kee Doogai, interviews by Omer J. Smith and Carmen R. Smith, July 20, 1976, Page, AZ. In author's possession.

———. Kee Doogai, interview by Omer J. Smith and Carmen R. Smith, October 16, 1977, Big Canyon, AZ. In author's possession.

———. Louis Evans, interview by Omer J. and Carmen R. Smith, October 6, 1980.

In author's possession.

———. Lorenzo Smith to James M. Smith, interview by Omer J. Smith and Carmen R. Smith, December 25, 1964. In author's possession.

———. Nephi Lot Smith, interview by Omer J. Smith and Carmen R. Smith, June 28, 1974. In author's possession.

———. Nephi L. Smith, interview by Omer J. Smith and Carmen R. Smith, September 1975. In author's possession.

———. Willard Smith and Karl Smith, interview by Omer J. Smith and Carmen R. Smith, October 2, 1975. In author's possession.

———. Willard Smith to Nephi L. Smith, interview by Omer J. Smith and Carmen R. Smith, June 28, 1974. In author's possession.

Smith, Philip. *Lot Smith.* Typescript. Utah State University Special Collections and Archives.

Smith, Sally. "A Choice Memory," Typescript. June 1946. Copy in possession of authors.

Smith, Sterling J. Alden Rice, interview by Sterling J. Smith, September 1979, Emmett, ID. In author's possession.

Smith, Thomas S. Deposition of Thomas S. Smith in Fort Limhi Massacre, April 15, 1858. Brigham Young Letterbooks, 1844–1877. Vol. 4. January 2–November 22, 1858. LDS Church History Library, Salt Lake City.

———. Diaries (1855–1864), holograph. LDS Church History Library.

Smith, William James. Biography, Typescript. N.p., n.d. In possession of authors.

Snay, Mitchell. *Gospel of Disunion: Religion and Separatism in the Antebellum South.* Cambridge: Cambridge University Press, 1993.

Sorensen, Steven R. "Alma Ash." *Pioneer* (City Creek Chapter, Sons of the Utah Pioneers) (July-August 1993).

Standage, Henry. Diary (1846-1847). Manuscript, LDS Church History Library, Salt Lake City.

Standifird, John Henry. *Diary, Typescript.* Special Collections, Northern Arizona University Library, Flagstaff, AZ; LDS Church History Library, Salt Lake City.

Steed, Thomas. *The Life of Thomas Steed From His Own Diary 1826-1910.* N.d. Manuscript, LDS Church History Library, Salt Lake City. Printed copy at Brigham Young University.

Steele, Mahonri M. Letter to parents in Arizona, February 17, 1887.

Stevenson, Joseph Grant, ed. *Porter Family History.* Delta, UT: Joseph Grant Stevenson, 1957; Provo, Utah: Joseph Grant Stevenson, 1983.

Stout, Wayne. *Hosea Stout, Utah's Pioneer Statesman.* Salt Lake City: Self-published, 1953.

Stowell, Brigham. *An Account of My First Trip Into Arizona in the Spring of the Year 1876, Subject to a Call Made by President Brigham Young, Typescript.* N.p., n.d. In possession of authors.

Sunset United Order (SUO) Committee Letterpress Copybook. LDS Church History Library, Salt Lake City.

Taylor, John. Letter, August 14, 1879. First Presidency Letterbook #17. Vol. 3, May 1879–January 1880. LDS Church History Library, Salt Lake City.

———. Letter to Elder Lot Smith and the Elders and Saints in New Mexico, December 13, 1877. First Presidency Letterbook, LDS Church History Library, Salt Lake City.

———. Letter to Lot Smith, November 27, 1878. Manuscript, Special Collection, Brigham Young University, Provo, Utah.

———. Letter to Wilford Woodruff, February 20, 1880. First Presidency Letterbook, 97. LDS Church History Library, Salt Lake City.

Taylor, Philip A. M. "Mormons and Gentiles on the Atlantic." *Utah Historical Quarterly*, 24: 195–214.

Taylor, Samuel W. *The Kingdom or Nothing: The Life of John Taylor, Militant Mormon*. New York: Macmillan, 1976).

Teeples, Nichalous Gourley. "Experience of the Paul Gourley Family with the Martin Hand-cart Company." Microfilm of manuscript. LDS Family History Library, Salt Lake City.

Terry, Thurzal Q. *The Great Utah War*. A-2152 for Utah History Contest, Utah State Historical Society.

Tidwell, Zelda E. "Jesse Wells Smith 1826-1896." Typescript, September 1990. Copy in possession of authors.

———. "William Orville Smith 1800-1849." Typescript in possession of authors.

Tietjen, Gary L. *Encounter with the Frontier, Typescript*. Albuquerque, NM: Self-published, 1969. Courtesy of Alvin "Mike" Steed.

———. Letter to Carmen R. Smith, August 1976. In author's possession.

Tinker, George H. *A Land of Sunshine, Flagstaff and its Surroundings*. Republished as *Northern Arizona in 1887, The People and Resources*. Glendale, CA: Arthur H. Clark, 1969.

Tracy, Albert. "The Utah War, Journal of Albert Tracy, 1858-1860." *Utah Historical Quarterly* 13 (1945).

Tullidge, Edward Wheelock. *History of Salt Lake City*. Salt Lake City: Star Printing, 1886.

Tyler, Sgt. Daniel. *A Concise History of the Mormon Battalion in the Mexican War 1846–1847*. N.p.: Privately printed, 1881; Chicago: Rio Grande Press, 1964.

Udall, David King and Pearl Udall Nelson. *Arizona Pioneer Mormon: David King Udall, His Story and His Family, 1851-1938*. Tucson, AZ: Arizona Silhouettes, 1959.

Utah State Archives & Records, Service, no. 908, no. 1264, no. 3432, February 19–27, 1851.

Walker, Ronald W. "Seeking the 'Remnant': The Native American during the Joseph Smith Period." *Journal of Mormon History*. 19, no. 1 (1–33).

Walker, William Holmes. *The Life Incidents and Travels of Elder William Holmes Walker and his association with Joseph Smith, the Prophet*. 2nd ed.. John Walker Family Organization, 1971.

Weekly Champion (Flagstaff, AZ), 1886, 1887, 1890.

Wells, Daniel H. "Narrative." *Utah Historical Quarterly* 6, no. 4 (October 1933): 817–18.

Wells, Daniel H. Letter to Lot Smith, October 17, 1857. University of Arizona Special Collections.

———. Letter to Lot Smith, April 28, 1862. University of Arizona Special Collections.

———. Letter to Robert T. Burton, October 18, 1857. University of Arizona Special Collections.

————. Letter to Thomas Callister, April 28, 1862. , Nauvoo Legion Letterbook, LDS Church History Library, Salt Lake City.

Whitney, Orson F. *Life of Heber C. Kimball, An Apostle, The Father and Founder of the British Mission.* 2nd ed. Salt Lake City: Stevens & Wallis, 1945.

————. *History of Utah.* Salt Lake City: George Q. Cannon & Sons, 1892.

Whitworth, Robert H. "From the Mississippi to the Pacific, An Englishman in the Mormon Battalion, the Journal of Robert Whitworth," edited by Gracy, David B. II, and Helen J. H. Rugeley. *Arizona and the West, A Quarterly Journal of History* 7, no. 2 (Summer 1965): 127–60.

Williams, James Van Nostrand, *Life Sketch of James Van Nostrand Williams, Typescript.* Utah State Historical Society, Salt Lake City.

Winder, John R. Letter to Major Lot Smith, May 11, 1864. University of Arizona Special Collections.

Winn, Norma B. "The Texas Expedition." *An Enduring Legacy.* Vol. 8. Salt Lake City: Daughters of the Utah Pioneers, 1985.

Wood, Daniel. Record Books. LDS Church History Library, Salt Lake City.

Woodruff, Wilford. Journal, Typescript. LDS Church History Library, Salt Lake City.

————. Letter to the Bishops Hunter and Hardy, October 29, 1879. LDS Church Library, Salt Lake City.

————. Letter to David Brinkerhoff, January 24, 1889. First Presidency Letterpress Copybooks, 1877–1949, LDS Church History Library, Salt Lake City.

————. Letter to David K. Udall, September 17, 1887. Letterpress Copybook, 1887 Sep–1893 Dec, Wilford Woodruff 1807–1898, LDS Church History Library, Salt Lake City.

————. Letter to John Bushman, November 25, 1887. Correspondence 1886–1887, Wilford Woodruff, LDS Church History Department, Salt Lake City.

————. Letter to Lot Smith, September 15, 1880. University of Arizona Special Collections, Tucson, AZ.

————. Letter to Lot Smith, December 14, 1880. University of Arizona Special Collections, Tucson, AZ.

————. Letter to Lot Smith, January 16, 1882. University of Arizona Special Collections, Tucson, AZ.

————. Letter to Lot Smith, January 31, 1882. University of Arizona Special Collections, Tucson, AZ.

————. Letter to Lot Smith, October 23, 1882. University of Arizona Special Collections, Tucson, AZ.

————. Letter to Lot Smith, November 10, 1882. P. T. Reilly Collection, Cline Library, Northern Arizona University.

————. Letter to Lot Smith, March 23, 1883. University of Arizona Special Collections, Tucson, AZ.

————. Letter to Lot Smith, September 18, 1887. Letterpress Copybook, 1887–1893 Dec, Wilford Woodruff 1807–1898, LDS Church History Library, Salt Lake City.

————. Letter to Lot Smith, January 24, 1889. First Presidency Letterpress Copybooks, 1877–1949, LDS Church History Library, Salt Lake City.

———. Letter to Lot Smith, March 14, 1889. First Presidency Letterpress Copybooks, 1877–1949, LDS Church History Library, Salt Lake City.

———. Letter to Lot Smith, June 27, 1889. First Presidency Letterpress Copybook, 1877–1949, LDS Church History Library, Salt Lake City.

Workman, Andrew Jackson. Andrew Jackson Workman History. Vol. 30 of *Utah Pioneer Biographies*. (Ogden, Utah: Historical Records Survey Project of the Works Progress Administration, 1936); Dixie College, Saint George, UT.

Young, Brigham. Letter to David P. Kimball, February 23, 1871. David Patton Kimball correspondence, Manuscript, LDS Church History Library, Salt Lake City.

———. Letter to George Q. Cannon, February 3, 1876. Brigham Young Letterbook, Box 21, LDS Church History Library, Salt Lake City.

———. Letter to Elder George Lake, July 13, 1877. LDS Church History Library, Salt Lake City.

———. Letter to Elder Lot Smith, September 13, 1872. Brigham Young Letterbook 13, LDS Church History Library, Salt Lake City.

———. Letter to Elder Lot Smith, July 29, 1876. Brigham Young Letterbook, LDS Church History Library, Salt Lake City.

———. Letter to John W. Hess, May 29, 1875. Brigham Young Letterbook, Box 13, Folder 5, LDS Church History Library, Salt Lake City.

———. To Captain Lot Smith and company, April 30, 1862. Microfilm. LDS Church History Library, Salt Lake City; Brigham Young University, Provo, UT.

———. Letter to Lot Smith, May 25, 1869. LDS Church History Library, Salt Lake City.

———. Letter to Lot Smith, May 29, 1875. Brigham Young Letterbook, Box 13, Folder 5, LDS Church History Library, Salt Lake City.

Young, Brigham, Jr. Diaries, Typescript. City of New York City Public Library; Manuscript, LDS Church History Library, Salt Lake City.

Young, John R. Memoirs of John R. Young. Salt Lake City: Deseret News, 1920.

———. Scrapbook of John R. Young. LDS Church History Archives.

Young, Richard W. "The Nauvoo Legion." *Contributor* 9, no. 4 (February 1888): 163-66.

Young, Samuel Claridge. "Treasures of Samuel Claridge Young," Typescript. Courtesy of Gary Tietjen, Los Alamos, NM.

Young, Seymour B. "Lest We Forget" and "Captain Lot Smith (Concluded)." *Improvement Era* 25, nos. 7, 8, 11 (1922): 609-614, 723, 726, 1006.

Index

A

Abbott, Thomas M., 41, 55, 57, 59, 198, 218, 242–44
Adams, Jerome J., 140, 170, 172, 210
Adams, Mary, 140
Adamson, 98
Aker, Saxon S., 167, 216
Alexander, E. P., 40, 53
Alexander, Moroni Woodruff ("Wood"), 82, 245
Allen, Alexander, 230
Allen, James, 3
Allen, William Coleman, 82–83, 119, 126, 148–49, 170, 179, 245, 254
Ambrosia branch records, 1
Ambrosia Settlement. *See* Hawley Settlement.
Antelope Island, 67–68
Argyle, Joseph, 103, 106–8
Arizona Stake of Zion, 137–38, 147
"Arizona Tramps," 118–19
Arnold, Orson P., 46–47, 241–43
Arrowsmith, John Taylor, 82–83, 245
Articles of Agreement/Association, 128, 148
Asay's Ranch, 123
Ash, Alma, 106
Ash, Thomas, 105–6
Ashurst, Edward B., 169, 177
Ashurst, Henry Fountain, 140–41, 169
Ashurst, Sarah, 140, 168–69
Ashurst, William H. ("Bill"), 140, 168–69, 177
Atkinson, James Isaac, 82, 245
Attwood, Richard, 245
Aztec Land and Cattle Company, 176

B

Bagley, John, 243
Bagley, William Henry, 245
Ballinger, Jesse O., 119, 126, 136–37
Bannocks, 23
Baptiste "LeChat," 48–49
Barlow, James Madison, 245

Barlow, Wilford and Laura, 119
Barnard, Lachon/Laconeus, 82, 245
Barney, Ron, xi
Barrett, R. W. ("Bill"), 43, 251
Barton, George H., 97
Baskin, R. N., 109–11
Bateman, Samuel, 46, 56–57, 59, 239, 241–44
Bates, Orville E., 233
Baugh, Elizabeth Ann Fereyhough, 106
Baugh, George Thomas, 106
Bean, James, 21–22
Beckstead, Henry, 243
Bennion, John Rowland, 82, 245
Bennion, Samuel Roberts, 82, 245
Benton, Senator Thomas H., 3
Bess, William, 83, 245
Big Elk, 21–22
Big James, 44
Big Table, 141, 157–58
Bigler, Andrew, 82, 85–86, 93, 245
Bigler, Henry W., 6, 11
Bigler, Jacob G, 113
Bigler, Mark, 49, 243
Bird, Henry, 82, 245
Black Hawk, 93–94
Black, George A., 111
Black, James L., 202, 215–16
Blakeslee, James, 1
Bliss, Harvey, 244
Bloomfield, John, 148, 165
Book of Mormon, 1, 8
Booth, Edwin, 44, 243
Box, Elijah, 103–4
Boyle, Henry G., 16
Bridger, Jim, 25
Bringhurst, William A., 82, 245
Brinkerhoff, David, 202, 208, 213, 230–33, 239
Brinkerhoff, James, 239
Brinkerhoff, Lydia Nelson, 231
Brookbank, Thomas W., 152, 179, 192, 205–6, 223, 233

Brown, Edwin, 82–83, 117–18, 125, 131, 245
Brown, Lorenzo, 58
Brown, Norman, 243
Buchanan, James, 39
Budge, William, 69
Buffalo Bill. *See* William F. Cody.
Bulkley, Newman, 4
Bullock, Thomas, 27
Bunker, Edward, 4
Burdick, Jerusha, 66, 115
Burk, Allen, 19, 65
Burk, Asahel, 177
Burk, Hubert R., 119, 140, 145, 153, 190, 192–93, 200, 206, 208
Burk, Laura, 140
Burnham, Charles Carrol, 82–83, 245
Burnham, Luther, 212
Burton, Ralph Smith, xi
Burton, Robert T., 21–22, 24, 30, 32–34, 57–58, 73–74, 77, 91, 108–9, 111, 113, 163–64, 219
Bushman, John Lewis, 137, 148, 170, 179–82, 192–93, 206–8, 254
Buss, Georgia Smith, xi
Butler, William, 243

C

Cahoon, Henry, 56, 244
Cahoon, John Farrington, 82, 245
Caldwell, Thomas S., 82, 85–86, 245
Calkins, Edwin, 4, 16, 17
Calkins, Theodore J., 82, 245
Call, Israel, 119, 124, 131
Call, Medora, 119
Callister, Thomas, 58–59, 63–64
Camp of the Saints, 187–89
Candland, David, 30–31, 38
Cannon, A., 113
Cannon, George Q., 108, 182, 207
Cantwell, Francis Robert, 82–83, 245
Cardon, Paul, 244
Carpenter, Alexander, 69
Carrington, Albert, 97, 101
Carter, Philo, 17–18
Chachos/Catchose, 228, 236
Chapin, Louisa Mercy/Maria, 70
Charbonneau, Jean Baptiste, 9–10
Cheney, Nathan, 128
Cherry, Jesse Yelton, 82, 245
Christensen, C. L., 136, 159, 212

Christensen, Julius Peter, 248
Christensen, Madse, 29
Christensen, Victor, 248
Clark, Amasa L., 28
Clark, Ezra T., 29
Clark, Hiram, 185
Clark, William, 42
Clemons, Hyrum B., 82, 87, 245
Cleveland, George W., 243
Cluff, W. W., 103
Cody, William F. ("Buffalo Bill"), 45, 80–81
Collins, William Oliver, 80, 81
Comaduran, 13
Comayazzie , 131, 158–59
Conover, Peter W., 22
Cooke, Philip St. George, 8–10, 12, 14–15, 145
Cornia, Peter, 80, 82, 85–86, 245
Cottrell, George, 82, 83, 245
Cournoyer, Pierre. See Peter Cornia.
Covert, Everett, 245
Cowley, Mathias F., 241
Cox, Amos, 12
Cox, Isaiah, 244
Cragun, James H., 82, 93, 245
Craig, Ellis, xi
Craig, James, 78, 80
Crawford, 100
Creswell, Rufus, 199
Crismon Jr., Charles, 82, 89, 245
Cumming, Alfred, 38, 40, 63–65
Cummings, B. F., 251

D

Daggs Brothers, 176, 177, 194
Daggs, John Franklin, 198
Daggs, William A., 195–98, 203, 225
Da-gha-hi Chi (Red Beard), 127, 158, 212, 231, 235
Dalton, Henry L., 30, 245
Davis, Albert Wesley, 245
    Draper, Parley Pine, 245
Davis, Daniel C., 3–4
Davis, Dan, 130
Davison, George W., 245
Dawson, John, 43, 251
Day, Abraham, 4
Day, Henry, 42, 243
DeCloss, L., 236
Dennett, Daniel Q., 4
Devil's Gate, 33–35, 81

Dewey, Albert P., 97, 107–8
DeWitt, Dan, xi
Dibble, Philo, 46, 243
Dickson, Albert D., 243
Digger Indian, 17
Dittenhoffer, Sam, 200
Dixon, Randy, xi
Dorsett, Ruth, xi
Dotson, Marshal Peter K., 64–65, 69
Douglas, Elder William M., 99–103
Duffin, Isaac ("Ike"), 216, 219, 222, 256
Dykes, George P., 12

E

Eardley, Josiah H., 84, 245
Eastern Arizona Stake of Zion, 147
Echo Canyon, 39
Echo Canyon War. *See* Utah War.
Eckles, Delana R., 64
Egan, Howard, 7–8, 62–63
Eldredge, Alma, 103
Eldredge, Horace Sunderlin, 104–5, 108
Ellinwood, Everett E., 224–25
Elmer, Elijah, 14
Esplin, Ron, xi
Evans, Charles M., 245
Evans, Ken, xi
Evans, Ralph, xi

F

Fairchild, Fletcher, 212–14, 219–20, 222–25
Farnsworth, Alonzo L. 212–13, 219–23
Farnsworth, Austin M., 202
Farnsworth, Cyrus, 220
Faust, Henry Jacob, 107
Fellows, Hyrum, 17
Felt, Joseph Henry, 82, 241–42, 245
Ferguson, James, 21, 23–25, 32, 64
Ferguson, Thomas H., 68–69
Ficklin, Benjamin F., 42
Fish, Joseph, 155–56, 179–82
Fisher, Joseph Armstrong, 82, 245
Flake, Chad, xi
Flake, S. Eugene, xi
Flake, William J., 138
Fletcher, Philander, 17
floods, 132-34, 142–43, 145
Flynn, Isham, 21
Folsom, William H., 114

Forrest, Earle R., 167, 174
Forsyth, William, 107
Francis, John W., 202, 225
Freeman, John B., 145
Fremont, John C., 16
Fuller, Will, 245

G

Gadsden Purchase, 16
Gardner, Franklin, 51
Garn, Samuel, 141, 165
Garn, Sarah, 140
Garr, Abel, 34
Geronimo, 192
Gibson, Jonathon, 245
Gibson, Moses Washington, 82, 245
Gilbert, Abel, 63
Goddard, Joseph, 82, 245
Golding, Irving, xi
Goodale, Tim, 77–78
Goodhart, George, 70–71
Gosiutes, 23
Gourley, Paul, 34, 243
Gove, Jesse A., 51, 65
Grant, George D., 21–22, 32–34, 57, 250
Grant, Heber J., 169–71, 241–42
Grant, Jedediah M., 31–32, 37
Grant, William, 82, 245
grasshoppers, 31
Green, James, 82, 84, 245
Greer, Bonnie, xi
Greer, E., 205
Greer, Gilbert, 205
Groo, George W., 107
Grover, Thomas, 19, 29
Guest, Edward Francis Mailon, 245
Gully, Samuel L., 3

H

Haight, Horton D., 41, 47, 243
Hale, Solomon Henry ("Sol"). 82–85, 87,
    89, 218–19, 242, 245, 256
Hall, Mark, 55, 243
Halliday, Abraham, 105
Halliday, Ben, 79
Hamblin, Jacob, 138
Hamilton, Henry S., 40
Hamson, George Frederick, 62, 244
Hancock, Levi W., 10

Hanks, Ebenezer, 18
Hanks, Ephraim K., 21, 24, 58–59, 65
Harmon, Mary Ann Blanks Smithson, 17
Harris, Thomas H., 82, 245
Harrison, Isaac, 4
Hash Knife, 176
   photograph, 199
Hatch, Ira, 125, 152
Hatch, Lorenzo H., 138, 144, 154–55, 173,
   179–82, 220, 237
Hatch, Meltair, 122
Hatch, Permelia, 122
Hawley Settlement, 2
Hayes, William, 130
Helm, John, 245
Henrie, James, 182
Hereford, Robert, 81–89
Herwood, 101–2
Hess, Chloe Knowlton, 64
Hess, Jane, 20
Hess, John W., 94, 110–11, 242
Hess, Moroni, 119
Heward, Stephen, 230–31
Heward, Susannah, 233
Hickman, Thomas J., 53
Hickman, William A. ("Bill"), 47–48, 53,
   70–71, 234
Hickok, James Butler ("Wild Bill"), 45
Hickory Grove Camp, 3–4
Hickson, James, 82, 84, 245
Higbee, Joseph, 21
Hill, Samuel, 82, 241–42, 245
Hill, William H., 244
Hinckley, Ira Nathaniel, 82, 143–44, 242, 245
Hoagland, John, 245
Hobbs, Henry, 130
Hodgett, William Benjamin, 34
Hoggan, James, 101
Hoggan, Janet, 101
Holbrook, Joseph H., 119
Holbrook, Joseph J., 119
Hooper, Talana S., ix
Hooper, William H., 73
Hopis (Oraibis, Moquis), x, 117, 126–27, 138,
   149–50, 152, 159, 169–70, 208, 227, 232
Hopkins, Charles, 4
Hoskinini, 228
Hoskinini-begay, Dinetcloth, 228
Hoskinini-begay, Dinet-tsosi, 228
Hough, Joel, 2

Hough, Riley, 3
Hough, Sarah Stillson, 2
Howe, Richard, 245
Hubbell, Thomas S., 201–2
Huffaker, Lewis Albert, 80–82, 84, 245
Hullinger, Harvey Coe, 245
Hunt, John A., 34
Hunt, John, 143, 184, 194
Huntington, Lot, 234
Hyde, Rosel, 69

I

Imlay, James Havens, 82, 84, 245
Irwin, John, xi
Ivins, Anthony W., 242

J

Jackson, Bill, 184
Jackson, Henry W., 12, 42, 244
Jacob Meeks Ferry, 88
Jacobs, H., 69
Jacobs, Henry Chariton, 98–103
Jacques, Elder John, 107–8
James, Joseph H. ("Joe"), 142 172, 190
Jensen, Lars, 82, 84, 245
Jenson, Andrew, 103
Johnson, Albert Sidney, 235
Johnson, Annie R., 187
Johnson, Henry M., 21
Johnson, Powell, 245
Johnson, Sixtus E., 188
Johnston, Albert Sidney, 64–65, 67
Johnston, Philip, 210
Johnston, William J., 11
Jones, Daniel, 34–35
Jones, Edward, 128
Jones, Elijah, 119
Jones, Malinda, 119
Jones, Maury, xi
Judd, Daniel, 140
Judd, Hiram, 4, 140, 148
Judd, Lyman P., 140
Judd, Zodak K., 4

K

Kahl, Cora Creswell, 199
Kane, Elizabeth, 16
Kane, Thomas L., 63
Kartchner, John, 190

Kearny, Stephen W., 5, 15
Kelly, Edward, 233
Kilfoyle, James, 243
Kimball Jr., Hiram, 82, 245
Kimball, Heber Chase, 27, 29, 31, 91–93, 95, 231
Kimball, Heber P., 68, 77
Kimball, William H., 21, 23, 32–33, 63
Knowles, Henry F., 130
Knowlton, Benjamin F., 64, 244
Knowlton, George Quincy, 28
Knowlton, John Quincy, 79–83, 85, 87, 97, 245

L

Lake, George, 119, 126, 137, 144
Lamanites, 127, 138, 152
Lamb, Preston, 216–17
Lamb, William, 214, 216–17, 222
Lance/Lancehall, William, 4
Larkins, James H., 82, 87, 245
Larson, Thurston, 245
Layton, Christopher, 13, 183
Lee, Ernest, 230
Lee, J. David, 184
Lee, John D., 7–8, 26, 210, 235
Lee, Joseph Hyrum, Jr. ("Jode"), 219, 231–32
Lee, Joseph Hyrum, Sr., 209–10, 233
Lefford, Jeff, 199
Lemmon, Leander, 246
Leonard, Glen, xi
Leroux, Antoine, 9
Lewis Robinson ferry, 76
Lewis, Samuel, 13
Life Guard Cavalry. See Minute Men.
Lightning, 149
Lincoln, Abraham, x, 71, 73–74, 80
Little Colorado Stake of Zion, 147–48
Little Soldier, 64
Loflin, JoJean, xi
Longstroth, William, 82, 246
Lost Well of Mormon Battalion, 9
Lutz, Thomas Jefferson, 82, 246
Lutz, William Wharton, 246
Lyman, Francis M., 178, 182, 255
Lynch, William, 246

M

Macdonald, Alexander F., 109, 183, 187–88
Maguire, Don, 158

Mahomet, 26
Majors and Russell, 40, 42
Marcy, Randolph B., 51–54, 58, 251
Marshall, John, 216
Martin handcart company, 32–35
Martineau, Albert, 184
Martineau, James H., 183
massacre of Mormons planned, 235–36
Maxfield, Elijah H., 246
Maxwell, William B., 184
McAllister, Daniel, 125
McAllister, J. D. T., 40–41, 55–56, 109, 111
McArthur, Daniel D., 63
McBride, Harlum, 4, 16–18, 22–23, 27
McKean, James B., 109, 111, 114
McMurry, Charles, 244
McNeil, David, 103
McNeil, James R., 140, 165
McNeil, John, 103
McNeil, Phoebe, 140
McNichol, Donald/Daniel, 82, 84, 246
Mecham, Lyman, 153
Melick, D. W., 118
Merrill, Edwin de Lafayette, 246
Merrill, Philemon C., 29, 144
Messenger, Charlotte Winifred (Kaberry), 116, 164, 247
Messenger, Howard William, 116, 164, 247
Messenger, William, 116
Michie, Robert E. L., 236
Miller, James R., 244
Miller, Reuban Parley, 246
Millet, Alma, 188
Minute Men (Life Guard Cavalry), 21–27, 32–35
Mission of San Diego de Alcala, 15
Mogollon Livestock Protective Association, 177
Moquis. See Hopis.
Mormon Battalion, 145
    "American Backbone," 12
    camps at Ojo de Vaca, 9
    celebration, 30–31
    Cimarron Desert, 7
    dips water with spoons, 10
    discharges members, 16
    foils power of Fremont, 16
    Fort Leavenworth, 5
    Gila River, 13–14
    importance of wagon route, 16
    Lost Well, 9

near present-day Derry, New Mexico, 9
near Wagon Mound, 7
raises US flag in Tucson, 13
reaches Las Playas and water, 11
reaches Mission of San Diego, 14–15
reaches Pacific Ocean, 14
Rio Grande riverside, 9
San Pedro Valley battle of the bulls, 12–13
Santa Fe, 8
separation at Vale of Tears, 7
St. Joseph, Missouri, 5
travels over Colorado Desert, 14
Arkansas River, 6
Pecos River Valley, 7
Warner's Ranch, 14
Weston, Missouri, 5
Mormon Island, 17
Mormon Volunteers, 16
Mortensen, James, 167–68
Mortensen, Karen, 170
Mortensen, Lauritz F., 179
Mortensen, Margaret, 254
Mortensen, Martin, 191
Mortensen, Morten P., 154, 156
Moss, Charlie, 199
Moss, Daniel, 119
Mountain Meadows Massacre, xi, 235
Moyes baby's death, 102–3
Murdock, John R., 21
Murphy, Mark, 82, 246
Myrick, Merrick Newton, 82, 246

N

National Centennial, 130
Nauvoo Legion of Utah Territory, 21–22
Navajo Code Talkers, 210
Navajos, x, 126–27, 131–32, 138, 159, 169,
    208, 211–12, 219, 231–32, 227–28, 235–36
Nebeker, Ashton, 200
Neff, Benjamin Barr, 246
Neff, John, 246
Nelson, Price, 145
Nielson, Frihoff G., 122, 119, 132, 136,
    142–43, 148, 161, 164–65, 192–93, 206,
    208
Nielson, Peter, 165
Noble, Edward Alvah, 82, 143, 188, 246
North, Hyrum Bennett, 246
Nowlin, Jabez, 22
Noyce, Gladys, xi

Nuttall, L. John, 143–44

O

Oglesby, 134
Ohio Volunteers at Pacific Springs, 80
"Old Bishop" (Ute), 20
Oliphant, C. H., 143
Oraibis. See Hopis.
Osborn, Lewis, 82, 246
Owens, Commodore Perry, 202–6

P

Pacheco, Francisco, 189
Pacific Ocean, 14
Pa-láh Sa-weéch-a-mee, 127, 232
Palmer, Alta, 20
Palmer, Andrea, 20
Palmer, George W., 227, 242
Palmer, Nephi, 20
Park, Hamilton G., 98–103
Park, Hugh D., 82, 84, 246
Parker, Elmont W., 175–76
Parry, Joseph, 242, 244
Patrick, Marshal M. T., 109, 111
Patten, George, 244
Pemberton, Pete, 199
Pendleton, A. J., 21
Penelope, 168, 221
Peteetneet (Payson), Utah, 22
Peterson, Charles S., xi, 147
Peterson, George H., 97
Pettigrew, David, 4, 10
Phelps, Alva, 4
Photographs
    Alice Ann Smith and children, 120
    Hash Knife cowboys, 199
    Lydia Smith's cabin, 217
    Smith's Farmington home, 20
    Smith's mission call holograph, 96
    Smith's Mormon Lake log trough, 140
Pickard, James, 244
Pipkin, Aser, 165
Pipkin, James Knox Polk, 136, 165
Platt, Francis, Jr., 246
Polmantur, Lewis L., 246
Porter, Annie, 140
Porter, Lyman W., 244
Porter, Mason [Marius], 140
Pratt, Addison, 114

Pratt, Orson, 113
Preston, W. B., 224
Prince, Francis, 82, 84, 246
Provo War, 20-22
Prusser, Pruitt or Henry, 199

Q

Qua-chequa, 209

R

railroad spur, 177
Randall, Alfred, 82, 246
Rankin (wagon master), 42
Rawlins, Joseph Sharp, 76, 78, 82–83, 243, 246
Raymond, Spence, 122–23
Red Cloud, 167, 221
Reformation, 32
Reynolds, George, 223
Rhead, Nona Smith, xi
Rhodes, William Henry, 82, 84, 246
Rice, Adelbert, 246
Rice, William Kelsey, 244
Rich, Charles C., 93
Rich, Joseph, 92
Rich, Landon, 82, 246
Rich, Thomas, 49–50, 58, 244
Richards, Franklin D., 32, 94, 173
Richards, Joseph H., 193
Richards, Martha Jane, 153
Richards, Mary, 94–95
Richards, Samuel, 29
Richards, Willard, 27, 94
Richardson, Charles Edmund, 172, 190
Richardson, Sullivan Calvin, 190
Richardson, Thomas, 4
Richland Township branch, 1
Rigby, John, 244
Riter, Samuel Harvey Wollerton, 78, 82, 246
Robinson, Jack, 81
Robinson, Joseph Lee, 249
Robison, Lewis, 40, 51, 58
Rockwell, Orrin Porter, x, 23, 38 , 40, 49–50, 70–71, 234
Rogers, Andrew Lo'ce ("Locy"), 119, 122, 140
Rogers, Aurelia Spencer, 119
Rogers, Clara, 136
Rogers, Henry, 140
Rogers, Samuel H., 188
Rogers, Thomas, 119, 243

Romney, George, 103
Romney, Miles P., 188
Roos/Ross, Andrus/Andrew, 244
Rose, Alley Stephen, 82, 84, 242, 246
Rupe, James, 40, 50

S

Sainsbury, Robert E., 202, 209, 220
Sanders, Martin, 191
Sanderson, George B., 6, 8, 10
Sarpee, Peter, 4–5
Savage, Levi M., 136, 148, 153, 155, 171, 188, 190–91, 254
Savage, Marintha, 153
Scandinavians, 29
Schwartz, ("Black Pete"), 199
Secrist, J. M., 241
Sessions, Alene, xi
Sessions, Keppler, family, 119
Shaffer, J. W., 109
Sharp, James, 82, 85–86, 98, 182, 241–42
Shipp, Milton B., 106
Shortfingers, Pat ("Stubbs"), 227–30, 236
Shoshones, 22–23
Shumway, Albert P., 103, 107–8
Shumway, Charles, 105
Shurtleff, Emerson Davis, 246
Sill, Daniel C., 246
Simmonds, A. J. ("Jeff"), xi
Simmons, Harlan/Harlow Edward, 82, 246
Simon, Ben, 64
Simpson, Lew, 45, 48, 251
Smith, Abiah Ann ("Bide"), 247
Smith, Abiah Ann (McBride), 1, 2, 30, 250
Smith, Alden B., II, xi
Smith, Alden Burdick, 164, 215–16, 224, 228, 247
Smith, Alice (Robinson), 247
Smith, Alice Ann Richards, 94–95, 122–23, 135–36, 143, 154, 156, 158–59, 170–73, 193, 200, 210, 212, 218, 241, 253
    "Big Alice," 114
    photo, 120, 248
Smith, Alice Mary Baugh, 106, 135, 192–93, 205, 210, 231–32, 241
    "Little Alice," 114
    photo, 248
Smith, Alice Roxey, 248, 256
Smith, Alma ("Al"), 211, 239, 248
Smith, Annetta (Udy), 247

Smith, Arza Lavell, xi

Smith, Azariah, 11

Smith, Bert, xi

Smith, Brigham, 248

Smith, Carmen R., ix

Smith, Charles Rich, 248

Smith, Charlotte Elizabeth ("Lottie"), 191, 248

Smith, Diantha, 205, 248

Smith, Dorthea Elizabeth ("Diantha"), 156–57, 184, 191–92, 205, 211, 214, 228–33, 241, 254

   photo, 248

Smith, Edwin Dilworth, 248

Smith, Elias, 38

Smith, Elizabeth Jane, 135, 248, 254

Smith, Emily, 248

Smith, Emily Abigail (Hess), 247

Smith, Emily Jane (Burk), 1–2, 19

Smith, Francis Mary (Short), 225, 248

Smith, Franklin Dewey, 248

Smith, George Albert, 39, 53, 91–93, 108, 113

Smith, George Albert (Lot's son), 171, 248, 254

Smith, Glade M., 118

Smith, Grant Gill, xi

Smith, Helaman ("Jim"), 248

Smith, Helen Mar ("Nell"), 247

Smith, Hyrum (Diantha's son), 191, 227–28, 248

Smith, Hyrum (J. Smith Jr.'s brother), 2

Smith, Hyrum (Lot's brother), 2, 19, 30, 250

Smith, Hyrum Burton, 192, 214, 216–19, 247

Smith, James Martin ("Jim"), ix, 162, 195, 248

Smith, Jane Walker, 20, 27–28, 67, 91, 95, 115, 135, 164, 218, 241, 250–51

   photo, 247

Smith, Jedediah Heber, 118, 135, 209, 214–16, 247

Smith, Jesse N., 143–44, 147, 151, 154, 179–85, 187, 190, 220, 223, 232, 240, 242

Smith, Jesse N., Jr., 190

Smith, Jesse Nathaniel, 220, 248

Smith, Jesse Nathaniel (Lot's son), 192, 220, 255

Smith, Jesse Wells ("Nick"), 1, 2, 67

Smith, Jessie, xi

Smith, Joel Hough, 1–2, 19

Smith, John H., 241

Smith, Joseph F., 114, 182, 207, 241–42

Smith, Joseph Howe, 210, 248

Smith, Joseph, Jr., 1–2, 4

Smith, Julia Adelaide, 247, 252

Smith, Julia Amanda, 247

Smith, Julia Ann Pence, 30, 67, 70–71, 91, 95, 114–15, 117, 164, 241, 251–52

   photo, 247

Smith, Karl, xi

Smith, Kate ("Katherine"), 232, 248

Smith, Kenneth B., xi

Smith, Laura Louisa ("Lollie"), 115, 164, 247

Smith, Laura Louisa Burdick, 67, 91, 94–95, 115, 164, 241, 251

   photo, 247

Smith, Andrew J., 6, 8

Smith, Lorenzo Lot ("Ren"), 194–96, 227, 248

Lot Smith

Smith, Lot

   accompanies Daniel H. Wells to Fort Bridger, 39

   acquires camp supplies, 135–36

   acquitted at Isaac "Ike" Duffin trial, 256

   acquitted at John Thistle trial, 256

   administers to sick and poor, 101–2

   Albuquerque, 162–63

   and Alonzo L. Farnsworth, 213–14, 222–23

   Alonzo L. Farnsworth suits, 220

   announces calls to Savoia, 165

   Antelope Island roundup, 252

   Arizona Stake organized, x, 137–38

   arrested for Isaac Duffin burning, 221–22

   arrested for John Thistle shooting, 224–25

   arrives back in Arizona, 193

   arrives in England, 253

   arrives in Utah, 18, 108, 249, 253

   asked to burn wagons, 40–41

   assigned as traveling elder, 98

   assists Alma Millet, 188

   assists Brigham Young, 110–11

   assists Miles P. Romney, 188

   assists Orrin Porter Rockwell, 23

   attends general conference, 162–63

   avoids arrest, 215, 221

   baptism, 250

   bear chase, 168–69

   Bear River trip, 91–93

   begins stockade, 133

   and Benjamin F. Ficklin, 42

   Big Canyon, 209, 256

   Birmingham Conference President, 103–7, 253

   birth, x, 1

   Black Hawk War, 93

blesses Orson P. Arnold, 46
blesses Martha Jane Richards and twins, 153
blesses Spence baby, 99
blizzard at Pacific Springs, 80
blizzard on Muddy, 56
blooded stock, 166
blue-bellied Yankee, 1
"brands" Jane Walker Smith, 28
Bridger Butte, 58–60
brigadier general, 93, 253
Brigham Young dispels weariness of, 61
Brigham Young's desertion strategy, 51
brings troops to Salt Lake City, 61
builds dam, 126
builds Farmington home, photo, 20
builds Farmington wall, 28
builds wall fence, 16
bullfight, 16
burns wagon trains, 42–46, 251
buys farm, 249
cabin at Mormon Lake, 139
call to British Mission, 253
called to colonize Arizona, 254
calls off chase, 85
calms Navajos, 131
camp at Sunset Crossing, 126
captain in Civil War, 252
captain of Life Guards Cavalry, 250
captain, 25
carries supplies for Thomas Callister, 58
censures Robert Hereford's profanity, 87
Circle S horses, 167
climbs Ben Lomond, 103
Collins regiment, 81
Colonia Diaz, 190
color bearer, 250
Color Bearer General of Nauvoo Legion, x, 24
and Comayazzie, 158–59
commissioner and assessor, 252
and Commodore Perry Owens, 206
confronted by cattlemen, 174–75
confronts Birmingham heckler, 105
Constitutional Convention, 253
cure from Wilford Woodruff, 162
Da-gha-hi Chi. See Da-gha-hi Chi.
and Daggs brothers, 175
dairy at Mormon Lake, x, 138–39
Davis County Assessor, 69
Davis County Sheriff, x, 29, 250
defends Bill Ashurst, 177

delegate to Constitutional Convention, 113
delegate to establish statehood, 112
difficulties with wives, 91
digs and carries water, 11–12
disbands Sunset United Order, 173–74
discharged, 16, 249
Donald McNichols drowning, 84
duty on Bridger Butte, 251
eats pepper bark, 14
Edinburgh, 98
and elderly Hopis, 149–50
enlists as Mormon Volunteer, 16
enters Utah War, 41
escapes capture, 51, 55, 210–11, 251
escorts Brigham Young, 37, 70, 251
expedition to Big Sandy, 79–80
expedition to Fort Bridger, 25
explores for lead and silver, 24, 250
explores Snake, 87
family prayers, 115
Farmington memorial services, 241–42
feared gunman, xi
fights Shoshones, 22–23
first war speech, 46
flees to Utah, 179–82
Fort Leavenworth, 5
Fort Moenkopi, 255
Fourth of July celebration, 81
Fourth of July oration, 130
and Frederick A. Tritle, 178, 255
funeral, 233
gathers troop's cattle, 48
general conference, 173
and George D. Grant, 32
and George Thomas Baugh family, 106
gives Brigham Young gold, 19
guards Brigham Young, 250
guards fence poles in Santa Fe, 8
guards murderer on train, 215–16
guards Robert Taylor Burton, 113
guides Brigham Young Jr. and Heber J.
   Grant, 169
and Hamilton G. Park, 98–103
hauls rock, 91
helps Wilford Woodruff escape arrest, 152–53
and Henry Chariton Jacobs, 98–103
Hoback Canyon, 83
horseback to Little Colorado, 184
House of Representatives candidate, 178
ill with violent cold, 57

indicted for attempted murder, 203
indicted for treason, 64, 251
initiates Circle S Ranch, x
interview with Craig, 80
interview with San Bernardino, 134
Isaac "Ike" Duffin cabin burning, 216–17
and Jesse N. Smith, 220
and John Quincy Knowlton, 82
and John Taylor, 148
and John Thistle, 198
John Thistle shooting, 194–98, 255
keeps tavern, 133
killed, 256
Las Playas, 249
last hours, 231–32
and Laura Louisa Burdick Smith, 115–16, 164
leads colonists to Arizona, 120–25
leads vanguard patrol, 41
leaves for mission, 97
Los Angeles, 16
"Luther" in Mormon Battalion, 249
major, 37, 251
marches around hill, 63–64
marries Alice Ann Richards, 94–95, 253
marries Alice Mary Baugh, 114, 254
marries Dorthea Elizabeth "Diantha"
    Mortensen, 156, 254
marries Jane Walker, 250
marries Julia Ann Pence Smith, 30, 251
marries Laura Louisa Burdick, 66, 251
marries Lydia Minerva McBride, 27, 250
marries Mary Merinda Garn, 141–42
and marshals at Mormon Lake, 177
Meeks Ferry, 88
memorial service and re-interment, 256
Mexico, 187, 255
military support for Peter K. Dotson, 69
and Minute Men, x, 38
mission call, 96
mission conference in London, 104–5
mission quarterly conferences, 137
Moenkopi, 255
Mormon Battalion, x
Mormon Battalion celebration, 30–31
Mormon Volunteer, 249
mule drowns with gold, 18
musters troops, 73
names baby after Wilford Woodruff, 154
obituaries, 234–35, 240–41
obtains food from miners, 88

on raft with Thomas S. Caldwell, 86
Oraibi village, 227
ordered to continue duty, 64
organizes Wilford Ward, 172
and Orrin Porter Rockwell, x, 49–50
peace bond, 223
peace with Wakara, 25–26
photograph, 110
polygamy raids intensify, 173
prayer circle, 67
president of 40th Quorum of the Seventy, 29
president of 74th Quorum of the Seventy, 94
president of Arizona Stake of Zion, x, 254
private, 249
proposes legislative bills, 113
Provo War, 20–22
punished for disobedience, 12
purchases Red Cloud, 167
purchases sixty-acre farm in North
    Cottonwood, 19
purchases Stoddard land, 251
purchases Weber Valley land, 67
pursues grizzly bear and cub, 79–80
quick temper, 136
Rankin's wagons, 42
rawhide footwear, 11
rebaptisms, 32, 118, 251
receives call to British Mission, 95
receives call to colonize Arizona, 117
receives counsel from Wilford Woodruff, 213
receives letters from Wilford Woodruff,
    171–72
Red Beard. See Da-gha-hi Chi.
refuses bribes, 178
refutes Elmont W. Parker death charge,
    175–76
re-interment, xi
relations with Indians, 159
released as stake president, 255
reports on colonization, 163
representative to legislature, 252
reprimanded, 144
reputation as killer, 174
rescues handcarts, x, 33–35, 251
rescues Henry Fountain Ashurst, 169
resettlement meetings, 205–8
retrieves Julia Ann Pence Smith, 70–71, 252
reward for capture of, 64, 251
rides train to Mexico, 183
rides unsaddled horse, 57

rides wild mule, 189
and Robert T. Burton, 77
roping exhibition, 80–81
roundup on Antelope Island, 67–68
Saint David, 255
Salmon River Expedition, 62
Salt Lake City, 89
San Diego, 249
San Luis Rey, 249
San Luis Rey Mission, 15
School of the Prophets, 94, 109, 253
scouts army, 62–63
senior president of seventies, 253
sergeant, 24, 250
set apart by Wilford Woodruff, 253
Seventy, 250
shares foodstuff, 154–56
shot in back, 229
Snake River Expedition, 81–89, 252
Song of 1857, 61–62
speaks at Robert T. Burton's benefit party, 113
St. George general conference and temple dedication, 136–37
St. George temple dedication, 136–37
and Stewart Van Vliet, 38
stake conference, 145
stampedes cattle, 49–50, 251
steel engraving, iix
summons for Isaac Duffin burning, 256
Sunset Crossing, 125
Sunset United Order, 190, 255
takes Moenkopi fort, 200–202
takes Wilford Woodruff to St. George, 155
tames Antelope Island horses, 67
teaches Hopis 149
teaches no deceit, 211
temper, 191
territorial legislature, 69, 111–13, 253
threshing injuries, 156–57, 161–162
throws cow off rails, 183
Tim Goodales's court martial, 77
tithing, 224
tours southern Arizona, 144–45
tours with Erastus Snow, 254
trains Stonewall, 24
traveling elder, 253
Tuba City, 205, 255
Tuba City bulletin, 224
twice injures leg, 254
United Order, x

Utah Volunteers, x
Utah War, 251
volunteers for Mormon Battalion, 4
voyages to America, 107
Walker War, 24–25
water dispute meetings, 208–9
white cloth for burial, 233
and William F. Cody ("Buffalo Bill"), 80–81
and William M. Douglas, 98–103
writes to John Hunt, 194
Smith, Lot P., 198
Smith, Lot Samuel, 27, 70, 91, 247
Smith, Louise Marie ("Tude"), 247
Smith, Lucy Effie (Palmer), 20, 247
Smith, Lydia May "Lillian" (Stoddard), 247
Smith, Lydia Minerva, 241
Smith, Lydia Minerva McBride, 27, 70, 91, 95, 217–18, 250, 252, 256
  photo, 247
Smith, Margaret Agnes (Palmer), 247
Smith, Martha (Schott), 205, 248
Smith, Mary Melissa (Carr), 248
Smith, Mary Merinda Garn, 17, 118, 136, 141–42, 151, 161, 164, 170–71, 173, 197, 210, 231, 237, 239, 241
  photo, 248
Smith, Melissa Packer, 201
Smith, Nannie Amelia (Ashcroft), 115, 211, 248
  photo, 120
Smith, Nathaniel, 96
Smith, Nephi, 191, 248, 255
Smith, Nephi Lot, 248
Smith, Omer James, ix
Smith, Phoebe, 70
Smith, Phoebe Vilate, 247
Smith, Rhoda Hough, 1–2, 249
Smith, Rhoda Jane (Hutchinson), 247
Smith, Rhoda Minerva, 248, 255
Smith, Robert Taylor Burton, 91, 247
Smith, Rock M., xi
Smith, Samuel, 248
Smith, Sarah Theresa, 247, 253
Smith, Wilford Woodruff, 154, 170–71, 248, 254
Smith, Willard, Jr., xi
Smith, Willard Richards, 152, 155, 194–97, 222, 248
  photo, 120
Smith, William B., 244

Smith, William James ("Bill"), 2, 96, 218
Smith, William Lot, 118, 247
Smith, William Orville, 1–3, 19, 249
Smoot, Abraham O., 38
Snow, Erastus, 127–28, 143–45, 148, 190–94, 208, 254
Song of 1857, 61–62
Spearman, Earl, 139
Spence, Charles Wright, 99–100
Spence, Elizabeth, 99
Spence, Jane, 99
Spence, Margaret Morrison, 99
Spencer, B. M., 222
Spencer, Howard Orson, 79–80, 82, 84–86, 246
St. Johns Ring, 178
Standifird, John Henry, 179–82, 244, 246
Starley, John J., 143
Stayner, Arthur, 94, 109–11
Steed, Alvin V. ("Mike"), xi
Steed, Fern, xi
Steed, James Henry, 246
Steed, Thomas, 31–32
Stevenson, James, 244
Stoddard (Farmington judge), 29
Stoddard, Judson, 38, 67-68
Stone, Ed, 200
Stout, Hosea, 39
Stowe, Samuel, 244
Stowell, Brigham, 122
Strock, John, 128
Sugar Creek Camp, 2
Sunset Crossing, 125
Sunset United Order, 141–42, 151, 153–56, 173–174, 193
Swank, William, 199

T

Tanner, Henry M., 181
Tanner, Seth B., 209, 233
Taylor, John (apostle and church president), xi, 39, 91–93, 113, 118, 137, 142, 147–49, 151, 156, 159, 182–83, 191–92, 213, 255
Taylor, John (bishop), 185
Taylor, Joseph, 58
Taylor, Joseph E. 240, 242
Taylor, Joseph James, 82, 246
Taylor, Stephen, 59, 68, 77, 244
Teasdale, George, 188, 190–91
Teeples, Nichalous Gourley, 34

Terakee, 22
Terry, James Parshall, 53–54, 62, 242–43
Terry, Joseph, 82, 246
Terry, William, 246
Thatcher, Moses, xi, 113, 182–84, 187
Thistle, John, 195–99, 224–25, 256
Thompson, John, 125
Thurber, A. K., 182
Thurston, Moses, 246
Tietjen, Ernest A., 165, 208, 211–12
Tinker, George H., editor, 176
Tracy, Albert, 65
transcontinental railway, 95
Trejo, Meliton G., 183
Tritle, Frederick A., 178, 255
Tullidge, Edward, 41, 65–66
Turner, James, 56
Tuttle, Newton, 55, 244, 246

U

Udall, David K., 155, 192, 206
Udy, Joseph, 256
US Army, 38, 59
Utah War, 66
Utes, 20–22, 25–26, 44, 64

V

Van Fleet, Elias, 94-95
Van Stewart, Urban, 23
Van Vliet, Stewart, 38
Vance, John, 41, 59, 243
Vasquez, Luis, 25

W

Wakara, 24–26, 250
Walker War, 24–25
Walker, Edwin, 16–17
Walker, John H., 246
Walton, William Harrison, 246
Ward, Elijah ("Barney"), 21–24
Warner, Juan Jose, 14
Warner's Ranch, 14
Washakie , 53, 75
Weaver, Miles, 24
Weaver, Pauline/Paulino, 9
Webb, Chauncey, 32
Weiler, Elijah Mahlon, 82, 246
Well, James H., 82, 246

Wells, Daniel H., 22, 37–41, 44, 47–49, 51, 55–57, 62, 66, 73–76, 95, 113–14, 127
Wells, Junius F., 164
West, Chancey W., 73
Westover, Joanna, 133
Wheelock, Angus, 34
Wheelock, Cyrus, 32
Whiting, Charles, 140, 190
Whiting, Edwin, 140, 190
Whiting, Verona, 140
Whitney, Brian, xi
Whitney, Newell K., 20
Whitney, Orson F., 103
Whitney, Orson K., 21
Wilcken, Charles H., 241
Wiley, Parley B., 119
Wilhelm, Bateman H., 143–44
Williams Ranch, 18
Williams, Bateman Haight, 246
Williams, Ephraim Henry, 246
Williams, George C. ("Parson"), 184, 187, 190
Williams, James V., 4
Williams, Narney, 200, 202
Willie handcart company, 32–35
Wilson, George D., 181–82
Wimer, John Peter, 246
Winder, John Rex, 91, 241–42
Wood, Edward J., 189
Wood, George C., 119, 125
Wood, J. C., 127
Wood, James T., 128, 130, 133

Wood, Peter, 119, 125
Woodruff, Abraham O., 118, 241
Woodruff, Wilford, x, 2, 66, 91–93, 95–96, 113, 145, 150–55, 162, 166, 192, 207–8, 213–14, 216, 218, 220–23, 232, 254
Woods, George L., 111–12
Woolley, John, 58, 244
Workman, Andrew J., 18
Workman, Cornelius, 17–18

Y

Yates, Richard, 111
Young, Brigham, x, 6, 19, 24–27, 30–32, 37–40, 43, 51, 58, 61, 65–68, 73–76, 89, 91–95, 108, 114, 117–18, 127, 132–33, 135–37, 141, 149, 159, 231, 240, 250–53
  Articles of Agreement, 128
Young, Brigham, Jr., 59, 68, 127, 162, 169–71, 173, 178, 182, 191–92, 194, 208, 244, 255
Young, John W., 137–38, 154, 250
Young, Joseph, 91–93
Young, Joseph A., 32, 34
Young, Joseph W., 112–13
Young, Seymour Bicknell, 66, 77, 82–86, 88, 241–42, 246

Z

Zabriskie, Jerome, 17, 18
Zedong, Mao, 15

Also available from
GREG KOFFORD BOOKS

"Swell Suffering":
A Biography of Maurine Whipple

Veda Tebbs Hale

Paperback, ISBN: 978-1-58958-124-1
Hardcover, ISBN: 978-1-58958-122-7

Maurine Whipple, author of what some critics consider Mormonism's greatest novel, *The Giant Joshua,* is an enigma. Her prize-winning novel has never been out of print, and its portrayal of the founding of St. George draws on her own family history to produce its unforgettable and candid portrait of plural marriage's challenges. Yet Maurine's life is full of contradictions and unanswered questions. Veda Tebbs Hale, a personal friend of the paradoxical novelist, answers these questions with sympathy and tact, nailing each insight down with thorough research in Whipple's vast but under-utilized collected papers.

Praise for *"Swell Suffering"*:

"Hale achieves an admirable balance of compassion and objectivity toward an author who seemed fated to offend those who offered to love or befriend her. . . . Readers of this biography will be reminded that Whipple was a full peer of such Utah writers as Virginia Sorensen, Fawn Brodie, and Juanita Brooks, all of whom achieved national fame for their literary and historical works during the mid-twentieth century"
—Levi S. Peterson, author of *The Backslider* and *Juanita Brooks: Mormon Historian*

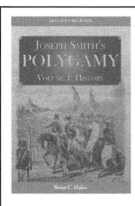

Joseph Smith's Polygamy, 3 Vols.

Brian Hales

Hardcover
Volume 1: History 978-1-58958-189-0
Volume 2: History 978-1-58958-548-5
Volume 3: Theology 978-1-58958-190-6

Perhaps the least understood part of Joseph Smith's life and teachings is his introduction of polygamy to the Saints in Nauvoo. Because of the persecution he knew it would bring, Joseph said little about it publicly and only taught it to his closest and most trusted friends and associates before his martyrdom.

In this three-volume work, Brian C. Hales provides the most comprehensive faithful examination of this much misunderstood period in LDS Church history. Drawing for the first time on every known account, Hales helps us understand the history and teachings surrounding this secretive practice and also addresses and corrects many of the numerous allegations and misrepresentations concerning it. Hales further discusses how polygamy was practiced during this time and why so many of the early Saints were willing to participate in it.

Joseph Smith's Polygamy is an essential resource in understanding this challenging and misunderstood practice of early Mormonism.

Praise for *Joseph Smith's Polygamy*:

"Brian Hales wants to face up to every question, every problem, every fear about plural marriage. His answers may not satisfy everyone, but he gives readers the relevant sources where answers, if they exist, are to be found. There has never been a more thorough examination of the polygamy idea." —Richard L. Bushman, author of *Joseph Smith: Rough Stone Rolling*

"Hales's massive and well documented three volume examination of the history and theology of Mormon plural marriage, as introduced and practiced during the life of Joseph Smith, will now be the standard against which all other treatments of this important subject will be measured." —Danel W. Bachman, author of "A Study of the Mormon Practice of Plural Marriage before the Death of Joseph Smith"

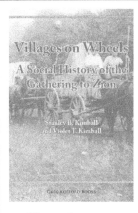

Villages on Wheels: A Social History of the Gathering to Zion

Stanley B. Kimball and Violet T. Kimball

ISBN: 978-1-58958-119-7

The enduring saga of Mormonism is its great trek across the plains, and understanding that trek was the life work of Stanley B. Kimball, master of Mormon trails. This final work, a collaboration he began and which was completed after his death in 2003 by his photographer-writer wife, Violet, explores that movement westward as a social history, with the Mormons moving as "villages on wheels."

Set in the broader context of transcontinental migration to Oregon and California, the Mormon trek spanned twenty-two years, moved approximately 54,700 individuals, many of them in family groups, and left about 7,000 graves at the trailside.

Like a true social history, this fascinating account in fourteen chapters explores both the routines of the trail—cooking, cleaning, laundry, dealing with bodily functions—and the dramatic moments: encountering Indians and stampeding buffalo, giving birth, losing loved ones to death, dealing with rage and injustice, but also offering succor, kindliness, and faith. Religious observances were simultaneously an important part of creating and maintaining group cohesiveness, but working them into the fabric of the grueling day-to-day routine resulted in adaptation, including a "sliding Sabbath." The role played by children and teens receives careful scrutiny; not only did children grow up quickly on the trail, but the gender boundaries guarding their "separate spheres" blurred under the erosion of concentrating on tasks that had to be done regardless of the age or sex of those available to do them. Unexpected attention is given to African Americans who were part of this westering experience, and Violet also gives due credit to the "four-legged heroes" who hauled the wagons westward.

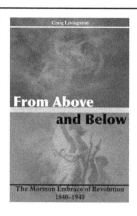

From Above and Below: The Mormon Embrace of Revolution, 1840–1940

Craig Livingston

Paperback, ISBN: 978-1-58958-621-5

**2014 Best International Book Award,
Mormon History Association**

Praise for *From Above and Below*:

"In this engaging study, Craig Livingston examines Mormon responses to political revolutions across the globe from the 1840s to the 1930s. Latter-day Saints saw utopian possibilities in revolutions from the European tumults of 1848 to the Mexican Revolution. Highlighting the often radical anti-capitalist and anti-imperialist rhetoric of Mormon leaders, Livingston demonstrates how Latter-day Saints interpreted revolutions through their unique theology and millennialism."
--Matthew J. Grow, author of *Liberty to the Downtrodden: Thomas L. Kane, Romantic Reformer*

"Craig Livingston's landmark book demonstrates how 21st-century Mormonism's arch-conservatism was preceded by its pro-revolutionary worldview that was dominant from the 1830s to the 1930s. Shown by current opinion-polling to be the most politically conservative religious group in the United States, contemporary Mormons are unaware that leaders of the LDS Church once praised radical liberalism and violent revolutionaries. By this pre-1936 Mormon view, 'The people would reduce privilege and exploitation in the crucible of revolution, then reforge society in a spiritual union of peace' before the Coming of Christ and His Millennium. With profound research in Mormon sources and in academic studies about various social revolutions and political upheavals, Livingston provides a nuanced examination of this little-known dimension of LDS thought which tenuously balanced pro-revolutionary enthusiasms with anti-mob sentiments."
--D. Michael Quinn, author of *Elder Statesman: A Biography of J. Reuben Clark*

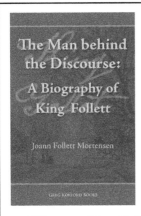

The Man behind the Discourse:
A Biography of King Follett

Joann Follett Mortensen

ISBN: 978-1-58958-036-7

Who was King Follett? When he was fatally injured digging a well in Nauvoo in March 1844, why did Joseph Smith use his death to deliver the monumental doctrinal sermon now known as the King Follett Discourse? Much has been written about the sermon, but little about King.

Although King left no personal writings, Joann Follett Mortensen, King's third great-granddaughter, draws on more than thirty years of research in civic and Church records and in the journals and letters of King's peers to piece together King's story from his birth in New Hampshire and moves westward where, in Ohio, he and his wife, Louisa, made the life-shifting decision to accept the new Mormon religion.

From that point, this humble, hospitable, and hardworking family followed the Church into Missouri where their devotion to Joseph Smith was refined and burnished. King was the last Mormon prisoner in Missouri to be released from jail. According to family lore, King was one of the Prophet's bodyguards. He was also a Danite, a Mason, and an officer in the Nauvoo Legion. After his death, Louisa and their children settled in Iowa where some associated with the Cutlerities and the RLDS Church; others moved on to California. One son joined the Mormon Battalion and helped found Mormon communities in Utah, Idaho, and Arizona.

While King would have died virtually unknown had his name not been attached to the discourse, his life story reflects the reality of all those whose faith became the foundation for a new religion. His biography is more than one man's life story. It is the history of the early Restoration itself.

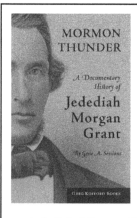

Mormon Thunder:
A Documentary History of
Jedediah Morgan Grant

Gene A. Sessions

Paperback, ISBN: 978-1-58958-111-1

Jedediah Morgan Grant was a man who knew no compromise when it came to principles—and his principles were clearly representative, argues Gene A. Sessions, of Mormonism's first generation. His life is a glimpse of a Mormon world whose disappearance coincided with the death of this "pious yet rambunctiously radical preacher, flogging away at his people, demanding otherworldliness and constant sacrifice." It was "an eschatological, pre-millennial world in which every individual teetered between salvation and damnation and in which unsanitary privies and appropriating a stray cow held the same potential for eternal doom as blasphemy and adultery."

Updated and newly illustrated with more photographs, this second edition of the award-winning documentary history (first published in 1982) chronicles Grant's ubiquitous role in the Mormon history of the 1840s and '50s. In addition to serving as counselor to Brigham Young during two tumultuous and influential years at the end of his life, he also portentously befriended Thomas L. Kane, worked to temper his unruly brother-in-law William Smith, captained a company of emigrants into the Salt Lake Valley in 1847, and journeyed to the East on several missions to bolster the position of the Mormons during the crises surrounding the runaway judges affair and the public revelation of polygamy.

Jedediah Morgan Grant's voice rises powerfully in these pages, startling in its urgency in summoning his people to sacrifice and moving in its tenderness as he communicated to his family. From hastily scribbled letters to extemporaneous sermons exhorting obedience, and the notations of still stunned listeners, the sound of "Mormon Thunder" rolls again in "a boisterous amplification of what Mormonism really was, and would never be again."

Hearken, O Ye People:
The Historical Setting of Joseph Smith's Ohio Revelations

Mark Lyman Staker

Hardcover, ISBN: 978-1-58958-113-5

2010 Best Book Award - John Whitmer Historical Association

2011 Best Book Award - Mormon History Association

More of Mormonism's canonized revelations originated in or near Kirtland than any other place. Yet many of the events connected with those revelations and their 1830s historical context have faded over time. Mark Staker reconstructs the cultural experiences by which Kirtland's Latter-day Saints made sense of the revelations Joseph Smith pronounced. This volume rebuilds that exciting decade using clues from numerous archives, privately held records, museum collections, and even the soil where early members planted corn and homes. From this vast array of sources he shapes a detailed narrative of weather, religious backgrounds, dialect differences, race relations, theological discussions, food preparation, frontier violence, astronomical phenomena, and myriad daily customs of nineteenth-century life. The result is a "from the ground up" experience that today's Latter-day Saints can all but walk into and touch.

Praise for *Hearken O Ye People*:

"I am not aware of a more deeply researched and richly contextualized study of any period of Mormon church history than Mark Staker's study of Mormons in Ohio. We learn about everything from the details of Alexander Campbell's views on priesthood authority to the road conditions and weather on the four Lamanite missionaries' journey from New York to Ohio. All the Ohio revelations and even the First Vision are made to pulse with new meaning. This book sets a new standard of in-depth research in Latter-day Saint history."

-Richard Bushman, author of *Joseph Smith: Rough Stone Rolling*

"To be well-informed, any student of Latter-day Saint history and doctrine must now be acquainted with the remarkable research of Mark Staker on the important history of the church in the Kirtland, Ohio, area."

-Neal A. Maxwell Institute, Brigham Young University

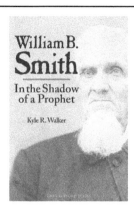

William B. Smith:
In the Shadow of a Prophet

Kyle R. Walker

Paperback, ISBN: 978-1-58958-503-4

Younger brother of Joseph Smith, a member of the Quorum of the Twelve Apostles, and Church Patriarch for a time, William Smith had tumultuous yet devoted relationships with Joseph, his fellow members of the Twelve, and the LDS and RLDS (Community of Christ) churches. Walker's imposing biography examines not only William's complex life in detail, but also sheds additional light on the family dynamics of Joseph and Lucy Mack Smith, as well as the turbulent intersections between the LDS and RLDS churches. *William B. Smith: In the Shadow of a Prophet* is a vital contribution to Mormon history in both the LDS and RLDS traditions.

Praise for *William B. Smith*:

"Bullseye! Kyle Walker's biography of Joseph Smith Jr's lesser known younger brother William is right on target. It weaves a narrative that is searching, balanced, and comprehensive. Walker puts this former Mormon apostle solidly within a Smith family setting, and he hits the mark for anyone interested in Joseph Smith and his family. Walker's biography will become essential reading on leadership dynamics within Mormonism after Joseph Smith's death." — Mark Staker, author *Hearken, O Ye People: The Historical Setting of Joseph Smith's Ohio Revelations*

"This perceptive biography on William, the last remaining Smith brother, provides a thorough timeline of his life's journey and elucidates how his insatiable discontent eventually tempered the once irascible young man into a seasoned patriarch loved by those who knew him." — Erin B. Metcalfe, president (2014–15) John Whitmer Historical Association

"I suspect that this comprehensive treatment will serve as the definitive biography for years to come; it will certainly be difficult to improve upon." — Joe Steve Swick III, Association for Mormon Letters

CPSIA information can be obtained
at www.ICGtesting.com
Printed in the USA
BVHW030541180419
545791BV00005B/92/P